THE
ELDER LAW HANDBOOK

A Legal and Financial
Survival Guide for
Caregivers and Seniors

Peter J. Strauss
and
Nancy M. Lederman

Facts On File, Inc.
AN INFOBASE HOLDINGS COMPANY

The Elder Law Handbook: A Legal and Financial Survival Guide for Caregivers and Seniors

Facts On File, Inc.
11 Penn Plaza
New York NY 10001

Library of Congress Cataloging-in-Publication Data
Strauss, Peter J.
   The elder law handbook: a legal and financial survival guide for caregivers
  and seniors / Peter J. Strauss and Nancy M. Lederman.
     p.   cm.
  Includes index.
  ISBN 0-8160-3082-0 (hc).— ISBN 0-8160-3410-9 (pb)
    1. Aged—Legal status, laws, etc.—United States—Popular works.
  I. Lederman, Nancy M. II.   Title.
  KF390.A4S755   1996
  346.7301'3—dc20
  [347.30613]   95-53937

Facts On File books are available at special discounts when purchased in bulk quantities for businesses, associations, institutions or sales promotions. Please call our Special Sales Department in New York at 212/967-8800 or 800/322-8755.

Cover design by M.R.P. Design

MP FOF 10 9 8 7 6 5 4 3 2 1

This book is printed on acid-free paper.

CONTENTS

DEDICATION AND ACKNOWLEDGMENTS

To my family, young and not so young, who created the framework for my values and ideas.

—P.J.S.

To my grandmother Freda Weinstein (1902–1992).

—N.M.L.

A lawyer's career is influenced by many persons, beginning with family, friends, and teachers in school, college, and law school, and later with mentors at the bar. This is certainly true for me, and I acknowledge my debt to all those who in their own way helped shape my life as a lawyer. But in particular, I wish to acknowledge the small group of lawyers who were the pioneers in elder law in the late 1970s when only a handful of us were working to develop this new area of expertise. Alan Bogutz of Tucson, Arizona, Steven Feldman of Philadelphia, Michael Gilfix of Palo Alto, California, Charles Robert of New York, and my former partner Robert Wolf of New York were just a few of those early practitioners who I worked with then to shape the development of elder law. To them and all the others who were part of the 1988 group of 26 founders of the National Academy of Elder Law Attorneys, I owe a great deal.

Before lawyers discovered the elderly, social workers and other gerontologists had served them for many years as counselors, advocates, and experts on the issues of aging. I was fortunate to have met these social worker–gerontologists early on and was deeply affected by their knowledge, expertise, and values. In the early 1980s I worked with the group that had formed the New York Network on Aging that later broadened its scope to build the National Association of Professional Geriatric Care Managers, an organization with which I have been proud to be affiliated for many years. Those first "care managers"—Lenise Dolen, Adele Elkind, Jerie Charnow, Sarah N. Cohen, Leonie Nowitz, Ellen Lurie Polivy, and Bernice Sheppard—have left an indelible mark on our senior citizen population as well as on me.

Lastly, I must recognize the physicians, nurses, and psychologists who have led the medical profession in creating the specialty of geriatric medicine. By acknowledging that the medical needs of the elderly are different from others', and developing approaches and treatment strategies that recognize their different needs while respecting their rights and values, they have contributed greatly to the quality of life of our aging population.

—Peter J. Strauss

I join with Peter in saluting the lawyers, social workers, and medical professionals who pioneered services for the elderly. Their work laid a foundation that changed forever the way this country views its older citizens and those with disabilities.

In addition, I would like to acknowledge my personal debt to the many friends and colleagues who influenced my own career in education and elder law, and helped me shape my legal work to the needs of clients rather than neat little pigeonholes of law. Among them are Anthony Alvarado, Selma Belenky, Doreen DeMartini, Ellen Estrin, Shelley Greif, Charles Schonhaut, Peter Strauss, Jane Stern, Robin Willner, and Carol Ziegler. An added note of thanks goes to Jeanne Frankl for her role at the inception of this project. I also pay tribute to Jack Lipson, who was my best friend and teacher.

My family deserves special mention, particularly my parents, Marilyn and Paul Lederman, my sisters, Sherri Mandell and Loren Fogelson, and my brother, Elliott Weinstein. A unique debt of gratitude is reserved for my grandmother, Freda Weinstein, who taught me what it is like to be an older person negotiating the world. As her caretaker in her final years, I drew much from her counsel and worldview as she benefited from my more "practical" help. This book is dedicated to her.

Sincere thanks go to our editors, Caroline Sutton, Bob Shuman, and particularly Drew Silver, for their help in shepherding this book to publication.

Lastly, I must thank those older friends, relatives, and clients who have generously helped me to see the world through their eyes.

—Nancy M. Lederman

PREFACE

"I've got enough money for the rest of my life, unless I want to buy something."
When Milton Berle says it, it's funny. For the rest of us, the financial and legal dilemmas of our later years are no laughing matter. That's why we've written *The Elder Law Handbook*—to give you something more than a punchline with which to face your future. This book provides what you and your family need, access to the vast array of legal rights, tools, and strategies available to face those dilemmas.

For both of us, writing this book represents a commitment spanning our professional lives and our personal beliefs. For Peter, it's the natural culmination of years spent on the front lines treating the problems of older people. When Peter first hung out his shingle as a specialist in legal problems of the aging, no one had ever heard of "elder law." It simply didn't exist.

There was only the growing subterranean culture of older Americans, neither rich nor poor, with multiple legal needs relating to aging. Peter's first "elder law" case, in 1980, gave him a memorable introduction to this world. Sally and David Franklin[1] were a retired couple faced with a common tragedy when David had a stroke. His condition left him needing help with simple tasks such as eating, toileting, and bathing.

The problem was money. The Franklins lived on a fixed income, nowhere near the price of the continued institutional care that David needed. They couldn't pay. Medicare wouldn't pay—not for the so-called "unskilled" care that David required. Medicaid would pay, but it was a welfare program. In order to qualify, David would have had to relinquish his income, leaving Sally with just over $300 a month on which to live. It was only a matter of time before she would be out on the street.

As a lawyer, Peter was able to devise a legal solution for the Franklins. Sally sued David for support, which rendered her court-ordered support immune from Medicaid. For the Franklins, it was a life-saver. For Peter, it was an eye-opener. Here were people who had believed in the American dream, worked and struggled their whole lives trying to earn some needed security in their later years. Yet the system designed for their care, Medicare, excluded the very coverage they actually needed.

It was the unfairness that troubled him. Who decided that acute care patients would be favored over those with long-term needs? Wasn't that the very heart of discrimination against the elderly, punishing them for the

---
[1] Not their real names.

very conditions to which they were most vulnerable? What kind of system, he asked himself, encouraged divorce, impoverishment, dependency?

Peter's questions led him away from courthouses and legal chambers to hospitals and nursing homes, to retirement communities and senior centers. He met couples trying to find help for their disabled children, older people trying to manage chronic illnesses on their own, patients fighting "the system" to get the care they wanted—and to end the care they didn't—and social workers trying to find patchwork solutions to insoluble problems. Again and again he heard how little was being done to meet the simplest needs of the elderly (and disabled people of all ages, often caught in the same trap). Over the next decade, elder law evolved as the Franklins' story was repeated again and again in law offices and hospital wards and the homes and communities of older people across the country.

For Nancy, a slip on the ice provided her entry to the world of elder law. Her 85-year-old grandmother Freda Weinstein was hospitalized for a month, then discharged to her home with no help. Nancy's years as an attorney didn't prepare her for the toll of caretaking. From finding home care to paying her grandmother's bills, making plans for future needs, dealing with doctors over medical treatment, and exercising her grandmother's health care proxy, Nancy was on the front lines, as a consumer and as her grandmother's advocate.

Although by this time Peter had been joined by other elder law practitioners working on the legal problems of the aging, for consumers there was little help or information available. What was available was generally useless, or worse, misinformation. Nancy was able to get the guidance she needed because of her legal experience in the field of public education, working on behalf of children and the disabled. As an attorney, she knew where to go. The contrast was stark: on the one hand, lack of information—and a ton of misinformation; on the other, information and help for those who knew how to get it.

So we teamed up to write this book, to get that information to the people who need it. It could not have been written 20 years ago. It had to wait for elder law to develop as a separate area. For both of us, elder law is about enforcing people's rights. Whether dealing with a crisis or planning for the future, we believe in forcing changes through traditional and not-so-traditional solutions and educating the community about their rights.

Education is key. Americans' rising awareness of the problems facing the elderly has forced the passage of dozens of laws on nursing home practices, patients' rights, age discrimination, and insurance reform. Today, David Franklin's bills would be paid and Sally Franklin would have a "community spouse resource allowance," which in New York would allow her to keep up to $76,740 of marital assets, monthly income of at least $1,918.50, and her home. These rights came into being *because of* Sally and David and all the others like her who fought back.

Some politicians are now advocating rolling back these reforms. Yet who could sensibly argue for return to a system that would allow David Franklin to be cared for in an unsafe or unsanitary nursing home? What moral argument could justify forcing Sally Franklin to the poorhouse?

Injustice invariably creates legends out of ordinary people caught in extraordinary circumstances. Elder law has just such a pantheon of heroes and martyrs:

- *Estelle Browning, the Florida widow whose living will was ignored by the hospital, which insisted on administering artificial hydration and nutrition against her expressed wishes.*
- *Jean Elbaum, the comatose patient who was continued on a feeding tube against her wish not to be kept alive by tubes and medication.*
- *Murray Elbaum, who was forced to court to enforce his wife Jean's rights and then given a bill by the nursing home for $120,000 for her medical care, care which had been administered over his objections and in contradiction to his wife's wishes.*
- *Edward Winter, who after watching his wife's death in horror, had executed a do-not-resuscitate order on his own behalf. Hospital workers ignored his written orders, causing him to live on in pain for two years after an unwanted resuscitation.*
- *John Kingery, the 82-year-old man suffering from Alzheimer's disease who was abandoned at a racetrack by a daughter unable to care for him.*
- *Maggie Kuhn, forced to retire from a church job at age 65, who went on to found the Gray Panthers.*
- *Karen Ann Quinlan, age 21, kept alive in a persistent vegetative coma by artificial feeding, whose parents' fight to disconnect their daughter's respirator led to the first judicial decision on the right to die.*
- *Nancy Cruzan, age 25, kept alive in a persistent vegetative coma by artificial feeding, whose parent's fought to the United States Supreme Court for the right of their daughter's wishes to determine her fate.*

The list goes on and on. Add to it Sally and David Franklin and Freda Weinstein and the thousands of anonymous older Americans relying on Medicare for their health care and unprotected when illness struck, or being tube-fed in nursing homes against their will, or left in the care of abusive caretakers, or left without any help at all for the simple tasks involved in managing their lives.

We dedicate this book to all of them and the rights they've helped win for all of us.

Peter J. Strauss
Nancy M. Lederman

INTRODUCTION: PLANNING FOR YOUR FUTURE

Planning for the future, once just a matter of a steady job and a savings passbook, today requires a cadre of experts to steer you through the unknown. The prospects are hardly glowing. As you grow older, you and your family face the possibility of reduced spending power, rising health care and insurance costs, loss of health benefits both on the job and in retirement, pensions in jeopardy, and changing housing needs. If you're feeling the pinch, you're not alone. According to a recent *New York Times* poll, three out of four workers expect they or their colleagues will face a financial crisis when they retire.

THE DEMOGRAPHIC IMPERATIVE

To some extent, this is the result of phenomenal demographic changes in the United States. During the last two decades the older population has grown more than twice as fast as the rest of the population. The median age in the country, now just under 32 years, is expected to reach 41.8 years by 2030. Life expectancy, less than 50 years at the turn of the century in 1900, reached an all-time high of 75.8 years in 1995.

In sheer numbers, the increase in staggering. At the beginning of this century, only 1 out of 25 Americans was over 65. By the year 2000, 1 out of every 7 will be 65 or older. The fastest-growing part of the population, those over 85, at 3 million now, will reach 8 million in the next 40 years.

FUTURE SHOCK, FUTURE ANXIETIES

These changes have been accompanied by a host of new problems that cut across all lines in American society. One of the greatest of these is health care. One third of the nation's annual health care expenditures—now reaching upwards of $1 trillion—goes to those over 65. Yet despite these enormous outlays, the health care system fails the elderly and people of all ages with disabilities because funding is not available for their long-term and custodial care—forcing them into poverty to obtain needed assistance from Medicaid.

The cost of this system has sent Congress scrambling for changes to limit Medicaid spending and force reforms in Medicare. Yet Medicare, the Great Society program designed for the elderly, does not provide enough. Worse, it discriminates against the elderly. Medicare funding is provided solely for acute illness and is not available for the long-term and custodial care that characterizes the needs of so many elderly people. It does not cover what they actually need—help with managing their lives. Nearly 70 percent seek or receive help with day-to-day tasks such as preparing meals or dressing or managing money.

An estimated 43 percent of Americans over 65 will need long-term care during their lifetimes. Only 1.5 million currently reside in nursing homes, four to five percent of the nation's elderly population. In the next five years, the number will reach 2 million; by the year 2025, 3 million beds will be needed to deal with a population of 60 million older Americans.

In the absence of home care and community assistance, caretaking falls disproportionately on wives and daughters—today's working woman. Of seven million caregivers in the United States, more than two-thirds are juggling careers or taking early retirement in order to provide care for an elderly relative. Nearly 40 percent of women workers over 55 are working part-time. Elder abuse, largely unreported, is on the increase both at home and in institutions—an estimated 1.5 million older Americans are victims of financial or personal abuse.

At the same time, medical technology has posed new dilemmas in medical ethics, raising issues about treatment at the end of life and pushing courts and legislatures to address a whole new batch of ethical questions about personal autonomy—your right to make decisions to control your life. And the questions become even more difficult for the increasing number of family and friends who are called upon to make decisions for others.

PLANNING LESSONS FROM ELDER LAW

If you're like most people, you've planned for good times and ignored the possibility of bad—hoping they wouldn't catch up with you. The irony is that the longer you live the longer the odds are against you, especially if you aren't prepared.

Consider these questions:

- Can I get decent care for my parents, in or out of a nursing home? Where will the financing come from?
- Is my money protected in the event of a health crisis in my family?
- Will my wishes about my health care treatment be respected if I'm incapacitated?

- How secure is the future of my disabled child?
- Will I be able to find appropriate housing or living arrangements as my needs change?

Elder law was founded on these dilemmas, to help find solutions for these problems and to find a way to safeguard your own future and the future of your parents and your children. This new and rapidly evolving area of law deals with legal and management problems that may result from aging, illness, or incapacity, reflecting the pace of change affecting older Americans.

The problems of older clients tend to fall into more than one category, creating multiple dilemmas that demand creative and unconventional strategies. Elder law attorneys along with other advocates have come up with solutions for many of these problems—on a short and long-term basis—making sure their clients get the full range of housing, health care, income and pension benefits they've got coming to them. They've pioneered advances, constructed solutions, and suggested strategies for the problems of older citizens that cut across traditional legal categories:

- living wills and health care proxies to ensure you have a say in your medical treatment
- powers of attorney and trusts to help manage your property and secure your assets
- enforcing rights to Medicare and other government benefits
- Medicaid planning to qualify for government benefits
- long-term care insurance and other financing tools
- home care and support programs for staying in the community
- nursing home reforms
- reverse mortgages to obtain financing on your home

Since Medicare and Medicaid were signed into law in 1965 and the Older Americans Act in 1966, laws passed on behalf of the elderly have included reforms in supplemental Medicare ("Medigap") insurance, long-term care insurance, nursing home reforms, guardianship protections, prohibitions on age discrimination and discrimination on account of disability (on the job and in housing), family leave laws, employee retirement laws, pension guarantees, fair housing laws, and living will statutes.

LEGAL STRATEGIES FOR SURVIVAL

Legal strategies for planning have become necessary to make decisions ranging from questions of health care to financial planning to basic living arrangements. Unfortunately, too little information about the legal aspects of these questions—or too much misinformation—has found its way to the general public. That's what the following pages are about. An understanding of elder law can help you identify your goals and formulate strategies to achieve them. We will help you to focus on your concerns and explain how the laws work for your benefit—so you can understand what your options are and how you can proceed.

Part 1: Planning for Your Health Care Needs

For older Americans and their families, health is their most precious asset—and the one most vulnerable. This part is devoted to a discussion of your health care needs—from identifying your needs and getting appropriate care to financing the health care you receive.

We begin in Chapter 1 with a brief tour of the health care system, including the doctors and hospitals who provide your first line of defense. In Chapter 2, we discuss your rights in making medical decisions about your care. Chapter 3 tells you about options for care in your home and the community, and Chapter 4 describes nursing homes and your rights and options under federal and state law.

Part 2: Managing and Paying for Health Care

For most people, the most important questions are how to find quality care and how to pay for it. These questions assume even greater urgency in a crisis. In Part 2, we show you how to make sure you can pay for the health care you need. In Chapter 5, we discuss your rights under Medicare, the insurance coverage provided by the United States government for those over 65 and younger persons with disabilities, and note some likely areas for change. In Chapter 6, we discuss supplemental coverage and other private insurance and explain current law and proposed legislation designed to help you hold onto that coverage.

In this section, we also introduce you to a number of tools which may be useful for long-term care financing. In Chapter 7, we take a look at the options which may be available to you through Medicare, reverse mortgages, life insurance, retirement communities, long-term care insurance—and a few other financing ideas you may not be aware of. In Chapter 8, we explain the ins and outs of Medicaid planning, to ensure you and your family won't have to be impoverished to receive the health care services you may need, and tell you of changes that may be in the offing. We describe some new programs that may offer protection you need at prices you can afford (Chapter 9).

Part 3: Life Planning for You and Your Family

Many people believe, mistakenly, that life planning is for the wealthy. But most people, rich or not, have the same goals—health, enough assets and income to ensure support for themselves and their spouses, and a cushion for a possible crisis or chronic long-term care needs.

Life planning is about tools that can help you achieve your goals. We start with health: In Chapter 10, we tell you about health care decision-making, how you can protect yourself with advance directives, and how these same documents can help you make decisions on behalf of others.

Then we turn to other planning tools. Chapter 11 tells you about financial planning—and the use of the power of attorney, perhaps the most important legal tool you'll ever need. We explain what a trust is, what it can and cannot do for you, how to avoid common pitfalls, and whether "avoiding probate" is really the best course for you.

Chapter 12 gives you a short tour of planning instruments for a disabled child. In Chapter 13, we talk about options available for those no longer able to make their own decisions—and who neglected to plan ahead—from guardianships to other protective services. We also discuss the increasing problem of personal and financial elder abuse, among families and in institutions, and describe options available for its many victims.

For many, making a will is the primary vehicle for financial planning for a spouse or children. This becomes even more difficult when you consider the possibility of your spouse's need for greater health care in the future—and how provisions you make may affect his or her eligibility for Medicaid benefits. We discuss wills and estate planning, and the implications for taxes and Medicaid, in Chapter 14.

Part 4: You and Your Taxes

One element of planning for the future is a consideration of potential tax obligations. Shifting funds for Medicaid planning, creating trusts, using financial strategies such as reverse mortgages or accelerated death benefits to reap cash flow—all of these may have significant implications for your tax situation. Chapter 15 discusses taxes for older citizens—including gift and estate taxes, income taxation of Social Security benefits, and the effect of tax laws on Medicaid planning.

Part 5: Working and Retirement

Recent years have seen a small revolution in work in the United States. The linear path from trainee to retiree has been replaced with a new and often bewildering maze of options. More than 13.5 million people over 55 are currently in the work force. Another 6 million unemployed Americans over the age of 55 are ready and able to work.

This section offers a short course on issues that you may face while you're working and after you retire. Chapter 16 tells you how to identify discrimination at work—there's more than one kind—and what to do about it. Chapter 17 discusses retirement decisions and protections for your pension and benefits. In Chapter 17, we give you the grand tour of Social Security retirement and disability benefits.

Part 6: Meeting Your Housing Needs

Surveys indicate that more than 86 percent of people over 55 want to remain in their own homes, and most do. For older people, housing expenses represent a major budget item. Those who do stay in their own homes often feel a financial pinch. For others, frailty and insecurity make other housing alternatives a necessity.

In Chapter 19, we discuss your status if you rent or if you own your home, explaining both the rights you have and the opportunities available to help you maintain control over your living arrangements. In Chapter 20, we discuss alternative housing arrangements for older Americans ranging from continuing care facilities to assisted living communities. As these have gained in popularity, they have become a $7 billion industry.

Part 7: Getting Help

In order for your rights to be respected, you have to know how to enforce them. In this chapter, we explain the process of filing claims and making appeals, how to go about finding a lawyer when you need one, and what agencies you may contact for help.

Resources

At the end of this book, we provide a comprehensive list of government agencies, not-for-profit organizations, legal advocacy groups, aging societies, and other sources that you may contact for information and support. We hope you will make ample use of the contact information in this section, which should prove an invaluable resource for any problems you may encounter.

HOW TO USE THIS BOOK

One of the keys to planning your future is identifying the problems and knowing the options available to you.

We help you sort through laws and regulations pouring forth from government to find the strategy fitted to your problem. Where state requirements vary, we point you to the law in your state. Where federal mandates rule, we tell you. We explain your rights at various levels of government, so you can deal with complicated requirements as well as understand the amendments and reforms being discussed. Where your future is concerned, you need information about your rights today—and the consequences of government action on your rights tomorrow.

Your rights depend on the actions you take to enforce them. Throughout this book, we explain how to enforce your rights, from keeping accurate records and making your grievances known to filing claims with the right agencies.

This book was not written to replace a lawyer or to provide legal advice for any particular case. Interpretation of laws often turns on the facts of a particular case. And, as we've pointed out, laws change. With 51 legislatures at the federal and state level, it would be hard to imagine otherwise. Although we note some likely areas for change, we can't predict all possible changes nor what they may look like. But we do promise that if you follow the advice we've laid out for you, you'll be better prepared for any changes that may come.

In many cases, we recommend getting the advice of a professional—whether a lawyer, accountant, financial planner, or private care manager. But regardless of who you call, the responsibility for your life and your future is yours. Don't leave it to chance or depend on others to make the best decisions for you. Start planning now, before a crisis. And keep planning and revising your plans. Control of your future depends on your taking action in the present.

A Final Comment

At all times, we will try to make sure you understand your rights and responsibilities as well as the options available to you. Some of what we have to say you may already know, but we guarantee that some of what we tell you will surprise you. We can't predict what the future will hold, but we can provide the legal framework to help you successfully negotiate your future. With the information in this book, you'll be better prepared to meet whatever challenges face you.

Part 1

■ ■

Planning for Your Health Care Needs

For older Americans and their families, health is their most precious asset—and their most vulnerable one. We begin this part with a blueprint for ensuring good health care, from identifying your needs to getting appropriate care to exercising your right to determine what treatment you will and will not receive. (Later on, in Part 2, we'll show you how to make sure you can pay.)

We start with a brief tour of the health care system. Chapter 1 describes the system you must deal with, healthy or ill, when you go to the doctor and when you enter a hospital. Chapter 2 discusses your right to determine your own treatment—and your right to refuse treatment. (We'll show you even more ways to protect your rights to make decisions about your health care in Chapter 7.)

In a health crisis, the most important question most people face is how to find quality care. Chapters 3 and 4 tell you about available home care programs and nursing homes, and describe your rights and options under federal and state law.

1

■■■

DOCTORS AND HOSPITALS

For most of us, the health care system is represented by doctors. They are the front-line troops who administer the prescriptions, the checkups, the sage advice that keeps us well when we're healthy and gets us better when we're not.

Doctors, specialists, and hospitals, along with nurses and lab technicians—that's the health care system. Other major players in the system are the insurance industry and the government. In today's medical marketplace, whether you can get access to the doctor you want or an experimental treatment or a specific facility often depends on your insurance. The government provides medical benefits for millions of Americans through the Medicare and Medicaid programs.

Don't forget the most important participant in the health care community—the patient. With all our technological advances, we're still likely to treat the patient as the problem to be solved rather than as a participant in finding a solution.

Seeking and getting health care today is not so much knowing the system as understanding the pieces of a puzzle. In order to take care of your health and your family's health, you need to know how the puzzle fits together—so that you can understand your options and exercise your rights and responsibilities as a consumer as well as a patient.

CHOOSING A DOCTOR

Your choice of doctor may be the most important health care decision you will make. Everything else flows from that one decision. Your primary physician is the one who in all likelihood will give you routine medical care, treat you in illness and emergencies, perform laboratory tests and make diagnoses, refer you to specialists, and find you other services and facilities as needed. In everyday matters and crisis situations, this is the doctor who will be monitoring your care and explaining your options to you.

People are often forced to search for a doctor when they are least capable of doing it. Either they are sick or they are in an emergency situation, forced to rely solely on a blind recommendation or the luck of the draw at the local emergency room. Part of good health care planning is choosing ahead of time.

It's important to have a doctor you know and trust, and one you can talk to. In searching for and choosing a suitable doctor, the recommendations of family and friends can be very useful. So can referrals from your county medical association or local hospital.

Even if you are joining a health maintenance organization (HMO) or are covered by an insurance plan that restricts your choice of doctors, you generally can choose a primary care physician from among a roster of participating doctors. Remember, before choosing a doctor or allowing one to treat you, there are certain things you are entitled to know.

Education and experience. A doctor has completed four years of medical school following college, most likely followed by two years or more of postgraduate practice in residency. Upon a qualifying examination, he or she is licensed to practice medicine by the state.

Theoretically that's all a doctor needs to perform even the most difficult procedures, like open-heart surgery. However, that shouldn't be enough to satisfy you (nor would it be allowed by most hospitals).

Board certification. A doctor with expertise in a particular area of medicine may have certification of the specialized knowledge and qualifications to practice in that particular area. Board certification provides an extra measure of assurance that a doctor is trained and proficient in an area of practice. In order to become a board-certified specialist, a doctor must complete a prescribed course of training as a resident in that specialty, pass an examination, and satisfy other requirements established by the board in question.

Primary-care specialties include internal medicine, pediatrics, and obstetrics/gynecology, as well as family practice for those who specialize in care of the individual or family. You can get referrals to local members from both the American Board of Internal Medicine (telephone 202/289-1700) and the American Academy of Family Practice (telephone 800/274-2237).

Certification in subspecialties is available from a number of boards. For example, the American Board of Internal Medicine certifies subspecialties in Gastroenterology and Medical Oncology. The American Board of Internal Medicine and the American Academy of Family Practice also certify competence in Geriatric Medicine. In order to have subspecialty certification, a doctor must first have certification in the umbrella specialty.

Certification is not available in some areas of practice and is relatively new in others. All together, approximately 124 specialty boards provide certification, although with significant variations in their requirements. The American Board of Medical Specialties is an umbrella organization of 24 specialty boards, such as the American Board of Internal Medicine, which are generally accepted as setting industry standards. In addition to specialty certification, member boards offer 50 subspecialty certifications.

How can I find out if my doctor is certified?

The American Board of Medical Specialties runs a special hotline certification number, at 800/776-2378. Call to check whether or not your doctor is certified with one of their boards.

If my doctor is Board-certified, does that guarantee knowledge of all the latest technology and advances in the field? Not necessarily. Your doctor's certification may be old, and once certified, not all doctors need to be recertified.

A number of specialty boards do require periodic recertification (for instance, in internal medicine, physicians must be recertified every ten years), but these are relatively new requirements. Many doctors who are currently board-certified were "grandfathered" in under old rules, meaning they do not need to be recertified to keep their standing. Good doctors do keep up with changes in their field, regardless of their recertification requirements.

Don't the states have some sort of recertification procedure?

No. A number of states do impose continuing education requirements that require doctors to complete a minimum number of continuing medical education course credits in order to keep their licenses. If courses are not taken, the doctor's license can be suspended or revoked. (State regulation is discussed later in this chapter.)

Is membership in a medical society or academy the same thing as certification?

Not all societies or academies are certifying boards, and it's difficult to distinguish among them. In general, membership in a medical society helps a doctor keep up with advances in the profession. There are some with rigorous requirements amounting to board equivalence.

Hospital affiliation. Affiliation ("privileges") with a particular hospital allows your doctor to admit you to that hospital and to treat you there as your attending physician (sometimes *voluntary physician*). An internist or other primary-care physician who is affiliated with a medical center is more likely to offer you greater access to a broad range of specialists. It's generally your primary care physician who makes these recommendations when you need them—and who will troubleshoot any medical problems you have.

A hospital can be held legally responsible for the actions of a doctor affiliated with it, especially where the hospital knew or should have known about any deficiencies in the doctor's performance. A hospital has an obligation to review the credentials of its attending physicians, including education credentials, any disciplinary actions and malpractice suits, and references. The hospital may limit an attending physician to those procedures the physician is qualified to perform, although there is no obligation that a hospital restrict a doctor's privileges for any given reason. Usually a hospital bases its decision on the type of practice the doctor has and whether the hospital will be able to handle admissions from that particular doctor.

Traditionally, attending physicians have been doctors in private practice. Recent changes in hospital organization have dramatically altered the relationship between hospitals and doctors, with more and more hospitals affiliated in networks with doctors. It is not clear how self-policing these networks will be, although both networks and member hospitals may be held to higher standards of responsibility for doctors with whom they are more closely affiliated.

Checking on your doctor

The general unavailability of public information concerning doctors is one of the disgraces of the medical profession. Oversight of doctors varies from state to state, and reporting requirements are generally minimal. Some states, such as New York and Pennsylvania, publish limited information on heart surgeons' mortality rates.

For the most part, however, reports concerning doctors with outstanding malpractice and disciplinary charges against them are not made available to the public. It's even harder to track those doctors who have been found guilty of professional misconduct in one state and moved to another. Hospitals have access to information on disciplinary actions against doctors through the National Practitioners Data Bank. Under law, the public is not entitled to this information.

You should check with your state department of health or licensing agency to determine whether your doctor has been charged with or found guilty of any disciplinary charges. Public Citizen's Health Research Group publishes a book called *13,012 Questionable Doctors*, which offers summary information on doctors who have been disciplined (see Resources section).

 GETTING THE MEDICAL INFORMATION YOU NEED

If you think your doctor is not paying enough attention to you, don't dismiss the thought as only in your imagination. Studies show that many doctors just don't listen to their patients. This is not just bad manners. It's bad medicine. It restricts the ability of the doctor to glean necessary information from the patient interview. This is especially important for older patients, who often have multiple complaints. A doctor who hears only the main symptom may be missing the big picture. Doctors who treat the elderly must be alert to underlying and additional symptoms.

Today's doctors have less time for patients in both managed care plans and traditional fee-for-service practices. Find one who will give you enough time. Don't let your doctor monopolize the conversation. You should do your part, too. Be prepared with a list of your complaints and symptoms, and have your questions written down in advance. Write down the doctor's answers, too, and any instructions you may be given.

Drug prescriptions present a related issue for older patients. The *Journal of the American Medical Association* has reported that almost one-quarter of patients 65 or older are given inappropriate prescriptions. In addition to specific drugs which should never be prescribed to them, older patients are more susceptible to undesirable interactions from multiple drug prescriptions. Don't assume a reaction is the result of your old age. Make sure your doctor takes a complete drug history and discusses all your medication and possible side effects with you.

Another area generally ignored by doctors is nutrition. Nutritional assessment and training have been shown to be useful in illness prevention and treatment for older patients. Yet doctors are for the most part uninformed about nutrition and fail to inquire about the nutritional habits of their patients. Insist that diet and nutrition be included in your discussions with your doctor.

One area too often avoided by both patients and doctors is anticipated treatment in catastrophic illness. A recent study found that many doctors routinely prescribed aggressive treatment in end-of-life cases, regardless of patient wishes. Only a small percentage of physicians even knew when their patients wanted to avoid cardiopulmonary resuscitation. Make sure your wishes are discussed with your doctor. (Your doctor should also be given a copy of your living will. Living wills and advance directives are discussed in Chapter 10.)

Is a second opinion always necessary before surgery?

Yes. It may also be the last bargain in medicine. You should seek another opinion before surgery and whenever your diagnosis is serious or uncertain, your treatment is undesirable or simply not working, or you have any questions about your doctor's competence. Insurers have learned to support second opinions, which often save unnecessary surgery and other costly and unwanted procedures. If you can't find a doctor, the Medicare hotline at 800/638-6833 will supply you with local referrals.

How can I find out more about my condition?

The information explosion has had one enormous benefit. Medical information once inaccessible to the layman is no longer unavailable. Not only are research journals easy to locate, but there are any number of agencies to give you information on specific diseases, conditions, and symptoms.

If you have access to a computer and modem, health-related information databases will let you research specific diseases and print out articles from medical journals. A number of private companies have also emerged which offer to conduct research for you, for a fee. These can be very expensive, however, and are not covered by insurance. Medical journals and public access databases may also be available at your public library. (See the Resources section at the end of this book.)

YOUR MEDICAL RECORDS

Reviewing your records increases your participation in and control of your health care. It also allows you to question or correct inaccurate information, a not uncommon occurrence. The use and dissemination of patients' medical records are regulated by the states. Many states have laws prescribing strict confidentiality concerning information and limiting release of your medical records.

Many doctors and medical facilities will give you copies of your records if you just ask for them. More than half the states have laws granting you direct access to your medical records, including Alaska, California, Colorado, Florida, Michigan, Minnesota, New Jersey, New York, South Carolina, and Wisconsin. In others, you may be restricted to a summary prepared by your doctor or the hospital, or you may have to obtain release through a physician or a lawyer. Federal law grants nursing home residents in Medicare and Medicaid facilities access to their medical records. Patients are also granted access to medical records held in federal facilities such as Veterans' Administration hospitals.

HOW YOUR DOCTOR CHARGES

Because of upheavals in the health care industry, many doctors are joining with other doctors in managed-care organizations and networks, changing their fee structures and the nature of their medical practice. In addition, government regulations are setting more requirements on doctors, while insurers are second-guessing once-sacrosanct medical decisions.

For consumers, it's a very confusing time. Some of the changes you may find at your doctor's office may affect the quality or cost of the care you receive, and should be considered when choosing your doctor.

Traditionally, doctors have charged patients on a per-service basis with few controls. This led to a spiral of rising charges for overtesting, overtreating, and overprescribing. There was little incentive for doctors to practice preventive care to keep healthy patients well.

HMOs and managed care. Many doctors have join managed-care organizations such as health maintenance organizations (HMOs) or more loosely configured networks of health care providers. In many of the groups, doctors or hospitals receive per-person payment instead of per-service payment. This is called *capitation*.

By joining, the doctor has agreed to accept certain lower fees. The patient may be liable for a small share of the cost, known as *copayment*. Under capitation, there is a shared financial risk and greater incentives for physicians to practice preventive medicine. The downside of this system is that it may result in less incentive to provide quality care on an individual basis.

Doctors' fees. A large portion of health care reform has focused on lowering health care costs in general, and doctors' fees in particular. Insurance companies apply fee limits through their reimbursement rates, paying a percentage of what they deem to be "standard and customary." We explain how to deal with your insurance company in Chapter 6, but remember that you can also negotiate with your doctor for lower rates so you won't be unreasonably out-of-pocket.

As a result of federal reforms, there are fee limits for the amounts *all doctors* can charge Medicare patients. A number of states also restrict fees. (For an explanation of fee limits for Medicare patients, see Chapter 5, Physician Fees.)

 CHOOSING A HOSPITAL

In choosing a hospital in non-emergency situations, you have two options. One is to have a doctor affiliated with a good hospital located near your home. Remember that when you pick your primary care doctor, you're picking a hospital, too. The hospital your doctor is affiliated with is not only where you may likely wind up if you need hospitalization, but where your doctor may send you for laboratory tests, CT scans, and other outpatient procedures. (Some doctors use "off-premises" facilities.)

The other choice (when you have time to plan for hospital services) is to go where the type of surgery or procedure you need is performed most often. You will generally be wiser to plan to go where the specialty is. The more complex the procedure, the more prudent to do so. Hospitals have specialties in which their work and reputations are excellent. Studies have shown that the more often a doctor or hospital does a procedure, the more likely the results will be better for the patient.

Another consideration for older patients is *discharge planning*. This is especially important for those going to rehabilitation services. Many hospitals offer special programs for senior citizens.

What information is available? Hospitals are evaluated and accredited by the Joint Commission on Accreditation of Healthcare Organizations, which accredits four out of every five of the nation's hospitals. Accreditation is dependent on inspection every three years, based on a variety of measures. The Health Care Financing Administration (HCFA), which certifies facilities for federal reimbursement purposes, publishes quality-of-care data for Medicare patients (generally over 65). States publish some information on hospital patients. New York has consumer information guides to its hospitals, which show the most common procedures and their cost.

IN AN EMERGENCY

Emergency rooms are busy places. In 1990, 90 million people went to an emergency room. As anyone who's gone to one recently can tell you, many of the people waiting are there for primary health care purposes. For them, the emergency room ("ER") *is* their health care system. Unfortunately, for them and for you, this drives up the cost of ER care—and makes getting in harder and more time-consuming.

Although most states do not require hospitals to admit you, under federal law any institution with emergency facilities must treat you if you have an urgent medical problem. This is commonly referred to as the "anti-dumping" law, although its formal title is the *Emergency Treatment and Active Labor Act*. It prohibits private hospitals from turning away uninsured patients needing emergency care.

No matter what the particular intake procedures of the hospital you go to, you will begin with *triage*, where someone—most likely a nurse or a physician's assistant—will make a preliminary evaluation of your medical condition. This evaluation determines how long you will wait. ER workers can be wrong. If you're in pain or think you need to see someone sooner, speak up! Keep at it. It's easy to be forgotten in an ER. Insist on having a doctor examine you to assess the urgency of your condition.

Do all hospitals have emergency rooms?

No. One response of strapped hospitals to anti-dumping laws has been to eliminate their emergency care service altogether. However, some states require all hospitals to have an emergency room. There are also proposals to require that all non-profit hospitals have emergency rooms.

In an emergency, am I entitled to be admitted for treatment?

You're entitled to treatment for an emergency medical condition. If you have an urgent medical problem and present yourself at a hospital with an ER, you have the legal right to be treated. And you can't be transferred to a different facility, unless you're in stable condition (or a doctor certifies that the benefit of transfer outweighs the risk and the receiving hospital has agreed to accept you). Make sure a doctor examines you to determine appropriate treatment. If you aren't treated and suffer damage, you may have grounds for a malpractice suit against the hospital. Some jurisdictions also provide penalties for hospitals which deny you emergency care.

Once the emergency is dealt with, you may need continued care. This no longer qualifies as an emergency, and whether you must be admitted to the hospital at that point varies from state to state.

Can I be refused emergency care if I can't pay?

No. You have a right to emergency treatment for an emergency condition regardless of your ability to pay. One little-known fact is that many hospitals receive construction funding under the federal Hill-Burton Act, passed in 1946, which requires them to accept a number of indigent patients free of charge. You can inquire at the hospital about eligibility and how to apply for these services. (If you can't pay, you may also be able to qualify for Medicaid. For more, see Chapter 8.)

HOW HOSPITALS ARE ORGANIZED

Hospitals are going through dramatic changes, as is the rest of the nation's health care system. In many parts of the country, hospitals are cutting costs, merging with other institutions and redefining the services they offer. In some communities, they are going under. Across the board, traditional notions of hospital structure—like the delivery of all health care services—are being questioned. These changes have both direct and indirect implications for consumers.

Traditionally, hospitals have been classified both as to ownership (whether they are public or private) and specialties. In regard to ownership, don't be confused by misleading nomenclature. *Voluntary* or *charitable* hospitals are generally private, albeit non-profit, organizations. Private hospitals are called *proprietary*. Not all hospitals provide all services. Specialty institutions may treat a particular disease or condition, such as heart disease. Some *teaching hospitals* maintain close affiliations with medical schools.

Although a hospital as a corporation is run by its board and management, your health care is in the hands of the medical staff. This may be either your private physician or resident doctors, or a combination of both. Your attending physician, if you have one, is in charge of your care. If you don't have an attending physician and you've been admitted to the hospital, there will be a doctor, generally a resident on staff, assigned that responsibility. You have the right to know who that person is.

Do I have to be examined by residents, interns, and medical students?

You can refuse to be examined by medical students or hospital staff such as interns and residents (now known as PGY-1, PGY-2, and so on, for their "postgraduate year"). The person with the responsibility to make decisions about your care is the attending physician. But remember, hospitals are caught between the dual missions of training doctors and providing patient care. Your care may be improved by the attention that comes with additional help.

PATIENT'S BILL OF RIGHTS

One of the first initiatives in the patient rights movement was the development of a bill of rights. This was developed over the years and has been adopted by the American Hospital Association as the Patient's Bill of Rights.

PATIENT'S BILL OF RIGHTS*

1. The patient has the right to considerate and respectful care.
2. The patient has the right to and is encouraged to obtain from physicians and other direct care-givers relevant, current, and understandable information concerning diagnosis, treatment, and prognosis.

    Except in emergencies when the patient lacks decision-making capacity and the need for treatment is urgent, the patient is entitled to the opportunity to discuss and request information related to the specific procedures and/or treatments, the risks involved, the possible length of recuperation, and the medically reasonable alternatives and their accompanying risks and benefits.

    Patients have the right to know the identity of physicians, nurses, and others involved in their care, as well as when those involved are students, residents, or other trainees. The patient also has the right to know the immediate and long-term financial implications of treatment choices, insofar as they are known.
3. The patient has the right to make decisions about the plan of care prior to and during the course of treatment and to refuse a recommended treatment or plan of care to the extent permitted by law and hospital policy and to be informed of the medical consequences of this action. In case of such refusal, the patient is entitled to other appropriate care and services that the hospital provides or transfer to another hospital. The hospital should notify patients of any policy that might affect patient choice within the institution.
4. The patient has the right to have an advance directive (such as a living will, health care proxy, or durable power of attorney for health care) concerning treatment or designating a surrogate decision maker with the expectation that the hospital will honor the intent of that directive to the extent permitted by law and hospital policy.

    Health care institutions must advise patients of their rights under state law and hospital policy to make informed medical choices, ask if the patient has an advance directive, and include that information in patient records. The patient has the right to timely information about hospital policy that may limit its ability to implement fully a legally valid advance directive.
5. The patient has the right to every consideration of privacy. Case discussion, consultation, examination, and treatment should be conducted so as to protect each patient's privacy.
6. The patient has the right to expect that all communications and records pertaining to his/her care will be treated as confidential by the hospital, except in cases such as suspected abuse and public health hazards when reporting is permitted or required by law. The patient has the right to expect that the hospital will emphasize the confidentiality of this information when it releases it to any other parties entitled to review information in these records.

---

*These rights can be exercised on the patient's behalf by a designated surrogate or proxy decision maker if the patient lacks decision-making capacity, is legally incompetent, or is a minor.

7.   The patient has the right to review the records pertaining to his/her medical care and to have the information explained or interpreted as necessary, except when restricted by law.

8.   The patient has the right to expect that, within its capacity and policies, a hospital will make reasonable response to the request of a patient for appropriate and medically indicated care and services. The hospital must provide evaluation, service, and/or referral as indicated by the urgency of the case. When medically appropriate and legally permissible, or when a patient has so requested, a patient may be transferred to another facility. The institution to which the patient is to be transferred must first have accepted the patient for transfer. The patient must also have the benefit of complete information and explanation concerning the need for, risks, benefits, and alternatives to such a transfer.

9.   The patient has the right to ask and be informed of the existence of business relationships among the hospital, educational institutions, other health care providers, or payers that may influence the patient's treatment and care.

10. The patient has the right to consent to or decline to participate in proposed research studies or human experimentation affecting care and treatment or requiring direct patient involvement, and to have those studies fully explained prior to consent. A patient who declines to participate in research or experimentation is entitled to the most effective care that the hospital can otherwise provide.

11. The patient has the right to expect reasonable continuity of care when appropriate and to be informed by physicians and other caregivers of available and realistic patient care options when hospital care is no longer appropriate.

12. The patient has the right to be informed of hospital policies and practices that relate to patient care, treatment, and responsibilities. The patient has the right to be informed of available resources for resolving disputes, grievances, and conflicts, such as ethics committees, patient representatives, or other mechanisms available in the institution. The patient has the right to be informed of the hospital's charges for services and available payment methods.

Most hospitals have adopted some version of it, and many states have adopted statutes enumerating patients' rights, including the right to know who's treating them, to reject care by students, to be informed about doctors' financial interests in hospitals if it would affect health care, to consent to or refuse treatment ("informed consent"), to be told the alternatives for treatment and surgery, and to receive a copy of hospital medical records. (See the box on p. 11 for the Patient's Bill of Rights.)

Federal law has also adopted some portions. Hospitals are required by federal law to notify patients of their right under state law to refuse medical treatment. (Federal law also sets forth rights for nursing home residents. See Chapters 4 and 10.)

How do I enforce my rights?

Because of inadequate training and education of health care providers, these rights are not uniformly enforced. Even where a written bill of rights is routinely distributed, patient rights may not always be respected. One of the advances that has most helped in this area is the "patient advocate," described in the next section.

 PATIENT ADVOCATES

Most hospitals have a *patient advocate* (also called a *patient representative* or *patient ombudsman*), who can provide the communications link between the patient and the hospital. Often this is just a matter of taking the time to explain to you and your family what is going on. If you have a complaint, the patient advocate will discuss it with you and take it to hospital administrators or doctors.

Patient advocates are knowledgeable about the options available to you and can explain your rights in exercising those options, help you obtain a second opinion, or assist you in challenging a hospital decision to discharge you. They can be of particular help in situations in which you are refusing treatment or making decisions on behalf of someone else. (See Chapter 10 on health care directives.)

One caveat: Patient advocates, social workers and others you encounter in a hospital may offer you helpful advice on qualifying for Medicaid. Before you follow *anyone's* advice on transferring or spending funds to make yourself Medicaid-eligible, make sure you consult a lawyer knowledgeable in the field. (Medicaid planning is discussed in Chapter 8.)

How do I find the patient advocate?

Information on how to find the patient advocate will be included in your hospital admission papers and posted or placed in your hospital room.

 REGULATING DOCTORS AND HOSPITALS

State regulation comes in a variety of forms. In the first instance, states license doctors and hospitals, usually under the authority of the state department of health. If standards or conditions of licensure are not maintained, licenses can be suspended or revoked. While action against a hospital is rare, an increasing number of doctors have been disciplined for professional misconduct by state regulatory agencies. In 1994, more than 3,600 American doctors received reprimands or had their licenses suspended or revoked.

A 1996 report by Public Citizen's Health Research Group, however, charges that only one third of those doctors found to have given substandard or negligent care were required to stop practicing temporarily or permanently; most retain their licenses and continue to treat patients. There is great variation in penalties from state to state.

Health care reforms and related economies are forcing states to look harder at their regulations. Hospitals, for example, are finding it harder to justify new or expanded services. Doctors who make referrals of patients for medical services in which they have a financial interest, a practice called *self-referral*, are finding themselves under criticism for conflict of interest. Under federal law, doctors are prohibited from referring Medicare patients for clinical laboratory and radiological services in which they have a financial interest, and current proposals would broaden the categories of prohibited services. Some states prohibit self-referrals or fee-splitting, while others have laws mandating disclosure.

If you have a problem with medical treatment or any other action by a doctor or hospital, you can make a complaint to the state department of health or your local medical society. Remember, complaints you make to the proper authorities may help protect the next unwary patient. (Check the Resources section at the end of this book.) If your complaint is of possible malpractice, you should also consult an attorney to determine if you have a valid claim or grounds for a lawsuit. (We discuss how to find an attorney in Chapter 21.)

2

■■■

MAKING HEALTH CARE
DECISIONS

Decision-making about one's life and medical care is a basic right of an autonomous human being. In health care as in many areas involving experts and professionals, individuals are only recently learning to make their own decisions and, perhaps more importantly, questioning the decisions of others in areas which have a direct bearing on their lives.

Each day medical science offers new technologies, new technologies offer new options, and new options create new dilemmas. With advanced technologies capable of keeping more and more people alive longer and longer, life-and-death issues have become both more complex and more common.

At the same time, patients have fought for and won the right to make decisions about their own health care, decisions which were formerly the exclusive province of medical practitioners. Compounding the difficulty for patients, they have to make these decisions at times of crisis, often under extreme stress.

Under optimal circumstances it would be hard to absorb all the information thrown at you—options, therapeutic benefits and risk factors, possible side effects—and all in scientific terms guaranteed to alarm even the most stout-hearted. Medical crises are rarely optimal circumstances. The more life-threatening the situation, the more difficult the decision; the more difficult the decision, the more stressful the situation. It's a vicious cycle.

While you're trying to determine what's best to do, others may be undermining your efforts, trying to take the choice away from you. When it comes to confronting life-and-death issues, there are no easy answers. But there are legal techniques that will empower you to assert your rights.

▌ THE EMERGENCE OF PATIENT RIGHTS

The history of patient rights is surprisingly brief. Not so long ago patients could be subject to experimentation by doctors, without their knowledge or consent. At the opposite end of the spectrum, the authority of today's doctors has been diminished to the point where insurance companies are using their control over the purse strings to exercise control over health care decisions.

As the decision-making role of the doctor has diminished, the role of the patient has expanded, to the delight of patient advocates and the lament of many doctors—and not a few patients. Patients have been transformed from unquestioning supplicants to wary consumers in dealing with doctors, hospitals, and insurance companies and making their own decisions about medical treatment.

Although the role of the patient has changed, the concept of patient rights is not new. As far back as 1914, in a landmark decision, New York's highest court ruled:

> Every human being of adult years and sound mind has a right to determine what shall be done with his own body; and a surgeon who performs an operation without his patient's consent commits an assault for which he is liable in damages.

The author of those words was Judge Benjamin Cardozo, renowned jurist of the New York State Court of Appeals who later served on the United States Supreme Court. In that one opinion, Judge Cardozo established your absolute right as a patient to determine your own treatment and the liability of those who fail to respect that right.

The case for patient rights and patient autonomy received renewed attention in the 1980s and 1990s from the *Cruzan* case. Nancy Cruzan was a young girl who at the age of 25 had a tragic automobile accident in Missouri. She fell into what doctors call a "persistent vegetative state" and was kept alive only by artificial feeding. When her parents sought to disconnect the feeding tube, citing their daughter's wishes in the matter, the hospital refused. The Cruzans went to court.

Cruzan provided the ultimate test between medical authority and patient rights. Eventually the Missouri case went to the United States Supreme Court, which in 1990 ruled that there was a constitutional right to refuse artificial life support. The liberty interests of the individual under the 14th Amendment were held to be paramount. Nancy Cruzan had the constitutional right to determine her own care (in this case through her surrogate).

Not everyone is comfortable with patients' and their families' exercising their rights to make these "medical" decisions. Despite the clear rule of law dating back to Judge Cardozo, changes to the traditional patient-doctor relationship are resisted both within and outside the medical community. There continues to be a large "care gap" between what patients want and what they get. That's why it's so important for patients to learn how best to exercise their rights—and the responsibilities that come with them.

CONSENTING TO TREATMENT

When you go to a doctor, there are certain assumptions that are understood by both parties. You have entered a relationship with expectations of each other.

- The doctor will examine you, either as part of a routine checkup or in response to specific complaints, or a combination of both.
- The doctor will evaluate your medical condition and, if appropriate, attempt to offer a diagnosis and possible treatment, or further tests to aid in diagnosis or treatment.
- The doctor will offer you treatment recommendations and options, fully explaining advantages and disadvantages, benefits and risks.
- You will decide whether to accept or reject the doctor's advice.
- You (or your insurance company, or Medicare) will pay for the service.

That's the extent of the relationship. If you don't want to have your blood drawn or an X ray taken, you can refuse. No one may force you. In a nutshell, that's *informed consent*. Before you undergo *any* medical treatment or procedure, you need to know what is planned for you and you need to agree to it.

Informed consent is an important concept to understand. Informed consent requires full disclosure to you, the patient, of the risks and benefits of the proposed treatment, as well as any possible alternative treatments. Without this information, your assent is worthless, because you haven't been given the information that would make your consent "informed."

The purpose of informed consent is best understood by how the two words work together.

- *Informed*: doctors provide information to patients to help them understand their condition and proposed treatments
- *Consent*: patients agree to a course of treatment before it starts, to protect doctors from liability for things that go wrong

The average encounter soliciting your approval for a procedure will have more emphasis on the *consent* side of the equation than on the *informed*. This is due to the inherently unequal nature of the doctor-patient relationship. Signed forms may be used as evidence of your informed consent should you decide afterwards to sue.

Most of the time that won't be necessary. But don't put your faith blindly in experts and professionals. Hospitals have systems to prevent errors, but systems break down. *Things go wrong*. Doctors prescribe medicines and forget to ask about allergies or other medications. Medicine gets delivered to the wrong patient, or the wrong patient gets delivered to the operating room. Paddy Chayefsky's movie *The Hospital*, starring Diana Rigg and

George C. Scott, offered a chilling portrayal of incompetence, larceny, and medical malpractice; one patient simply died from being left on a gurney in the hall and forgotten. Unfortunately, such horror stories are not confined to the movies.

According to one study published in the *New England Journal of Medicine*, thousands of hospital patients have suffered similar negligence. In 1995, three well-known institutions received national publicity for performing the wrong surgery on patients, with tragic results. Don't assume that a procedure that you haven't approved is intended for you at all. Make sure anything that your primary doctor has not discussed with you before-hand is in fact intended for you.

And always get a second opinion before you agree to any high-risk treatment. Most insurance policies now require this, because it cuts down on unnecessary surgery.

Is informed consent required by law?

Yes. Treating you without consent may constitute assault or battery. It may be grounds for a malpractice lawsuit. The right to informed consent is included in the American Hospital Association's Patient Bill of Rights (see page 11). Written consent is merely documentation of your agreement. In most cases other than experimental treatments, writing itself is not required by any statute or regulation.

Nevertheless, you can wind up signing as many as three or more consent forms when you're in the hospital. Whether or not any of these is legally valid depends on the circumstances. Although a signed form can be used as "evidence" of informed consent, it does not necessarily preclude you from bringing a suit after treatment.

How specific does informed consent have to be?

You need to be informed of the risks and potential benefits of planned treatments, and of alternative treatments or procedures. These include the option and probable outcome of receiving no treatment. Serious side effects, however unlikely, should always be disclosed.

Consent is not simply a blanket agreement to treatment. If you're undergoing surgery, you have the right to authorize what will be done to you—and the right to say what will *not* be done to you. The law grants some leeway to surgeons confronting unexpected problems. If there is any question, discuss these matters with your surgeon beforehand.

For the most part, general consent forms prepared by hospitals have limited legal validity. The more specific your consent, the more likely it will be upheld as valid in any subsequent court proceeding. From a legal point of view, what counts is whether or not you were given the information you needed to make your consent meaningful.

Are there exceptions to the requirement that a patient give informed consent?

In an emergency situation, where there is no one available to authorize treatment, doctors may proceed without consent. This emergency authority is sometimes abused in institutional settings to give unwanted medication. Problems also arise in emergency situations when elderly people are given treatment by doctors and other personnel without knowledge of or in disregard of contrary prior instructions.

In cases where the patient is unable to give consent due to incapacity, doctors may sometimes proceed with consent from family members (*substituted consent*). Many adults with mental illness receive experimental drug treatments with the consent of relatives or friends. (See "Surrogate and Family Consent," later in this chapter.)

Doctors sometime cite "therapeutic privilege" to withhold information. This may be done in limited circumstances when the doctor believes that disclosing it would have an adverse effect on the patient's condition, for example, on a depressed or critically ill patient.

My doctor is pressuring me to sign a consent form. What are my options?

If no medical emergency exists, the first thing to do is get a second opinion. This is always your right. Your consent must be voluntary, without any coercion. Most insurance companies will back you up on this. Ask to talk with the hospital's patient advocate, who will explain your rights to you. Ask for time to think about it. And remember you can always alter the form, deleting or editing the words that make you feel uncomfortable.

The most important step to take with a consent form, as with any other paper you may be asked to sign, is: *read it before you sign*. Your signature signifies both your understanding and your agreement.

- Don't sign what you don't understand.
- Don't sign what you don't agree with.
- Always get a copy of what you sign.

You are as important as the physician standing before you and your wishes and requests for information must be respected and honored. That's only fair—and it's the law!

Remember, signing does not keep you from changing your mind during your treatment or bringing a lawsuit afterwards if you were not properly advised or if you received negligent treatment.

 EXPERIMENTAL PROCEDURES

Codes of behavior against human experimentation date back to two philosopher-physicians practicing in the 11th and 12th centuries, when Avicenna, who was Islamic, and Maimonides, who was Jewish, warned against using patients for medical discoveries and not treating them for their own good. Unhappily, this advice has not always been taken. In the United States, notorious examples of such experiments include syphilis treatment withheld from black sharecroppers at Tuskegee in the 1930s, penicillin withheld from servicemen in the 1950s, and cancer cells injected into elderly patients as recently as the 1960s, all in the name of research.

The doctrine of informed consent was developed in part to remedy this sorry history of human experimentation. In cases where experimentation is involved, more detailed and complete information is required. In the first place, the patient must fully understand the experimental nature of the proposed treatment, the existence of other approved treatments in the protocol of the trial, the potential for known and unknown risks, and the probability of success.

In the institutional setting, federal regulations mandate review by an "institutional review board" established to approve and monitor research projects. Specific review criteria must address the rights and welfare of the individual research subjects, the methods used to obtain informed consent, and the risks and potential benefits of the investigation. Approval by the institutional review board only signifies approval of the research being conducted; it does *not* mean that you have to consent to being a part of it.

 REFUSING TREATMENT

The corollary to informed consent is the right to refuse treatment. *If you have the right to consent to treatment, it necessarily follows that you have the right to refuse it.*

Traditionally, the right to refuse treatment has been based on your common-law right to bodily integrity, your constitutional right to privacy, and, under certain circumstances, your constitutional right to the free exercise of your religion. Theoretically at least, treatment performed against your will could be a form of negligence or assault.

According to the law—upheld in the Supreme Court's 1990 *Cruzan* decision—the decision to reject life-saving treatment is protected by the guarantee of the right to liberty embodied in the 14th Amendment to the Constitution. The right to refuse treatment is included in the American Hospital Association's Patient Bill of Rights (see page 11), and included in most individual hospitals' patient bill of rights. Hospitals are required by federal law to notify patients of their right under state law to refuse medical treatment.

What kinds of treatments can I refuse?

Any kind. Whether it's good or bad for you, you can refuse it. You are free to refuse treatment even if it puts your life in jeopardy.

Is there any exception?

Only a very limited one, to protect public health, as in vaccinations required by the board of health. Even this kind of requirement may be overridden in some cases by objections based on religious belief.

Is the right to refuse lost when a person becomes incompetent?

No. If a person's wishes were expressed when he or she was competent, either through a document such as a living will or orally to another person, those wishes must be respected. Decisions for incapacitated adults or children who have not expressed their wishes are usually made by relatives pursuant to *family consent laws* or the doctrine of *substituted judgment*. You can preserve your rights though a health care proxy, in which you can designate an agent in advance to make decisions on your behalf if you later become incapacitated. We discuss these issues in Chapter 10, Advance Directives for Health Care.

 IN THE HOSPITAL AND NURSING HOME

Under federal law signed in 1990, all hospitals, nursing homes, home health agencies, hospices, and prepaid health care organizations receiving federal aid must notify patients of their right to receive or refuse medical treatment. The Patient Self-Determination Act mandates that health care facilities that participate in Medicare and Medicaid must

- Provide *written information* to all adult patients as to their rights under state law to make decisions about their medical care, including the right to accept or refuse care and their right to sign advance directives—living wills and health care proxies—for health-care decisions
- Provide a *written description* of state law and their own internal policies governing patients' rights
- Inquire whether any advance directives have been signed, document the existence of any directives, and avoid discriminating in the kind of care provided based on whether or not the patient has executed advance directives
- Ensure compliance with state law on advance directives

Most states and hospitals, as we discussed earlier, have adopted a patient's bill of rights that includes the right to refuse treatment.

Under federal law, health care facilities which do not comply risk loss of funding. Hospitals and nursing homes are not required to provide forms for patient use. The law provides for staff education and informational materials for the public prepared by the Department of Health and Human Services.

Under what circumstances can I leave a hospital?

If you want to leave the hospital, the hospital can't stop you. Some people prefer not to stay in the hospital, risking unwanted infections; others want to be far away from possible extraordinary life-saving measures. Provided you're of sound mind, you can leave anytime. You can sign yourself out of hospital "AMA" (against medical advice).

Most hospitals will ask you to sign a form saying "discharge against medical advice." You don't have to sign this or any other form to leave the hospital, even if you haven't paid the bill. Keeping you against your will would be false imprisonment.

Can the hospital kick me out for not following its advice?

No. The hospital cannot discharge you for other than medical reasons. Anti-dumping laws guarantee that the hospital will continue to provide medical care if you need it. You can be transferred to another hospital only if you're in stable condition.

THE "RIGHT TO DIE"

The phrase "right to die" means different things to different people. It is used and misused by advocates and opponents alike. What it means to patients who assert their rights when they are critically ill—and to the lawyers who help them—is this: *it is your right to determine what treatment you will get and what treatment you may refuse.*

In simple terms, this is just an extension of the "informed consent" rights you've had all along to situations in which refusing treatment could result in your death. The "right to die" assumes a greater significance when you consider how many acute and long-term illnesses result in prolonged discussions and negotiations among patients, their families, and their doctors about how much treatment to pursue and when to call a halt. An estimated 70 percent of deaths today are "negotiated" in this manner.

Why is this so? People with chronic diseases live longer, sicker lives. The terminally ill, once left at home to die among their loved ones, are now ensconced in hospitals and nursing homes, at the mercy of technology available to save them and strangers ready to administer it.

Before we go on, there are some common misperceptions about the right to die to clear up. The most common misunderstanding is the notion that determining your own treatment means only determining that you will cease treatment. Those cases have achieved more publicity, it's true, and may be more common. But your right to determine the medical interventions you will and will not allow may include determining that you want to continue treatment, even though doctors may not want to continue. What's called the right to die can also be called the right to treatment as you choose.

So important is this point that two nationwide organizations at the forefront of the right-to-die movement, Concern for Dying and the Society for the Right to Die, merged to form Choice in Dying. (Choice in Dying can provide you with information about life-sustaining technology and how to enforce your wishes. For information, telephone 212/366-5540 or 800/989-WILL.)

The right to treatment is not unlimited. There is a point at which further treatment may be so medically futile that it should be ended, although where society will draw the line between appropriate and futile treatment is thus far unresolved. In a recent Virginia case, a federal appeals court ruled that doctors are *required* to treat and stabilize all emergency conditions, regardless of their medical belief that no treatment is warranted, under the federal anti-dumping law.

What's the difference between right to die and suicide?

Refusing treatment is not suicide. The right to die does not mean the right to kill yourself, or to be assisted in your own hastened death. It is *not* the right to suicide, or to assisted suicide. *It is the right to determine what treatment you will get, and what treatment you may refuse*, in accordance with your personal values and wishes. (Assisted suicide and recent rulings on the rights of terminally ill patients to hasten their deaths are discussed in Chapter 10.)

Do I have to have a living will to enforce the right to die?

No. You enforce your right to die, or your right to determine what treatment you'll accept or refuse, by telling the doctor your decision and discussing it with him or her. (Advance directives—living wills and health care proxies—are your protection when and if you become incapable of making or communicating decisions about your health care. We discuss these in Chapter 10.)

 ENFORCING YOUR RIGHTS

Laws and policies protecting patients, however well-motivated, are not generally what lawyers call "*self-executing*." Nor are they the types of laws for which you can scream "Call a cop!" and expect enforcement.

Rather, these are laws which require the participation of the people they're designed to protect in order to ensure that they are followed. They are civil laws with remedies available through bureaucratic processes, agency hearings, and administrative law.

This applies generally to all the topics we discuss in this book, but especially so in health care decision-making, when your health is at stake—raising the ante at a time when you're least likely to be in a position to fight recalcitrant agencies.

What can you do? Well, for starters, there are some basic principles to apply. These may sound simple, but you'd be surprised how often people neglect to do just these things that would in fact directly deal with the problem.

- **Assert your rights.** You have them. Shyness is not appropriate here. We're talking about your health and your life. Talk to your doctor and nurses and the hospital administrators. Tell them your wishes. Ask questions, even if you think they are dumb. And if you don't understand the answer, get a clearer one. Make sure to ask this question: "Do you agree to respect and honor my wishes?"

- **Make yourself heard.**   Studies show that doctors often ignore patient wishes, especially in administering aggressive treatment for terminally ill patients. Insist on the care you want and the care you don't want for you or your spouse or parent—and keep insisting on it. Repeat yourself until you are sure the message is getting through.
- **Write it down.**   Make a record of both the treatment or care you're objecting to and the conversations you have about it—including *who* you're dealing with, *when* the conversation or action takes place, *what* people say to you and what you say to them. And be prepared to put it in writing—to the doctor or the hospital. One of the things we do as lawyers is to write letters for people. You'd be surprised how often that makes a difference.
- **Get a lawyer.**   You may want to consult a lawyer to be sure of your grounds and to help you assert your rights against a recalcitrant bureaucracy. The mere presence of a lawyer may get you action. (For more on seeking legal help, see Chapter 21.)
- **Plan ahead.**   We can't say this often enough. Waiting to deal with these matters until you are hospitalized, especially for critical care, is a mistake. There are a number of techniques—living wills, health care proxies—which will help you avoid some of the problems discussed here. (See Chapter 10 for a discussion of these advance directives.)

Don't wait to get outside help. Start with the patient advocate in the hospital, who can help you cut through any number of problems. If he or she is unable to help you, see if there is a hospital ethicist or ethics committee, and contact them. You may try to be transferred to another doctor or facility. This is generally your right, if a doctor or hospital will not comply with your legal wishes. Although it may feel like you are fighting the entire medical establishment in trying to assert your legal rights, remember that the law is a powerful ally.

3

■■■

HOME CARE

Many people need care for a chronic condition or recovery from an illness but dread the prospect of a nursing home. Although in some cases nursing home care may be necessary, it is by no means the only option for all cases. The care you (or your spouse or your parent) need may be available at home or in community settings other than an institution.

With increased pressure on hospitals to discharge patients quickly and an increased demand for trained home care workers, home health care has mushroomed into a $27 billion a year industry with more than 17,000 home care agencies. The number of home health agencies is expected to double in the next decade. Hundreds of communities across the country have developed programs that provide specific services to elderly residents in their homes. An estimated two million home care aides are currently working in the United States.

Home care that is not provided directly through government programs is often financed by government benefits, making recipients vulnerable to budget and service cuts. Current deficit reduction proposals envision massive cuts, potentially forcing thousands of home care patients into nursing homes. In New York City alone, as many as 20,000 home health care recipients may be affected.

Yet many of those who need home care services don't receive them. Home health care is allotted only a small portion of the billions spent for long-term care under Medicare and Medicaid, most of which goes to more costly nursing home services. A 1991 report by the National Institute of Medicine estimated that if all those entering nursing homes waited an extra month, the United States would reap $3 billion in savings. (For more on financing home care, see Chapters 7 and 8.)

▌ IDENTIFYING YOUR NEED

The warehouse model is of little appeal to most people with any choice in the matter. One reason the nursing home population has more than doubled in the past quarter of a century is that the Medicare and Medicaid laws are structured to encourage institutionalized rather than community-based care. The result is less money to help you stay at home.

Most older people—even most of those over 85—live at home and get some kind of help for both their medical and functional problems. One third of them live alone. According to a recent survey, more than three quarters of older people report changing their behavior and using other strategies to adapt to their changing needs as they age. Some try to cope on their own, or limit their activities. Although only 23 percent have problems with basic activities of daily living, nearly 70 percent seek or receive help with day-to-day tasks such as preparing meals or dressing or managing money.

You may be one of them. Or you may need greater monitoring of your health situation. Depending on your circumstances, alternatives may be available to meet your specific needs, and at lesser cost than institutionalized care.

What many of the home care options discussed in this chapter have in common is that they are modeled on individual needs, not the needs of an institution into which you must fit yourself. And by providing services at home and in the community, they operate to maximize independence and autonomy.

ACTIVITIES OF DAILY LIVING (ADLs)

Home care is often prescribed for people recuperating after illnesses or hospital stays and requiring some medical services and the assistance of trained medical personnel. But home assistance is needed just as urgently by many who don't need these skilled interventions but who do need help with *activities of daily living*. These ADLs, as they are known, are the many functional tasks of everyday life, the performance of which may diminish with age.

ADLs include activities as basic as walking, dressing, bathing, eating, breathing, dressing, transferring (moving from bed to chair), cooking, shopping, and daily money management. Cooking, shopping, and money management are sometimes called *instrumental activities of daily living*, or IADLs. You'll note that a number of ADLs refer to activities requiring mobility. In fact, more than a quarter of older people report that their biggest problem as they age is walking.

Assessment of a person's ADLs provides a *functional* measurement. The reliance on ADLs came about largely because of the efforts of advocates to replace unhelpful labels with professional assessment techniques to identify people's specific needs. With proper assistance, many people with functional disabilities (whether physical or cognitive) can continue in their homes and their lives with help tailored to their needs. Often all they need is task-specific help—and recognition of that fact.

You'll see ADLs mentioned throughout this book. ADLs are an important concept for you to understand, for they are used to measure a person's level of functioning in a number of situations and determine the appropriate level of assistance, such as

- Determining the need for a guardian
- Providing long term care insurance benefits
- Making nursing home assessments
- Making accommodations at work
- Finding appropriate housing in a retirement community

TYPES OF HOME CARE PROGRAMS

Some home care programs provide traditional care, delivered in the home, and others provide services in community settings convenient to the home. A third category offers help for family members—spouses, adult children, and others—who care for their relatives at home.

From home care to a variety of forms of assisted living, a number of options may be available through public and private agencies in your area:

- At-home services, including meal programs, home repair services, transportation
- Personal care and homemaker services, including shopping, bathing, cleaning, cooking
- Home health care, either live-in 24-hour care or part-time
- Adult day care centers
- Daily money management services
- Foster homes
- Respite services for caretakers

Home health care can include both health-related nursing services as well as help with ADLs by home health aides, on a full- or part-time basis. If it is not covered by insurance or government benefits, it can be very expensive. (But you may be able to qualify for financial help. See Chapters 7 and 8.)

Not all the services listed above are offered in the home. Senior centers in your community may have a host of services to offer, including a social worker and other therapists. Of increasing importance are *respite services* for the caretaker. Respite programs provide a home care professional or aide to substitute for a caretaker, who gets a much-needed break. Some plans offer a three- or four-hour break once or twice a week, or a month. These are especially welcome for caretakers of people with chronic conditions such as Alzheimer's disease.

Adult day care in particular provides much-needed care and activity for patients and respite for caretakers. Adult day care is not the same thing as a senior citizen's center; it is a place for people to go during the day where more intensive services, such as nursing care, are offered. There are approximately 2,200 adult day care programs in the country, generally affiliated with churches and other not-for-profit local community agencies.

FAMILY HELP

The first line of help for many older people is their families. Yet caretaking for older people puts enormous burdens on a family's resources, emotional as well as financial. Caretaking is a stressful responsibility, often falling on the family member least able to handle the frustrations and difficulties.

- **The young old.** Many caretakers are themselves older, the so-called "young old," who at 65 find themselves taking care of their 85- and 90-year-old parents. According to a study by the Commonwealth Fund, more than one-quarter of the 32 million Americans 65 and older are caring for a relative or friend who is disabled.
- **The sandwich generation.** Many women performing caretaking chores are working as well, often part of the "sandwich generation" tending both children and elderly parents. These women perform superhuman feats. Other older workers have been forced to leave their jobs to tend older relatives.

For many caretakers, respite care is the only break they get, while the patient is in attendance at an adult day care program. A number of corporations have begun to offer respite care and other services for their employees that may be available for you.

For those acting as or relying on working caretakers, the 1993 Family and Medical Leave Act also gives employees up to 12 weeks of unpaid leave to tend to a parent or other immediate family member with a serious health condition. This time need not be taken consecutively, but can generally be used in smaller time periods to tend to the needs of a chronically ill parent. (For more on this law, see Chapter 16.)

If you are taking care of an older relative or you are being taken care of, you should consider helpful life planning tools such as a power of attorney. (For more, see Part 3, "Life Planning for You and your Family.")

Caretaking often falls to family members poorly prepared for or inadequate to the task; thirty percent of domestic abuse occurs within the family. One recurring problem in such families is personal and financial elder abuse. There are a number of programs and services available to provide information and needed intervention. (See Chapter 13.)

HOW TO FIND HOME CARE

Many home care and community programs are available through the Older Americans Act which provides grants to State and Area Agencies on Aging and to more than 10,000 senior centers. These programs include meal and transportation services, respite care, housekeeping and personal care services, shopping, money management, and related caregiving services, all of which help maintain people in the community. Services in these centers are usually free, although limited by funding and staff.

Limited home care is available through Medicare and Medicaid approved agencies. One concept which has been tested in a few areas is the "social HMO" for the elderly, which provides home care services under plans modeled on those of HMOs. (See Chapters 7 and 8.)

A number of states have developed home care options for elderly with disabilities. Oregon has pioneered home care as part of its assisted living program, which provides daily help for Medicaid patients formerly in nursing homes. Wisconsin provides an ambitious array of services, on a sliding scale, to keep people in their homes. New York State's model home care program cares for more than 200,000 elderly.

According to the National HomeCaring Council, of the approximately 17,000 home care agencies, half are certified to provide Medicare services. Thousands of other programs deliver services to the home, both on a formal and an informal basis.

Nearly 700 Area Agencies on Aging nationwide have been set up under the Older Americans Act to administer non-medical services. Many offer case management services, and may be able to coordinate services for you. Your Area Agency on Aging can refer you to available services in your community. Another possibility is a private care manager, discussed below. (See the Resources section at the end of this book for a list of State Agencies on Aging.)

A number of home care and community services are also available through other program and funding sources in your state and locality. One possible source of information is your employer. A number of corporations have set up programs to counsel employees caring for elderly parents and to make referrals. You can also try the Administration on Aging's National Eldercare Locator at 800/677-1116, which makes referrals for adult day care.

HOW TO EVALUATE A HOME CARE AGENCY

Approximately 45 percent of home care is funded or paid for by public programs, and 55 percent is paid for privately. All together, there are an estimated 17,000 home health agencies across the nation. In evaluating an agency to meet your needs, there are a number of things to keep in mind.

Certification. Approximately half of the home care agencies in the United States are Medicare or Medicaid Certified Home Care Agencies (CHAs). This certification means that Medicare or Medicaid will pay for home care provided by them. Although certification is not conclusive, it means the agency has met certain minimum requirements imposed by the federal government in patient care and finances.

Certified agencies can provide specified home health services for both Medicare and Medicaid recipients. You can inspect a copy of an agency's Medicare Survey Report by contacting your state health department.

Licensure. Home health care agencies are licensed in many states. Licensure means it is subject to state standards and regulation, although as a general rule, oversight of even licensed facilities is generally poor and not a good indicator of quality.

Accreditation. As with doctors or hospitals, accreditation is available for home care agencies as well. There are a number of accrediting agencies for home care, depending on the services provided. Check to see whether an agency is accredited by the Community Health Accreditation Program (telephone 800/847-8480), the Joint Commission on Accreditation of Healthcare Organizations (telephone 312/642-6061), or the National HomeCaring Council (telephone 202/547-6586). If so, it has voluntarily submitted to compliance with standards promulgated by the accrediting organization.

Staff qualifications, selection, and training. As a general rule, certified agencies are more selective and demanding in their hiring, in part due to government-imposed requirements on who may work as home health aides under their programs. Federal law requires aides to pass competency tests in patient care and to have at least 75 hours of classroom and practical training. Training and testing requirements vary by state, and may be stricter in your locality. For example, New York's model home care program has rigorous requirements in training, certification, and benefits for home care workers.

Training is important to ensure that all workers can perform the tasks necessary for your needs. Non-certified agencies may charge lower fees, but without certification requirements, they often provide less training and less trained staff. The National HomeCaring Council has developed standards for home care services, which require adequate training. It also offers a national certification program for home care aides.

Note that terminology for home care workers is often a function of funding source and not function. For example, "home health aides" are generally employed in certified agencies to perform health-related services, while "home attendants" perform so-called personal care. As a practical matter, both may perform the same services.

Plan of care. An important service is a written plan of care, detailing the services that will be provided and the specific tasks performed. A copy of this plan should be available for you and your family.

Availability of staff in emergency. This is very important. Check what the agency's plans are to deal with emergency care, if needed, and whether 24-hour backup help will be available.

Information. Check to see if family members are informed about care, any other services are provided or if you are given any written information, including a bill of rights for patients and information about fees and charges.

Ask for and consult references. Inquire in the community and at local senior centers. If you are seeking help following a hospital stay, remember to consult with professional staff at the hospital such as discharge planners or social workers.

 ## PRIVATE CARE MANAGERS

One new profession that has emerged along with the aging population is *private geriatric care management.* A private care manager is a professional with training in gerontology, usually as a social worker, nurse, or psychologist, who specializes in assisting older people and their families with long-term care arrangements. You can hire a private care manager to help you with managing your care needs.

A private care manager can evaluate your needs, formulate a care plan, locate appropriate services, and arrange care for you—even fill out the applications for you. The care manager can help you evaluate the options available to you and can also monitor care after it's been arranged. These services are particularly useful for people caretaking their parents in faraway cities.

The case management approach is beneficial for elderly patients. With community and medical services coordinated, care is assured and problems that arise may be identified promptly. Private care managers are skilled in finding and coordinating needed care, and despite the emphasis on geriatric care, may also be useful for people trying to find services for persons of any age with disabilities.

Private care managers have raised some ire in the traditionally non-profit social work community, but they perform a useful and valuable function. Professional standards for practice have been developed by the National Association of Professional Geriatric Care Managers. You can find a private care manager from social service agency referrals, or you can contact the National Association (telephone 602/881-8008).

PAYING FOR HOME CARE

You can always pay for home care yourself, which may be an option if your needs are limited and you're not strapped for cash. But costs mount up swiftly, year in and year out, and you should be aware of other options open to you.

Some home care is available through the community or the government, either free or for a limited charge. Many of the programs available through the Older Americans Act are not means-tested, which means you don't have to plead poverty to qualify. Some require fees, payable on a sliding scale according to need.

Home care is also available under Medicare and Medicaid, subject to stated conditions. Medicare especially tries to limit home nursing care. We discuss your coverage under Medicare and Medicaid, and how much the government is paying for care, in Chapters 7 and 8. Even if you're already receiving services you pay for, don't neglect Medicaid planning! Broader coverage for home care services is also included in more recent long-term care insurance polices. (See Chapter 8.)

 WHERE TO COMPLAIN

If you have a complaint about home health care services, you should always start at the source, with the agency itself. If the agency does business in your community, it will be in its best interests to respond promptly and fully to your complaint.

If the agency is Medicare-certified, you can complain to Medicare. If your agency is licensed by the state, you can also notify the appropriate state agency, usually the state department of health. Certified and licensed agencies are required to comply with federal and state standards for operations.

 WHEN YOU NEED MORE

If home is not a viable option, even with home care, there may be a variety of intermediate independent and assisted living arrangements available to you other than nursing home care. (We discuss assisted living residences, continuing care communities, and other housing options and adult communities in Chapter 20 and nursing homes in Chapter 4.)

4

NURSING HOMES

The longer you live, the more likely it is you will spend some time in a nursing home. If you're a woman, your chances are even greater. Women not only live longer than men, they care for men outside of institutions in far greater numbers than they are cared for. Not surprisingly, women account for nearly two thirds of the nursing home population.

According to studies, nearly half of those turning 65—43 percent in a 1991 survey—will use a nursing home in the future. One out of four will spend one year in a nursing home, and one out of eleven will spend as long as five years in a nursing home. By the year 2000, an estimated 2 million people will be living in nursing homes, a one-third increase in the span of a decade. And that's *before* the onslaught to come as this century's baby boomers turn into next century's senior citizens.

The good news is that the nursing homes of the past—badly managed, badly staffed, frightening places for warehousing souls—are no longer the rule. Today, with federal and state reforms spurred by heightened consumer awareness and greater treatment options for many older patients, many nursing homes are well-run places. Nevertheless, problems persist. According to a survey by *Consumer Reports* in its August 1995 issue, a significant number still offer a poor or questionable level of care. And some legislators want to turn back reforms, eliminating federal protections along with Medicaid benefit cutbacks.

The search for a nursing home therefore poses these questions: (1) how to find a good nursing home, (2) when you do, what your rights are to quality care and services, and (3) how to enforce those rights. (The all-important question of cost and your options for financing long-term care are discussed in Chapters 5 to 9 of Part 2 of this book.)

IDENTIFYING YOUR NEED

A nursing home provides nursing, rehabilitative, and other health-related services, along with room and board. Depending on your circumstances, other alternatives may be available to meet your specific needs and at lesser cost.

We've seen that health care is available in settings other than a nursing home. In today's competitive marketplace, some nursing homes are beginning to offer specialized services in addition to custodial and skilled nursing care (e.g., assisted living services, adult day care). If a facility doesn't offer health services, however, it's *not* a nursing home. (Chapter 3 describes the number of options available in home and community-based care. For more on adult living communities, see Chapter 20.)

If institutionalized nursing care is needed, then by all means follow our recommendations in this chapter. But make sure you explore whether the alternatives may be the answer for you—or your spouse or parent. For most people seeking to maintain their independence and autonomy in later years, a nursing home is the least desirable option.

FINDING A NURSING HOME

Your first source for facilities in your area may be the social worker at the hospital, senior center, or other agency with which you have contact. If you're in a hospital, your discharge plan will seek to locate and identify an appropriate facility. In addition, your State or Area Agency on Aging or local or state aging department should be able to provide you with a list of nursing homes in your area. You can also try the Administration on Aging's Eldercare Locator, at 800/677–1116, which will provide referrals in your area.

One helpful resource may be your state's long term care ombudsman. Under the Older Americans Act, the long term care ombudsman serves as an advocate for those in nursing homes and will know of those facilities which have been subject to repeated complaints or found to provide substandard care. (See the Resources section for contact information.) The August 1995 issue of *Consumer Reports* also provides ratings for national chains and not-for-profit groups operating 4000 nursing homes.

No matter what the source, you must visit and inspect the facility in person. If you cannot go, send someone in your place. An on-site visit is critical to an informed decision about whether to enter a particular facility—and offers the added benefit of a display of concern.

HOW TO EVALUATE A NURSING HOME

Some people need nursing home care during short-term rehabilitation following illness or injury. Others need day care while family members work. Others need round-the-clock medical care or custodial care or both. Few nursing homes offer a complete range of services, although services may be coordinated with outside agencies. Other specific services include rehabilitation programs specifically for older people, assessment services and social work programs.

Credentials. Facilities are both licensed by the state and certified by Medicare and Medicaid. More than 10,000 nursing homes are certified by Medicare. A nursing home that is not certified may not meet minimum standards of care required for federal reimbursement.

Quality of care, services, and activities. Quality is critical to your health. In a nursing home, you need good nursing and medical services, as well as adequate food and shelter.

As important as the physical structure of the facility and the extent of its services are the staff providing them. It's important to know whether medical staff and supervisors are on premises or "on call." Find out about staff levels and schedules of nurses, assistants, social workers and other full and part-time staff. Are rehabilitative services furnished by nursing home staff or outside providers? Is there an activities program to meet your interests as well as your physical, mental, and psychosocial well-being? Is there a qualified therapeutic recreation specialist or activities professional on staff? Remember, you should be receiving social services designed to meet your needs.

Physical environment. The ideal nursing home will provide a safe, clean, and homelike environment, allowing you to keep and use your personal belongings to the greatest extent possible. Federal regulations require housekeeping and maintenance services to keep rooms not just sanitary but comfortable, clean bed and bath linens in good condition, with adequate and comfortable lighting levels in all areas, and comfortable sound and temperature levels (generally between 71 and 81°F). You are entitled to private closet space in your room.

Be sure to check the physical conditions of the nursing home, inspecting for sanitation and comfort. Rooms, furnishings, common areas, toilet and bathing facilities should all be on your check-list.

Rules and restraints. Another area of concern is rules. A nursing home has policy and rules that govern such aspects of resident life as eating, sleeping, participation in activities, use of telephone and mail. You want to examine these rules to gauge whether they are flexible enough to meet your needs or unduly restrictive.

Of special note is a nursing home's policy on restraining devices—both the physical and chemical variety—for patients. It should be unacceptable at the close of the 20th century that we continue to allow our elder citizens to be routinely subjected to this horrible indignity. Yet restraints are commonplace in nursing homes, where they are almost always used, improperly, for the convenience of staff rather than the welfare of patients. Despite reforms, a substantial proportion of facilities continue to use restraints on their patients inappropriately and illegally. Make sure you ask about the home's policy—and observe whether patients are indeed free of restraints. (We discuss the law on using restraints later in this chapter.)

Shopping for a nursing home, whether for yourself or a relative, is a very traumatizing experience for most people. If possible, go with a friend or family member when you make your inspection—and take notes. Ask questions and write down the answers. If you proceed in a deliberate way, you maximize your chances of making an informed and wise decision.

Subjective attributes. A nursing home may be a home, but it is not your home. Even with recent improvements, nursing homes by nature are impersonal places, designed to offer production-line, albeit humane, services marketed to the least common denominator.

We say this not by way of criticism, but to remind you that personal contact, caring, and interest are qualities that are hard to measure but very important for you to consider. A facility that has compassionate staff, that manages to engage its residents in activities of interest to them, that establishes some sense of warmth in individual quarters and common rooms—these are things that cannot be quantified but will be invaluable, literally life-saving, to residents.

Visit as many nursing homes as you can. Be sure and schedule a weekend or evening visit, as well. Observe the staff and the residents, and ask them about staffing, activities, and scheduling. Their comments should prove extremely useful to you.

You can also get copies of annual state reviews and quality care surveys of individual facilities. These reviews should provide valuable information on quality of life and quality of care issues. Copies of the most recent survey are supposed to be available at the nursing home, and you should ask to see one. They are also available from the state. (See the discussion of state regulation, later in this chapter.) However, don't let an inspection report substitute for a personal visit.

One last comment. For most people, their most important human right is freedom. Loss of autonomy is the greatest indignity imposed by a stay in a nursing home. A few years back, the National Citizens Coalition for Nursing Home Reform surveyed residents for qualities they thought important in a good nursing home. The responses included food, activities, staff—and choice and autonomy. Whether you are shopping for yourself or your spouse or parent, it's important to ask administrators and staff their attitudes about personal rights of residents in the home and to make your own observations about rights being exercised by residents.

NURSING HOME REFORMS

The Nursing Home Reform Act of 1987 enacted a comprehensive series of standards for nursing homes. The law was designed to address the most prevalent abuses occurring in the nursing home industry as well as to establish a basic standard of care and rights due to all nursing home residents.

The rights established by this law include basic human rights to dignity, choice, privacy, and autonomy, as well as to quality services. Just as important, the Act outlaws discrimination against residents who are or may become Medicaid recipients.

The reforms cover a number of areas:

- Increased staff qualifications
- Quality of care
- Residents' rights
- Use of restraints
- Information and access

The Nursing Home Reform Act is sometimes referred to as OBRA '87, because it was passed as *part of* the Omnibus Budget Reconciliation Act of that year. The law applies to all nursing facilities and their owners and operators who receive Medicare or Medicaid funds.

Legislative note. Along with proposed Medicaid changes, there are proposals now being considered in Congress to eliminate federal standards, letting the task of regulation fall to the states. Many states in fact do have nursing home laws paralleling federal protections. In other states without such laws, this regressive action could reverse twenty years of progress.

 THE NURSING HOME CONTRACT

When you enter a nursing home, a contract (the "admissions agreement") is signed. There are a number of considerations in signing this contract, which we describe below. Remember that entering or admitting someone to a nursing home is an act done in a time of stress. In the urgency of the moment, you may not be exercising your best critical abilities. A number of nursing home contracts routinely include illegal clauses, such as those concerning advance payments or requiring guarantees.

Often, such clauses are unenforceable. But not always. Be aware that nursing home admission agreements are contracts, and should be read and considered in detail before signing.

Don't confuse a nursing home with a *continuing care facility* (sometimes called a *lifecare community*). These generally provide housing and some medical care—less than a nursing home—for an unspecified, lifetime term. Some of these facilities do have nursing homes as well. Many states provide some regulation of continuing care facilities, governing items such as entrance fees, probationary periods, and refunds. (Some of the protections in these statutes may apply to nursing home contracts as well.) If you are applying for entry to a nursing home, you should not be asked to sign a lifecare contract. (For more on continuing care facilities, see Chapter 20.)

ADMISSIONS AND DISCRIMINATION

Discrimination against Medicaid recipients is prohibited by federal regulations banning discrimination on the basis of source of payment. This discrimination is sometimes referred to as *Medicaid discrimination*. The prohibition applies to admissions, services, transfer, and discharge.

Despite these prohibitions, residents applying under private pay rates, which are not regulated, will find it easier to obtain nursing home care. Although in theory all applicants have equal access to quality care, courts have been generally unwilling to hold nursing homes to identical standards for Medicaid and non-Medicaid applicants due to lower reimbursement rates provided by Medicaid.

Some safeguards against discrimination based on source of payment are described below. Prohibitions against discrimination that are mandated by other federal, state, and local laws continue to apply in nursing homes.

WAITING LISTS

Many nursing homes have waiting lists. Whether a bed is available is a function of where you live and the quality of the facility. It may also be a function of payment—if you are a private payer, you will find it easier than if you (or your parent or spouse) are already on Medicaid. The pressures on hospitals to discharge Medicare patients has led to increased referrals to nursing homes.

In some cases (and depending on where you live), it may also be a function of the extent of services needed or anticipated, and government reimbursement structures. For example, the less care you need, the more likely you are to find a bed. However, some states encourage facilities to take residents needing greater care by providing higher reimbursement rates for them.

Many states require a minimum percentage of Medicaid patients. For example, New York requires that the percentage of Medicaid patients in a nursing home be at least 75 percent of the percentage of Medicaid patients in nursing homes in the county as a whole. A nursing home's admissions policy should be available upon request, including an explanation of its waiting list, where one is used.

DEPOSITS AND PAYMENTS

Under the reform law, if you enter a nursing home covered by either Medicare or Medicaid, you cannot be asked for a "security deposit," "contribution," or any other form of advance payment.

This is what the law says. It is not what happens. Typically nursing homes do ask for upfront payments and other forms of "guarantees" from applicants or their relatives. These may run in the thousands, in some areas reaching $10,000 or $20,000. Some homes try to charge you for a minimum number of days or months. These deposits and charges are against the law.

The law also says that you cannot be asked to sign anything giving up any of your rights to Medicaid. For example, some homes ask that you agree not to transfer your personal funds or to apply for Medicaid for a given period of time. This is illegal. (Keep in mind, however, that giving away your funds could make you ineligible for Medicaid. We discuss this in Chapter 8.)

If you are a friend or relative helping a nursing home applicant in the admissions process, make sure you don't sign anything making you personally responsible for payment. These third-party guarantees are also illegal.

Residents who are covered by Medicaid may nevertheless be asked to pay for "extra" services, such as laundry or hair care, which in fact are covered by government benefits. These supplementary fees are also illegal. (Note that some added fees may not be illegal, such as for a TV in your room. But they cannot be required for your admission, either.)

Many states also have laws restricting or banning nursing home deposits. Check with your long term care ombudsman for the requirements in your state. (See Resources section at the end of this book.)

My stay is not covered by Medicare and I'm not eligible for Medicaid. The nursing home wants a deposit. Is this permitted?

In most states, yes. Under these circumstances, your ability to pay is a legitimate concern for a nursing home. However, many states limit the size of the deposit that can legally be requested. For example, Florida provides for a $1,500 maximum security deposit. Some (Connecticut and California) establish an outright ban on security deposits.

Make sure that you really are not covered by Medicare. You have the right to ask that a "demand bill" be submitted to Medicare for a determination concerning your coverage.

 ## QUALITY OF CARE

The difference between quality services and inadequate services can be as critical as getting adequate medical treatment or being afforded the dignity of your own personal space. Reforms have attempted to codify both a process and plan for providing quality services for nursing home residents. Your involvement, as a resident or a family member, ensures that nursing home staff get the information they need to provide quality services.

Preadmission screening and annual resident review (PASARR). Screening and review are mandated to ensure that individuals with mental illness or retardation are not inappropriately placed in nursing homes.

Assessments. Individual patient assessment is critical for the delivery of quality patient care. Assessment measures a patient's ability to function and perform activities of daily living (ADLs), including abilities as basic as walking, dressing, bathing, eating, and breathing.

Each resident must be assessed by the nursing home staff at the following times:

- Within 14 days of admission and
- At least once a year thereafter and
- Upon any significant change in mental or physical condition. In such cases subsequent three-month reviews are required

The assessment must be administered or coordinated by a registered nurse (RN). In addition, each person performing a portion of the assessment must certify its accuracy. The form and content of the assessment is specified by state requirements, in compliance with federal regulations.

Plan of care. A plan of care spells out strategies, tasks, and responsibilities, as part of an overall design to allow each resident to maintain the highest practicable physical, mental, and emotional well-being. The plan of care should address both medical and non-medical issues, including daily schedules, staff, personal care, medications, and activities. A program of activities must be provided to meet the interests and physical, mental, and psychosocial well-being of each resident.

The law requires that a written comprehensive plan of care be prepared by the attending doctor, an RN with responsibility for the resident, and any other facility staff who may be involved in a resident's care, as well as the resident and a family member or lawyer as his or her representative.

A plan of care (also called a "care plan") must be done within seven days of an assessment. Care plan conferences must occur every three months and whenever there is a significant change in a resident's mental or physical condition.

Physician choice. You are entitled to free choice of an attending physician. The nursing home can't prevent you from exercising this right by imposing unreasonable practice rules before allowing your doctor to see you on the premises.

Staff requirements. Federal law requires minimum nursing staff 24 hours a day, including an RN as director of nursing, an RN on duty at least one shift a day, and a licensed nurse on duty at all times. Homes with more than 120 beds must also employ full-time social workers. In many cases, however, these requirements have been circumvented by waivers.

Nursing home administrators must be licensed by the state. The law specifies training and competency requirements for both full- and part-time workers in nursing homes. States are made responsible for training and evaluating nursing home nurses' aides. Training is required for all nurses' aides employed more than four months. Retraining and reevaluation is required after more than two years' absence.

States must also establish and maintain registries of nurses' aides who have completed training and evaluation. Registries must also include individuals who have neglected or abused residents, or misappropriated resident funds. Nursing homes must check state and other available registries for employee history of patient neglect or abuse.

Rehabilitation, dental, and pharmacy services.   You must get any physical therapy or other rehabilitative services specified in your care plan. This may include speech language pathology, occupational therapy, and mental health rehabilitative services. The nursing home can either provide the service by staff or arrange to have it furnished by qualified outside personnel. You must get necessary routine and 24-hour emergency dental care (for which Medicare patients may be charged). This includes a prompt referral for residents with lost or damaged dentures. If necessary, you are entitled to assistance in making appointments and arranging transportation to and from the dentist's office. You must also be provided with medication, as needed.

Other services.   Dietary services are prescribed as to the number and time of meals. The physical environment is also regulated. A room can have no more than four beds, and a minimum amount of space must be allotted for each resident. Rooms must be adequately furnished, with toilet and bathing facilities nearby and accessible. There must also be a system in place for residents to summon help.

 ## CHEMICAL AND PHYSICAL RESTRAINTS

In an industry long noted for abuses, the biggest abuse is one that continues to this day. That is the practice of keeping nursing home residents "under control," a euphemism for the physical and chemical restraints that keep thousands of institutionalized persons "roped up and doped up" for the convenience of those who tend them.

Federal law prescribes the use of both *physical restraints* and *chemical restraints*. Physical restraints are ropes, jackets, and mittens which tie a patient to a chair or bed. Chemical restraints are psychotropic drugs. They are both used for the same purpose, keeping the patient subdued and passive.

Hospital and nursing home operators who routinely order restraints justify them as needed to prevent patients, especially elderly patients, from falling or injuring themselves or pulling out tubes. But restraints are mostly used as a convenience for staff rather than to safeguard the health of patients. In egregious cases, they have been used as discipline for "misbehaving" residents. In nursing homes, especially, antihistamines have been misused to keep patients drowsy and tractable.

In some cases, restraints can keep patients from harming themselves. But there are alternatives. Reducing the use of restraints may require training staff to meet individual needs through innovations such as environmental alterations, positioning devices, or redeploying nursing assistants. As simple an idea as a regular walking program can benefit many residents. The Jewish Home and Hospital for the Aged in New York City has proved that a restraint-free environment can lead to more independence and autonomy, without increasing and in fact lessening injuries and accidents. (JHHA has developed programs seeking to minimize the use of restraints. You can also get information on reducing restraint use from the National Citizens' Coalition for Nursing Home Reform in Washington, D.C. See the Resources section for contact information.)

Under federal law, blanket orders for restraints "as needed" may no longer be issued. Before restraints may be used on a patient, there must be an individual order *for that patient* that explains the need for restraints and when their use will be discontinued. Orders for drug restraints are good for no longer than 12 hours.

Except in an emergency situation to protect patient life or safety, restraints must be ordered by a doctor, in writing, specifying the need and the duration. Under no circumstances should restraints ever be used as "discipline." Nursing homes are required to report on alternatives and plans for ending restraints.

BED-HOLD AND BED RESERVATIONS

An important factor for residents in a nursing home, and one with potentially serious consequences, is the facility's *bed-hold and bed reservation* policy. If a nursing home resident has to be hospitalized, what are the resident's rights to have his or her bed held open until he or she returns from the hospital? What are his or her rights to the next available bed?

The answer is tied to money. Homes will generally hold beds for as long as they are paid for. If you are paying privately, this is covered by your pocketbook or by your insurance. Note that charging you for holding a bed is *not* a violation of law. As a general rule, Medicaid will cover a minimum number of days. For example, in New Jersey it will cover 10 days. A resident who remains in the hospital longer becomes entitled to the next available bed in the same nursing home. Generally, the hospital will keep him or her until the next bed is available.

Residents have a right to know the nursing home's policy. They have a right to readmission to the next available bed.

Many state laws also govern bed reservation and bed-hold policies. Some require that beds be held for a minimum number of days (7 days in California for Medicaid patients; 15 days in Florida, 30 days for private pay).

If I am waiting in the hospital for a space in a specific nursing home, can I decline another nursing home offered me?

If you decline an appropriate placement without a good reason, you will be obligated to pay for your hospital stay. An "appropriate" placement is one within a 50-mile radius of your home.

TRANSFERS AND DISCHARGE

Under the law, there may be no arbitrary transfer or discharge from a nursing home. Transfers and discharges against your will (known as "involuntary transfers") are only allowed under certain conditions:

- If you present a risk to the safety or health of yourself or others
- If you regain your health, making a nursing home stay inappropriate
- If you fail to pay (for Medicare and Medicaid residents, this applies only to allowable charges)
- If the nursing home closes

If you are to be transferred or discharged, you must be given 30 days advance notice. You have the right to appeal a transfer or discharge through an appeal process established by the state and to be granted a hearing. (This right does not apply to transfers to other floors or rooms within the same facility.) Procedures for a hearing apply to all nursing home residents, regardless of the source of payment.

My elderly uncle is being discharged from his nursing home for being disruptive. Is this legal?

Not if he doesn't present a risk to his own or others' safety or health. At least one court has ruled that merely being disruptive is not cause to discharge a resident from a nursing home.

RESIDENTS' BILL OF RIGHTS

By its nature, a nursing home robs people of their independence and their autonomy. Once in a nursing home, a resident's whole life is subject to regulations and schedules imposed by others. The new resident loses control of such simple things as choosing meals, taking medication, and keeping personal possessions.

This situation has been partly addressed by provisions in federal law that seek to establish a minimum standard of personal rights—a "bill of rights" for nursing home residents. Among the most important rights are:

A statement of your rights.   You are entitled to a copy of your legal rights when you enter a nursing home, and any revisions thereafter. This includes a statement of your right to make a complaint to the state about abuse or neglect. You have the right to a description of how your personal funds will be protected.

A written statement of fees, charges, and services. You are entitled to this before entering. If you are on Medicaid or Medicaid-eligible, you must be informed of available coverage as well as all other fees and services.

Quality of life, dignity, and self-determination. You are entitled to receive care in a manner and an environment that promotes maintenance or enhancement of your quality of life, dignity, and respect in full recognition of your individuality.

Self-determination means that you have the right to choose activities, schedules, and health care consistent with your interests, assessment, and plan of care. You are entitled to interact with members of the community both inside and outside the facility, and make choices about aspects of life in the facility of significance to you.

Right to privacy. Privacy is the most sought-after and elusive goal in a communal setting like a nursing home. You have the right to privacy in your room (although not to a private room), as well as in telephone calls, mail, and visitors. You also have rights to confidentiality concerning your medical records.

Financial control. You have the right to manage your own finances to the extent that you can. As protection of resident funds, the law provides that you must be given information about your personal funds.

Visits. You have the right to visitors at any reasonable hour. You also have the concomitant right *not* to have visitors—to refuse to see family or friends if you don't want to.

Access and visitation. Reasonable access must be granted to anyone providing you service, such as legal services. Your personal physician and a long-term care ombudsman or other state representative must be given immediate access to you. The patient's attorney or state officer can examine the resident's records, with the resident's permission.

Meetings and participation in resident and family groups. You and your family have the right to meet to discuss problems or any matters that concern you. You and your family also have the right to form councils to discuss your problems and to bring them to the attention of administrators, as necessary. The nursing home is required to make space available and to designate a staff person responsible for providing assistance and responding to written requests that may result from group meetings.

I am considering nursing home services, which I may need for an undetermined period of time. If I enter a nursing home, do I have the right to come and go as I please?

Yes. You are a resident, not an inmate. Except where your health renders you incapable to leaving the facility, you have an absolute right to leave whenever you want. This includes shopping excursions or visits to friends.

The nursing home can be held liable for your supervision, however, and some nursing homes will limit your right to remain in the home if you stay away for an extended period of time. You should make sure you know the nursing home policy in regard to leaving the premises.

If I am in a nursing home, what rights do I have concerning my medical treatment? Do I have go along with whatever "the doctor orders"?

No. You have the right to participate in making your plan of care. You also have the right to give or refuse consent to any treatment or procedure, as you would outside the nursing home. Make sure that you, your representative, and your health care proxy, if you have appointed one, are aware of your rights in this regard. (See Chapter 10 on health care directives.)

If I enter a nursing home, will I lose the right to manage my finances?

Not because you enter a home. You still have the right to manage your finances, although your cash allowance within the home may be limited. However, this does not restrict your right to manage, direct, and otherwise administer your business affairs and your assets and income.

 ## REGULATING NURSING HOMES

Nursing homes are licensed by the state and must be inspected yearly. States are now required to conduct annual reviews and perform quality care surveys of nursing homes under federal guidelines.

All states have a long-term care ombudsman, whose powers and duties are set forth by statute. States must investigate complaints of violation and allegations of neglect and abuse and monitor deficient nursing homes. Where facilities have been found to provide substandard care, notice is required to the long-term care ombudsman, administrative licensing board, and the attending physicians of residents.

Under federal law, each state must maintain a registry of nursing aides who have been found abusive. Other health care professionals, including nurses, doctors, and administrators, who have been found guilty of abuse, neglect, or misappropriation of funds must be reported to the appropriate state agency.

States have their own nursing home statutes, many with nursing home bills of rights (either parallel to the federal law or adding specific rights). These generally include a requirement that the law be posted in the nursing home, a process for making complaints, and sanctions for non-compliance with standards, including Medicaid sanctions, other fines and penalties, and licensure suspension or revocation for violations. Many also specify a prohibition on discrimination in nursing home admissions and services based on age, race, national origin, handicap, or sex.

Some states provide express protection for nursing home deposits. Connecticut and California, for example, establish an outright ban on security deposits. By contrast, Florida's statute sets a $1,500 maximum on the permissible deposit amount. Under New York law, any deposit remains your property and must be treated as such. In several states, separate funds have been created to protect nursing home residents, financed by fees and penalties.

 ## ENFORCING YOUR RIGHTS

Implementation of the federal law has not been easy and is still ongoing. Reforms cost time and money. Federal rules have been delayed and at least one state, California, has publicly announced that it would not comply with the law. Others have dragged their feet. Education and training are needed for nursing home administrators and staff as well as state inspectors. The bottom line is that these reforms will take place over time, possibly several years.

How does this affect you? It makes your active participation all the more important. Oversight is as much a responsibility of the individual as of the government. It's crucial that individuals know their rights, and their closest friends and relatives know what those rights are, so that objections can be voiced strongly when standards of care, basic quality services, and legally mandated rights are not met.

You should be aware that there are specific sanctions in place for violation of the law. Where defects have been found, states may order a plan of correction and take steps to ensure compliance (under threat of loss of federal Medicaid funds). In some cases, facilities may be closed and residents moved.

One of the problems with sanctions for nursing homes is that the cure may be worse than the disease. Even with substandard facilities, it is often not in the best interest of residents for a facility to be closed. Other possible sanctions that may be imposed by government officials include fines, denial of payment, and temporary takeover of management. Federal law provides specific monetary penalties for fraud involving patient assessments.

• *Complaints and grievances within the nursing home or institution.* A statement of rights is good only if you have a mechanism that backs it up. A nursing home must have a formal complaint and grievance procedure in place for dealing with complaints from residents. This means that you should be able to identify the place and the person to whom you should make your complaint, and what the home's responsibility is to investigate and respond. Nursing homes are required to provide immediate efforts to resolve resident grievances.

Don't think that because someone has a title, that individual knows what he or she is talking about. Remember, many of these reforms are very new and implementation has been sporadic. Often, what seems to be a violation of your rights and flagrant disregard of law is merely ignorance. Your job at the outset is to make your complaint. If the officials with whom you speak profess lack of interest or ignorance, your job is to educate them. Both the residents and the facility staff should know the requirements of the law. Residents have the right to voice grievances without reprisal.

• *State investigation.* Each state must institute a process for investigating complaints of violation and allegations of neglect and abuse. The state regulatory system must provide for corrective plans where needed and appropriate sanctions. State action can originate from inspections and surveys, or upon a complaint by an individual.

State action can lead to improvements—or to closings. Investigations by regulators in Oregon upheld charges of negligence in six deaths in homes run by Beverly Enterprises, which operates the nation's largest nursing home chain, forcing the company to sell out its holdings in the state.

• *Long-term care ombudsman.* Every state must have a long-term care ombudsman, who serves as an advocate for those in nursing homes and other long-term care facilities. This is required under the Older Americans Act. (See Chapter 13 on the long-term care ombudsman's role in elder abuse and protective proceedings.)

• *Other state agencies.* Your state department of health regulates and licenses nursing homes, and may be some help. The state also licenses nursing home administrators, nurses, nurses' aides, and other health care professionals. State human rights agencies are given responsibilities for enforcing discrimination laws.

• *Criminal action.* Medicaid fraud and other financial irregularities have long been the object of criminal investigations and prosecutions in the nursing home industry. Although not as common, an increasing number of prosecutions has been initiated against nursing home administrators and staff charging neglect or abuse of residents so flagrant as to constitute criminal misconduct.

• *Private action.* If neglect or abuse or serious injury has occurred, you may have a private right of action. Depending on the circumstances, you may bring a lawsuit based on negligence, breach of contract, or violation of the statutory requirements (or a combination of those). It may be difficult to pursue this types of lawsuit—or to find a lawyer willing to take it on—but there have been successful suits where aggrieved parties have won significant awards. In one well-known case, Beverly Enterprises was required to pay $250,000 in damages for neglect in one of the nursing homes in its chain.

A number of states provide an additional private right of action for violation of their nursing home residents' rights statutes. In states such as Florida or Missouri, for example, an aggrieved resident can sue for violation of statutory protection, although damages may be limited. If you believe you have a case warranting a private lawsuit, you should consult an attorney for advice.

Part 2

■ ■

Managing and Paying for Health Care

In our free enterprise system, medical care is a commodity, bought and sold like any other. Yet it is a commodity whose economic fortunes have the power to affect every part of your life. Health care costs can influence your choice of doctors, the frequency of your medical check-ups, and the kind of care you and your family will receive during an illness. If you need to protect health care insurance coverage you receive through employment, the impact of medical costs may dictate where you live and work.

Health care costs have accelerated at an unprecedented pace over the last decade. For both crisis situations requiring high-tech interventions and chronic conditions demanding long-term care, costs have risen exponentially. In New York State, the average daily cost of a nursing home is $178; that translates into $65,000 yearly. Across the country, as many as 2.8 million people can be expected to use a nursing home during the course of a single year—fewer than half covered by Medicare and insurance.

This section shows you how to make sure you can pay for the health care you need. Chapter 5 discusses Medicare, the insurance coverage provided by the United States government for people over 65. Chapter 6 describes supplemental coverage and other private health insurance, and details current law and proposed legislation designed to help you hold onto that coverage. In Chapter 7, we review long-term care insurance and lesser-known tools which may be useful for long-term care financing. In Chapter 8, we explain the ins and outs of Medicaid planning, to ensure that you and your family won't have to be impoverished to receive needed care. We also introduce you to some new programs that may offer protection you need at affordable prices (Chapter 9).

One cautionary note. As we go to print, Congress is debating changes in both the Medicare and Medicaid programs (described in the following chapters). Some of these proposals, such as increasing Medicare costs for recipients or offering medical savings accounts, may have immediate effect on your pocketbook. Others, involving block grants for financing Medicaid, might have more far-reaching effects on the nursing home industry and your ability to pay for long-term care.

5

MEDICARE

Medicare has been an accepted part of later life for thirty years, so much a feature of the health care landscape that even today's legislators intent on changes to the program are still wary of the political fallout. When it was signed into law in 1965 it was historic legislation. President Lyndon Johnson took the occasion to predict:

> Every citizen will be able, in his productive years when he is earning, to insure himself against the ravages of illness in his old age. No longer will illness crush and destroy the savings they have so carefully put away over a lifetime so that they might enjoy dignity in their later years.

If you're over 65 and retired, Medicare is your primary health insurance. Under Part A (hospital coverage) and Part B (medical insurance), more than 37 million disabled and elderly have Medicare coverage, providing payment to doctors and hospitals, either directly or via reimbursement to patients.

At its creation, Medicare was a revolutionary scheme by the government to insure older people, with contributions provided by citizens when they are working and after their retirement. The financing of Medicare reflects the shared responsibility of employer and employee, citizen and insured. Medicare's hospital coverage (Part A) is financed by payroll taxes of 2.9 percent per worker, split between the employer and the worker. The medical insurance program which covers doctor fees (Part B) is paid for in part from general tax revenues and from monthly premiums paid by enrollees.

Health care costs attributed to Medicare have been staggering, and the program faces an uncertain financial future. The hospital insurance trust fund is in jeopardy and predictions are that its funds will be depleted by 2002. Tax revenues are hard-pressed to keep pace with growing costs. Benefit cuts are all but certain, and there are various proposals to encourage participation in HMOs and to increase premiums and copayments paid by Medicare beneficiaries. Even then some predict insolvency within a decade.

Yet for all the expense, Medicare has failed to fulfill the promise articulated by President Johnson. Medicare pays only for "skilled" care for "acute" illness, contributing to only 44% of personal health care expenses. With no coverage for 'unskilled" care such as help with personal hygiene or household chores, and insurance picking up only some of the gap, the burden of health care costs on American families today looms greater than ever.

 ELIGIBILITY FOR MEDICARE

Medicare consists of two programs: Part A, hospital insurance, and Part B, medical insurance. Each program involves different kinds of treatment for which enrollees are partially or fully covered.

You're eligible for Medicare if you're

- Over 65 and entitled to retirement benefits under the Social Security Act (even if you don't actually receive benefits because you've earned too much income)
- Under 65 but permanently and totally disabled for 24 months

Legislative note. One current legislative proposal would increase the age of Medicare eligibility over a period of years until it reached 67 in the year 2027. This would parallel the increase in the age of Social Security eligibility already enacted (described in Chapter 18).

Can I get Medicare if I'm not a citizen?

Medicare is available only to United States citizens or permanent aliens who have resided here more than five years.

My spouse has enrolled in Medicare. Am I eligible for Medicare as a spouse?

Medicare benefits are available only to the 65-year-old individual applying for them. If one marital partner is 65 and the other is not, the younger spouse is not eligible to purchase Medicare insurance. Don't give up private insurance for yourself or your spouse until you know you are both covered by Medicare.

My son was injured in an accident more than two years ago. Is he eligible for Medicare?

It depends on the severity of the injury. Your son qualifies if he has been permanently and totally disabled for 24 months. Although our emphasis throughout this book is on the elderly, what we say about government entitlements is generally applicable to the disabled as well.

 ENROLLMENT (PART A HOSPITAL COVERAGE)

For most people, enrollment in Medicare is a fairly straightforward process that accompanies enrollment in the Social Security system. The Social

Security Administration handles applications to both Social Security and Medicare. Once you've established your entitlement to Social Security, you should be enrolled in Medicare without having to file a separate application. Social Security disability recipients who receive benefits for 24 months are also enrolled automatically. You'll automatically receive Part A hospital coverage. Part A covers all in-hospital services, discussed later in this chapter. (Social Security is discussed in Chapter 18.)

If you're not enrolled in Social Security, you must file an application for Medicare with the Social Security Administration. Apply during your *initial enrollment period*, which begins three months before the month of your 65th birthday and runs for seven months (through the three months following your birthday month).

Applying is as simple as making a phone call to your local Social Security office. All you have to supply is proof of eligibility, including your age and some record of your earnings. The Social Security office does the rest—it even fills out the forms for you.

It pays to enroll before the month of your birthday. If you do, coverage will begin on the first day of the month of your 65th birthday. If you wait until your birthday month, coverage won't begin until the next month; if you enroll in the following months, coverage will begin in the second month following your enrollment; and if you wait until the last two months, coverage will begin in the third month following your enrollment.

After you've enrolled, your contact with Medicare will be primarily through claims filed with your *intermediary* or *carrier*. These are private insurance companies under contract with Medicare to process claims and handle information requests. Whether you will be dealing with an intermediary or a carrier depends on the type of claim you're filing: intermediaries handle Part A claims and carriers are responsible for Part B claims. (It's a distinction without a difference; a company can be both an intermediary and a carrier.) Intermediaries and carriers report to the Health Care Financing Administration (HCFA), the federal agency that administers Medicare.

I'm not eligible for Social Security benefits. Can I purchase Medicare privately?

Yes. You can buy Medicare insurance if you're 65 or older. The premiums are expensive, but may well be worth it when you factor in the rising cost of health insurance and the scarcity of other forms of insurance available to the elderly. In 1996, Part A coverage comes to $289 a month. For those with 30 quarters towards Social Security, there is a reduced $188 monthly premium. (For more on Social Security, see Chapter 18.) The premium cost for Part B is the same as for Medicare-eligible enrollees.

Medicare can't refuse to accept you because of your previous health history. Don't underestimate the importance of this guarantee. If you live in a state that allows medical underwriting, this may be the only insurance you can get.

Will I be notified by the government when it's time for me to apply?

Don't count on the government to tell you you're eligible or remind you to enroll. One way the government saves money is by neglecting to do just that. If you're not automatically enrolled as a Social Security recipient, you'll have to make that call to Social Security.

Can I get retroactive benefits?

Yes, for Part A hospital coverage. If you apply within six months, benefits will be retroactive to the first month of eligibility. If you apply later, they'll be retroactive to the sixth month of potential eligibility. In order to receive retroactive benefits, you must apply for them. (Only living individuals can apply; estates are not eligible for retroactive benefits.)

 ## ENROLLMENT (PART B MEDICAL INSURANCE)

Part B medical insurance covers physician and surgeon services and other specified services (discussed later in this chapter). Enrollment in Part B is automatic with your Medicare enrollment. No separate application is necessary.

Part B charges premiums like those you would pay for traditional medical insurance. The rates, which are established by statute, increase each year. In 1996, the monthly premium is $42.50. (The premium amount is scheduled to rise to $60.90 by 2002.)

Legislative note. *This amount may increase considerably, if legislative proposals to increases premiums for higher-income Medicare recipients come to pass. At present, premiums cover less than one third of program costs for the average elderly participants. Under some proposals, the monthly amount would more than double.*

Premiums are deducted from your monthly Social Security check. If you're not receiving Social Security, premiums will be billed directly to you on a quarterly basis.

Part B coverage is optional. If you don't want Part B coverage, you can opt out. The Social Security Administration will send you a letter granting you a specific time, at least two months, for you to decline.

If you don't enroll in Part B during your initial enrollment period when you reach age 65, you can enroll thereafter only during a *general enrollment period* from January 1st to March 31st of each year, with coverage to start July 1st. There is a *premium penalty* of 10 percent for each year in which you're eligible but fail to enroll. (There is no penalty for those covered by a company plan after reaching age 65.)

Medicare Part B is administered nationwide by 32 carriers, including Blue Shield plans and private insurers such as CIGNA, Aetna, and

Transamerica. Carriers are responsible for paying your claims and providing information on your coverage.

Can I get retroactive benefits for Part B?

No. Retroactive benefits are available for Part A hospital coverage only. There are no retroactive benefits available for Part B.

If I'm working, do I have to pay for Medicare Part B?

No. Part B is optional, whether you are working or not. And there's no premium penalty for older workers who delay enrollment because they're covered under group health plans through their (or their spouses') current employment. If you are covered by a company plan, you needn't enroll in Medicare Part B. When you stop working, you can apply through a *special enrollment period*.

Are Part B costs tax deductible?

Yes, Part B premiums are tax deductible to the same extent that medical insurance premiums are.

MEDICARE BUY-IN PROGRAM

If you can't afford Medicare premiums, you may be able to have the government pick up the check. Under the Medicare Buy-in Program (also called the *Qualified Medicare Beneficiary Program*, or *QMB*), states cover specified Medicare charges for qualified individuals. In order to qualify, you must be Medicare-eligible with an income less than the poverty level. (In 1995, this benefit was extended to those with income up to 120 percent of the poverty level.)

The potential for savings is great. The Medicare Buy-in Program pays for premium costs, as well as deductibles and copayments. This can run into the thousands. (Deductibles and copayments are discussed later in this chapter.)

An estimated 4 million elderly poor are believed to be eligible. If you think you or a member of your family may be eligible for the Medicare Buy-In, contact your local Medicaid office and ask for an application. Or call Medicare's toll-free hotline at 800/638–6833. The Buy-in Program is separately administered from Medicare, through your state's Medicaid program.

I'm 65 years old. I'm not on Medicaid and I can't afford Medicare. Can I get help?

The Medicare Buy-in Program may pay for your Medicare premiums—and also cover your deductible and copayment. This is like getting Medicare *and* supplemental insurance. Call now to see if you're qualified. You don't have to be on Medicaid to qualify for the program.

COVERAGE AND EXCLUSIONS

What does Medicare insurance provide? Coverage under both Part A and Part B entitles participants to a number of services. One caveat: in order to qualify for coverage, all services must be provided in an appropriate facility and by personnel with Medicare certification and licensed by the state.

Part A hospital insurance covers in-patient hospital care, including:

- Semiprivate room and meals
- Special care units
- Diagnostic procedures, X-rays, laboratory services
- Anesthesia
- Operating and recovery rooms
- Rehabilitation services
- Post-hospital skilled nursing facility care (under specific conditions only)
- Home health care (under specific conditions only)
- Hospice care
- Blood

Part B medical insurance covers

- Physician and surgeon services
- Clinical laboratory services
- Ambulatory (out-patient) services
- Physicians' assistants and nurse anesthetists
- Psychiatric social services
- Physical and speech therapists
- Chiropractic care
- Ambulance services
- Screening mammograms for older women
- Injectable drugs to treat osteoporosis
- Durable medical equipment, medical supplies, and prosthetic devices
- Blood
- Home health care (under specific conditions only)

It's also vital to know what's not covered by Medicare. Medicare does *not* cover
- Long-term nursing home care
- Full-time home nursing care or personal care
- Homemaker services (except hospice patients)
- Home-delivered meals
- Check-ups and preventive care
- Routine eye exams, eyeglasses, and contact lenses (except for some cataract surgery patients)

- Hearing exams, hearing aids and fittings
- Routine foot care and orthopedic shoes
- Dental care and dentures
- Over-the-counter drugs
- Prescription drugs used at home (except hospice patients)
- Self-administered injections such as insulin
- Most immunizations
- Experimental procedures
- Chiropractic services
- Acupuncture
- Private hospital rooms
- Private duty nursing

These exclusions can be fairly daunting to those in need of the care they represent—and in some circumstances even the care included on the list of covered services may be denied. Medicare coverage for home health care and post-hospital care in particular is limited in most cases due to extensive restrictions. Be prepared to fight for benefits you're entitled to. You may need to appeal an adverse decision or seek professional legal assistance. Appeals are discussed later in this chapter. (See Chapter 7 for information on obtaining Medicare for home health and post-hospital care.)

 DEDUCTIBLES AND COPAYMENT

Medicare is a cost-sharing program, its expenses borne by the government and contributed to by Medicare participants. These contributions are in the form of premiums (discussed above) and deductibles and copayments for which participants are liable.

Deductibles. A deductible is the amount you must pay before Medicare assumes responsibility for payment. For medical services under Part B, you have to pay the first $100 in charges each year. For hospital care under Part A, you have to pay a deductible ($736 in 1996) for *each* benefit period.

A *benefit period* is a measure of your use of hospital services. A benefit period starts when you're admitted to the hospital and ends after you've been out of the hospital (or the skilled facility you went to after leaving the hospital) for 60 days.

If you're readmitted to the hospital within the 60 days following your discharge, that counts as part of the same benefit period. If you're readmitted more than 60 days after your discharge, you've entered a new benefit period—and you'll have to pay a new $736 deductible. After the new deductible is met, you once again have a full 60 days at full reimbursement before copayment is required.

Copayment. Copayment requires you to pay a share of the costs. Under Part B, you generally have to pay 20 percent of the approved amount of doctors' costs. For Part A hospitalization, you have to pay a set amount

($184 a day in 1996) after 60 days. If you need more than 90 days, you will have to use a one-time bank of 60 "lifetime reserve" days, for which you have to pay $368 per day (in 1996). You are responsible for total costs over 150 days. (We'll explain how Medicare supplemental insurance can pay these amounts in Chapter 6.)

For skilled nursing facility expenses under your Part A coverage, you have to pay a set amount after 20 days ($92 a day in 1996). Beyond 100 days, you're liable for total costs.

Watch out for hospital outpatient costs! Under Part B, if you receive outpatient services at a hospital, you are responsible for paying 20 percent of whatever the hospital charges, not subject to any Medicare-approved rate. In recent years, as outpatient care has increased, hospitals have raised these costs to the detriment of unwary patients. Remember to find out what the charges will be before you agree to any outpatient procedures.

Legislative note. Deductibles and copayments are also under congressional scrutiny. Current proposals include an increase in deductibles to as high as $200 within the next five years. Copayments may also be increased and extended to other non-doctor Part B services, such as laboratory services, which are currently fully covered.

 PHYSICIAN FEES

Under Medicare Part B, the patient is responsible for paying an initial $100 deductible and 20 percent of the approved amount of the doctor's fee. As a Medicare patient, your costs will be dependent on

- The approved rate set by Medicare
- Whether your doctor participates in Medicare
- Fee limits imposed by federal and state law

Medicare-approved rate. This is the rate set by Medicare for the particular medical service performed by the doctor, whether it is an office visit or outpatient or in-hospital surgery. The Medicare-approved rate governs how much the doctor may bill Medicare and how much the patient will be charged. Depending on the state you live in and your choice of doctor, patient charges may range from 20 to 35 percent of the Medicare-approved rate (not including liability for the yearly $100 deductible).

Participating doctors. A participating doctor is one who accepts assignment for all patients, who will then be charged at the Medicare-approved rate. By accepting assignment, the doctor agrees to accept the Medicare-approved rate in full payment for services rendered. The doctor submits all Medicare claim forms to HCFA for direct payment, and the patient is billed for any deductible and copayment unpaid by Medicare.

With a participating doctor, there is no cost to you above the $100 Part B deductible and 20 percent copayment. Participating doctors must take assignment on all the services they render.

A doctor who doesn't accept assignment or who accepts it in select cases only is a *nonparticipating* doctor. If your doctor refuses assignment, you may have to pay the whole amount of your doctor's charge (subject to fee caps, discussed below) and wait for Medicare to reimburse you. You'll be responsible for the annual deductible and 20 percent copayment amount, plus the cost over what Medicare approves for the service. This is called *balance billing*.

If your doctor is nonparticipating but accepts assignment on your case, for all practical purposes it works the same as with a participating doctor. The doctor must submit the bill to Medicare, and you will be charged only the applicable deductible and copayment of 20 percent of the Medicare-approved rate.

Fee limits. Whether or not a doctor accepts assignment, the federal government and a number of states have imposed additional fee limits (also called *fee caps*) on the amount doctors may charge Medicare patients.

Federally imposed fee limits apply to all doctors treating Medicare patients, even if they don't accept assignment:

- A doctor who accepts assignment is limited to the Medicare-approved fee. Medicare will pay 80 percent, which leaves you liable for 20 percent.
- A doctor who doesn't accept assignment can charge you more than the Medicare rate, but *no more than 115 percent* of the Medicare approved rate. Medicare will still pay 80 percent, which leaves you liable for no more than 35 percent.

A number of states specify more restricted fees than the federal law or eliminate additional fees ("balance billing") totally:

- **Fee restrictions.** Massachusetts requires doctors to accept assignment for all Medicare patients. Pennsylvania prohibits any billing above the Medicare-approved rate. As of 1995, New York imposes fee limits of 105 percent of the Medicare-approved rate (limits are not applicable to home and office visits).
- **Means-tested restrictions.** Rhode Island requires assignment for all those below a certain income. Connecticut and Vermont also have eligibility requirements by income. (Vermont does not apply limits to home and office visits.)

How can I find a participating doctor?

A directory of participating physicians is made available to all Medicare recipients. Between one quarter and one third of physicians are participating doctors. Even if your doctor is not a participating doctor, you can always try to negotiate with your doctor to accept assignment on your case.

My doctor does not participate in Medicare and insists on my paying upfront. Are there any limits on the fees I can be charged?

Yes. Fee limits set by federal law apply to *all* Medicare patients, regardless of whether your doctor is a participating doctor or accepts assignment in your case. Your state may impose additional restrictions on the amount you are charged.

What do I do with these Medicare forms?

Under recent law, all doctors must fill out and submit Part B Medicare forms for their Medicare patients, whether they've accepted assignment or not. The law allows doctors one year to file a claim.

I have an insurance policy that will pay the balance above the rate allowed by Medicare. What should I tell my doctor?

If you are covered by insurance, your doctor can bill your insurance company for the extra amount, despite the fee limits. But with statutory limits on the fees you can be charged anyway, why pay extra for that kind of coverage.

The doctor I used to go to refuses to accept Medicare patients. Is this legal?

Yes. Doctors are not obligated to treat Medicare patients.

My doctor has joined an HMO. Can he still treat me? What options do I have?

You have the right to join an HMO in lieu of Medicare services. More than three and a half million Medicare recipients nationwide have joined HMOs. (For more on managed care and Medicare, see the next chapter.)

 ## HOSPITAL COSTS, TREATMENT, AND DISCHARGE

Once you're in the hospital, you have the right to the treatment and services you need. Medicare Part A covers these in-patient hospital services, subject to your deductible and copayments not covered by insurance. This is what you will pay.

Don't confuse your charges with the amount Medicare pays the hospital. In order to control hospital costs, Congress has established a payment system based on patient diagnosis. When you enter the hospital, a flat fee is determined in advance by whether you're being admitted for a hernia or heart surgery or any one of nearly 500 different groups (called *Diagnosis Related Groups*, or *DRGs*). Under this "prospective payment" or "DRG system," the hospital gets the same flat rate from Medicare no matter how long you stay in the hospital or how many or how few services you receive.

How does the DRG system affect your treatment? Theoretically, it shouldn't. If you need treatment, you are legally entitled to it even if your "DRG days" are used up. When the DRG system was first introduced, critics charged that hospitals were discharging patients "quicker and sicker." Although the prevalence of these abuses has since lessened in response to intense consumer outcry and government monitoring, the economic incentive for hospitals is still there—and so is the opportunity for abuse. Remember, your discharge date must be determined by your medical needs, not by your DRG category or Medicare coverage.

You will have to pay, however, for any service or treatment you receive that isn't approved by Medicare. Medicare pays only for hospitalization that is medically necessary. If the hospital believes the particular treatment or service you're being prescribed is not covered by Medicare, it must inform you in writing.

- If you haven't already been treated, you'll have to forego the service or pay privately. The Catch-22 of this alternative is that if you can't afford and don't pay for the service, you have nothing to appeal later.
- If the decision on your treatment amounts to a denial of your right to remain in the hospital, you can appeal your discharge as premature to the hospital's Peer Review Organization (PRO) through an *immediate review* process designed to help you remain in the hospital if discharge is inappropriate. You can make this appeal whether you're being discharged to a skilled nursing facility, to home health care, or to your home.

You have the absolute right to *discharge planning* before you're discharged from the hospital. What services will or won't be covered should be discussed at your consultation. The plan must be discussed with you and placed in your record. Under law, it must be finished in time for arrangements to be made for your transfer to a nursing home or skilled nursing facility or to your home with home care services before discharge. (See Chapter 7 for information on your rights in this regard.)

The hospital wants to discharge me, but I'm still sick. Can they do this?

It depends on your medical condition. In more egregious cases, patients have been transferred from the hospital before their conditions were stable. This kind of "dumping" is strictly against the law.

Am I limited to the number of days in the DRG for my illness?

No. You're not limited to the number of days in your DRG and you cannot be charged extra if your stay exceeds them. So long as your medical condition requires hospital care, the hospital cannot discharge you.

The hospital has billed me $1,000 for outpatient care, 20 percent of a $5,000 bill. Isn't it limited by the DRG system?

No. The DRG system doesn't apply to outpatient services, which are covered by Medicare Part B. And because of a quirk in the law, the hospital can charge whatever it wants for outpatient services and you will be liable for a full 20 percent.

The hospital wants to discharge me but I don't have a bed to go to. Can they charge me?

If you're awaiting placement in a skilled nursing facility, you're entitled to stay in the hospital without charge until a skilled nursing bed is available. It's the responsibility of your doctor and the hospital to find an appropriate placement for you. That doesn't necessarily mean the facility of your choice. You will not be allowed to remain in the hospital once an appropriate nursing home bed is found, even if it's not where you'd prefer to go.

 EXPEDITED REVIEW BEFORE DISCHARGE

Once you've received a decision turning down a claim submitted to Medicare, you can challenge that decision through an appeals process set forth in the Medicare law (and described in the following section). However, if you are in the hospital and the decision amounts to denial of your right to remain in the hospital, you may also be entitled to an *expedited review*.

If you receive a "Notice of Noncoverage" while you're in the hospital, one option is to stay on and pay privately, appealing later if you wish. Another option, for those unable to foot the bill even temporarily, is to ask for an immediate, or *expedited*, review.

How to proceed with your expedited review depends on whether your doctor agrees or disagrees with the hospital's determination to discharge you.

- **If the hospital and your doctor agree** that you should be discharged, you must request a review by noon of the first workday after you receive the written Notice of Noncoverage. You can make your request by phone or in writing, but the deadline is very important. If you meet the deadline, you can't be made to pay hospital charges until a committee called the Peer Review Organization (PRO) reviews your case.

  The PRO is a group of doctors who review treatment decisions on behalf of Medicare. Although these are usually statewide groups, some PRO decisions are made by hospital utilization review committees which have been delegated that task.

  The PRO will ask your views before making its decision, which it will communicate to you by phone or in writing. If it agrees with you, you'll be allowed to remain in the hospital without paying. If not, you're not billed until noon of the day after you receive their decision.

  You can gain at least one day more of coverage if you do not appeal on the day you receive your notice but wait until the morning of the following day. If your appeal is denied on the dame day, you are liable as of noon of the next day. You must file before noon.

- **If the hospital and your doctor disagree** about your discharge, your case has probably already been reviewed by the PRO. With your doctor opposed to discharge, the PRO had to agree with the hospital for a Notice of Noncoverage to have been issued. Because of this, the hospital is allowed to bill you as of the third day after you receive your notice, even if you've requested another review.

  To limit your potential liability to one day, you should request reconsideration immediately, by phone or in writing. The PRO has three working days to complete its review.

If you receive a Notice of Noncoverage while you're in the hospital, contact the hospital's patient representative immediately. The patient representative (also called *patient advocate* or *ombudsman*) will help you understand the notice and explain the options available to you if you want to stay longer.

I've received a Notice of Noncoverage from the hospital. What happens now? What are my legal obligations?

If you don't request a review, the hospital may bill you for all the costs of your stay beginning the third day after you receive the written notice.

The hospital says I'm not covered by Medicare for any more time, but I haven't received anything in writing. Am I legally obligated to pay?

If you don't receive a written Notice of Noncoverage, you don't have to pay.

I want to request my review right away. Why can't I just go ahead and do that?

You can. But there are financial reasons to delay. If you do request an expedited review and it's decided against you right away, you may lose those extra days that delay might gain you.

What happens if I don't ask for an immediate review and stay in the hospital and pay for the noncovered days?

You can still appeal Medicare's decision to end payment later on, through the regular appeals process described in the following section.

 APPEALING A MEDICARE DECISION

As noted above, Medicare contracts out its claims administration to private insurance companies, called *intermediaries* and *carriers*. (Intermediaries process Part A claims; carriers process Part B claims.)

Once you've submitted a claim and received an initial determination from the Medicare carrier or intermediary, you can challenge that decision through an appeals process set forth in the Medicare law. If you go to a participating doctor or if your doctor has accepted assignment for your treatment, the doctor handles appeals; you only have to appeal on unassigned claims.

You can appeal decisions about

- Doctor bills under Medicare Part B
- In-hospital admission or continued hospital stay
- Decisions about hospital payment
- Admission to skilled nursing facility and continued stay
- Home health agency coverage and payment

The Medicare appeal process is multilevel. The rules differ slightly depending on whether you're appealing a Part B claim decision, a Part A claim decision for in-hospital services, or any other Part A claim decision.

Each step has different rules, including minimum amounts that must be "in controversy" and deadlines which must be observed. The time runs from the receipt of the prior decision. (See chart below.)

MEDICARE APPEALS		
PART B CLAIMS		
Steps	**Deadline to file (from receipt of prior decision)**	**Minimum amount in controversy**
Initial denial		
Review	6 months	None
Fair hearing	6 months	$100 to $500
Administrative hearing	60 days	$500
Appeals Council	60 days	$500
Federal Court	60 days	$1000
PART A CLAIMS (IN-HOSPITAL)		
Steps	**Deadline to file (from receipt of prior decision)**	**Minimum amount in controversy**
Initial denial		
Reconsideration	60 days	None
Administrative hearing	60 days	$200
Appeals Council	60 days	$200
Federal Court	60 days	$2000
PART A CLAIMS (ALL OTHERS)		
Steps	**Deadline to file (from receipt of prior decision)**	**Minimum amount in controversy**
Initial denial		
Reconsideration	60 days	None
Administrative hearing	60 days	$100
Appeals Council	60 days	$100
Federal Court	60 days	$1000

Although the appeal process uses different nomenclature for different steps (e.g., "review" of Part B claims, "reconsideration" of Part A claims), there is no legal significance to the names used. They are primarily used to identify one appeal step from another. Medicare provides forms to request review, reconsideration, or appeal. These forms are not required; you can use any other forms or letters that state your case. However, you may wish to use them for your convenience or as a guide to help prepare your appeal.

1. Review and reconsideration

Review of Part B claims. You should request a review if Medicare denies your coverage of a Part B claim, or if it pays you less than 80 percent of your doctor's (or other health provider's) charges. This happens when Medicare says the "reasonable charge" is less than what your doctor billed.

You can get a review simply by requesting it within six months after the date of the initial denial. Simply write to your Medicare carrier. The carrier will have your claim reviewed by a different employee than the one who made the initial determination. You'll get a written response within six to eight weeks.

Always request a review if your claim is denied. There is no minimum amount that need be in dispute. More than 63 percent of Part B reviews are successful at this first review level, winning money for the claimants.

Reconsideration of Part A claims for inpatient hospital care. For determinations concerning the necessity of inpatient hospital care, you may request reconsideration by the PRO.

You can get a reconsideration of your claim upon request within 60 days. Expedited review of admission or continued-stay denials is also available upon request by the patient. The PRO will issue its written reconsideration determination within 30 days, within 10 days for skilled nursing facility patients, and within three days for admissions candidates and hospital patients. There is no minimum dispute amount for reconsideration.

Reconsideration of Part A claims for other than inpatient hospital care. You may request reconsideration by the intermediary. Again, there is a 60-day period in which you must make your request for reconsideration; there is no minimum dispute amount. These will be decided "on paper," which means you don't have to appear anywhere. The decision will be made by an intermediary employee, *not* the one who made the initial determination. The reversal rate for these appeals is only 15–20 percent.

2. Fair hearing (Part B claims only)

If the review of your Part B claim has not been successful and your claim is between $100 and $500, you're entitled to a fair hearing from the carrier. You must request a hearing within six months of the review determination.

For this kind of hearing, courtroom rules of evidence do not apply. The hearing officer is appointed by the carrier, usually a paid employee. The hearing officer has no subpoena power. In making a decision, the hearing officer applies Medicare policies and guidelines. The hearing is recorded and transcribed.

The hearing is usually held at the carrier's office or a Social Security office, although it can be held elsewhere on request. The hearing may be in person or "on the record," which means the appeal is decided solely on documents submitted to the hearing officer.

Your odds on success at a fair hearing are good. The reversal rate for claimants at a Part B hearing is 60 percent.

3. Administrative hearing

If you're still not satisfied after your review and/or hearing, you're entitled to an administrative hearing before an administrative law judge (ALJ) employed by the Social Security Administration. You may bring a lawyer.

You must request an administrative hearing within 60 days of the prior determination made concerning your claim. The minimum amount that must be in dispute depends on the type of claim: $500 for a Part B claim, $200 for a Part A inpatient claim, and $100 for all other Part A claims.

An administrative hearing is similar to a regular civil suit, including sworn testimony by the parties. You have the right to submit testimony, the opportunity for cross-examination, and the right to object to admission of evidence. An ALJ can issue subpoenas on the written request of counsel, made at least five days before the scheduled hearing date. Your doctor may be required to testify.

The hearing is usually held near your home, although you may be required to travel up to 75 miles. You or your lawyer will get 10 days notice of the time and the place of the hearing from the ALJ.

The hearing may be in person or "on the record." There is a 40 percent success rate for those who request in-person hearings.

4. Appeals Council review

Within 60 days of the ALJ's decision, you may appeal the ALJ's decision to the Social Security Appeals Council. There is no additional dollar minimum. Review by the Appeals Council of a decision by an ALJ is usually based on errors of law, abuse of discretion, and policy issues. For the most part, it's an on-the-record hearing. The Appeals Council is the last step required before you go to federal court.

5. Federal court

If the Appeals Council rules against you or if it refuses a hearing, you may appeal to the federal courts. If you meet the minimum amount requirements ($2,000 for in-hospital Part A claim, $1,000 for all others), you or your lawyer can request a federal court hearing. If the district court finds in your favor, it can reverse Medicare's decision or order a new hearing.

Medicare denied my claim. How do I decide whether to appeal?

In most appeals, the question being reviewed is the medical necessity of your care. In order to show that your treatment or care meets that standard, you will have to produce letters from your doctor attesting to your condition as well as any other medical documentation. In later stages of an appeal, your doctor may be called to testify.

Other possible issues include whether Medicare covers the particular treatment or service, whether you're entitled to it under the rules, and what amount you're entitled to. You might be arguing about deductibles, copayments, days used in a benefit period, or duration of a benefit period. Whatever the issue, it's important that you focus on that question and not get sidetracked by extraneous matters.

How can I appeal when I don't know why they denied my claim?

You have a right to the information on which Medicare based its decision. You should ask for a copy of your file when you request a review or recommendation.

I missed the deadline for review. What do I do?

Requests for review or reconsideration, or other appeal, must be filed within certain time limits set forth in the law. The time limits are important, although a late filing may be allowed for "good cause." What constitutes good cause may be death or serious illness in the family or misunderstanding, but there is no requirement that you be allowed a late filing. The safest bet is to meet the deadline in the first place.

My claim is for $2000. Can I go directly to federal court?

You have to take your turn, starting with the first step of the appeals process (review or reconsideration) and proceeding to each subsequent step in order. Before going to court, you must first complete the administrative process. This is called *exhausting your remedies*.

Of course if you prevail at any step, you stop at that stage. If Medicare doesn't appeal, then you win. If Medicare appeals, you have to continue onto the next step.

Should I get legal help?

You may represent yourself throughout the entire process, or use a lawyer for each step. As a general rule, the initial stages of appeal don't require sophisticated legal help. In admission and continued stay determinations, where the consequences are more immediate and the stakes are higher, you may welcome professional assistance at early stages.

A number of Medicare advocacy programs provide free legal services. AARP has a Medicare assistance program, which helps with Medicare problems, processing payments and paperwork. Assistance is also available with Medicare appeals. (See the Resources section at the end of this book for a listing of agencies which may be of help.)

▌ MEDICARE'S FUTURE

With health care changes on the horizon, the immediate future of Medicare is of concern to many older Americans. At this writing, changes to reduce spending growth are inevitable.

The mechanics of Medicare—its basic structure of enrollment, eligibility, coverage, and related rights—will likely stay the same as described in this chapter. Within that basic structure, individual standards may change. At least one proposal envisions means-testing for eligible individuals with incomes above $60,000 ($90,000 for couples) while another would gradually push the eligibility age up to 67 over the next three decades.

Expect to see costs go up. You will be paying more out of pocket, both in Part B premiums and, perhaps, in payroll tax increases to support Part A. Increases in deductibles and copayments are also on the table.

Benefit cuts are all but certain, and obtaining access to skilled nursing care and home health care may be even more difficult than at present. At the same time, more managed care plans are expected to be offering comparable benefit packages to Medicare recipients, who may be availing themselves of newly authorized "medical savings accounts." The anticipated increase in controls will affect availability of hospitals, doctors, and services across the board.

6

■ ■

HEALTH INSURANCE

For most older retired Americans, primary health insurance is provided by Medicare. For charges that Medicare does not cover and charges that it covers only in part, they rely on other insurance supplemental to that primary coverage.

Insurance made available through employment provides the primary coverage and protection for many older workers, retirees, and their spouses. For those age 65 to 69, that insurance is their primary coverage and protection. For those with other insurance coverage, Medicare provides secondary coverage, covering services and charges not paid for by their private carrier. At age 70, no matter what your employment status, Medicare becomes your primary insurance coverage.

No matter which category you fall into, an understanding of the protection afforded by hospitalization, major medical policies, Medigap supplemental policies, and long-term care policies (discussed in the next chapter) is crucial to your health care planning.

This is especially true now, when corporations and insurers are experimenting with new arrangements to keep costs down, including self-insurance, health maintenance organizations and managed care, direct administration of company plans, and utilization review and monitoring. You need to be able to assess what type of insurance will meet your needs, and know how to evaluate policies, what your rights are, and how to assert them. There's no excuse for ignorance—and less for not asserting rights you've paid for.

Your benefits depend on these factors:

- The type of coverage you have
- The terms and conditions of your individual policy
- The fiscal integrity of your insurance company
- Laws affording you protection as a consumer

A number of laws govern the benefits you receive and rights you are afforded under health policies, including HMO and managed care plans and Medicare supplemental insurance (Medigap). At this writing, Congress is contemplating legislation to guarantee "portable" health insurance. But you may already have rights under various federal and state laws to coverage when you change jobs and when you stop working. These legal protections are described in this chapter.

 ## TYPES OF HEALTH INSURANCE

Hospital-surgical insurance covers inpatient hospital services and surgical procedures. Charges for room and board, surgeons' fees, nursing services, X-rays, and lab and diagnostic tests should also be included. Almost always excluded are services provided outside the hospital, even follow-up visits.

Your coverage under a hospital-surgical policy may be limited to a fixed number of days in the hospital. Double-check reimbursement rates. This type of policy often pays at the low end of the scale, leaving you with a hefty balance due.

Comprehensive/major medical insurance provides coverage for basic hospital services and for doctor services in and out of the hospital. Coverage generally includes room and board, operating and recovery, doctor visits, nursing care, lab tests, X-rays, anesthesia, and other costs commonly associated with hospital services.

Policies vary widely. Some offer supplemental items such as prescription drugs or post-hospital coverage. If you're over 65 and receiving Medicare benefits, comprehensive policies may be needed for your under-65 spouse's coverage.

Managed care is a fairly recent innovation combining insurance and health care services under one roof. It's designed to cut costs by eliminating the incentives provided in the typical fee-for-service doctor-patient encounter by charging a flat fee for your health care, no matter what your needs are, and emphasizing preventive care.

Medigap insurance and long-term care insurance are also recent strategies designed to supplement Medicare coverage for older people and to provide some protection against catastrophic illness requiring prolonged care either in a nursing home, other long-term care facility, or at home. (We discuss these later in this and the next chapter.)

These are the most common forms of insurance. Stick with a basic hospitalization plan, or a comprehensive major-medical if you can get one. Others include the following:

- *Hospital indemnity policies* pay a fixed dollar amount for each day you're in the hospital. Some are designed to pay a fixed amount per service. Coverage is often linked to a waiting period for which you cannot collect benefits, and the amounts are often too small to cover hospital costs.
- *Dread disease insurance* is linked to the possibility that you might catch a specific disease. You can buy cancer insurance, or insurance against other specific diseases. Not only are the odds against your contracting the particular disease for which you're covered, the benefits

are usually pitifully small, the premiums comparatively high, and there's usually a qualification period of six months or more before you would be eligible to collect benefits. These are banned in New York and a number of other states.

 POLICY TERMS AND CONDITIONS

An insurance policy is a contract. It binds both you and your insurer to certain obligations which are enforceable under the law. The terms of your policy determine whether or not you'll collect on any claims, and how much you'll collect.

Your policy may have exclusions for eligible expenses, limitations for pre-existing conditions, deductibles and copayment amounts, and newly-instituted review boards. There are any number of possible variations, and it's important for you to know what coverage you have and what coverage you're buying.

Eligible expenses. Health coverage is typically linked to a determination by the insurance company of eligible expenses. An eligible expense is one for which the treatment or service is covered by your policy. It's generally subject to the condition that the treatment must be *medically necessary*, often limited to treatment of an illness or injury, as defined by the insurer.

Even if the procedure is determined to be medically necessary, you have another hurdle to cross. Your expenses are limited to *reasonable and customary charges.* What constitutes a reasonable and customary charge differs among insurers and among policies. The amount is theoretically set on doctors' fees in your area. You're liable for what the doctor charges above the insurance company-determined eligible expense.

Make sure you know how much your insurance will pay before you commit to any high-ticket procedures. If the amount is appreciably out of sync with your doctor's fee, you should ask why. Either your doctor is overcharging or your insurance company is not paying enough. You can negotiate with your doctor or your insurance company, and ask them to reconsider their decision.

Pre-existing conditions and waiting periods. Pre-existing conditions are health problems for which you were diagnosed or received advice or treatment prior to the effective date of your insurance. With a pre-existing condition, you may have difficulty finding a policy. Or you may only be able to get one at higher premiums or with an "exclusion rider" expressly excluding coverage for that pre-existing condition.

Insurance companies often will issue a policy that (1) defines a pre-existing condition as one diagnosed or treated within a specified period of time before the effective date of coverage, and (2) requires a waiting period before allowing coverage for pre-existing conditions. The length of time for defining a pre-existing condition generally varies from six months to two years before coverage begins. Waiting periods may vary from 90 days to as much as two years.

A number of states limit both the length of time prior to coverage for a pre-existing condition and the waiting period after coverage begins to a specified duration. About half the states limit the length of time for pre-existing conditions to the six-month period before coverage, and another 11 states limit it to 12 months in laws governing small employer health insurance. Waiting periods after the effective date of coverage are restricted to a maximum of 12 months in half the states, and to six months in six states.

A number of states have additional "portability" provisions, in which waiting periods and limitation or exclusion of coverage for pre-existing conditions are waived for individuals who have had continuous health insurance coverage for up to 30 or 60 days (in some states, 90 days) prior to the date of new coverage. Some states prohibit waiting periods and limitations in coverage for pre-existing conditions altogether.

It's very important to disclose any pre-existing conditions on your insurance application. In some states, insurance companies are permitted to delay checking on an applicant's medical history until a claim is filed. This is called *medical underwriting*. If you have a pre-existing condition which is later uncovered, the company could rescind your policy.

Legislative note.   *Current health bills before Congress would guarantee "portability" for health insurance by ensuring that group coverage would be available for those changing jobs, by prohibiting waiting periods for more than one year for a pre-existing condition diagnosed or treated within the previous six months (and reducing the allowable waiting period one month for each month of coverage under a prior plan). Similar protection would be afforded those seeking individual plans, requiring insurance companies to offer individual policies to anyone who had coverage under a group plan for 18 months (with exceptions for those otherwise eligible for a group plan or who have not exhausted their continuation coverage under COBRA).* (For more on COBRA, see Continuing Coverage When You Stop Working, later in this chapter.)

Am I covered for preventive care such as check-ups and routine examinations?

Probably not. Most traditional forms of insurance cover only medically necessary care, defined as treatment for illness or injury. Alternative forms of coverage such as managed care are beginning to include coverage for preventive care. Some state laws require coverage for specific items such as pap smears, mammograms, and other screening services. If so, your policy will state this. (See HMOs and Managed Care later in this chapter.)

I told my insurance agent about my condition and was told to leave it off the application—I would be all right. Should I follow my agent's advice?

No. Lying on an application is fraud. Remember, your prior treatment is a matter of record. It doesn't do you any good to get a policy that won't pay later.

The Medical Information Bureau maintains a database on more than 15 million insurance applicants. The information is disseminated to nearly 700 insurance companies, which may in turn base coverage decisions and premium charges on it.

These files often contain errors. It's a good idea to obtain a record of your application and policy claims information to make sure the contents are accurate. You can obtain a copy of the record of your insurance coverage by calling the Consumer Information Office of the Medical Insurance Bureau at 617/426–3660.

I'm changing jobs. Do I have to worry about changing insurance?

It depends. A new job may give you benefits even if you have a medical problem, but there might be a waiting period for a pre-existing condition. And you may not be covered for some period of time, often six to 12 months. (Pending federal legislation, if passed, may reduce this time to 0.) You may need to get "continuation" or "conversion" coverage from your former employer to cover you in the interim. (We discuss these later in this chapter.)

Deductibles and copayment. You will be reimbursed subject to your deductible and copayment share. The deductible is the amount you pay before the insurance company reimbursement begins. The higher the deductible, the lower the premium.

The copayment is the portion or amount of medical charges you are required to pay once the deductible is met. Many policies pay 80 percent of eligible expenses, leaving your copay share at 20 percent. Other policies provide 70–30 or 50–50. More recent policies, including many managed care policies, require a higher percentage if you don't use panel-approved doctors or hospitals.

An upper cap on the copayment amount you're liable for per year is called a *stop loss*. Above a given amount, for example, $5,000 or $10,000, 100 percent of eligible expenses will be paid. With stop loss protection, your maximum outlay is limited to the total of your premiums, deductible, and copayments within a given range. Some policies exclude certain expenses, such as for mental health, from stop loss protection. (One proposal before Congress would require coverage for mental illness to be equivalent to that provided other conditions, eliminating it as a category for seperate treatment.)

Case management/utilization review. More and more insurance companies are issuing policies requiring review for your health care to be covered. A case management or utilization review program incorporated into your health insurance policy is intended to ensure that proposed medical services are necessary, reasonable and cost-efficient: the most "appropriate" level and amount of care at the least cost. This kind of review is similar to the controls established by HMOs and other managed care organizations.

Often the case management requirement is limited to inpatient hospital treatment. Preadmission review or admission review following emergency admission commonly includes second opinions (covered by insurers), pre-certification and testing. There may be a penalty when the insurance company is not notified of an inpatient stay.

Many policies, which include an appeals process for claim conflicts, set up an additional, special appeals process to handle denials of this kind. Check your policy: *it may require a special appeal to be made within as short a time as 24 hours.* If you miss this deadline and go ahead with your treatment without utilizing the special appeals process, you can avail yourself of the regular appeals machinery later on. (See "Filing an insurance claim," below.)

Renewability.   An insurance policy is a contract, in force for a period of time specified in the contract. Some *optionally renewable* policies can be cancelled by the insurer at the end of the policy year or premium period, for no reason at all. In a *conditionally renewable* policy, the contract can be cancelled only if all other similar policies in your group, category, or state are cancelled. A policy that's *guaranteed renewable* cannot be cancelled, but this kind of policy is harder to find. A number of states have included "guaranteed renewal" protections within recent reform legislation applicable to insurance obtained through small employers.

I have a health insurance policy that is guaranteed renewable. I missed a few payments and the insurance company cancelled it for lack of payment. Can they do that?

Yes. Even if your policy is guaranteed renewable, it can be cancelled if you fail to pay your premiums. (One exception: some long term care policies provide for a waiver of premiums if you're collecting benefits. See Chapter 7.)

Am I protected once my rate is set?

Insurers set premiums for the contract period, generally one year. There's little protection against premium raises, which can force strapped policy-holders to cancel. However, the law allows insurance companies to raise rates only by class of policyholders; your company cannot raise your rates just because you've made numerous claims.

There's limited protection for older workers in federal law, which grants to those who work for employers of 20 or more the right to the same coverage offered to those under 65 and under the same conditions, whether or not they're covered by Medicare.

CHECKING THE INSURANCE COMPANY

When you buy an insurance policy, you're buying an insurance company. Unfortunately, failures of health insurers—an average of 10 per year in the

1980's—have become more common. The U.S. General Accounting Office reported 46 failures in 1991. Most of these failures occurred in four states: Illinois, Louisiana, Pennsylvania, and Texas.

You don't want to be left in the position of paying the bill for that failure. While all the states have established guarantee associations to fund benefits and limited coverage for those whose insurance companies have failed, there are significant gaps in the protections afforded you by those funds. Policyholders have been held responsible for unpaid claims.

How can I tell if an insurance company is fiscally sound?

First, check with the insurance company. Ask for copies of financial statements filed with your state's insurance department. Check with your state insurance department to find out if the health insurance company is licensed in your state. The insurance department can also provide you with information on pricing and service. Insurance departments also conduct financial reviews of insurers within the state. Ask about any problems or complaints. (See Resources for a list of state insurance departments.)

Make sure you check with a rating service. Although not perfect, they're an indispensable source of information if you're researching a company. Among the companies which furnish reports on insurance companies' solvency are A.M. Best (telephone 908/439–2200 or 212/439–2200, which gives you an ID number for another phone call at 900/420–0400), Standard & Poor's (telephone 212/208–1527), Moody's Investors Service (telephone 212/553–0377), and Duff & Phelps (telephone 312/368–3157).

Highest ratings for each company are

- Standard & Poor's   AAA
- Moody's   Aaa
- Best   A++
- Duff & Phelps   AAA

A.M. Best charges a $2.50-per-minute fee for its services; the other companies provide free information, and additional information on request (and possibly a fee). A newer entrant in the field, Weiss Research, provides a rating for a $15 minimum fee (telephone 800/289–9222). Rating reports are available in public libraries. (See Resources section for rating service addresses and phone numbers.)

Am I protected if the company is backed by a larger insurance company?

Not necessarily. Check with the larger company about its relationship with the smaller one. Don't take it for granted that because it's written in a brochure it must be so. In some cases, companies have claimed to be guaranteed by a respectable-sounding insurance company, or to have links with one, which on closer examination turned out to be tenuous.

Are there any protections from government?

Some state insurance departments are vigorous monitors on behalf of consumers. Others don't see their function the same way. Still others are underfunded and can't perform adequate oversight. State "guarantee associations" are supposed to absorb the liability of bankrupt companies and provide some benefits and coverage for stranded policyholders. Check with your state insurance department to see if your insurance company has contributed to your state's fund.

My employer is part of a MEWA. Am I protected?

Small businesses and their employees should watch out for pooled fund plans called "multi-employer welfare arrangements," or MEWAs, in which a health insurance provider sells otherwise unavailable insurance to a group of small companies or acts as administrator for them.

The trouble with these arrangements is they're often not regulated. Although many MEWAs are legitimate, mismanagement and fraud have accounted for hundreds of millions in unpaid claims and stranded many people without any insurance at all. A number of MEWAs are currently under federal and state investigation. Michigan has issued regulations governing MEWAs and many states are moving forward to regulate them.

I work for a firm that is "self-insured," but the plan is administered by Blue Cross. Does this make Blue Cross my insurer?

No. Don't confuse your insurer with your insurance plan administrator. Many health plans are administered by third-party administrators, which may be local insurers or Blue Cross. If so, it doesn't mean your plan is underwritten by the insurance company or subject to state regulation; self-insured plans are exempt from state standards. More than half of all employees in the United States work for companies that are fully or partially self-insured. Businesses like self-insurance because it saves money in premiums and assets can be used to pay claims.

I have coverage from Blue Cross, but have read reports about its finances. Are the "Blues" sound?

At least a dozen of the 73 Blue Cross-Blue Shield plans have reported financial problems, and one Blue Cross in West Virginia went broke in 1990, leaving nearly 50,000 policyholders with $40 million in unpaid claims. Unfortunately, only a few have been rated. One possible source of information is the financial statement of the company filed with your state insurance department. You could also check the Blue Cross and Blue Shield Association, which issues performance standards for its member plans, to see if the plan in your area is on its "watch" list (telephone 312/440–6000).

FILING AN INSURANCE CLAIM

When a claim is filed with an insurance company, it's generally reviewed based on (1) whether the service is covered under your policy and (2) whether the service was "medically necessary."

Services must be included in your contract coverage for you to receive payment for them. States often have express requirements for health insurance policies which insurers must write into their policies. For example, on the theory that preventive care saves money in the long run, some states require that mammograms or other preventive tests be covered by all insurance policies. If the terms of your policy conflict with state law, the law overrides the provisions of the policy.

Once a claim is made and meets the test of medical necessity, the actual charges are reviewed based on a standard of "customary and reasonable." The company will provide reimbursement at the contract rate (for example 80 percent) against that standard. Unlike Medicare, there are no restrictions on fees charged in relation to the insurance reimbursement or approved rate.

Check in advance. With an eye on the corporate bottom line, more and more insurance companies are rejecting claims, in whole or in part. If at all possible, check in advance about your basic coverage and the amount you will be covered for.

Research costs. If a portion of your doctor's charges is disallowed as unreasonable and you believe your doctor's fees are similar to those of other doctors in the same geographic area, write a letter to your insurance company asking it to review the reasonable and customary allowance. Get letters from your doctor and survey costs in your area. (If it turns out your doctor's fees exceed charges in your area, you can ask your doctor to lower the charges.)

Keep a record. Remember to put everything in writing. If you make a telephone call, keep a record of it. Maintain a log of your medical treatment, payments made and received, and copies of claims submitted to your insurance company. These will be essential for any appeal.

Appeal. You have the right to appeal any decision by your insurance company. It never hurts to appeal an adverse decision. An estimated 30% of insurance company rejections are the result of error. Insurance companies will back down if they get reasonable, written objections.

The process you will have to follow will be in the policy, and it may also be explained in the company's letter to you. You will also be given instructions on when and where to appeal. Check out your appeal rights before you sign up. Remember to file by the deadline!

Pursue your claim. If you can't get any action from the insurance company or feel you're not being treated fairly, try contacting the president of the insurance company, your state insurance department, or your Congressional representative. Your employer or plan administrator may also be of help. Remember, most people are too busy or too intimidated to pursue their complaints—and companies rely on that.

*My insurance company has given me less than half of my doctor's charges,
based on their estimation of "reasonable and customary charges," less my 20%
copayment. Is this legal? Is there anything I can do about it?*

It's legal, but that doesn't mean there's nothing you can do about it.
Ask the insurance company to provide you with the supporting data it
used to arrive at its determination. Compare the data and your own
survey results of doctor's charges. If the company doesn't reconsider,
file a formal appeal.

▎ INSURANCE REGULATION

Insurance regulation is a primary responsibility of the states, which oversee
the activities of insurance companies operating in their jurisdictions through
their state insurance departments.

States license insurance companies, setting standards for financial
operations and approving rates and policies issued by insurers. Policies
are also subject to review to make sure they comply with state minimum
requirements for benefits and other safeguards. Insurance agents are also
licensed by the state.

More than 30 states have passed limits on rate increases for people
with costly illnesses, while a smaller number have passed laws mandating
uniform rates. New York, for example, requires insurance companies to
accept all applicants, individuals and small companies, at the same
"community rate," regardless of age, gender, or health history. Other
states with similar laws include Hawaii, Vermont, Maine, and Oregon.

States vary in terms of their monitoring activities, which in some cases
is limited. Some states are more active than others on behalf of consumers, providing closer oversight and monitoring of insurance companies.
All state insurance departments have review procedures to assist consumers and investigate their complaints.

The National Association of Insurance Commissioners has adopted
accreditation standards which have accredited some two thirds of the
states, but have stirred opponents in state legislatures that have refused to
adopt the Commissioners' model laws. The General Accounting Office has
found the Commissioners' accreditation standards inconsistent. New York,
New Jersey, and Connecticut are among the states not accredited.

If you have a complaint against an insurance company, make sure you
notify your state insurance department by phone and in writing. And make
sure the company knows it, by forwarding it a copy of the letter. Your letter
may provide just the leverage you need to get the response you want from
the insurance company.

We mentioned the guarantee associations states have set up to provide
help for ex-policyholders. Some states also have programs to provide

subsidies toward insurance or managed care for uninsured residents who don't qualify for other insurance or Medicaid benefits.

 CONTINUING COVERAGE WHEN YOU STOP WORKING

The loss of a job no longer has to mean the loss of health insurance. If your job is in jeopardy, you may be eligible to continue in your group plan or convert to an individual policy.

Contract. You may be able to continue your policy under the terms of the policy itself. Some insurance contracts have special provisions allowing retirees or others to continue or convert their coverage after they leave their employment.

Whether you or the company will pay the premiums depends on the language of the contract. Make sure you consult your policy before you agree to any other arrangements. Don't sign away health insurance benefits that are rightfully yours.

Federal law. Under the "Comprehensive Omnibus Budget Reconciliation Act" (COBRA), if your past employer has more than 20 employees, you can remain in the same group plan for 18 months or longer. You'll pay a monthly premium, which is figured at 102 percent of your current premium cost and subject to the same deductible.

You must apply for continuation coverage during an election period that begins before your initial coverage ends and extends at least 60 days after it would end or when you've been given notice, whichever is later. Continuation coverage begins the date your prior coverage ends.

If you're an employee, you're entitled to continuation coverage for 18 months

- If your employment is terminated (except for gross misconduct)
- If your hours are reduced so that you no longer qualify for coverage

You're entitled to 29 months continuation coverage

- If you're disabled and eligible for Social Security benefits *when your employment ends* (You may have to pay as much as 150 percent for the additional months of coverage.)

You're entitled to continuation coverage for 36 months

- If your former employer commences bankruptcy proceedings (These rules and time periods apply to employees and to their spouses and dependent children.) If you're the spouse of an employee, you're entitled to 36 months continuation coverage
- If your spouse dies, or becomes entitled to Medicare

If you divorce or become legally separated (These rules and time periods also apply to dependent children.)

If you're the dependent child of an employee, you're entitled to 36 months continuation coverage

- When you lose dependent child status and exceed the age for coverage under the employee's plan

Continuation coverage is commonly purchased for those who lose their jobs, or whose spouses are not yet eligible for Medicare. It's also useful for those who are changing jobs but have a pre-existing condition not covered for a period of time under their new employer's policy.

Proposed federal legislation, described before in this chapter, would prohibit waiting periods for those moving to new group coverage and would provide additional coverage options for those seeking individual coverage after exhausting their COBRA rights. (See p. 71.)

State law. Even if COBRA doesn't apply, a number of states mandate that you be given continuation benefits—at your employer's expense or your own—for a limited period of time ranging from three to as many as 26 months (Connecticut). Your state department of insurance will be able to tell you what your state requires and what your rights are.

Once your continuation coverage ends, you may be able to convert to an individual policy from the same insurance company under state law. A majority of states require that you be offered a conversion option allowing you to convert to an individual policy. (Remember that this right may be included in your insurance contract.)

Employers who offer leaving employees conversion policies must also make them available to former employees when their continuation coverage under COBRA ends. You'll usually be given a time limit of 30 days for enrollment in a conversion policy. But you may be better off with a new policy. Keep in mind that the benefits offered under conversion policies may not be as good as your employer's group policy.

My new employer's health insurance plan has a waiting period of 12 months for pre-existing conditions. Any suggestions?

Maintain your continued coverage under COBRA during the waiting period, and use the new plan for the rest of your health bills. (That waiting period may be banned if Congress acts on basic portable insurance.)

I thought that when I got Medicare my company had to cover me the same as before. But I'm told by my former employer that my coverage is going to end. Is this legal?

Under the law, your right to continuation coverage ends when you become entitled to Medicare or obtain coverage under a new policy. If your COBRA coverage is better than Medicare will be, you might try arguing with your employer that "entitled to Medicare" requires you actually to enroll—and that until you do, you're still entitled to your continuation coverage. Your benefits are also not protected when your former employer goes out of business and discontinues health insurance for other workers.

My former employer has fewer than 20 employees. Do I have any right to continuation coverage?

Although you're not covered by federal law, which is limited to businesses with 20 or more employees, some states require continuation benefits for three to as many as 26 months. If not, you may have to buy a new policy. Check with your state insurance department.

My former employer is self-insured. Does he have to provide continuation coverage?

Yes. Although employers who serve as their own health insurers are generally exempt for insurance regulation, they are still required to cover you for these purposes.

 HMOS AND MANAGED CARE

More and more employees are leaving traditional insurance plans and enrolling in managed care programs, from health maintenance organizations (HMOs) to wider networks of doctors and hospitals offering discounted fees. HMOs and other managed care organizations now enroll as many as 50 million Americans, an increase of nearly 40 percent in five years. According to one survey, nearly two out of three employees and their families are now enrolled in managed care plans. So prevalent have they become that many doctors who have resisted participating are now trying to get in. The resistance of many groups to including all comers has resulted in a legislative push for statutes requiring managed care organizations to allow in any and all doctors who want to participate.

An HMO is not insurance in the traditional sense, but an alternative to insurance. It's an organization of health care providers—doctors, surgeons, hospitals, and other professionals and facilities—that offer comprehensive services for a fixed prepaid fee. It functions both as insurance and as the health care delivery system for its members.

One reason for HMOs' success is cost. HMOs are dedicated to maintaining your health rather than paying for your illness. The emphasis on prevention and early diagnosis is both a cost and health measure. However, perceptions of reduced time, services, and quality of care persist.

If you're eligible for Medicare, you have the right to enroll in an HMO in lieu of Medicare services. About 10 percent of the 37 million Medicare recipients are currently enrolled in and receiving their health care benefits through HMO plans nationwide.

Legislative note. One current proposal would grant Medicare recipients 65 or older a fixed amount to purchase their health care coverage by enrolling in an HMO, opening a medical savings account, or purchasing private insurance. Some analysts predict that the future of Medicare lies in offering competitive managed care plans.

Joining a Medicare HMO. As a Medicare recipient, you can join only an HMO that has a contract with Medicare. The premium for the HMO is paid by the Health Care Financing Administration (HCFA). You have to be enrolled in Part B as well as Part A—that's where payment is coming from. The government pays the HMO to provide you with coverage; the HMO pays the doctors and hospitals and does the paperwork. You continue to pay your Medicare Part B premium, but you don't have to pay any deductibles or copayments. You can't be denied enrollment in an HMO because of your health.

Resuming Medicare coverage. If you're not happy with the HMO, you can always drop out and return to Medicare. If you choose to disenroll or move out of the service area, your standard Medicare coverage automatically resumes on the date of the termination of your plan, which can be as early as the calendar month following your request.

Retroactive disenrollment is also possible under certain circumstances. If you go to a hospital outside the network and your HMO refuses to cover you, you can get Medicare to pay if you prove you did not know the rules.

HMO coverage. An HMO provides nearly all of a person's medical needs, through designated doctors and hospitals. All costs are covered by a preset monthly premium, which is the same no matter how much or little medical care you receive. The only requirement is that members must use only HMO doctors and facilities to be covered (except for emergency care or urgently needed care outside the HMOs geographic service area).

Some HMOs charge a nominal fee per visit (such as $2 or $5); other than that there are no deductibles or copayment requirements. Theoretically, there's no limit based on duration or intensity of care, even if you have to go to a hospital. However, utilization review may be tougher than with regular insurance, limiting your stay and care.

The HMO must provide you with a "low option plan" at least equal to Medicare benefits (without deductibles and copayments). If you want any services provided by the HMO which Medicare doesn't cover, you may have to pay an extra premium for them.

HMO basic benefits provided under federal law include

- Physician services, including consultant and referral services
- Hospital services, both inpatient and outpatient
- Diagnostic laboratory and therapeutic radiology services
- Home health services
- Preventive health services, including periodic health exams
- Medically necessary emergency health services
- Short-term outpatient mental health services
- Alcohol and drug-abuse treatment and referral
- Supplemental services provided by that HMO's individual plans, such as prescription drugs or dental services

Your Medicare HMO rights. As a Medicare recipient, you have these rights:

- You can't be denied enrollment in an HMO because of your health (although you can be limited to a low-option plan).
- Your HMO coverage cannot be terminated because of health or treatment.
- Emergency services must be available 24 hours a day.
- You're entitled to the HMO's written procedures for resolving complaints—which you may utilize in addition to the appeal rights you have under Medicare.

Does my employer have to give me an HMO option?

Federal law requires that all employers with at least 25 employees (living in the service area, full or part-time) and having some health benefit plan provide the option of enrolling in an HMO. Your employer must contribute an amount equal to the contribution it would have made on your behalf to a health insurance plan, as well as for supplemental continued benefits for any services you can't get through the HMO. A number of HMOs and other managed care plans are also available to individuals, during a prescribed open enrollment period.

I was approached by an HMO, which promises to let me pick my own doctors. Is this legal?

In today's market-driven health care environment, a number of types of organization have been created. *Preferred provider organizations* (PPOs) are groups of doctors and other health care providers who continue in their private practice, but have contracts with employers, insurers, or other third-party payers to deliver services, usually to employee groups, at reduced rates. With a PPO you can generally choose a doctor from a wider range of participating doctors. If you use a designated doctor, you get a discount and may not have a copayment; if you choose from off the list, you'll have to pay more in co-insurance. A PPO is not prepaid, but reimbursed as with traditional insurance.

There are also hybrid systems, sometimes called *managed medical systems* or *competitive medical plans.* These combine elements of managed care with provisions allowing you to choose nonparticipating providers for a greater fee. Each has its own set of rules and regulations, which you should be fully familiar with before enrolling.

Can I check on an HMO like an insurance company?

The A.M. Best Company is the only rating agency to offer this service for HMOs. Best's rating reflects the financial soundness of an organization as well as its ability to deliver services; ratings do not measure quality of services provided. The National Commission of Quality Assurance, which sets accreditation standards used by about half the country's HMOs, has announced plans to provide quality-of-care and service report cards for HMOs. Thus far, it has reported on 26 larger managed care plans. (See Resources section for contact information.)

I'm on Medicare and have supplemental "Medigap" insurance. I plan to switch to an HMO. How does this affect my Medigap insurance?

For Medicare recipients, it eliminates the need for Medigap insurance. (See Medigap Supplemental Insurance below.)

Will the services be the same?

You have to check with your specific HMO. Not all HMOs have 24-hour medical care available. Check the HMO hours, and whether the HMO offers 24-hour access to medical attention, with doctors on call.

Also, you should note that an HMO is not for frequent travelers. You're not covered for services outside the HMO area except for severe emergency. Even then, you'll have to get approval by phone. If you're a frequent traveler, you may also want to get Medigap insurance with the foreign travel emergency benefit (see below).

MEDICAL SAVINGS ACCOUNTS

One recent innovation is the *medical savings account*, in which money is earmarked for an individual's medical expenses by an employer, who funds all or part of the account.

The medical savings account is not insurance. When combined with health care coverage (usually with higher deductibles for a lower premium), the medical savings account provides a savings for employers while giving "account holders" an incentive to "save" rather than spend the amounts in their accounts. At the end of the year, the balance in the account can be retained by the employee.

For people with few health care needs, it may save money, but it is potentially more expensive for those with greater needs. For one thing, the money in the accounts is taxable to the employee. And if the use of medical savings accounts becomes widespread, there is also a potential indirect cost as greater numbers of healthy people in cheap account plans would leave older people and others in need of services paying higher costs. Even more troublesome, medical savings accounts may operate to discourage the preventive care that might keep you healthy now and avoid the need for costlier treatment down the road.

Medical savings accounts have elicited significant political interest among those who believe they will help curb heath care spending. At least one quarter of the states have passed bills authorizing the use of medical savings accounts.

Legislative note. There is legislation pending to make medical savings accounts tax-exempt and allow carryover of a balance from year to year. And the principle of medical savings accounts is incorporated into current proposals for increased choice and competition in Medicare, offering recipients a fixed amount to purchase a medical savings account, private insurance, or join an HMO.

We cannot predict what form legislation will eventually take, but we can warn you to examine very carefully any health care package or "deal" you're offered, whether by your employer, an insurance company, or the government.

Make sure you consider and understand what services are being offered—with what guarantees, under what conditions, and at what cost to
you.

*My employer has a flexible plan which establishes a tax-free medical benefits
account for me. Is this the same as a medical savings account? Is it a good deal?*

Many employers already offer "flexible plans," which allow employees
to put some part of their pay into a tax-exempt account for medical benefits;
however, in those plans, money not spent generally goes back to the
employer. If you are right on target in estimating your costs, you can save
on your tax bill, but if you're not, you can lose money you've earned. It's
a good deal only if you keep your deposits into the account on the low end.
If you're betting your salary against your health, it's not a fair deal.

MEDIGAP SUPPLEMENTAL INSURANCE

Medicare supplemental insurance, often called "Medigap," supplements your
Medicare coverage by picking up the tab for a large portion of your health care
and treatment that Medicare doesn't cover. Depending on your policy, it pays
for coinsurance and deductibles, additional benefits not covered by Medicare
such as prescription drugs, and charges exceeding Medicare-approved rates.

Medigap coverage is only supplemental to what Medicare covers. If you
have expenses not covered in the first place by Medicare (such as non-essential
cosmetic surgery), your Medigap policy generally won't pay for the coinsurance
or deductible. As a general rule, Medigap policies don't cover custodial care
or long-term nursing home or home care.

The law guarantees the availability of Medigap policies to all new Medicare
enrollees without any medical examination if you enroll within six months of your
65th birthday. You can't be denied a policy or charged more because of your
health. In those states that have eliminated medical underwriting entirely, you
don't have to worry about the six-month limitation.

There's a six-month limitation on the time you can be excluded from
collecting benefits or otherwise limited for a "pre-existing condition." If you
switch your policy, any pre-existing condition you have will be credited with
the time elapsed under your original policy.

You have the right to return a Medigap insurance policy within 30 days of its
delivery. You're also entitled to a full refund of any premiums you've paid. Your
Medigap policy is renewable yearly as long as you pay the premiums.

As a result of abuses in sales of Medigap policies, federal law allows the sale
of only 10 basic Medigap model policies (called A through J), as shown on the
chart on page 85.

Each policy must offer you these basic benefits, provided in plan A:

• Part A hospitalization coinsurance for 60–90 days and one-time "lifetime
  reserve" for days 91–150

- 365 days lifetime hospital days (100 percent reimbursable) after Medicare benefits ends
- Part B doctor bill coinsurance
- Three pints of blood yearly

MEDICARE SUPPLEMENTAL INSURANCE MEDIGAP POLICIES AND BENEFITS										
Plan ▶ Coverage ▼	A	B	C	D	E	F	G	H	I	J
Part A co-insurance (for Days 61–90 and Lifetime Reserve Days 91–150) 365 lifetime hospital days Part B co-insurance 3 pints of blood yearly (Parts A & B) *Core policy*	◆	◆	◆	◆	◆	◆	◆	◆	◆	◆
Skilled nursing care co-insurance (for Days 21–100)			◆	◆	◆	◆	◆	◆	◆	◆
Part A deductible		◆	◆	◆	◆	◆	◆	◆	◆	◆
Part B deductible			◆			◆				◆
Excess Part B bills						◆	◆		◆	◆
Foreign travel emergency			◆	◆	◆	◆	◆	◆	◆	◆
At home recovery				◆			◆		◆	◆
Prescription drugs								◆	◆	◆
Preventive care					◆					◆

The menu of benefits available in Plans B through J offers:

- *Plans C–J.* Skilled nursing care coinsurance (in 1996, $92 a day for days 21–100)
- *Plans B–J.* Part A deductible
- *Plans C, F, J.* Part B deductible
- *Plans F, G, I, J.* Excess of Part B doctor bills beyond Medicare limits. (All are 100 percent reimbursable except G, which is reimbursable at 80 percent.) These are of limited value, given the limits on doctor fees to Medicare patients. Changes to the law in 1995 made it illegal for doctors to charge Medigap insurers more that 115 percent of Medicare's approved rate

- *Plans C–J.* Foreign travel emergency (80 percent of costs after a $250 deductible, up to a lifetime benefit of $50,000)
- **Plans D, G, I, J.** At-home recovery. This is somewhat limited, offering up to eight weeks beyond Medicare coverage, limited to 28 hours a week, at $40 an hour, up to $1,600 a year. You can receive these benefits only if you receive Medicare home care benefits
- *Plans H, I, J.* Prescription drugs. This is expensive, offering only a 50 percent copayment and subject to a $250 deductible. Plan H and I have a $1,250 annual limit; Plan J goes up to $3,000

Plans E, J. Preventive care such as flu shots and tests for cancer, diabetes, and hearing disorders, up to $120 a year

These are now the only Medigap policies that may be sold. Not all insurers supply all policies, although each must give you the basic plan.

Which of the ten models is best?

Every additional benefit increases the premium. You should buy a policy based on your individual medical history and expenses. Why spend extra dollars for foreign travel benefit if you never go anywhere? On the other hand, prescription drug expenses may be of greater importance to you. If you want to ensure benefits for the future, you may want to purchase comprehensive policies now.

If the policies are uniform, does that mean I don't have to shop around for rates?

No. Coverage is uniform, but premiums may vary considerably among different insurers. Over the past few years, the price of Medigap policies has risen at an alarming rate. At a cost averaging between $700 and $1,200 yearly, and with new comprehensive policies reaching beyond $2,000 yearly, you should investigate thoroughly before you buy a Medigap policy. The new law should make comparison you buy a Medigap policy. The new law should make comparison shopping relatively easy, with a ready basis for comparison provided by the 10 models.

You can get a list of carriers offering Medigap insurance from your state insurance department or office of aging. Use the chart to compare what you're being offered from different insurers, and make sure you try at least three or more companies before purchasing a policy. Some policies purchased through organizations such as AARP may be less expensive because there are no sales commissions built into the premium.

I'm disabled and getting Medicare. Should I buy Medigap coverage?

Medigap coverage has generally been available only to Medicare-eligible people over 65. Some states do allow Medigap insurance to be bought through their pool (a big help to the disabled who are otherwise ineligible), and a few companies do offer it.

I have a health plan from my former employer. Do I need a Medigap policy?

Check your coverage. Often, health care plans available through your employer supply more supplemental coverage than you can get through a Medigap policy.

Can my Medigap policy be cancelled?

By law Medigap and long-term care insurance policies must be guaranteed renewable.

I'm moving to Florida next year. Can I buy new Medigap insurance?

You can, but it's not necessary. You have the right to keep the same Medigap policy you have for the rest of your life, regardless of where you move.

How do I know what I'm getting?

Under the law, you can get help in deciding about Medigap policies through counseling programs set up through your local Social Security office. These should provide an objective source of information on Medigap policies. You can also call the Medigap Hotline at 800/638–6833.

 ## MEDICARE COVERAGE WHEN YOU'RE WORKING

For employees aged 65 to 69 and covered by insurance, and for their spouses covered by the employer's health plan, Medicare is the secondary payer.

The employer's plan must be the primary payer. Medicare will pay the difference between what the primary payer approves and pays and the doctor's charges, up to the Medicare-approved amount. At age 70, Medicare becomes the primary payer.

Medicare is also secondary to any automobile, liability, or no-fault insurance you may have, as well as to workers' compensation. If you are trying to collect through the courts, your medical expenses will be advanced by Medicare, which you must reimburse from the eventual settlement or judgment.

MEDICARE AND LONG-TERM CARE

Medicare's role in long-term care planning is a limited one. Restrictions on Medicare eligibility and benefits (for both home health care and skilled nursing facility) limits its value, and for cases involving so-called "custodial" care, it may be unavailable. However, this doesn't foreclose Medicare in all cases. (For more on Medicare and long-term care financing, see Chapter 7.)

■■■

7

FINANCING
LONG-TERM CARE

Long-term care comes in many forms, with interventions available along a continuum of services that range from home care services to services in a skilled nursing facility. Whether the care takes place at home or in a nursing facility, it will be expensive.

Although most nursing home stays average less than a year, with costs for long-term care averaging $40,000 a year and approaching as much as $100,000 annually in some areas, financing home care or even a short stay in a nursing home can mean a quick trip to the poorhouse. Studies show the average family spends its resources in a health care crisis *in 13 weeks.*

What many do not realize, often to their detriment, is that Medicare and health insurance do not cover long-term care. Medicare, even supplemented by Medigap insurance, covers skilled care only and that only for a limited time.

With spiraling health care costs and no hope in sight for more help from the government, planning for long-term care is critical. Fortunately, there is some good news. The universe of financing options for you to consider is greater than ever, including long-term care insurance and government benefits, reverse mortgages, retirement communities, and Medicaid benefits.

THE ROLE OF MEDICARE

As we described in Chapter 5, Medicare provides you with basic hospital care, home health care benefits to a maximum of 35 hours a week, and post-hospital skilled nursing facility benefits up to 100 days. Days 21 through 100 in a facility require some payment from you, but with Medigap insurance you receive 100 percent coverage.

You should apply for these benefits if you are eligible or think you may be. The potential savings can be significant. In 1995, an estimated 3.5

million people received health care under Medicare, more than double the number from a decade before.

However, Medicare's role in long-term care planning is a limited one. For purely custodial cases, coverage may be wholly unavailable. Restrictions on coverage and benefits (for both home health care and care in a skilled nursing facility) limit Medicare's value as a planning tool.

 ## POST-HOSPITAL CARE UNDER MEDICARE

If you need further care after being in the hospital, Medicare Part A also covers post-hospital care in a skilled nursing facility, including:

- bed and board
- nursing care by registered nurses
- medical care by interns and residents
- physical, occupational, or speech therapy

Up to 100 days in a skilled nursing facility may be covered per benefit period. Days 1–20 are fully paid by Medicare; days 21–100, you pay $92 a day in copay. (Medigap insurance may be available to pay this amount, which increases each year; see Chapter 6 for more information.) After day 100, you must pay all costs.

There are several restrictions on receiving this benefit:

- Your post-hospital care must be for skilled nursing care or rehabilitative services.
- Your care must be received daily in a skilled nursing facility.
- You must enter within 30 days after having had a hospital stay of three days or longer.

Prior hospitalization/spell of illness. In order to qualify for Medicare coverage the same condition ("spell of illness") must necessitate your stay in the hospital and your admission for post-hospital care. Without a hospital stay prior to entering a skilled nursing facility, you will not be covered under Medicare.

Skilled nursing care. The difference between skilled and custodial care is crucial. Basically, your care will be deemed "custodial" if it is the kind of care that a lay person can perform without special professional training or experience. For example, helping you to dress is custodial care.

Because Medicare doesn't cover custodial care, you must be receiving daily skilled care or rehabilitative services which can be provided only on an inpatient basis. It is not required that a patient be capable of recovery or even improvement for services to be covered. Physical therapy to prevent deterioration is enough to justify the provision of skilled care.

Skilled nursing facility. A critical requirement for Medicare coverage is that you must need and receive care in a skilled nursing facility (SNF). An SNF is engaged primarily in providing skilled nursing care or rehabilitative services such as physical or occupational therapy to help restore a person's health. It provides RNs, LPNs, and nurses' aides on a 24-hour basis. Medicare covers care at the skilled level only, in a Medicare-certified program. It does not cover care in a custodial or residential care facility.

Changes in your status. If the SNF believes a service is not covered by Medicare, it must inform you in writing. You have the right to demand that the SNF bill Medicare regardless, and you don't have to pay for the service until Medicare denies payment.

When a level-of-care determination "demotes" you from skilled to non-skilled, ending your Medicare coverage, you have the right to an immediate review. An appeal from an SNF must be decided within 10 days.

Can I enter a nursing facility directly from home and receive coverage from Medicare?

No. Your admission must follow a hospital stay.

Do I have to be admitted to the hospital again for the same thing?

Only one hospital visit is necessary. Should you leave the skilled nursing facility and have to return for continued services for the same condition within 60 days, you don't need to satisfy the three-day hospital requirement again.

Should I appeal?

If you have the resources to stay in a nursing home and pay for services after Medicare cuts you off, you can still appeal the payment decision. The skilled versus custodial care battle is one Medicare loves to fight. Only 2% of all nursing home stays are Medicare-covered. But appeals are a good bet. A large number are successful.

HOME HEALTH CARE UNDER MEDICARE

Medicare's home health care benefit provides some coverage for care in your home. Although it often follows a hospital stay, prior hospitalization is not required for home health care benefits.

Home health care benefits include

- Part-time or intermittent skilled nursing care
- Physical therapy, speech therapy, and occupational therapy
- Home health aides, part-time or intermittent
- Medical social services
- Medical supplies and equipment

Home health benefits are provided under both Part A and Part B. Assuming you're covered, Medicare pays the full amount of these services, subject only to the $100 deductible for Part B services. There is a 20 percent copayment you have to make on medical equipment only.

The purpose of home health care is to supply you with some of the medical services that will allow you to remain at home. To qualify under Medicare's rules, there are a number of conditions that must be met.

- You (or the patient) must be homebound, confined to home except for going for medical treatment with some kind of assistance. You do not have to be bedridden, but you do have to be confined to home.
- You must need and receive either skilled nursing care, physical therapy, or speech therapy. This means that you may get the services of a home health aide (for your custodial care needs) only if you need one or more of these skilled services.
- Your condition does not need to be "curable" or even capable of improvement; what is required is that you need care or therapy to maintain your condition without deterioration.
- Your care must be provided by a home health agency certified by Medicare.

Medicare will cover up to 35 hours per week of part-time or intermittent care. Medicare will cover up to 35 hours per week of *combined* home health aide and skilled services if you're required to have at least intermittent skilled services pursuant to a home health plan set up by your doctor. Intermittent skilled care must be for fewer than five days a week and may be as infrequent as once in 60 days. If services are needed for a finite and predictable period up to 21 days, then up to seven days a week are allowed, and as many as 56 hours in the week may be covered. That's what the law says, but the coverage you can expect to get is a lot more limited. Medicare guidelines try to limit number of visits and hours per visit. Be prepared to fight for what the law allows.

Before the plan is established, the agency makes an evaluation visit, which operates to limit the prospective services to what the agency anticipates will be covered by Medicare. As a result, visits are generally limited to a few hours weekly, not really sufficient to maintain a patient at home.

Check with your local aging agency to see if your state or locality has any programs that provide similar assistance which may be of help to those needing home health care services, such as Meals on Wheels or transportation to get medical services. (See Chapter 3 for more on home care programs.)

If the agency says Medicare won't cover the care and payment is demanded in advance for services which you believe should be covered, you must decide whether to accept or decline those services.

- You are entitled to demand that the home health agency bill Medicare, so you can appeal any adverse decision.

- The reversal rate for home health care decisions on appeal is quite good, as high as 70 percent.
- If you don't get the service, there's nothing to contest—and no appeal process.

What if I need another type of service?

You must need and receive one or more of the three specified services (skilled nursing care, physical therapy, or speech therapy). Coverage is also available for occupational therapy, but it must be linked to a need for skilled nursing care, physical therapy or speech therapy. Once established, occupational therapy may continue after these other services have lapsed.

May I receive personal or custodial care from a Medicaid health aide?

Incidental household chores performed by a covered home health aide are permissible.

My doctor is part owner of a home health agency. Can he refer me there?

Under federal law, your doctor cannot certify the need for treatment in any home health agency in which he or she may have a share (unless it is the only one in the community).

LONG-TERM CARE INSURANCE

Long-term care insurance can provide a shield for the high costs of health care. This is a brand of insurance that's intended to fill in the gaps left by general insurance coverage and government benefits, paying for your care in a nursing home or at home. Depending on the policy, long-term care insurance can be extremely valuable, offering coverage not just for nursing home care but for home care, adult day care, and care in assisted living facilities.

Long-term care insurance differs from Medicare and general health insurance in several ways. First, it's intended to cover you for custodial, non-skilled care. It also is designed to provide benefits for a longer period of time. Benefit periods in long-term care policies generally provide three years coverage for nursing home care and six years for home health care. Longer benefit periods and lifetime benefits are available.

The virtue of a longer benefit period is twofold. In the first place, it pays for your nursing home care during a crucial period—and the typical three-year coverage is more than the average person will need.

The other real advantage to long-term care insurance is that *it buys you time.* If Medicaid will ultimately have to finance your long-term care needs but you don't wish to transfer funds to make yourself eligible at the present time, purchasing long-term care insurance now will allow Medicaid transfers to be postponed until a later date. (Under present Medicaid rules, you generally need to wait as long as three years between transferring money and applying for Medicaid benefits. We explain transfers and qualifying for Medicaid in Chapter 8.)

If you then need care, the three years of insurance coverage gives you a financial cushion to pay for it while transfers can be made and Medicaid eligibility kicks in. With long-term care insurance, planning must be done now, but transfers can be made later.

One question is cost. Long-term care policies are expensive and considered most suitable for middle income buyers. Wealthier individuals have resources to cover their expenses, and will probably not need Medicaid in the future, while annual premiums of $1000—and approaching $4500 for an initial purchase at age 75—may be too costly for those with less in assets and less income. Long-term care insurance is generally recommended for those with incomes of more than $20,000 yearly and assets of more than $100,000.

Long-term care insurance is still a relatively new product. But with budget cuts on the horizon, long-term care insurance offers more appeal to consumers worried about future home care and nursing home care needs. Cutbacks and changes in Medicaid laws may spur innovations and increased interest.

One innovation pioneered in Connecticut and available in some other states is the "public-private partnership." We discuss public-private long-term care financing programs in Chapter 9.

 EVALUATING THE LONG-TERM CARE POLICY

According to the Health Insurance Association of America, long-term care insurance business has grown from 100,000 policies sold in 1986 to two million sold by 1990. In the same period, the number of insurers selling long-term care policies nearly doubled, to more than 130. Major sellers include Travelers, John Hancock, Unum, CNA, and Amex Life Assurance.

Nearly all the states have passed laws and regulations governing long-term care insurance. While many of these laws are similar, modeled on recommendations of the National Association of Insurance Commissioners, specifics vary from state to state. Policies offer various options in coverage, benefits, deductibles, and protection, leaving you with a number of factors to consider when shopping for a long-term care policy.

The insurance company. The most important consideration is the fiscal soundness of your insurer. You do not want to be in a position in which your insurer fails and you are left holding a stack of unpaid claims. Check with your state insurance department, which is responsible for monitoring the solvency of insurers operating within the state. Make sure you check with one or more of the insurer rating services as well: A.M. Best, Standard & Poor's, Moody's, Duff & Phelps or Weiss Research. And make sure you know how each rating service ranks companies—rating systems differ. (For more on insurer solvency and rating services, see Chapter 6.)

Level of care. You want to make sure the policy covers both nursing home and home health care. Some policies now cover adult day care and assisted living as well. Check what benefits are paid for each level of care.

The home care benefits under the policy should be of particular concern to you. Policies differ significantly in the "triggering event" which determines your coverage and how quickly they will pay on it. Some companies may utilize a "care manager," who may or may not be an employee of the insurer, to review your claim and determine the care you will get.

Conditions covered. Early policies covered only certain medical conditions and excluded others such as Alzheimer's disease. Make sure the policy includes language providing coverage for cognitive impairment and functional impairment as measured by activities of daily living (ADLs).

Restrictions on coverage. Some policies restrict benefits by mandating preconditions, for example, requiring prior hospitalization or skilled services before coverage will be provided. This is unacceptable—and now illegal in many states. Another restriction which is not acceptable is that you receive nursing home or home care from Medicare or otherwise "certified" facilities.

Medical necessity. In all policies, there is the *triggering event.* The triggering event is the injury, illness, or condition that must occur before coverage is provided and a claim is payable. It may be based upon establishment of so-called medical necessity, but that should take into account either cognitive impairment or functional disability (for ADLs such as dressing, eating, and transferring).

Post-claims underwriting. This is a practice under which a company insures you but requests more detailed information about your application upon your filing a subsequent claim. At that time, it can then try to rescind the policy. This is illegal in some states. Avoid these policies.

Pre-existing conditions. Policies may restrict benefits for conditions for which medical advice was or should have been sought within a given period of time preceding the effective coverage date. For older people, many with multiple ailments, this may exclude the very condition or conditions for which they seek coverage. Make sure that any restriction on pre-existing conditions is itself subject to a fixed period with a so-called "sunset clause," after which coverage will be granted.

Benefit payouts and deductible period. Payouts should be daily, starting at $100 a day. The *elimination* or *deductible period,* measuring the number of days before you can begin receiving benefits, may be anywhere from 0 to 100 days. Make sure the benefit is realistic. A nursing home benefit of $75 a day will do little good if the daily cost in your community if $150 a day, unless you can afford to pick up the difference.

Since the cost of care will certainly increase over the years, you need *inflation protection* in the form of an inflation rider so that the benefit will increase each year. The most common form of this benefit is a five percent annual increase in the daily benefit, at either simple or compounded interest, although a compounding increase rider is preferable. Some policies also offer the right to purchase additional coverage later on with no medical examination necessary.

Duration of benefits. This refers to the maximum benefit period allowed under your policy. Although three years of nursing home care or six years of home care (with various combinations) is the most common, some policies offer variations ranging from two years to lifetime benefits. Your age, resources, and projected costs should be factors in your consideration. Remember that if you are using long-term care insurance as a delaying strategy to allow you time to transfer funds for Medicaid eligibility, you must have a minimum benefit period of three years to cover the application look-back period.

Fees. The older you are, the more your insurance will cost. With rising costs, you need to know about future increases. Two provisions are of importance: *inflation protection* and *waiver of premium* for collection of benefits. Inflation protection ensures that rising costs will not outstrip future payments. A waiver of premium allows you not to have to pay the premiums while you are collecting benefits.

Premium costs. The older you are, the more your insurance will cost you at the time of purchase. Under the law, long-term care policies are *guaranteed renewable.* This means that the policy can't be cancelled, as long as you pay the premium. The law does allow an insurance company to increase the premium for the class of *all* policy holders with the same policy, although this is likely to happen rarely.

The only time you don't have to pay the premium is if the policy has a waiver of premium feature, which allows you to stop paying when you are receiving benefits under the policy.

Group policies. A few, mostly larger, employers are beginning to offer *group* long-term care policies for employees. There are a number of considerations which may make this a better deal for you. The premium cost may be substantially lower under a group than for an individual policy, even if you are asked to contribute in whole or in part to the premium cost. And the benefits may be better, regardless of premium costs.

Some group policies are offered *guaranteed issue*—meaning you can purchase the insurance even if you are not healthy (although you will probably have a pre-existing condition waiting period). One disadvantage, however, is that if your company drops the plan and you have no conversion privilege, you may not be able then to buy an individual policy.

If you are considering a group policy, be sure to check the terms to see if it can be cancelled, and if so, what your rights are to convert to an individual policy. State law may also provide additional protections for you.

 REVERSE MORTGAGES

Another option for financing long-term care is the reverse mortgage. For older homeowners who are house-rich but cash-poor, home equity conversion mortgages, or reverse mortgages, permit them to tap the equity in their homes without having to sell them. With a reverse mortgage, you *receive* payments—either in a lump sum or at monthly intervals over the course of a fixed term or your lifetime. The total amount generally becomes due when you sell or leave your home.

Reverse mortgages may be a source of funds for financing long-term care. It may provide the additional cash you need to pay for help in your home, to cover premiums on long-term care insurance, or to place your spouse or parent in a nursing home or other living facility. On the minus side, once your home equity is spent, it is no longer available to you. And your home is protected only as long as you live in it.

For a full discussion of reverse mortgages, see Chapter 19.

 RETIREMENT COMMUNITIES

Thanks to a growing number of older people who seek added security and assistance that cannot be provided in their own homes, the retirement community industry has been transformed into a $7 billion industry. Unlike the retirement villages of the past, some adult communities today offer a full-service menu, a place to live, three meals a day, and nursing care as needed.

This is one way to finance your long-term care needs. All-inclusive life-care facilities provide traditional long-term care as part of their package. Others provide modified services or fee-for-service options, including medical services, hospital services, and support and social services.

A number of rental and condominium developments for older Americans offer assisted living packages. Depending on the services they offer, they may be called *continuing care facilities, congregate housing,* or *assisted living communities.* For more on adult living communities, see Chapter 20.

 USING LIFE INSURANCE

One idea that has gained popularity in recent years is the receipt of death benefits under a life insurance policy *before death.* This is also known as *living benefits* or *accelerated death benefits.*

Holders of existing life insurance policies and purchasers of new policies are being offered living benefits riders. Over 200 companies now offer them.

Triggering event. As with long-term care and health insurance, policies pay living benefits upon the occurrence of a triggering event. Some policies, especially earlier ones, required proof of terminal illness before benefits could be paid out. Over the years, these requirements have altered, some allowing payouts upon a need for long-term care, and states have moved to provide some regulation. For example, New York does not allow living benefits to be used for patients with non-terminal conditions, although they are authorized for patients with AIDS.

Determination of benefit. The amount of benefits you can receive, usually a percentage of the face value of the policy, depends on the controlling language of the policy. It may vary from 25 to 100 percent of the full benefit under the life insurance policy.

Accelerated death benefits are regulated by the states. To some extent, payouts are limited. With a living benefits rider, you can get either a lump sum benefit or payment through installments. Installments are preferable for those entering long-term care.

I have a standard life insurance policy, without riders. Can I get an accelerated benefit payout?

You may be able to "sell" your policy to a company that will give you a *viatical settlement.* Viatical settlements are based on the same concept as accelerated benefits riders, allowing you to collect on your policy in advance of death. The policy is *viaticated,* i.e., sold by the owner to the company, at a discounted rate. As a general rule, payout under a viatical settlement is conditioned on terminal illness (or permanent transfer to a long-term care facility). Often, a life expectancy of no more than two years is required. The percentage the owner gets depends on his or her life expectancy, the shorter the greater in cash terms. Payouts are generally from 60 to 80 percent of the policy death benefit.

Viatical settlements are regulated in California and New York, as well as Kansas and New Mexico, where they were originally pioneered. Viatical settlements are prohibited in Utah.

 MEDICAID

Medicaid is the government health care program signed into law at the same time as Medicare. Medicaid provides health care coverage for the poor—and you have to be poor to qualify for its benefits. It also provides long-term care and home care benefits generally unavailable through Medicare.

For that reason, many people "spend down" to qualify for Medicaid purposes. If you're considering other financing alternatives, you should understand that the amount of funds under your control—whether you're transferring, receiving, or maintaining access to them—may affect your

Medicaid eligibility. If funds qualify as income or assets for Medicaid purposes, they may disqualify you from receiving benefits. Benefit rules may change without your knowledge. This is of considerable importance to your long-range planning and requires consultation with a lawyer or financial expert knowledgeable about Medicaid issues. (We discuss "spending down" and other techniques for qualifying for Medicaid benefits in the next chapter.)

 ## TAX ISSUES

An important consideration in evaluating your long-term care financing options is the effect on your taxes. If you are considering a reverse mortgage, long-term care insurance, accelerated benefits, or a viatical life insurance policy, you must review

- Whether payments count as income for tax purposes
- Whether payments count as income for determining tax liability on your Social Security income
- Whether premium payments are tax-deductible

Consultation with a lawyer or accountant familiar with long-term care planning is required for any financing option that involves structuring payments to you, on either a lump-sum or periodic basis. Don't forget that tax rulings in this area are subject to swift change. (See Chapter 15 for a discussion of taxes.)

If long-term care benefits count as income for tax purposes, do they also count for Medicaid purposes? Can my long-term care benefits disqualify me for Medicaid?

To the extent long-term care benefits pay your bills, they may count against you in states allowing spend-down and render you ineligible in income cap states. In general, if you're receiving long-term care benefits, you won't need Medicaid for long-term care. (See the next chapter for a full discussion of Medicaid and long-term care.)

8

■■

MEDICAID AND
LONG-TERM CARE

Medicaid is a public assistance grant program, the twin Great Society benefit signed into law along with Medicare by President Lyndon B. Johnson in 1965. Financed jointly by federal and state moneys, it provides health benefits to 35 million low-income people who are aged, blind, or disabled as well as those who are poor.

Although designed to serve low-income people of all ages, Medicaid has become a lifeline for the elderly, providing essential services that Medicare doesn't—home health care and long-term nursing home care.

Medicaid is the major payer of long-term care for those who can't afford the average yearly cost of $40,000 or more (more than double that amount in some areas). Medicaid covers the "non-skilled" but unbelievably expensive custodial care services that Medicare doesn't. Thousands of middle-income Americans have found themselves divesting themselves of their assets or "spending down" to eligibility levels in order to qualify for benefits under Medicaid. Medicaid pays for 42 percent of all nursing home costs nationwide. It covers over 60 percent of all nursing home patients.

Administered by the states, Medicaid represents the fastest-growing component of many state budgets. States pay approximately 45 percent and the federal government 55 percent of Medicaid costs. The federal share amounts to six percent of federal outlays. Nearly one-third of Medicaid spending goes to home health services and long-term nursing home care. Total costs for Medicaid reached $142 billion in 1994.

Medicaid rules must be understood in context. One target for budget cuts has been the benefits furnished to middle-income people who have made themselves eligible for Medicaid to avoid the astronomical costs of long-term care. Stricter eligibility rules have made qualifying for benefits harder than ever before, and service and program cuts have affected both home care and nursing home care as well as programs such as adult day care. Additional changes and restrictions are being contemplated by Congress and several states. These events make it more important than ever that you understand the rules and how Medicaid works.

Legislative note. Proposals for block grants to the states have called for repeal of many federal mandates prescribing eligibility and benefit protections, such as the minimum spousal assets and income protections described in this chapter. Although Medicaid is scheduled for reform, elimination of these protections is far less likely.

█ MEDICAID COVERAGE

Before learning how to qualify for Medicaid, you should understand what the benefits are you're trying to obtain. In general, Medicaid pays for doctors and hospital stays, like Medicare. It also provides coverage for long-term nursing home care not covered by Medicare. Nursing homes operate according to a Medicaid plan which requires doctor certification of the need to enter the facility and periodic review of the need for continued care.

Medicaid also covers home health care services, medical supplies, and equipment. It commonly pays for at-home services supplied under state plans for people who would otherwise be institutionalized, covering part-time skilled nursing, home-health, and homemaker services provided by certified home health agencies.

A number of limitations are imposed by states to restrain costs and eliminate unnecessary and inappropriate treatment. Depending upon where you live, this may include copayments for mandatory as well as optional benefits, restrictions on physician visits, and limits on other services such as lab tests, prescriptions, or transportation costs. A number of states have enrolled Medicaid recipients in HMO and managed care plans and instituted other program restrictions.

What else does Medicaid cover?

Each state has its own program, providing a different menu of services, subject to minimum federal standards. Your state's program may cover dental care, medical equipment, prescription drugs, foot care, optometry services, eyeglasses, clinic services, and various diagnostic, screening and rehabilitative services, as well as transportation to obtain medical care.

Who needs Medicaid?

The poor and the not-so-poor. This includes people who do not have Medicare, who cannot get or cannot afford health insurance, and who need Medicaid for all of their health care needs. Those who do have Medicare (and Medicare Supplemental Insurance) but have long-term care needs not met by Medicare are also turning in increasing numbers to Medicaid as the payer of last resort.

"SPENDING DOWN" FOR MEDICAID

For millions of older Americans, Medicaid is the only means by which long-term custodial care can be supported. Each year half a million people "spend down" their assets in order to qualify for long-term care assistance available under Medicaid. Some actually pay for their care until their assets are used up. Others purchase "exempt" items or transfer their assets, all legitimate Medicaid-planning strategies to allow them to keep their independence and autonomy without sacrificing their life savings.

These strategies all follow from one basic rule. *All* your income and assets above specified levels must be spent to pay for care before you will qualify for Medicaid. Various planning strategies using statutory exemptions, spousal protections, and asset transfers are described below.

Plan ahead! This is one area in which advance planning is critical. Depending on your circumstances, it may take time to spend down or otherwise divest yourself of your assets in order to meet eligibility levels—and the law imposes penalty periods after transfers before you can qualify for benefits. Last-minute action may not work.

Although financing long-term care in this manner is entirely legal, Medicaid planning has become a major political issue. So many people have been forced to try to qualify for Medicaid benefits that the various methods for achieving that goal are under continuous attack.

APPLYING FOR MEDICAID

Medicaid is administered by state or local Medicaid offices. States have their own application processes to ensure eligibility, including applications which are often lengthy and complex. (Only those who qualify for Medicaid based on their SSI status, as described in the next section, don't have to make a separate application.)

Applying for Medicaid entails verification of your financial resources as well as citizenship and residency requirements. You must be a United States citizen, lawfully admitted permanent resident, or residing permanently in the United States under color of law.

Financial requirements are strict. You will be asked for your bank statements, tax returns, and other financial records reflecting your income, assets, and expenses. Often this will be required in a short time period, although extensions can be granted. Make sure you have the documentation you need—and make sure you go to any scheduled interviews. Eligibility determinations can go against you solely on your failure to provide required documentation or to appear at interviews.

More and more older people seeking Medicaid for nursing home and home care services are enlisting professional help in obtaining Medicaid, using lawyers or social workers familiar with the process and its requirements. We recommend this approach highly. Regardless of whether you need to avail yourself of other Medicaid planning strategies to protect assets, you want to ensure that you get the health care coverage you need.

 ## QUALIFYING FOR MEDICAID

As we've described, Medicaid is a *means-tested* program. In order to qualify, you must establish financial eligibility by meeting income and assets tests set by the states. Depending on where you live, you can qualify for Medicaid under one or more of these programs:

Categorical needy program. All states provide health care coverage for those who meet the financial eligibility tests and are either aged, blind, or disabled. In 37 states and the District of Columbia, income and asset standards match guidelines for the Supplemental Security Income (SSI) program, which is welfare provided by the federal government for the aged, blind, or disabled. In these states, if you qualify for SSI, you automatically qualify for Medicaid. (See Chapter 18 for more on SSI.)

In the remaining 13 states, guidelines differ from those for SSI; most are more restrictive, although some are less so. (The 13 states are Connecticut, Hawaii, Illinois, Indiana, Minnesota, Missouri, Nebraska, New Hampshire, North Carolina, North Dakota, Ohio, Oklahoma, and Virginia.)

Medically needy program. In 37 states, people whose incomes are too high to qualify for "categorically needy" Medicaid coverage but whose medical bills are so great that in effect they've reduced their incomes to that level, may qualify for Medicaid under this standard. States have "spend-down" provisions that generally operate in the applicant's favor. (This category includes California, Massachusetts, and New York.)

Income caps. Some states do not have a "medically needy" program at all. According to the Medicaid laws in these states, if your income is one cent above the state's "income cap," you cannot get Medicaid at all. (In most cases, the cap is set at three times the federal SSI benefit, a limit of $1,410 a month in 1996.) Income cap states include Arizona, Colorado, Florida, Kansas, Nevada, Oregon, and Texas.

Eligibility rules in the states are confusing even for experts. Many states distinguish between nursing home and other home- and community-based care in determining Medicaid eligibility for those services. In some states there is a "medically needy" option for nursing home care only but not for general services. In seven states there is a partial "medically needy" program for services other than nursing homes. These are Arkansas, Florida, Iowa, Kansas, Louisiana, Oklahoma, and Texas.

The income cap has caused much hardship and generated even more controversy, although the harshness of these rules has been universally acknowledged. In 1993, Congress provided a way for people living in income cap states to set up certain kinds of trusts (called "Miller" trusts) to allow them to qualify for Medicaid despite the harsh income cap rules. We discuss trusts and Medicaid planning later in this chapter.

 ## YOUR HOME AND OTHER EXEMPT ASSETS

Medicaid allows you to hold on to certain resources. Under the rules, these assets are *exempt*, which means that you can keep them and still qualify for Medicaid. An individual may retain

- $2,000 in assets (slightly higher in a few states)
- A burial fund of $1,500
- Certain assets, including a car, jewelry, and clothing
- A home

A couple applying for Medicaid can retain

- $3,000 in assets (slightly higher in a few states)
- Two $1,500 burial allowances
- Certain assets, including a car, jewelry, and clothing
- A home

If my home is exempt, can I transfer it to my adult child and still qualify for Medicaid?

No. Owning exempt assets doesn't mean that you can transfer these assets without penalty. Your home is yours, and is not counted so long as you, your spouse, or your minor, blind, or disabled child resides there. If an individual is on or applying for Medicaid, it cannot be transferred without losing Medicaid eligibility unless it is transferred to

- A spouse
- A child under 21 or who is blind or disabled
- A child living there for two years prior to institutionalization who cared for the parent, enabling the parent to remain at home
- A sibling with an equity interest who has resided there for one year prior to institutionalization

Transfers of your home and transfers of other kinds of assets are discussed later in this chapter.

PROTECTING SPOUSAL RESOURCES

At one time, a married couple faced impoverishment when one partner went into a nursing home. In 1988, Congress acted to protect assets and income of people whose spouses are institutionalized.

When one member of a married couple moves to a nursing home and applies for Medicaid, the couple's total resources are reviewed for Medicaid purposes. A "snapshot" of the total assets of the couple is taken (leaving out exempt assets). The rules state that the *total assets* of both the spouse who enters a nursing home (the *institutionalized spouse*) and the spouse who remains at home (the *at-home* or *community spouse*) are considered available for the institutionalized spouse's care, except for the *community spouse resource allowance* (CSRA).

The CSRA is deducted from the couple's total assets. Assets above the allowance are deemed excess. The CSRA is determined by a set of complicated regulations and varies from state to state.

The community spouse may retain

- A community spouse resource allowance (CSRA) of up to $76,740 in assets (maximum amount is less in some states)
- The home and other exempt assets

The institutionalized spouse may keep:

- The exemption amount ($2,000 in most states)
- A burial account of $1,500

Allowances are indexed for inflation; they are increased each year by the same percentage as Social Security benefits. These figures are from 1996.

Community spouse resource allowances vary considerably from state to state, from as low as $15,348 to as high as $76,740. (The income allowance is discussed in the next section.)

My husband requires long-term nursing home care. Must all our assets except for the CSRA be spent on his nursing home care before Medicaid takes over?

No. There are a number of steps you can take to protect yourself and your assets. The CSRA can be increased via a court order or an order obtained through a Medicaid "fair hearing," in cases of hardship or special need or to permit you to have enough assets to earn the spouse's allowable monthly income allowance. (The income allowance is discussed in the next section.)

Depending on where you live, other techniques may be used. For example, in some states you can invest the excess assets (the assets over the CSRA) in an annuity payable to you for your lifetime which would not need to be spent down on your husband's care. And in some states, you are allowed to "refuse" to use the excess assets for your spouse's care. This is called a *right of refusal.* In those cases, Medicaid must pay for your institutionalized spouse's care but has a right to take you (the at-home spouse) to court and seek a support order.

If I do refuse support, is Medicaid likely to seek a support order?

In some states it will. In these cases, however, the courts tend to be fairly protective, requiring proof that you as the at-home spouse can truly afford to pay for the care.

PROTECTING SPOUSAL INCOME

Medicaid applies a "name on the check" rule, counting only the income that is paid directly to the ill spouse as his or hers for eligibility and spending-down purposes. If income is received in both names, each is considered to own one-half of the total amount. The community spouse may retain his or her income in most cases.

The states must establish a *monthly income allowance* for the community spouse (technically called the "minimum monthly maintenance needs allowance"). In calculating the amount, the states are given an option, under which the income allowance must be at least

- A *basic allowance* of 150 percent of the non-farm poverty level for a family of two, amounting to $1,296 a month in 1996, plus an *excess shelter allowance* for housing costs for the spouse's primary residence (equal to the amount by which combined rent, taxes, utilities, and related expenses exceeds 30 percent of the basic allowance), or
- A flat $1,918.50 monthly (in 1996).

There is also a family income allowance for minor children. Amounts are indexed to inflation and increase each year.

If the community spouse's separate income is below the monthly income allowance, enough of the institutionalized spouse's income will be automatically assigned to the community spouse to raise his or her income to that state's income allowance. The community spouse's monthly income allowance can also be raised above the state allowance in cases of hardship or special need, through a court proceeding or Medicaid fair hearing. (For this to occur, the institutionalized spouse must have more income that can be assigned to the at-home spouse.)

TRANSFERRING ASSETS

One of the ways in which an applicant with assets above the specified amount can qualify for Medicaid is to transfer them to another person. Medicaid has rules about these kinds of transfers. Making a transfer triggers a period of ineligibility, called a *penalty period*, before Medicaid will pay for care. Any transfer, *other than to your spouse or blind or disabled child*, creates a penalty period.

The penalty period is triggered only if you make a transfer within 36 months of making an application for Medicaid benefits. This 36 months is called the *look-back period*. When you apply, you will be asked for your financial records dating back 36 months. A transfer within that 36 months will trigger the penalty period. A transfer before that time will not. (These rules apply to transfers made after August 1993; transfers before that date were subject to a 30-month look-back period.)

Transfer Penalties

If you apply for Medicaid within 36 months following the date of transfer, you will be ineligible for Medicaid for a period of time determined by dividing the value of the property transferred by the monthly cost of nursing home care in your area. (This cost is determined by the state Medicaid agency.)

For example, if you transfer $60,000, and the average cost of nursing homes in your area is $3,000 a month, you would divide $60,000 by $3,000. The resulting number, 20, is the number of months you are ineligible for Medicaid.

The penalty period begins on the first day of the month in which the transfer takes place. Thus, if the $60,000 transfer described above was made in the first month of the 36-month look-back period and it is now 25 months later, the penalty period will have passed and the person who made the transfer would be eligible. In other words, you don't have to wait 36 months in all cases, just until the month after the number of penalty period months has passed.

If you apply for Medicaid within the look-back period, there is no limit on the duration of the penalty period. Although there once was a 30-month limit on ineligibility, the law has changed. As of August 11, 1993, there is no maximum period. For example, in a state with a monthly cost factor set at $3000, if you transfer $200,000 and file your application before 36 months have gone by, you would be ineligible for 66 months.

If you apply for Medicaid after 36 months following the date of transfer, there is no penalty period. You need not disclose the transfer and it will not be considered in your application.

It is critical never to apply within the look-back period if the amount of the transfer is more than 36 times the state's average cost factor.

Transfer Rules for Spouses and Disabled Children

Exceptions to the above rules are made for transfers to spouses and blind or disabled children. An institutionalized spouse can transfer resources at any time to his or her spouse or to a child who is blind or totally and permanently disabled without limit or penalty.

It's important to distinguish between transfers *to* a spouse and *by* a spouse. Transfers by the spouse of a person who receives or applies for Medicaid within 36 months can also disqualify the applicant.

Transfers of jointly held assets are also treated as transfers by the applicant. The full value of the assets will be treated as a transfer unless the co-owner can show contribution.

Home Care and Community Services

Individuals who transfer assets and seek non-nursing home Medicaid benefits (such as home care or hospital benefits) are not subject to any federally-imposed period of ineligibility.

Your state may choose to apply transfer prohibitions in determining eligibility for these "community" Medicaid benefits.

If a person remaining in the community receives Medicaid and subsequently enters a nursing home, Medicaid may be cut off if transfers have been made within the 36-month look-back period and he or she is admitted within a penalty period.

Trusts

Different rules apply to transfers to certain types of trusts, making them subject to a look-back period of 60 months. This 60-month period applies to both revocable and irrevocable trusts. A recent addition to Medicaid law, this provision is not at all clear.

Remember, it's not just the look-back period that's critical but the penalty period. Thus, if you transferred $150,000 to a trust where you will get the income on the trust for your life but cannot access the principal, and the "average cost factor" for your state in $3,000 a month, the look-back period will be 60 months—but the penalty period will be no longer than 50 months.

(In fact, the value of the "Medicaid transfer" to the trust will be less than $150,000 because it is reduced by the value of your lifetime right to the trust income. This reduction will be based on your age and life expectancy as set forth in tables used by Medicaid. If you are age 70 when you set up this "income-only" trust the value of the transfer to the trust for penalty period calculation purposes would be only $59,250, resulting in a penalty period of only 19 months.)

How does the look-back period relate to transfers?

Ineligibility is measured from the date of a transfer made within the look-back period. Once the penalty period passes, you may apply for Medicaid.

A transfer made before the look-back period is not used to figure eligibility. For sufficiently large amounts, you may just wait the 36 months before making an application, at which time you need not disclose the transfer.

Do all transfers result in a penalty?

No. Remember, there is an exception for transfers to spouses and blind or disabled children. In addition, only transfers for which there was no consideration will be penalized. For example, selling something is not a Medicaid transfer. Giving something to a child who gives you something in return is not a Medicaid transfer to the extent of the value of what you get back. If you give your daughter $50,000 but she promises to allow you to live with her for your lifetime, you will not have a penalty period so long as the "value" of your right to live with her approximates $50,000.

If you make a transfer for reasons having nothing to do with Medicaid (for example, giving a $25,000 wedding gift to your grandchild when you are perfectly healthy), it will not result in a penalty period should you subsequently need to apply for Medicaid. Only transfers that were intended to make you eligible for Medicaid result in a penalty. But you must be able to show that your gift was not intended to qualify you for Medicaid.

TRUSTS AND MEDICAID PLANNING

One of the earliest and still common forms of Medicaid planning is to establish a trust. A trust works by establishing a fund to be administered under the direction of a trustee or trustees. In broad outline, a trust makes provision for distribution of the income, usually on a regular basis to the named beneficiary, and eventual disposition of the principal.

By this means, ownership of assets can be transferred away from the Medicaid applicant—and away from Medicaid—and yet remain within reach. For these purposes, trusts are used in two basic types of situations:

Third-party trusts. These are trusts set up by one party to benefit another. For example, a parent may set up a trust to benefit a disabled adult child, or an adult child may establish a trust for an aging parent or a sibling. Since the person setting up the trust has no obligation to support the beneficiary, the trust can specify that it be used to supplement, not replace, Medicaid benefits for the adult child, parent, or sibling who is the beneficiary. (These "supplemental needs trusts," discussed later in this chapter, may be established during your lifetime or by your will.)

Self-settled trusts. These are trusts by which a person in need of Medicaid seeks to protect his or her own assets. The rules governing these trusts are much more restrictive. In general, you cannot set up a trust with funds that belong to you or funds to which you're entitled, have them remain "available" to you, and gain protection.

Depending on the purpose of the trust, the degree of discretion granted to the trustees, and restrictions on that discretion or use of the funds, trust principal can be sheltered and will not disqualify the trust donor once the statutory period of ineligibility following transfer of assets into the trust has expired.

Revocable trusts. For Medicaid purposes, the resources in a revocable trust are considered available to the creator of the trust, who can revoke or undo the trust, and therefore count as his or her assets in determining eligibility. Income paid from the trust to any person is considered income of that person. Payments to others are treated as transfers subject to the transfer rules.

Irrevocable trusts. Theoretically an irrevocable trust, which by definition cannot be revoked, removes all control from the trust's creator. Subject to the trust provisions, the property is out of his or her hands. Therefore, only the income and principal that can be paid to the creator from the trust would be counted as available to the Medicaid applicant for eligibility determining purposes.

Discretionary trusts were always subject to challenge by the government, which argued that any possible exercise of discretion by the trustees would make trust assets available and therefore countable as assets of the potential beneficiary when he or she applied for Medicaid. It doesn't matter whether the trustee has actually exercised discretion or not. The mere possibility operates to disqualify the applicant from eligibility for benefits. These so-called *Medicaid qualifying trusts* are really *Medicaid disqualifying trusts.*

Recent changes in the law seem designed to prohibit this sort of trust, and it may be that the assets in trusts with no discretion to invade principal will count against the Medicaid applicant.

Because of the proliferation of so-called Medicaid qualifying trusts, Congress acted in 1993 to tighten the rules of eligibility for transfers involving trusts. Tougher new Medicaid rules for trusts create a 60-month look-back period (and possible longer penalty periods) for transfers and other restrictions on their use. The new rules apply to trusts created with assets of the individual regardless of whether the trust is established by

- The individual
- The individual's spouse
- A person with legal authority to act in place of the individual or individual's spouse, such as a guardian or attorney in fact
- A person acting at the direction or request of an individual or individual's spouse, such as a guardian or attorney in fact

Despite restrictions, trusts may work in limited situations. A properly drafted "income only" trust, in which the trustee has no power to use any of the principal for the income beneficiary, will protect the trust funds after a penalty period (figured on the trust's "remainder value").

Medicaid rules apply to living trusts only. Trusts created by wills, called *testamentary trusts,* are not subject to these restrictive Medicaid rules. (Testamentary trusts are described in Chapter 14.)

Supplemental needs trusts. These trusts are traditionally set up for the use of disabled persons, often from the assets received from judgments or settlements arising out of accident or medical malpractice suits, or from assets accumulated by the disabled person before becoming ill. In the past, people would often be rendered ineligible for Medicaid by their ownership of these assets or settlements, which would dissipate quickly and not last the course of their lifetime.

New law protects assets of a Medicaid applicant placed in these trusts so long as the state's Medicaid outlay will be repaid out of the total amount of money left in the trust upon the individual's death. Two types of such trusts are authorized under law:

- A trust set up for a disabled person under age 65 by a parent, grandparent, legal guardian or court
- A trust established and managed by a not-for-profit association for the benefit of a person of any age

Assets placed in either type of trust are not treated as "available" for Medicaid eligibility purposes and can be used to pay for the "supplemental" needs of the disabled person. (See Chapter 12.) Transferring assets to such trusts is not subject to the transfer penalty rules, *if* the trust beneficiary who is applying for Medicaid is under age 65 at the time that person's assets are placed in the trust. A transfer by a person more than 65 years old to such a trust could result in a penalty period, but the look-back period will be only 36 months.

Trusts are legal instruments governed by complicated rules. A person cannot and should not draw up a trust without the advice of a lawyer expert in estate and trust planning and Medicaid eligibility. For a full discussion of trusts, see Chapter 11; Chapter 12 describes setting up a trust for a disabled child.

 CLAIMS ON RECIPIENTS' ESTATES

Under Medicaid law, states are now required to have estate recovery programs, whereby assets from an individual's estate may be sought for Medicaid outlays made on his or her behalf.

How can a Medicaid recipient have an estate if he or she is not allowed more than nominal assets to be eligible in the first place? In most cases there will be no "estate," but in some, there may be. For example, the home is exempt and may be owned by the Medicaid recipient at the time of death. Medicaid law also instructs the states to seek recovery from those assets in which the recipient had any interest at the time of death, raising complicated legal issues.

I have a life estate in my former house, now owned by my child. Is the house vulnerable to state action?

This part of the Medicaid law is poorly written and very confusing, even to Medicaid experts. State interpretations vary. One interpretation is that the state can seek recovery from "non-probate" assets such as trusts and annuities from which you received some benefits during your lifetime even if those benefits pass to someone else later on. Another is that the state has the right to go after jointly owned property or real estate in which the recipient has a life estate. If you have exempt assets or a partial interest in any assets, you need to get competent legal advice.

 APPEALING A MEDICAID DECISION

Under Medicaid, you have the right to a fair hearing, with due process guarantees, for a denial of application for benefits or for termination, suspension, or reduction of eligibility or covered services.

Basically, almost any denial, downgrade, or cessation of benefits can be appealed. (One exception: The state can always terminate optional benefits for lack of funding without giving you a hearing.)

The process for appeal under Medicaid is different than that of Medicare, which relies on its intermediaries and carriers to make determinations and hear appeals. In Medicaid, an appeal is made directly to the government.

Notice. Under federal regulations, you're entitled to receive ten days notice before cessation or reduction of your benefits takes place. The notice must specify the action to be taken, the reasons for it, the legal grounds supporting the action, and your rights to a hearing and to continuation of benefits pending a hearing. You should also be informed of any legal assistance available to you.

The notice will also inform you of the date by which you must request a hearing. Your request should be in writing. Upon request, you should also be allowed access to your file at a reasonable time in advance of the hearing, and to any other relevant documents to be used at the hearing.

Fair hearing. A fair hearing is an informal process, conducted by an impartial hearing officer. The burden of proof is on the government to show that its action was supported by applicable law and regulations. You have the right to appear in person, to be represented by counsel, and to call and cross-examine witnesses. Formal rules of evidence don't necessarily apply.

The law states that the hearing must be held and a written decision issued by the hearing officer within 90 days of your initial request for a hearing, although these rules are not always followed. If the decision goes against you, you may file for a rehearing or administrative appeal. Any further appeal is made to the courts for judicial review.

Don't be misled into thinking you don't need a lawyer. Despite the informal nature of administrative review, Medicaid eligibility rules are extraordinarily complex and state regulations sometimes more so. If at all possible, you need the assistance of a lawyer familiar with Medicaid cases. This is an adversarial proceeding, and depending on the circumstances, the consequences may be severe.

What happens to my benefits during the hearing?

You usually have the right to continuation of your benefits pending the hearing, but *you must ask for it*. You must claim your right by asking for continuing aid when you request a fair hearing appeal. If your request for continuing aid is received within 10 days, your benefits must be continued.

MEDICAID FOR MIDDLE-INCOME FAMILIES

Don't make the mistake of thinking that Medicaid benefits are limited to the very poor. Medicaid is a complex, confusing, but important government program which has become the lifeline for many middle-income families who need help paying for long-term care in order to avoid impoverishment.

Originally intended for the poor, it has become the payer of last resort for persons of modest means. Spousal protections for resources and income clearly indicate Congressional intent that Medicaid continue as a program for middle-income Americans. Yet the use of Medicaid to finance long-term care, particularly nursing home costs, has had a profound impact on state budgets and resulted in attempts to restrict access to the program and limit benefits through calls for block grants (at this writing, still in the proposal stage).

Despite intended overhaul, with the federal government unlikely to increase Medicare benefits in the foreseeable future, Medicaid is likely to continue as the only government-funded program that deals with long-term care.

There may be any number of reasons not to apply for Medicaid, including personal, family, and psychological reasons, quality-of-care issues, and tax consequences. Nevertheless, it is an option that deserves serious consideration. While access to Medicaid is complicated and may not be available to or right for everyone, it is a possible source of financing for long-term care—even for those who may not now imagine they can take advantage of it.

MEDICAID'S FUTURE

At this writing, proposed changes to the Medicaid program contemplate decreased federal regulation and increased authority to the states, which will have responsibility for determining enrollment and eligibility standards.

The specter of block grants to the states raises many questions and concerns. Proposals include eliminating the quality assurances for nursing home care and prescreening of residents. Although set-asides are contemplated to preserve some level of funding for low-income elderly and low-income blind or disabled, it's not at all clear what assurances will accompany these funds. Most states will be receiving even less federal money than anticipated.

A number of states already impose restrictions on benefits and services to restrain costs and treatment. Even if the Medicaid structure remains intact and federal guarantees stay in place, the poor can expect to feel the pinch in access to health care, with many being moved into managed care programs.

The real change for older Americans of modest means may be expected in eligibility for and access to long-term care under Medicaid. Spousal protections are slated to stay in place. However, we can predict that access will be more limited and many transfer rules will be tightened. That makes it imperative for you to start planning now—and consult with an experienced attorney about your plans.

9

PUBLIC-PRIVATE
LONG-TERM CARE
FINANCING

An innovative project pioneered in Connecticut and also available in California, Indiana, and New York, is the "public-private partnership" for long-term care financing.

If you live in one of these four states, the "partnership" offers you the opportunity to

- Buy long-term care insurance and
- Get Medicaid after your insurance benefits are used up—without having to "spend down" or give away your assets.

If you have and use this long-term care insurance and its benefits, you may be able subsequently to qualify for Medicaid *automatically*, without having to spend down. Three states—California, Indiana, and Connecticut—match your protection dollar for dollar. In the fourth state, New York, your asset protection through this program is unlimited.

PARTNERSHIP POLICIES

Under the partnership, public agencies join with private insurers to market long-term care policies that guarantee certain minimum benefits. An "approved" partnership insurance policy must meet certain standards, including at a minimum these basic components:

- Coverage for at least three years' nursing home benefits or six years' home care benefits (two days of home care equal one day of nursing home coverage)

- A minimum daily benefit of $110 for nursing home care and $60 for home care, with a 5 percent compounded inflation rider (these are 1995 minimums)

 MEDICAID BENEFITS AND ASSET PROTECTION

Once you use up the policy benefits, your assets will be protected as follows:

- In California, Connecticut, and Indiana, your assets will be protected up to the amount that your insurance pays for your medical expenses. Thus, if your insurance pays for $150,000 of nursing home costs, you can keep $150,000 of your assets (in addition to your home) and still be eligible for Medicaid.
- In New York, all your assets will be exempt and fully protected. New York's program gives you unlimited asset protection.

Can I buy a partnership policy in New York and use its benefits if I move to Florida and become ill there?
Yes and no. If you purchase a partnership policy, the home health and nursing home care insurance benefits can be used anywhere, subject to your qualifying for them. However, if you subsequently apply for Medicaid and wish to protect your assets under the plan, you must apply for benefits from the state which approved and sponsored the partnership policy.

 INCOME RESTRICTIONS

Although you receive assets protection, your income is not protected under the partnership programs. In fact, you may have to spend down your income. This may not be critical if you are single and living in a nursing home, but it will be a problem if you are married and your spouse will need your income to continue to live in the community.

 FUTURE PARTNERSHIPS

The public-private partnership is designed to encourage people to buy long-term care insurance. Because the average nursing home stay is two and a half years, the states expect to achieve savings through reduced Medicaid costs covered by the policies purchased under the program. Depending on your circumstances, it may also be of great value to you as a private individual, saving you a considerable amount of your resources.

Unfortunately, the federal government has seen fit to bar additional states from adopting new partnership programs. In 1993, it acted to restrict the program to the four states in which it now exists. (At this writing, there is legislation pending in Congress to lift this bar.)

Part 3

■■■■■■■■■■■■■■■■■■■■■■■■■■

Life Planning for You and Your Family

Many people believe, mistakenly, that life planning is for the wealthy. But most people, rich or not, have the same goals—good health, income and assets to ensure security for themselves and their spouses, and a cushion for a possible crisis or chronic long-term care needs. Planning can help identify those goals and formulate strategies to achieve them.

In Chapter 10, we'll tell you about tools for health care decision-making, how you can protect yourself with advance directives, and how these same documents can help you make decisions on behalf of others. Chapter 11 tells you about financial planning—and the use of the power of attorney and trusts, among other property management systems. In recent years, living trusts and other trust instruments have become increasingly popular among financial planners and advisers to the elderly. We explain what a trust is, what it can and cannot do for you, and how to avoid common pitfalls. Chapter 12 gives you an introduction to planning strategies for a disabled child. In Chapter 13, we talk about options available for those no longer able to make their own decisions, from guardianships to other protective services.

For many, making a will is the primary vehicle for financial planning. This becomes even more difficult when you consider the possibility of your spouse's needing increased health care in the future—and the Medicaid implications. We discuss the implications of wills and estate planning in Chapter 14.

1 0

■■

ADVANCE DIRECTIVES
FOR HEALTH CARE

In Chapter 2, we described your rights to determine what medical treatment you will get and what treatment you will refuse. The decision by the United States Supreme Court in the *Cruzan* case upheld your constitutional right to determine your own care, including the right to refuse life support.

If you're otherwise fine, and able to communicate with your doctors, you can tell them your views on the treatment they offer. In the best of all possible worlds, they'll make a diagnosis, discuss treatment options and their advantages and disadvantages with you, and give you ample time to come to a decision after obtaining a second and even a third opinion and discussing the options with your family and loved ones.

Unfortunately, medical decisions are not usually made at leisure. Nor are they always made when the patient is in a position to understand, make, and communicate decisions about his or her health.

Your right to have your wishes respected continues even if you are incapacitated. If you are no longer in a position to state them, others may assert them on your behalf as your *surrogate*. In the *Cruzan* case, Nancy Cruzan's parents spoke on behalf of their daughter, who was in a persistent vegetative coma and incapable of articulating her wishes. The decision made it clear that she had that right—that her own prior statements were in fact the best evidence of her present wishes, were she able to communicate them.

If a person's wishes are expressed when he or she is competent, either through a document such as a *living will* or orally to another person, those wishes must be respected. In this chapter, we discuss the use of living wills and *health care proxies*, and what happens when decisions must be made on behalf of incapacitated adults or children who have not expressed their wishes through such *advance directives*.

The rules may vary, depending on the state you live in. We've tried to note some of the differences here, but be aware that state legislatures make frequent changes in this area. If you're in a surrogate situation occasioned by incapacity—making decisions for someone else or having decisions made for you by someone else—doctors, hospital administrators, and other health care professionals may be overzealous in resisting your legal rights. That's when you'll need help in enforcing your rights. Advance directives such as living wills and health care proxies will empower you to assert your rights on behalf of yourself and others.

 THE THREE BASIC DIRECTIVES

To deal with possible future incapacity, lawyers have come up with documents called *advance directives* which allow people to make their wishes known when they are no longer in a position to express them themselves. Advance directives commonly used include:

- **Living will.** The living will states your desires concerning future medical care, specifying what procedures you want or don't want. These are sometimes called *health care directives*, *medical directives* or *instructional directives*. We use the expression living will because that's what most people call them.
- **Health care proxy.** Also called a *durable power of attorney for health care.* The health care proxy allows you to designate an agent in advance to make decisions on your behalf if you later become incapacitated. The proxy designates someone else to *ensure that the wishes you have expressed—in your living will or otherwise—are carried out*, and to *make health care determinations on your behalf, if you're not capable or don't have a living will, or for things not anticipated in your living will.* The power of attorney for health care is sometimes combined with a living will.
- **Power of attorney.** This is an advance directive primarily for use in financial planning. (This type of power of attorney is discussed in Chapter 11.)

With the help of lawyers and the courts, patients have learned to use legal documents like living wills and health care proxies to assert their rights to receive or refuse medical treatment according to their values and wishes.

 LIVING WILLS

The best known advance directive is the living will. If Nancy Cruzan's death provided the legal authority to recognize patients' wishes expressed through living wills, the deaths of Jacqueline Onassis and Richard Nixon further publicized their use. That both the former First Lady and the former President had living wills serves to illustrate how accepted living wills have become.

How does it work? If you're well enough and competent, you tell your doctors what you want and don't want. If you're not able, your living will does it for you.

Consider the words:

living—because it's useful when you're still alive;

will—because it gives instructions expressing your will.

A living will speaks for you when you can't. It ensures that your family and your doctor—and any other doctor or medical facility treating you—knows your wishes in the event you aren't able to make your own medical decisions. It protects you if you are in a coma or incompetent.

What do you need to know about a living will?

- *When* and under what conditions it becomes effective
- *What* medical care is authorized and what medical care is not authorized
- *How* the living will itself is sanctioned, by what form and with what necessary signatures

Living wills are governed by state law. Forty-seven states and the District of Columbia have specific laws authorizing and regulating their use. The other states recognize them and rely on interpretation of court decisions. Whether you live in a state with or without a living will statute, it's important to understand that *all states recognize living wills.*

Remember, you should talk about your wishes ahead of time—that's why your written expression of your wishes is called an "advance directive." A living will is your protection when and if you become incapable of making or communicating decisions about your health care.

When does a living will becomes effective?

When you're incapable of making or communicating the necessary health care decision. In other words, when you have lost the capacity to give informed consent. If you could speak for yourself, you wouldn't need that piece of paper.

What is the definition of capacity? For health care purposes, a person with capacity would be one who is able to understand the illness, the nature and effect of the proposed treatment, and the risk in accepting or refusing it.

Several states impose restrictions on the use of living wills. In most states, the statutes say a living will may be used only if the patient is terminal *and* death is imminent. The intent of these statutes is to preclude using the living will to refuse treatment for a patient who is seriously ill and with no hope of recovery, but not on the brink of death. Thus, a person in an irreversible coma or with advanced Alzheimer's might be given artificial hydration and nutrition even against his or her wishes.

Language such as this is clearly not binding. Under the *Cruzan* decision, you have the right to refuse treatment, through stating your wishes or through your living will, whether you are in a terminal condition or not. You do not have to agree to "heroic measures" which you do not want. (The model living will in this chapter covers a broad set of circumstances.)

Many states impose very specific requirements concerning use of a living will. Colorado's statute, for example, requires the person be terminal for seven days, and then imposes a 48-hour waiting period on removal of life-sustaining treatment. Alaska, Arizona, and California also have requirements concerning the duration of the patient's condition and additional procedures for certifying it. Other states are becoming more and more flexible, broadening the circumstances under which a living will may be invoked in the wake of the *Cruzan* decision.

Once I've signed a living will, can my doctor "pull the plug" at any time?

No. A living will (and any other medical directive you may sign) becomes effective only when and if you are incapable of making or communicating decisions about your health care. If you are so incapable *and* you are terminally ill, in a persistent vegetative state, or suffering persistent mental incapacity, *then* it can be used as an indicator of your wishes.

Can the state prevent my wishes from being honored? What do I do then?

You (or your family acting as your surrogate) may need a lawyer to enforce your rights. In Florida, Estelle Browning left specific written instructions not to give her tube feeding. Because she was in a vegetative condition but death was not imminent, as she specified in her living will, her instructions were ignored and she was kept alive against her wishes. Subsequent legal action, unfortunately too late for Mrs. Browning, upheld her right to refuse all life-sustaining treatment.

One important lesson of the *Browning* case is that the language of your living will should not be limited to preconceived ideas about your state law, but should express your views so that they may stand as the true expression of your intentions.

 SPECIFIC TREATMENT INSTRUCTIONS

People do not generally think about the specifics of illness and dying. They generally say something like "I don't want to be kept alive like that," "that" referring to anything from being mentally incapacitated to receiving artificial respiration. Drafting and executing a living will forces you to confront these issues.

In cases of serious or terminal illness, doctors may prescribe diagnostic tests ranging from relatively straightforward procedures such as blood tests, X-rays, MRI and CT scans to biopsies and exploratory surgery. Other possible treatment choices may include radiation, chemotherapy, or hormone therapy, all of which have potentially undesirable side effects. Or comfort care may be ordered to deal exclusively with alleviating pain.

A living will usually discusses these kinds of treatment and life-support options—procedures, medicines, technologies, foods, or any combination of those—and whether or not the individual wants them, and under what conditions. Treatments and other options often discussed in a living will can include respirators or ventilators, nutrition and hydration, cardiopulmonary resuscitation (CPR) and so forth.

Treatments don't have to be painful or unpleasant to be specified in a living will. For example, antibiotics have relatively harmless side effects but are commonly refused because of their very effectiveness in prolonging lives.

Your living will applies also to treatments that you would want to help you. At least one hospital has gone to court for permission to take someone off life-sustaining treatment because the hospital thought that continued treatment was futile. The court refused the hosiptal's request, specifically citing the patient's expressed desire for continued treatment.

In drafting your living will and discussing its provisions with your lawyer or your family, don't gloss over the specifics. Remember, details count. They count when you're deciding to accept or refuse treatment. They count even more when you're in no position to make the decision, and someone else has to make it for you.

Do I have a right to demand treatment through my living will?

Yes, at least to the extent you have the right to demand it at all. As we discussed in Chapter 2, the limits to "treatment on demand" are still uncertain. More than one court has refused to take a patient off life-sustaining treatment, despite medical evidence of its futility. Treatment has also been ordered by courts for patients who are brain-dead or in a persistent vegetative state. New Jersey laws sanction continued treatment for those of Orthodox Jewish faith who believe that the cessation of heart and lung function, rather than of brain activity, determines legal death.

Forcing doctors to treat patients in medically unacceptable ways creates numerous ethical dilemmas as yet unresolved. At least one lawsuit has been instituted charging a failure to provide requested care and more may be predicted. A disturbing survey reported in the *New York Times* found that 80 percent of doctors had withdrawn care over the objections of family members and 14 percent had withheld or withdrawn care they considered "futile" without discussion.

Are there any special rules for pregnant women?

Many states exclude pregnant women from their living will statutes, and do not allow them to refuse life-sustaining treatment during pregnancy. Some expressly make viability of the fetus or viability with life support the point at which treatment cannot be refused. Arizona, Maryland, and New Jersey allow pregnant women to refuse life support.

How do religions feel about living wills?

Mixed. While organized religion for the most part respects the right to die in dignity, without prolonging suffering by artificial means, some

Catholic, Orthodox Jewish, and fundamentalist Protestant groups are opposed. One organization has drafted a living will form for use by Orthodox Jews, which includes a hierarchy of rabbinical boards to determine issues of Jewish law for end-of-life decisions. The validity of this document in court is open to question.

Statutes deal with religion in two ways. First, they exempt physicians and hospitals from having to comply with directives which go against their personal religious beliefs. A number of court battles start because patients are under the care of doctors and institutions who are unsympathetic to their views. Under these circumstances, the patient can either seek another doctor or transfer to another institution. The Patient Self-Determination Act addresses this problem by requiring health care facilities to take certain steps to ensure that advance directives are respected.

Second, some statutes modify the definition of death (usually "brain death") for those whose belief system would insist the person is still alive. In New Jersey, for example, an otherwise-dead person whose heart and lungs are still functioning may be considered alive. This has obvious implications for when to end life support.

▌ INSTRUCTIONS ON NUTRITION AND HYDRATION

People have special feelings about eating and drinking. Although many people have no qualms about refusing medication or ending heroic measures for very ill patients, they balk at ending basic support of nutrition and hydration.

Although no distinction was drawn by the *Cruzan* court between nutrition and hydration and other forms of life-sustaining treatment (such as respiration), problems arise with artificial or tube feeding.

The ability to withhold or withdraw artificial nutrition and hydration is of concern in drafting a living will. Most state statutes are silent on the subject. In some states, you must expressly indicate in your living will that you don't want nutrition and hydration. This is the requirement in Alaska, Florida, Maine, Minnesota, Oregon, South Dakota, and Tennessee. In Kentucky, Ohio and Washington, the authority to withhold or withdraw nutrition or hydration is prohibited under certain circumstances, and in Missouri, it is expressly precluded.

Conformity with a state's statute is generally recommended in drafting a living will. In those states where withdrawal of nutrition and hydration is not authorized, courts have split on recognizing the patient's wishes. A generic living will may also be prepared, which may help as an added precaution. (See our model living will in this chapter.)

What is the difference between withdrawing and withholding life-sustaining treatment?

From a legal or moral point of view, there is no difference. Yet withdrawing treatment is often resisted by health care workers who feel more deeply implicated morally by actually turning off a machine than by just not turning it on in the first place. Drafting your living will to address both possibilities can help alleviate this problem.

"DO NOT RESUSCITATE" ORDERS

"DNR" stands for *do not resuscitate,* a code for an order commonly used in a hospital or nursing home. DNR indicates that if the patient's heart or breathing stops, he or she is not to be revived. These orders are known as *DNR codes, No codes,* or *Hollywood codes.* Hospitals used to routinely enter DNR on the charts of severely ill elderly patients, without asking.

Living wills can specify DNR orders, naming resuscitation as one of the life-sustaining procedures refused. Many states have laws requiring hospitals and nursing homes to withhold emergency cardiopulmonary resuscitation from patients who note their refusal in advance.

Interestingly, New York, which has no living will statute, has a DNR law covering hospitals and nursing homes as well as non-hospital DNR situations. Extending DNR regulation to homes as well as hospitals was intended to benefit many people with advanced medical conditions who die at home or in hospices. Emergency medical rescue workers are no longer required to resuscitate them.

A number of other states have passed laws prescribing guidelines for DNR orders outside health care facilities, including Arizona, Colorado, Florida, Illinois, Maryland, Pennsylvania, and Virginia.

These laws are fairly new and implementation has been uneven. A DNR order outside the hospital or institutional setting is hard to enforce. Emergency workers generally have no knowledge of a patient's wishes unless the patient is in a position to tell them, and often, this is not possible. The *Hemlock Quarterly* once advised people to tattoo a DNR order on their chests, where emergency service workers would be sure to see it, but we don't go so far. Some patients wear bracelets with the order noted on it, or carry a card in their wallet. Laws generally grant immunity to health professionals who carry out a DNR order in good faith, as well as to those who attempt resuscitation unaware of the order.

Make sure your doctor understands your wishes, and, if you are in a hospital, make sure they are entered in your medical chart. In a study reported in the *New York Times,* although three out of 10 patients said they didn't want cardiopulmonary resuscitation, 80 percent of their doctors either ignored or misunderstood their instructions. Nearly *half* the patients requesting it did not get DNR orders entered on their charts.

Does "do not resuscitate" mean "do not treat"?

DNR should not be confused with DNT ("do not treat"). In practice, some hospitals or health care providers may be casual about the difference, assuming that if you sign a DNR, meaning you don't want resuscitation, you don't want treatment. But this is not necessarily so. You may very well want continued treatment, for infections or for life-threatening situations other than cardiac arrest. Not all ways to go are equally bad. Make sure the people who are treating you know the difference.

What if I am resuscitated against my will? Do I have any recourse against the hospital?

Not under current law. Edward Winter saw his wife die after painful resuscitation years before, and determined to avoid that fate himself. The Cincinnati man left clear instructions that no such effort was to be made on his behalf, and when he was hospitalized they were entered on his chart and posted behind the monitor. Nursing personnel were not informed and acted against his instructions, resuscitating him and saving his life for two more years. He brought a personal injury suit against the hospital, charging "wrongful living." The suit was dismissed by the court.

However, several newer cases—and an appeal by Mr. Winter—have challenged the right to give aggressive treatment such as CPR in the face of express refusals, citing theories of negligence, intentional infliction of emotional distress, and battery.

 PHYSICIAN RESPONSIBILITY AND LIABILITY

As a general rule, state laws relieve doctors and families of responsibility in the patient's decision, specifically providing that withholding or withdrawing life-sustaining treatment in compliance with a living will does not constitute assisted suicide or homicide. Often the statute provides immunity from liability for health care providers.

A bigger problem is the number of doctors who ignore the instructions in the advance directives of their patients. A number of states impose penalties upon doctors for failure either to comply with medical directives in a living will or to transfer a patient to a facility that will comply. Some states sanction health providers for failure to record the terminal condition with criminal misdemeanors and penalties.

An interesting question of liability arose in the unfortunate case of Jean Elbaum, who was given medical services over her express objections. The nursing home said her wishes were not expressed in a way that met New York's "clear and convincing" standard of proof and kept her alive through a series of legal battles until the courts ruled that the treatment was unwanted and should be discontinued. The nursing home then presented her husband with a bill for more than $120,000. Astonishingly, the obligation of Mr. Elbaum to pay the bill—*even for treatment that was found to be unwanted*—was upheld by New York's highest court.

LIVING WILL AND HEALTH CARE DECLARATION

Know all people by these presents that I,   , residing at   ,
hereby declare my will with respect to my medical care and treatment in the
event I am unable for any reason to make known my will at the time medical
decisions must be made.

1. *Directive to forego or discontinue life-prolonging medical treatment when
   recovery is unlikely.*

   In the event I suffer from an injury, disease, illness or other
   physical or mental condition, including intractable pain, which renders me unable to make health care decisions on my own behalf,
   which leaves me unable to communicate with others meaningfully,
   and from which there is no reasonable prospect of recovery to a
   cognitive and sentient life (even if my condition or illness is not
   deemed to be "terminal" and even if my death is not imminent), I
   direct that no medical treatments or procedures (except as provided
   in paragraph 3 below) be utilized in my care or, if begun, that they
   be discontinued.

2. *Definition of medical treatment.*

   By "medical treatments or procedures," I mean interventions by
   medical doctors, nurses, paramedics, hospitals, residential health care
   facilities or any other health care provider, in the care of my body and
   mind, including all medical and surgical procedures, mechanical or
   otherwise, treatments, therapies, including drugs and hormones, which
   may substitute for, replace, supplant, enhance or assist any bodily function. This specifically includes maintenance of respiration, nutrition and
   hydration by artificial means. With respect to all medical treatments or
   procedures, I include both existing technology and any methods or
   techniques which may be hereafter developed and perfected.

3. *Provision for pain control.*

   I ask that medical treatment to alleviate pain, to provide comfort, and
   to mitigate suffering be provided so that I may be as free of pain and
   suffering as possible.

4. *Determination of prognosis.*

   My Health Care Agent acting pursuant to my duly executed
   Health Care Proxy shall follow my directions as set out in this Health
   Care Declaration whenever my Agent has ascertained by applying
   reasonable medical standards that my condition is as described in
   Section 1, above. In the absence of the instructions of my agent, any
   persons or institutions who are called upon to make decisions affecting my care shall comply with my directions contained herein. In the
   event of uncertainty or ambiguity as to how my wishes are to be
   interpreted or applied in any particular situation, any persons or
   institutions who are treating me shall comply with the interpretations
   and directions of my Health Care Agent.

5. *Acknowledgement of effects of this Declaration.*
   I make and execute this Declaration knowing that, if complied with, my death may occur sooner than it would were all available and appropriate medical treatments considered and used. I accept this as a necessary result of a decision to avoid dependence and pain. And I make the decision now, for myself, after careful consideration, to assure that I will have the level of medical care which I want, and to relieve others of the burden of decision.

Dated: _____ , 199___   _____

Statement of Witnesses

   I declare that the person who signed this document is personally known to me and appears to be of sound mind and acting of his or her own free will. He or she signed (or asked another to sign for him or her) this document in my presence.

_____ Address _____

_____ Address _____

More recently, several lawsuits have sought to challenge doctors, hospitals, and health care providers who have ignored living wills and other advance directives, and hold them liable for damages. In one case, a Michigan woman was awarded a verdict of $16.5 million for unauthorized treatment by a hospital against the patient's wishes.

LIVING WILL STATUTES AND LEGAL FORMALITIES

Let's clear up one common misunderstanding right now. There are states with so-called living will statutes and states without such statutes. But all states *recognize* living wills. All states are subject to the *Cruzan* decision of the United States Supreme Court allowing self-determination in refusing life-sustaining treatment.

The states with statutes authorizing living wills look to their statutes to determine issues that arise. The fact that the state you live in has no law concerning living wills does not mean that you shouldn't have one. Those states without living will statutes look to prior court decisions. A living will can be just as important, if not more so, in a non-statute jurisdiction, where it will count as evidence to the court of the patient's intentions.

The states without statutes authorizing living wills are New York, Massachusetts, and Missouri (Nancy Cruzan's home state). New York, for example, has no living will statute, but in fact the New York Court of Appeals, the state's highest court, declared in a landmark decision that the ideal situation to establish a patient's intentions to decline medical assistance would be one in which the person's wishes were expressed in some form of writing such as a living will when he or she was still competent. (The court found that "mere statements" about not being maintained on artificial life support were not sufficient to constitute the "clear and convincing" level of proof needed to assure the court that the patient had indeed made this determination.)

The *Cruzan* court authorized states to establish their own standards of proof concerning a patient's intentions. *A properly executed living will meets those standards in all states.*

How does a living will becomes effective?

In states with a living will statute, the statute usually contains form and execution requirements. There is usually a requirement that the living will be witnessed by two persons at least 18 years of age who are not relatives by blood or marriage, heirs, health care agents or otherwise financially responsible for the person's medical care. (Check local laws.) Notarization is not always required but it can't hurt.

Some states impose additional requirements. For example, California requires that a nursing home patient's living will be witnessed by a patient advocate or state-designated representative. Delaware and South Carolina have similar provisions. In Georgia, the living will of a person in a hospital or nursing facility must be witnessed by the medical director or a member of the medical staff not involved in the declarant's care.

Most states with statutes require certain formalities for execution, but allow you to use your own words. On the other hand, Oregon's statute mandates use of its statutory form. A few statutes, including those of Virginia, Louisiana, and Texas, specifically authorize oral declarations. Remember that in all states, oral statements can always be used as evidence of the speaker's wishes.

The important thing to remember about a living will is that it is implemented by others. The person who signs a living will is not in a position to enforce it. Someone—a spouse, a child, a friend—will be enforcing it on his or her behalf. Once you have signed your living will, you must communicate its existence to those upon whom you would rely, and either distribute it or leave it where it can easily be found.

An especially important resource to use is Choice in Dying, a national organization which counsels people facing these issues—and gives them the resources to deal with doctors, hospitals, and others. Choice in Dying publishes living will forms good for your state, and will send you free copies. (See the Resources section at the end of this book.)

What kind of living will should be prepared for states without living will statutes or with restrictions on withholding certain treatments?

We recommend the general form (such as the sample form on pp. 126–127), especially for states with statutory restrictions on withholding nutrition and hydration. Remember, your constitutional right to refuse treatment overrides any state attempts to restrict it. But you must express your wishes through a living will in order to make sure your rights are respected.

Is a living will valid state to state? Should I prepare separate documents?

It depends. For example, Arizona recognizes out-of-state documents that comply with its statute. Other states such as Texas give "full faith and credit" to living wills executed in accordance with the laws of other states.

A living will prepared out of state may not be valid as an alternative to the living will required by the state's law. However, any living will may be taken as evidence of your intent, and used in that respect. A validly signed document offers some proof of your intentions.

It makes no sense to sign 50 documents. If you move to a new residence or buy a vacation home in another state, you should review the validity of your living will in your new state and execute a new one, if needed, in accordance with the requirements of that state.

Where should I keep my living will?

Keep the original in an easily accessible place, and give copies to your primary doctor and close members of your family. Copies should also be given to other doctors and hospitals, and attached to your medical record.

Some people carry miniature copies of their living wills with them. In Minnesota, you can note on your driver's license that you have a living will. (Whether emergency workers will find these declarations is another question.) The Patient Self Determination Act requires that if you're in the hospital, your living will must be included in your record.

Choice in Dying maintains a registry of living wills and health care proxies, to which you may subscribe. Louisiana has set up a registry, but it is unpublicized and doctors are not required to consult it. Creation of other registries may be anticipated; one entrepreneur has obtained a patent on a living will data bank.

Who should have copies?

For starters, your family and your doctor. If your doctor is not someone you trust to carry out your wishes even with a copy of your living will, then you should consider changing your doctor. It is important that you agree on appropriate measures.

In some states, the living will must be made a part of your medical records, but *you* have to inform your doctor. This is the rule in Alabama. If you go into a health care facility, the Patient Self Determination Act requires that you be asked if you have advance directives. If you do, they must be made a part of your permanent medical record.

How do I make sure a living will is current?

Under most state laws, a living will is current if it has not been revoked and no other action is required. There are exceptions; California's Natural Death Act requires that a living will be re-executed every five years. If you want to make sure that everyone is assured of your intentions, you could reinitial your signed living will and date it on a periodic basis, perhaps yearly.

Can my living will be revoked? How do I revoke it?

Yes. Generally, you can just destroy the old document and execute a new one. You must signify your intent to revoke it, and you should inform anyone who has a copy.

HEALTH CARE PROXIES

What happens if you're incapacitated and your living will doesn't cover the situation? If doctors are unaware of patient's wishes, they can be more or less aggressive than the patient would want.

With a *power of attorney for health care*, you can designate a friend or relative to take responsibility for treatment decisions. Unlike a living will, which is often limited to termination of life support, a power of attorney or *health care proxy* covers a broad spectrum of nonterminal medical situations.

Statutory authority for health care decisions is a relatively recent phenomenon, but each of the states recognizes some kind of health care power of attorney. The Supreme Court in *Cruzan* also suggested that a chosen surrogate would have the same power to refuse treatment as the patient.

Theoretically, the living will is for those with terminal illnesses or long-term persistent mental incapacity from which recovery is not expected. The health care proxy can be used for any incapacity, however temporary. Because health care proxies are governed by state law, requirements as to form and execution vary from state to state.

- *Living will statute.* One kind of health care proxy is part of some states' living will statutes, and is generally subject to the same requirements as the living will. These statutes generally provide for a combined form of living will-health care proxy. States with such statutes include Arkansas, Delaware, Idaho, Minnesota, Maine, Virginia, and Wyoming.
- *Durable power of attorney statute.* Some states include health-care decision-making in a larger durable power of attorney statute. These states include Alaska and Pennsylvania.
- *Durable power of attorney for health care statute.* Another kind of health care proxy is authorized by a separate statute, usually one enabling a durable power of attorney for health care. These are found in California, Florida, Indiana, Kansas, Kentucky, Michigan, Mississippi, Missouri, Nevada, New Hampshire, South Carolina, North and South Dakota, Ohio, Oregon, Rhode Island, Tennessee, Texas, Vermont, West Virginia, Wisconsin, Wyoming, and the District of Columbia.

- *Health care proxy statute.* Massachusetts and New York have statutes specifically authorizing a health care proxy.

What is the difference between a health care proxy and a power of attorney for health care?

There is no difference. The statutes differ in terminology, so that what is called a "health care proxy" in one state is called a "power of attorney for health care" in another. When we talk about a health care proxy or a power of attorney for health care, we are talking about the same thing.

I have power of attorney over my spouse's financial affairs. Does this cover health care decisions as well?

The answer, in most states, is no. Don't confuse a power of attorney for health care with the power of attorney used in financial affairs. (Alaska and Pennsylvania are exceptions, in that they have a durable power of attorney statute that does extend to health care decision-making.) The financial power of attorney is explained in Chapter 11.

When does a health care proxy becomes effective?

A health care power of attorney, like a living will, is used when the declarant is incapable of making and communicating decisions. If you are capable of making and communicating your own decisions, there is no need for your proxy to be invoked.

 APPOINTING A HEALTH CARE AGENT

One additional element not present in the living will is the appointment of a person to make decisions for you. This person is usually called the *health care agent.* You are the *principal*; your *agent* is authorized to act on your behalf.

Theoretically, designating a health care agent may be more useful than preparing a living will, because a person rather than a document will be advocating on your behalf. Remember, too, that when you make out your living will you are unable to anticipate every situation that might develop. The health care agent can interpret and apply your wishes as the situation warrants.

Appointment of an agent for health care purposes is regulated by state law. In certain circumstances, this may take on great importance. Some states give additional statutory authority to health care agents. In West Virginia and Wisconsin, for example, an agent may arrange for nursing home placement or home health care. A few states which include health care proxies in their living will statutes try to restrict the agent's authority to interpret the patient's living will. A number of states forbid the appointment of a patient's physician or other health care provider as a designated agent.

New York Health Care Proxy

(1) I, _____

hereby appoint _____
(name, home address and telephone number)

as my health care agent to make any and all health care decisions for me, except to the extent that I state otherwise. This proxy shall take effect when and if I become unable to make my own health care decisions.

(2) Optional instructions: I direct my proxy to make health care decisions in accord with my wishes and limitations as stated below, or as he or she otherwise knows. (Attach additional pages if necessary.)

_____

(Unless your agent knows your wishes about artificial nutrition and hydration [feeding tubes], your agent will not be allowed to make decisions about artificial nutrition and hydration. See instructions on reverse for samples of language you could use.)

(3) Name of substitute or fill-in proxy if the person I appoint above is unable, unwilling or unavailable to act as my health care agent.

_____
(name, home address and telephone number)

(4) Unless I revoke it, this proxy shall remain in effect indefinitely, or until the date or conditions stated below. This proxy shall expire (specific date or conditions, if desired):

_____

(5) Signature _____

Address _____

Date _____

Statement by Witnesses (must be 18 or older)

I declare that the person who signed this document is personally known to me and appears to be of sound mind and acting of his or her own free will. He or she signed (or asked another to sign for him or her) this document in my presence.

Witness 1 _____

Address _____

Witness 2 _____

Address _____

Withdrawal of life-sustaining treatment is also an issue for health care agents. The right of an agent to authorize withholding or withdrawing artificial nutrition and hydration is recognized in more than half the states. However, many states require specificity in granting this authority. In Florida, the Life Prolonging Procedure Act, which sets forth comprehensive rights in advance directives, authorizes both a living will with a proxy and a separate health care proxy (called *health care surrogate*). However, the surrogate may order withdrawal only if that power is authorized in a living will. Under New York law, an agent may exercise authority over nutrition and hydration only if the agent knows the wishes of the principal in this regard. To provide evidence that this standard has been met, the health care proxy should include language that the principal has discussed his or her wishes in regard to nutrition and hydration with the agent. (See New York's health care proxy form above.)

Who should I appoint as my health care proxy?

Someone you trust to carry out your wishes. And make sure you've asked the person you intend to name. A person can't be compelled to act as your agent—he or she must voluntarily accept the responsibility. More to the point, only someone you've discussed your wishes with can know how to act as your agent. If you don't have someone you trust for these kinds of intimate and painful decisions, don't appoint anyone.

Is it all right to designate more than one person as my agent or my alternate?

The question of how many agents should be named entails both legal and practical considerations. Legally, some states in fact allow only one agent. Usually, an alternate, not a co-agent, may be designated.

This makes sense from a practical point of view as well. You are only asking for trouble if you leave your health care up to a committee. You can ask your proxy to consult with people, and you can specify that consultation in your proxy instrument. But the best method is to choose one person. Pick one and one only. Pick one and only one as an alternate. Don't be misled by thinking it's "only fair" to designate your two children or your three sisters as co-agents. If they argue, you will suffer.

Should I execute both a living will and a health care proxy?

Yes, if possible. There are potential problems if the power of attorney for health care conflicts with the living will, and they must be reconciled or chosen one over the other. Connecticut, for example, provides that the power of an agent must be in accordance with the living will. Contrast Florida, where to authorize withdrawal of life-sustaining treatment, you need express authority in the living will. The rules for resolving conflicts can be similarly varied. A number of states, including Arizona, Rhode Island, South Dakota, Texas, and Vermont, provide that the document signed more recently controls. Choice in Dying recommends you use the health care proxy only in Wisconsin.

An agent must follow your wishes, and is your best defense against unsympathetic medical personnel, with or without a living will. But an agent may die, become disabled, or refuse to act. And not everyone has someone to appoint. In that case, we say don't appoint anyone, but do execute a living will to make sure there is some memorial of your wishes.

 PROXY FORMALITIES

State requirements regarding the validity of a document differ in substance and procedure. Usually they require two witnesses or notarization, or both. A statutory form may also be prescribed. For example, Rhode Island requires the specific statutory form and prohibits the use of all others.

There may also be restrictions on who can be a witness. A number of states provide that the witness may not be a health care provider or facility, an heir or a person responsible for health care costs.

Is the health care proxy valid state to state?

Portability is limited. States are not obliged to recognize a health care power of attorney from another state. A few states—New York, Kansas, Texas, Utah, and West Virginia—grant statutory recognition to health care powers of attorney from other jurisdictions. This shouldn't deter you from executing a power of attorney for health care in full confidence. Remember that your designated agent may be highly persuasive in expressing your wishes even if his or her status as proxy is not officially sanctioned.

If you move to a new residence or buy a vacation home in another state, you should review the validity of your health care health care power of attorney or proxy in your new state and execute a new one, if needed, in accordance with the requirements of that state. If you want to execute separate proxy documents for different states, designating the same person as your agent in both documents will avoid conflict later on. If it doesn't make sense to designate a person in a far-off state, make sure each document clearly indicates who is your agent in that jurisdiction.

Where should I keep it?

Keep the original in an accessible place, and give copies to your primary doctor and close members of your family. Copies should also be given to other doctors and hospitals, and attached to your medical record. Remember, federal law provides that you be asked whether you have one, and that your health care proxy be made part of your permanent record when you enter the hospital.

Who should have copies?

Don't forget to give a copy to the person who is named as your decision maker. And the alternate.

How do I make sure it's current?

In most states, a health care proxy will remain in effect indefinitely, unless you revoke it. A few states limit its effectiveness to a fixed period of time. For example, a proxy in Ohio remains in effect for seven years (unless you're incapacitated at that time, in which case it will remain in effect until you regain capacity). Also, a divorce or separation may operate to suspend or revoke a proxy designation of a spouse. This rule applies in a number of states, including California, Florida, Massachusetts, and Michigan.

Updating your health care proxy is not required, and no other action is required. If you want to make sure everyone is assured of your intentions, you can reinitial your signed proxy and date it on a periodic basis.

Can it be revoked?

Yes. To revoke your health care proxy, or to designate a new health care agent, you can destroy the old document and execute a new one, signifying repeal of all prior documents.

You don't actually have to rip up the old document. But you must signify your intent to revoke it, and you must notify both the agent and any other family members, lawyer, or doctors who have copies of the original document. Some states provide that the signing of a new proxy revokes the old one automatically, and this seems to be the logical meaning of the new proxy.

 SURROGATE AND FAMILY CONSENT

What happens when there is no living will, no health care proxy, and no evidence of the patient's wishes? In some states, another form of surrogate decision-making is established by laws setting forth a hierarchy of relatives to make medical decisions for an incompetent person, in the absence of instructions to the contrary.

This type of surrogacy is commonly used for limited consent in emergency rooms across the country and other instances of mental incapacity. It's invoked when

- The patient is not competent
- There is no guardian, or none available
- There is no health care agent designated pursuant to a health care proxy

Someone must decide. Under a doctrine of "substituted judgment," courts have long recognized the common principle that consent must be obtained from someone, except in cases of emergency. Who is that someone? Usually a family member or relative. Where there is no applicable state law or regulation, institutional policy also may spell out who may give consent by next-of-kin. As with your health care agent, the choice of surrogate is important. The difference is that in a surrogate situation, the choice is made for you, and generally with no flexibility or discretion at all.

Approximately half the states have statutes that specify who can make these decisions for you. The statutory priority is usually: (1) guardian, (2) spouse, (3) adult children, (4) parents, and (5) adult siblings. As a general rule, only one person's consent is needed. Some statutes require unanimous consent from all those within the same category (for example, adult children).

Some states add other people to the statutory list. New York's statute, for example, adds "close friend" to the list of possible surrogates, as do Arizona, Colorado, Florida, Illinois, and Maryland. Idaho allows consent by an attending physician if no one else is available. West Virginia authorizes public agencies or public guardians as the choice of last resort.

Surrogate and family consent laws provide a last resort, relying on categories of kinship which may be irrelevant to many people's lives. For this reason alone, you want a proxy you've chosen yourself. Remember, children have no choice in who makes decisions on their behalf. If you want to ensure that you do have a choice, the solution is to execute a health care proxy, in which you name your own decision-maker.

Is there any difference, from a relative's or other surrogate's point of view, between consenting to treatment and refusing treatment?

Legally, no. From a practical viewpoint, however, refusing recommended treatment is more difficult. The authority of next-of-kin to *consent* to medical treatment recommended by physicians almost always goes unquestioned. In cases where consent is refused, physicians and hospitals are more likely to go to court.

In some states, surrogate authority is circumscribed by statute. For example, New York's statute allows surrogate consent for DNR orders only. West Virginia's statute applies only to nursing home and home care decisions.

What if I'm estranged from my family or have different views from them?

You don't want to rely on surrogate and family consent laws if you can't rely on your family. What you do want is a health care power of attorney, which in most states takes precedence over any statutory hierarchy (except yourself or your guardian). In Maine, even if you don't have a person to appoint as a health care proxy, the law provides that you may designate that a particular person *not* serve as a decision-maker for you.

What about incompetent adults with no statutory surrogate decision-making help?

A court order is usually required before medical treatment can be ordered for incompetent adults without guardians or family members to give consent. In New York, the Surrogate Decision-Making Committee program empowers volunteer members of decision-making committees, or panels, to make these decisions in accordance with the best interests of the patient. The committees are composed of health care practitioners, lawyers, relatives of mentally disabled persons, and mental health advocates.

ORGAN AND TISSUE DONATION

Under laws in effect in every state, a person 18 years or older can donate any or all parts of his or her body for the advancement of medical or dental science, medical or dental research or education, or therapy or transplantation for an individual.

Every state has some version of the Uniform Anatomical Gift Act (a model act), authorizing organ and tissue donation and providing the process for ensuring consent by the donor or by the family. Laws generally limit the authorized recipients to: a hospital; a doctor or surgeon; an organization for transplantation; an accredited medical or dental school, college or university; or an individual for needed therapy or transplantation.

A declaration of intent to donate can be included in your will or set forth on a donor card, available from organ donor programs (listed in the Resources section of this book). Like a will, a donor card requires that your signature be witnessed by two people. You can make a general donation or specify recipients, impose limitations on how organs may be used, or make other conditions as you may wish to impose. A donor card carried on your person is potentially more useful, because it is more likely to be discovered in the event of sudden illness or accident.

Donation cannot take place until a person is declared legally dead by a doctor, which is generally based on a medical standard of "brain death." Note that people in a persistent vegetative coma, whether they are on artificial feeding or not, are *not* considered dead. Organ or tissue donation is not considered unless a person's death is imminent and the condition irreversible. Donors are screened for medical suitability and no one is required to accept organs.

In addition to the well-known procedures involving solid organs such as the heart, liver, kidney, pancreas, and lungs, transplantation of other body parts such as heart valves, skin, corneas, tendons, bones, and cartilage can also help people hurt by illness or accident. Despite the benefits, organ donation has been resisted by the vast majority of Americans young and old. Whether out of fear, misunderstanding, or ambivalence, fewer than one out of five have signed donor cards. The liver transplant of Mickey Mantle prior to his death brought much-needed publicity to organ and tissue donation.

If I die without signing a donor card, can my family authorize that my organs be donated?

Yes. In the event a potential donor dies, the family will be asked whether they wish to donate organs. As with other forms of family consent, the order of priority of relatives who can consent is set forth in state statutes. As a practical matter, the family will be consulted regardless of whether you sign a card. It's advisable to make your intentions regarding organ donation known to your family.

If I sign a donor card, does that mean I won't have a burial?

No. After a part or parts of the body are removed, the remains are turned over the family for burial.

THE ASSISTED SUICIDE DEBATE

Your right to die does not mean the right to kill yourself, or to be assisted in your own hastened death. It is *not* the right to suicide, or to assisted suicide. It's important to repeat: *the right to die is the right to determine what treatment you will get and what treatment you may refuse when you are critically ill, in accordance with your wishes and your values.*

Whether your right to determine your treatment may extend to a "right" to assisted suicide is currently a matter of national debate. Dr. Jack Kevorkian, a retired Michigan pathologist, has become notorious in recent years for helping as many as 27 people kill themselves through the use of Rube Goldberg-style contraptions belching carbon monoxide fumes or dispensing lethal drugs. Dr. Kevorkian's crusade, which has earned him the nickname "Dr. Death," has contributed to raising questions about the laws and ethics of assisted suicide in this country.

First, let's define our terms.

- *Suicide.* The taking of one's life by one's own hand.
- *Assisted suicide.* In an assisted suicide, someone helps someone else to their death. Called physician-assisted suicide when it is a doctor who assists.
- *Euthanasia.* Literally, a "good death." The term is used to connote a person's active participation in someone else's death, upon request or on their own initiative. Also called *mercy killing.*

What do these terms have in common? They're all about dying. The differences among them lie in who makes the decision and who carries it out. With suicide, clearly the person taking action has made the decision to do so. But concerns arise with both assisted suicide and euthanasia, for which help is required—and for which the legal and ethical capacity of a suicidal person to request or consent to help is not so certain.

Advocates for physician-assisted suicide cite compelling reasons of humanity and basic principles of patient autonomy, which demand that patients afflicted with unending and unendurable pain and agony be allowed the lethal means to end their suffering. Dr. Timothy Quill, a respected internist from Rochester, New York, who provided a lethal dose of sleeping pills to a long-suffering leukemia patient, gained widespread sympathy after his experience was described in the *New England Journal of Medicine.* A grand jury failed to indict him and no disciplinary action was taken by the State Department of Health.

On the other side, physician-assisted suicide triggers the specter of doctors playing God, exercising too much power with too few safeguards. Opponents cite the "slippery slope" argument that if assisted suicide were legalized, it would have an immediate effect on the obligations felt toward the elderly, especially those of limited means, who might feel coerced to "choose" suicide to spare loved ones. Then there would be those who want to extend the "option" to people who aren't terminally ill, just chronically ill, such as those suffering from AIDS or Alzheimer's disease.

Is there a consensus in the United States? Thirty-two states have laws prohibiting assisted suicide, most carrying a criminal charge of manslaughter or its equivalent. Some dozen others criminalize assisted suicide through other laws, leaving a handful of states in which the law is unclear. According to a 1987 poll, 62 percent of Americans would support a law allowing doctors to end the life of a terminally ill patient in distress who asks to die.

In the fall of 1994, voters in Oregon became the first state in the United States to legalize assisted suicide, narrowly approving Ballot Measure 16, an aid-in-dying bill that would allow doctors to provide lethal doses of drugs under the following conditions:

- The patient has six months or less to live, as certified by two doctors.
- The patient makes his or her request on more than one occasion, with at least a 15-day interval, and follows it up with a written request. The written request must be witnessed by two people, one of whom is not a family member.
- The doctor does not perform the procedure. The patient takes his or her own life.

Court challenge has stayed implementation of Oregon's assisted suicide law. Similar proposals have been considered without success in Alabama, Oregon, California, Washington State, and the District of Columbia. In 1994, the New York State Task Force on Life and the Law, a state advisory panel (the same panel that proposed the health care proxy law that was later adopted) unanimously recommended keeping the state ban on physician-assisted suicide, citing the potential for widespread abuse.

If voters or legislators don't act, judges may. In March 1996, a federal appellate court overturned Washington State's ban on assisted suicide as a violation of liberty protections granted under the 14th Amendment of the federal Constitution. (This is the same constitutional provision cited by the court in the *Cruzan* case.) This stunning ruling, upholding an individual's right to decide "how and when to die," is applicable in states under that court's jurisdiction, including Alaska, Arizona, California, Hawaii, Idaho, Montana, Nevada, and Oregon, as well as Washington. The constitutionality of Oregon's assisted suicide law, struck down by the lower courts, will be decided by the same appeals court.

A similar challenge in New York was also successful in federal court, which ruled that the state's ban on physician-assisted suicide was unconstitutional because it didn't treat individuals equally. The court reasoned that terminally ill patients not on life support weren't granted the same protections that patients on life support were. To the court, prescribing drugs to hasten death was no different than honoring a patient's request to disconnect life-support systems.

These two decisions make it clear that eventually, the U.S. Supreme Court will have to decide the matter. In Florida, a challenge to that state's law on assisted suicide is currently before the courts. If these challenges are upheld, states may be able to regulate but not prohibit assisted suicide. A number of states will be closely watching the fate of Oregon's assisted suicide law.

What is the experience of the Netherlands, where euthanasia was made legal in 1993?

Under Dutch law, the request for euthanasia must be made entirely of the patient's free will; the law requires patients to be experiencing unbearable suffering and have a lasting longing for death. The patient's doctor must consult with a second doctor who has dealt with euthanasia before.

Even before the law was passed, euthanasia in the Netherlands was tolerated by prosecutors and doctors. Yet studies reported that despite regulation, more than 1,000 people (many mentally incompetent) were killed in a year without consent. This was termed "nonvoluntary euthanasia."

The Dutch experience has received intense scrutiny in the Netherlands and around the world. The Royal Dutch Medical Association, attempting to deal with continuing concerns, issued guidelines in 1995 recommending that, wherever possible, doctors should preferably have terminally ill patients administer the fatal drug to themselves.

What is the legal status of suicide in the United States?

Suicide is no longer a crime anywhere in the United States. Suicide is a real problem among the elderly, and increasing among them at alarming rates. White men have the highest rate of suicide, although the latest studies show the sharpest rate of increase among black men.

What are the consequences to a physician or other person who "assists" a person in a suicide?

Potentially severe. On the criminal side, and depending on the circumstances, he or she could be charged with manslaughter, murder, or a variant in more than half of the states. Despite publicized cases like those of Dr. Kevorkian and Dr. Quill, a number of people have been convicted and jailed for helping loved ones. Doctors could also face discipline by state licensing or professional boards, as well as action for malpractice.

On the civil side, there may be other consequences. For example, the law's prohibition on a person's profiting from wrongdoing may operate to disinherit an heir who aids a suicide. In one Pennsylvania case, a woman who aided her sister in suicide was barred from inheriting from her sister's estate.

ENFORCING YOUR RIGHTS

Plan ahead. We can't say this often enough. If you utilize the techniques we've discussed in this chapter—living wills and health care proxies—you'll be able to avoid most of the problems encountered in trying to assert your rights against an uncooperative medical establishment. As the New York State Court of Appeals said, the "ideal situation" to establish a patient's intentions in declining medical assistance would be for his or her wishes to be expressed in some form of writing such as a living will while he or she was still competent.

This is still an evolving area of law, however, and even with advance planning, you may need outside assistance. There are a number of groups that can advise you on your rights and how to pursue them. We've mentioned Choice in Dying, which will act as a resource and refer you to others. Other organizations that may be of help are listed in the Resources section at the end of this book.

If none of these measures is successful, get a lawyer. While a legal fight may not be what you want, unfortunately it may be necessary. It is still common to see medical practitioners resisting alternatives to aggressive treatment, such as pain relief at home, for end-of-life patients, even in the face of written instructions to the contrary. The mere hiring of a lawyer will often get doctors and hospitals to take notice of your demands and comply with them. There are any number of lawyers who specialize in this area. There are agencies that can advise you and make referrals to local lawyers. Choice in Dying, local bar associations, and senior citizens' organizations may also refer you to legal help.

11

##

PROPERTY MANAGEMENT
SYSTEMS

We've seen how critical a power of attorney can be for health care decisions—designating someone to speak on your behalf in the event that you're unable to do so yourself. By planning ahead and choosing the person best able to act in your interest, you arm yourself against the well-intentioned meddling of others—medical professionals, family members—who might act counter to what you perceive your interest to be.

The same holds true in managing your finances—your property, your assets, your income. And the same type of instrument, the *power of attorney*, is as valuable to ensure your future control over these important areas of your life.

The power of attorney is the single most important document you can use to protect your interests. It's absolutely critical for your future independence in the event of illness or incapacity. Without it, you risk having your affairs being managed by a stranger, under court supervision, and without any input from you. You will lose control.

The power of attorney, along with the living will and the health care proxy, are the cornerstones of your plan to ensure that your wishes will be respected even if you are not able to act for yourself.

POWER OF ATTORNEY

What does it mean when you give someone power of attorney? It means that you've designated someone to act in your place and on your behalf, under certain circumstances. A power of attorney is a written document whereby you appoint someone to manage your financial affairs in the event you are ill or incapacitated and cannot act for yourself.

In a power of attorney, the person executing the power of attorney (called the *principal*) names another (the *attorney-in-fact*, *proxy*, or *agent*), who then can manage the principals's financial affairs. This can be your spouse or a child, or anyone you want. (The term power of attorney is something of a misnomer: the person named does not have to be an attorney nor is he or she required to do any specifically law-related transactions.)

With a power of attorney, the person you designate can pay your bills, make banking transactions on your accounts, even bring a lawsuit—all in your name. Generally the power of attorney spells out in detail the specific powers the agent will have.

As with many legal documents, the requirements for a power of attorney vary from state to state. Powers of attorney are governed by state law, which spells out the process required for executing a valid power of attorney, the powers which may be granted under one, and other provisions concerning validity and duration of a power of attorney.

DURABLE POWER OF ATTORNEY

Traditionally, a power of attorney was perceived as a limited tool, useful for delegating authority to someone traveling to another town to transact business on your behalf. It did not survive the death or disability of the principal, thereby making it useless for future planning purposes.

Thus, the *durable power of attorney* evolved, so called because it survives the principal's incapacity. This is doubly important because the use of the durable power of attorney is most important as an easily used and inexpensive alternative to the appointment of a guardian or conservator. (These are discussed in the next chapter).

The durable power of attorney is now recognized in all 50 states and the District of Columbia. In order to achieve the level of "durable," it must contain words to the effect that

> This power of attorney shall not be affected by subsequent disability or incapacity of the principal.

The specific requirements for the wording differ from state to state. In a few states, such as Louisiana and Georgia, the power of attorney is automatically durable unless the written document provides otherwise.

SPRINGING POWER OF ATTORNEY

As a rule, a power of attorney takes effect immediately. This presents a problem for someone who doesn't want to grant broad powers to someone else who could act now, yet still wishes to provide for the management of his or her financial affairs should it be necessary in the event of a future disability.

The solution is the *springing power of attorney*. The springing power of attorney is a delegation of power which can be exercised only at some specified time in the future or upon the occurrence of a specified event, such as incapacity. Thus the power can be made effective only when it is needed—and only for the duration of the need.

Under the Uniform Probate Code (a model law which states can adopt), for a springing power of attorney to be effective, it must contain language expressly providing that "this power shall become effective upon the disability or incapacity of the principal."

Not all states allow a springing power of attorney. Connecticut and South Carolina do not. The springing power of attorney is authorized by statute in Alabama, California, Delaware, Idaho, Illinois, Kansas, Massachusetts, Michigan, Montana, Nebraska, Nevada, New Jersey, New York, North Carolina, Ohio, Oklahoma, Tennessee, Utah, Vermont, Virginia, Washington, and Wisconsin. It is presumably sanctioned in states whose laws do not mention it, such as Florida, Georgia, Maryland, Texas, and West Virginia, although a local attorney's advice should be obtained in those states.

One difficulty that occurs in utilizing the springing power of attorney is the determination of the triggering event. How is it determined, and by whom? This is the subject of much debate among lawyers, without any clear-cut answers. But there are some clear guidelines.

- The disability should be clearly defined. (New Jersey's statute in fact defines disability in the law itself.)
- The determining agent or event should be named. For example, a judicial determination or a declaration by two doctors.

As a corollary, it is generally not a good idea to have a determining agent be the same as the agent named as your attorney-in-fact in the instrument.

Remember the great advantage of this technique is that if you don't wish to grant broad powers over your property to another *at the present time*, you don't have to. The springing power of attorney becomes effective when and only when it is needed, upon disability.

APPOINTING AN AGENT

One of the rules of a power of attorney is that you should give it only to a person you trust. Most powers of attorney are not springing, but effective immediately upon signing. Yet even with a person they trust completely, many people are still justifiably wary of about giving someone immediate power to manage their affairs. Obviously, there's a risk of abuse, so it's important that you appoint only someone you trust implicitly.

Be sure that you appoint someone who will be willing to do the job, and who lives in your geographic vicinity—so he or she can do it. Nieces and nephews in distant cities may love you dearly, but not want the burden of being a long-distant agent.

Of equal importance to *who* you name as your agent is *what* powers you give to your agent. Some states have statutory forms of powers of attorney that enumerate the powers that may be granted an agent and define the extent of those powers, while others limit the power in specific circumstances.

A power of attorney may include the rights to

- Deal with real property
- Make gifts
- Purchase, transfer, sell life insurance
- Handle banking and securities transactions
- Collect and forgive debts
- Disclaim trusts and inheritances
- Deal with retirement plans
- Deal with taxes
- Create and amend trusts
- Make charitable contributions

Depending on the state, it may be necessary for you to expressly include some powers or your agent will not have them. In New York, for example, the power to make gifts, important to tax and Medicaid planning, must be expressly included. Similarly, in states such as Illinois and Mississippi, you must give express authority to amend or revoke a trust.

Is it all right to designate more than one person as my agent?

Opinion differ. If you're unsure about the trustworthiness or ability of your designee, designating to people who must act together may be a good idea. They could act as a check on each other. This is not allowed in all states. And it may make the power of attorney ineffective as a practical matter. Another possibility is successive appointments, someone to replace your first choice as agent if he or she fails to act.

Are there any powers an agent can't have?

An agent cannot change your will, make a will on your behalf, or revoke your will. Some states, notably Florida and Georgia, do not allow an agent to delegate his or her authority under the power of attorney to another person.

What is the effect of a guardianship on a durable power of attorney?

In most jurisdictions, the agent becomes accountable to the guardian. In a few states, such as Connecticut and South Carolina, the appointment of a guardian terminates the power of attorney. In others, the court has the power to revoke the power of attorney. States which allow continuation of the power of attorney differ on whether the guardian has the power to revoke a power of attorney.

What kind of document should I draft?

Although it comes in a number of formats, the power of attorney is basically simple; in most states a standard form is available in most legal

DURABLE POWER OF ATTORNEY

KNOW ALL MEN BY THESE PRESENTS, that I, _____, residing at _____, appoint hereby _____ _____, residing at _____, as my true and lawful attorney-in-fact, to act, manage and conduct all my affairs for me and in my name, place and stead, and for my use and benefit as my act and deed, and for that purpose I give and grant unto my said attorney full power and authority to do and perform all and every act, deed, matter and thing whatsoever regarding my property and affairs as fully and effectually to all intents and purposes as I might or could do myself if personally present, the following specially enumerated powers being examples of the full, complete and general powers granted herein, and not in limitation or definition thereof:

1. To buy, receive, lease, accept or otherwise acquire; to sell, convey, mortgage, hypothecate, pledge, quit claim or otherwise encumber or dispose of, or to contract or agree for the acquisition, disposal or encumbrance of, any property whatsoever and wheresoever located, be it real, personal or mixed, or any interest or right therein or pertaining thereto, upon such terms as my attorney shall think proper;

2. To take, hold, possess, invest, lease or otherwise manage any or all of my real, personal or mixed property, or any interest therein or pertaining thereto, to eject, remove or relieve tenants or other persons from, and to maintain, protect, preserve, insure, remove, store, transport, repair, rebuild, modify or improve the same or any part thereof;

3. To make, do and transact all and every kind of business of whatever kind or nature, including the receipt, recovery, collection, payment, compromise, settlement and adjustment of all accounts, legacies, bequests, interests, dividends, annuities, rents, claims, demands, debts, taxes and obligations, which may now or hereafter be due, owing or payable by me or to me;

4. To make, endorse, accept, receive, sign, seal, execute, acknowledge and deliver deeds, bills of sale, mortgages, assignments, agreements, contracts, certificates, hypothecations, checks, notes, bonds, vouchers, receipts, releases, documents relating to life or other insurance policies and such other instruments in writing of whatever kind and nature, as may be necessary, convenient or proper in the premises;

5. To make deposits or investments in, or withdrawals from, any account, holding or interest which I may now or hereafter have, or be entitled to, in any banking, trust or, financial investment institution, including postal savings depository offices, credit unions, savings and loan associations and similar institutions, to exercise any right, option or privilege pertaining thereto, and to open or establish accounts, holdings or interests of whatever kind or nature, with any such institution, in my name or in my said attorney's name, or in our names jointly, either with or without right of survivorship;

6. To institute, prosecute, defend, compromise, arbitrate and dispose of legal, equitable or administrative hearings, actions, suits, attachments, arrests, distresses or other proceedings, or otherwise engage in litigation in connection with the premises;

7. To act as my attorneys or proxies in respect to any stocks, shares, bonds or other investments, rights or interests, I may now or hereafter hold;

8 To engage and dismiss agents, counsel and employees, and to appoint and remove at pleasure any substitute for, or agent of, my said attorneys, in respect

to all or any of the matters or things herein mentioned, and upon such terms as my attorneys shall think fit;

9. To prepare, execute and file gift, income and other tax returns, claims for refund covering all or a portion of any taxes paid and other governmental reports, declarations, applications, requests and documents;

10. To appear for me and represent me before the Treasury Department, or any state taxing agency in connection with any matter involving federal or state gift, income or other taxes for any year to which I am a party, giving my said attorneys full power to do everything whatsoever requisite and necessary to be done in the premises, to receive refund checks, to execute waivers of the statute of limitations and to execute closing agreements as fully as the undersigned might do if personally present, giving my said attorneys authority to appoint attorneys to represent my said attorneys in connection therewith with full power of substitution and revocation at any time; and

11. To enter any safe deposit box or other place of safe keeping or deposit which I may now or hereafter occupy or possess;

12. To disclaim or renounce any property interest pursuant to the Internal Revenue Code of 1986, Section 2518 or any similar provision of any successor law.

13. To waive benefits and/or elect out of survivor annuity payment(s) under Section 417 of the Internal Revenue Code of 1986, or any similar provision of any successor law, and the regulations promulgated thereunder.

I hereby appoint my _____, _____, to serve as successor attorney-in-fact, TO ACT, in the event that _____shall be unable or unwilling to serve or to continue to serve as my attorney-in-fact, in which case _____shall be fully authorized to serve hereunder and shall have all of the powers granted originally to _____.

My successor, _____, shall execute an affidavit that _____ is unable or unwilling to serve or to continue to serve, after the occurrence of such event, and such affidavit shall be conclusive evidence insofar as third parties are concerned of the facts set forth therein. Any person acting in reliance upon such affidavit shall incur no liability to my estate because of such reliance.

Notwithstanding any other provision of this instrument, this power of attorney shall not be revoked by my disability through physical or mental incompetence, and any acts done by my attorney or successor pursuant to this power during any such period of disability or incompetence shall have the same effect and be as binding upon me and my heirs, devisees and personal representatives as if I were competent and not disabled.

I hereby ratify all that my said attorney shall lawfully do or cause to be done by virtue of this power of attorney.

I hereby declare that any act or thing lawfully done hereunder by my said attorney shall be binding on me, and my heirs, legal and personal representatives and assigns. To induce any third party to act hereunder, I hereby agree that any third party receiving a duly executed copy or facsimile of this instrument may act hereunder, and that revocation or termination hereof shall be ineffective also to such third party unless and until actual notice or knowledge of such revocation or termination shall have been received by such third party, and I for myself and for my heirs, executors, legal representatives and assigns, hereby agree to indemnify and hold harmless any such third party from and against any and all claims that may arise against such third party by reason of such third party having relied on the provisions of this instrument.

I certify that the following signature is the signature of my attorney-in-fact,
_____.

_____

_____

    IN WITNESS WHEREOF, I have hereunto set my hand and seal
on   , 199 .

_____

Signed in the presence of:

_____   Address _____

_____   Address _____

_____   Address _____

                                        _____

STATE OF   )
                      :   ss. :
COUNTY OF   )

    On   , 199 , before me personally came   , to me known,
and known to me to be the individual described in and who, by his mark, executed
the foregoing instrument, and duly acknowledged to me that he executed the
same.

                    _____
                                Notary Public

stationery stores and many large general stationery stores. Be sure to follow
the instructions on the form. You can also have your lawyer draw up a
durable power of attorney, tailored to your situation and your needs, which
is what we recommend. We've included a generic form (see pages
146–148), which you can use as an interim measure, but it's preferable to
get one authorized specifically for your state.

    A number of powers may or may not appear on the form commonly used
in your state. Most states with statutory short forms allow modifications.

Among them are Alaska, California, Connecticut, Minnesota, New Mexico, New York, and North Carolina.

Is the power of attorney valid state to state? Should separate documents be prepared?

There is something called *reciprocal recognition*, in which a limited number of states recognize powers of attorney validly executed in other states, according to the laws of that state. However, even then the power may be restricted, especially when dealing with real estate. If you spend a considerable amount of time in another state, it would be wise to have a dual set of documents.

 ## LEGAL CAPACITY AND FORMALITIES

Any document, whether a will or a trust or a power of attorney, is valid only if it is executed by a person with *legal capacity*. A person with legal capacity is one who has the ability to understand the nature and significance of what he or she is doing.

Only a sufficiently competent person possessing the requisite capacity may execute a valid document such as a power of attorney. Does this mean the technique is not available for those severely incapacitated by dementia or other disorder? Generally yes, although an individual who is lucid at intervals may be legally competent to sign a power of attorney during one of those times. In such a case, however, documentation by doctors of the individual's capacity is imperative.

State laws vary on execution requirements, and most are silent as to who must witness a power of attorney, and whether it should be notarized or recorded. In some states, the power of attorney must be witnessed, in some notarized, and in some, both. In a few states, the notarization must be in a special form known as "acknowledgement." Fewer than a dozen states contain specific execution requirements.

Real estate creates special problems in making sure your power of attorney is effective. Often, more formalities in the execution of the durable power of attorney are required to ensure that the agent will in fact have the power to convey or dispose of real estate. In the case of real property, the law of the site of the property controls real estate transactions.

Under the law of some states, a description of the real estate must be in the power of attorney. Others require witnesses (Connecticut and Florida require two) in addition to notarization, recording of the power of attorney as a deed, or execution like a will.

Where do I keep my power of attorney?

One solution is to sign a power of attorney but keep it under your control. However, if you trust a person enough to name him or her as attorney-in-fact, you should trust that person enough to give a copy or tell where it is. If you don't, then that person shouldn't be named. Remember, too, if you've signed a springing power of attorney, it only becomes effective when and only when it is needed, upon disability.

How do I make sure it's current?

Can a power of attorney become stale? Theoretically, it's a legal document, valid on its face, with no time limit. The Uniform Probate Code provides that a power of attorney is not effected by a lapse of time since execution, and remains effective unless it states a time of termination. We know one man whose wife recently tried to use the power of attorney he left with her when he went overseas to fight in the Korean War.

The whole point of the durable power of attorney is that it can be used at an unspecified time in the future, with luck the distant future, without resistance.

The real problem is that although the document may be valid, your agent may have a difficult time using it. Banks, investment firms, and other financial institutions are uncomfortable in the first place with powers of attorney, and often seek to limit their effectiveness through arbitrary policies. An arbitrary rule of one year is a common practice (that is, the power of attorney is accepted only within one year of its signing).

One possible solution is to update it regularly, just changing the date and signature or simply re-initialing it on a yearly basis. Remember, a current document should comply with full notarization and other formal execution requirements of your state.

 DEALING WITH BANKS

A common problem with a power of attorney is getting other parties to acknowledge it. Often banks and other institutions are wary of recognizing the authority in a power of attorney. Or they require their own form, displaying misplaced confidence in their own lawyers' ability to protect them from harm. This can be a serious problem when the maker of a power of attorney is no longer well enough to sign the bank's form.

Some states have incentives to encourage reliance. New York's statute requires banks and the state pension fund to accept the statutory short form power of attorney. In other states, such as Alaska and Minnesota, parties who refuse to honor powers of attorney may be held liable.

You can always contact your bank and any other financial institution with which you have an account and ask what forms and procedures they require. And don't assume their forms will fulfill your needs. Make sure they have the necessary *durability* language.

REVOKING A POWER OF ATTORNEY

In theory, you can revoke a power of attorney merely by tearing up the document and conducting yourself in a manner inconsistent with the power. Theory, however, is not as reliable as verifiable communication. You want to make sure that institutions, such as banks and investment houses, that may have received your power of attorney receive notice of its termination.

To revoke your power of attorney and make sure your revocation is recognized, you should

- Clearly put the revocation in writing, expressly revoking the powers
- Send copies of the revocation to all parties who have received the original power of attorney, notifying them of the revocation (You should keep a record of the institutions to which you and your agent give copies)
- Execute the revocation with the same formalities, such as notarization or acknowledgment, as you did the original power of attorney

Send letters certified mail, return receipt requested. (Always send legal documents that way.) And always keep copies. In case there is any question, get a written acknowledgment that your revocation was received.

 TRUSTS

A trust works by establishing a fund to be administered under the direction of a trustee or trustees. The creator of the trust makes provision for distribution of the income, usually on a regular basis to the named beneficiary, and eventual disposition of the principal. Assets such as funds or other property are deposited into the trust. The trustee, or trustees, manages the property in accordance with the instructions set forth in the trust instrument.

A number of trust instruments have been developed for financial planning purposes. Today's trusts are designed for a multitude of reasons—tax avoidance on future estates, enabling Medicaid eligibility for those in need of long-term and custodial care, or securing benefits for a disabled child or adult. (See Chapter 8 on Medicaid, Chapter 12 on planning for a disabled child, and Chapter 14 on wills.)

This section describes basic trusts, and highlights points to consider if you are evaluating the value of a trust as part of your planning strategy.

A word of caution. Creating a trust requires the expertise of a lawyer. There are innumerable forms of trusts, and hybrids within each category. And in today's world, it requires the expertise of a lawyer versed not only in the traditional world of "trusts and estates," but also in government entitlements. The rules are changing as rapidly as you're reading this page.

Creating the trust. A trust is created by a *settler*, also called a *donor* or *creator*. As with a will, the person setting up a trust must have legal capacity to do so. For the trust to be funded, property must be transferred or deposited into the trust. The trust document or trust instrument establishing the trust does not automatically fund the trust.

Purpose. Trusts are commonly established for a purpose, and contain instructions to the trustees to enable them to carry out their duties.

The purpose of a trust must be carefully crafted. You want to be meaningful enough so the trustees understand your intent. At the same time, if the trust you are establishing is to accomplish a legal function for estate tax or Medicaid qualifying purposes, it must satisfy those other legal requirements as well.

Trustee or trustees. The trustee (or trustees) manages the trust property, administering, investing, and otherwise supervising all the assets of the trust, including cash, real estate, and any other property deposited into the trust.

In performing the job of trustee, the trustee has certain *fiduciary* responsibilities. He or she must undertake the task of managing the trust in accordance with the instructions set forth in the trust instrument. The trust instrument will also spell out the authority of the trustee to act.

Beneficiary. A trust must have a beneficiary, who will receive the income from the trust. In all states but New York, you or your spouse can be both trustee and beneficiary of a trust you have created. Upon a designated event, *e.g.,* the death of the income beneficiary, the principal then goes to a designated future beneficiary or beneficiaries (or *remaindermen*). These can be children, grandchildren, charity, or any person or institution you choose.

Instructions. The trust instrument must set forth a statement of purpose and instructions. It must also spell out the amount of discretion granted the trustee to distribute funds, invade principal, or otherwise act, as well as any restrictions on distribution of funds or their use.

THE ROLE OF TRUSTS

Trusts can serve a number of purposes. In Chapter 8, we described the use of trusts for Medicaid purposes, shielding assets that would otherwise result in ineligibility for benefits. As a general rule, those trusts which are revocable are vulnerable to being counted as available assets for the purpose of determining Medicaid eligibility, while those which are irrevocable are better shielded from being considered as assets. Some forms of trusts stipulate that income should be withheld if the result would be disqualification for government benefits.

Testamentary trusts, created by wills, are used to save considerable estate taxes. Instead of assets passing outright—and taxed—income can be used without incurring estate taxes. Testamentary trusts are also not subject to many of Medicaid's eligibility rules. (See Chapters 8 and 14.)

Living trusts, created by you to take effect during your lifetime, are used to create tax savings in a number of ways. For example, income tax savings may result if principal is sheltered and income directed to someone in a lower tax bracket.

Other types of trusts include:

- **Qualified terminable interest property (QTIP) trust,** used when it is anticipated that future care may be needed by a surviving spouse, who will be unable to manage the money or be in no position to do so. A "Q-tip" trust qualifies for the marital deduction. (See Chapter 15.)
- **Charitable trust,** which may qualify for estate tax charitable deduction. (See Chapter 15.)
- **Supplemental needs trust,** created for a disabled child or adult. This is a discretionary trust set up to supplement government benefits. (See Chapters 8 and 12.)

 JOINT ACCOUNTS

Many people hold bank accounts, real estate, and other forms of property with other people. A common form of joint property is property owned by two or more people, each with a survivor interest.

Joint ownership is extremely common with married persons. Property is also often held jointly with children and grandchildren.

Joint ownership has advantages and disadvantages. Children or grandchildren can easily withdraw funds and use them to pay bills on your behalf; by the same token, they could legally deplete hard-earned assets. There may also be unknown and unwanted gifted tax implications when property is placed in joint ownership. (See Chapter 14.)

Potential problems extend beyond financial ones. If a "convenience account" is set up for the purpose of enabling a child to use the money for the benefit of a parent, it may, when the parent dies, wind up as a windfall for one child to the unintended exclusion of others, engendering bitter family conflict.

Joint property is not a good idea when Medicaid planning may need to be considered. Joint accounts can play havoc with your eligibility even before the death of a spouse. All the money in a joint account will be treated as belonging to the person applying for Medicaid, unless it can be proven that the non-applying joint owner contributed to the account.

If you place property you own into joint ownership, you lose control. While in the case of a joint bank account you have the power to withdraw 100 percent of the account funds at any time (as does your co-owner), this is not true with other types of assets. If you place 100 shares of AT&T stock in the names of your son and yourself as joint owners, you will need your son's consent to get it back or to sell it. If it is sold, your son owns half the proceeds.

I have a bank account "in trust for" my granddaughter. Can she use the money in it to help me pay my bills?

Not unless she also has your power of attorney. Many people commonly put their funds "in trust for" their children or their grandchildren. This common form of ownership of bank and investment accounts places title and ownership in one person's hands, held in trust for another person or persons.

These kinds of accounts are called *Totten trusts*, named after the owner of a New York bank account at the turn of the century. They are not joint accounts. Until the account owner dies, the person named as beneficiary has no legal rights or interest in the property at all. Upon the owner's death, the money is passed directly to the named beneficiary. In that, it resembles a jointly owned account (described in Chapter 14). Totten trusts are sometimes referred to as "poor men's wills."

A Totten trust provides no estate tax savings. The full amount of the account is included in the account owner's estate.

DESIGNATING A REPRESENTATIVE PAYEE

If you wish, you can designate someone as a representative payee, for receiving Social Security or Supplemental Security Income (SSI) checks on your behalf. This a limited form of a power of attorney, but a very useful management tool for people who are not able to present checks themselves. (Programs offering money management services may also be available in your community. See the next chapter.)

12

■■■

PLANNING FOR THE
DISABLED CHILD

In an ideal world, all children would lead healthy lives, without risk of harm. Adequate support networks would provide medical, rehabilitative, and social services as needed.

If you are involved in planning for your disabled child or children, you face a series of special challenges. In addition to meeting your child's present needs, you must consider and plan for the long-term needs of a child who may need to have care for a lifetime—in many cases, long after your death. You need to look to the "how" and the "who" of providing such care.

Financing is a primary concern. Where will the money come from to pay for care? The source may be either your private funds or the government—most likely a combination of both. In addition, planning for a child with disabilities will involve you in decisions concerning future medical care and treatment, your child's place of residence, finances and daily management, and other services which may be available for your child's benefit.

 ## SERVICES AND ENTITLEMENTS

Unless your private funds are plentiful, your major concern is making sure your disabled child will be entitled to necessary government services, such as Supplemental Security Income (SSI) and other entitlements necessary to provide appropriate care.

Before going into the various options, you should understand a bit about the universe of government assistance. Assistance for the disabled has evolved from charity or basic welfare provisions into a range of social programs and benefits. (In retrospect, costs made this evolution inevitable; at the same time, the costs of these programs make them a continuing target for budget and service cuts.)

In addition to Social Security and SSI for the disabled, there are other programs and benefits, including housing, which you or your child may qualify for. For parents of children with disabilities, the social safety net is more secure by virtue of other available support. (See Chapter 18 and the Resources section at the end of this book.)

One caveat: as a general rule, parents are responsible for their children, unless they are institutionalized. In theory, sound public policy would support maintaining children with disabilities in the home and community. During the Reagan years, so-called "Katy Beckett" waivers were issued so that health care benefits could be granted where institutionalization would clearly be necessary. Nevertheless, Medicaid benefits are still easier to obtain for children who are institutionalized than for those who are kept at home.

SETTING UP A TRUST

Since money left for a disabled child must last a lifetime, most experts suggest creating a trust. A trust works by establishing a fund under the direction of a trustee or trustees. A basic trust instrument names a beneficiary, which in this case would be your child, and makes provision for

- Income to your child on a regular basis
- Use of the principal in appropriate cases for your child's benefit
- Eventual disposition of the principal

Income distribution may be subject to the discretion of the trustee. The trustee may also be given discretion to "invade" the principal, sometimes with guidance from the trust document.

The advantage of setting up a trust is that it is a mechanism that will provide continuing support for your child after you have died. At the same time, a trust avoids guardianship for the child and the uncertain outcome and possible delay occasioned by protective proceedings. And by setting it up, you can provide for continuity in the provision of income and principal distributions.

Supplemental needs trusts are commonly used to coordinate a financial plan for a disabled child with the child's receipt of public benefits. As benefits are often a function of need, measured in income and assets, the amount your child inherits, directly or through a trust, may cause a number of undesirable results, including reduced benefits, ineligibility, or being charged for benefits.

That's why the level of discretion a trustee has in invading the principal for use on behalf of the disabled child-beneficiary is important to the courts. The kind of trust you'd set up for a disabled child is akin to the "spendthrift trust" designed to protect wastrel heirs from squandering their family fortunes by limiting the moneys available to creditors.

In a landmark New York case, the court ruled that public assistance was a right, and the trustee could not be compelled to invade an otherwise uninvadable trust to pay for government benefits otherwise available to the beneficiary of the trust. As a general rule, the power given to the trustee must be extremely limited and totally discretionary in order to avoid takeover.

How will transfers under trusts interfere with my entitlement to any benefit programs?

Transferring assets to an individual child who is blind or permanently and totally disabled does not result in any ineligibility or penalty under Medicaid rules for the transferor. Transfers to a disabled child or to a trust established solely for the benefit of a disabled child, or to a trust for the benefit of a disabled individual under 65, are exempt. However, recent rulings by Medicaid severely limit the kinds of trusts that will be treated as "for the sole benefit" of the disabled child and thus considered exempt. Outright gifts to your child or trusts for his or her benefit that are not properly drawn will make the child ineligible for some government benefits.

What about a court settlement on behalf of a disabled child?

Court settlements are, happily or unhappily, not uncommon when dealing with the disabled of any age. Your lawyer should be able to structure the settlement so that it is paid into a trust and not directly to the beneficiary, thereby avoiding jeopardy to any government entitlements.

APPOINTING TRUSTEES

As with any other document designating someone to do your work for you, one of the most important questions is who to pick. The question of who to appoint is almost as difficult as the question of whether to appoint. Your first choice is generally an individual, if there is one who is competent and qualified and willing to do it. The question of whether to impose this burden on a sibling is not an easy one. Professionals can also act as trustees, including banks and trust companies.

Can't I just leave my money to a trusted friend or relative to care for my child?

You can try to create a so-called *constructive trust*, but relying on a close friend or a sibling of a disabled child to take care of the child is not a good idea. Any number of things could happen to derail your intentions, and it's not at all certain there would be anyone to speak up for your child's interests. Your relative could die, divorce, or go bankrupt, and the assets that you have set aside for your child could wind up as a windfall for somebody who knows and cares nothing about your arrangements for your child's future.

Wouldn't a guardianship work just as well?

Maybe. Guardianship covers personal care as well as financial, but may not be necessary. Unless a court is petitioned to have a legal guardian appointed, your child is competent in the eyes of the law at the age of majority. The drawbacks to guardianship include continuing supervision by the courts, added administration costs, and the loss of flexibility in providing for your child's care. Some courts have denied guardians the right to set up supplemental needs trusts on behalf of their wards. (Guardianship is discussed more fully in Chapter 13.)

 HOW A TRUST WORKS

A legal document creating a trust usually has a statement of objectives, which serves a number of purposes. Ideally, the trust should have flexibility, providing income and principal in the trustee's discretion. Distributions should not be made for any benefits available through a government program, unless the trustee believes the government services are inadequate or of poor quality. You may make specific provision for what the government will not pay for, such as state-of-the-art systems in communication and transportation and "quality-of-life" purchases. Certain distributions could result in a loss of some SSI benefits, a primary consideration in creating a trust for a child with disabilities.

There is a statutory exception for trusts containing the assets of a disabled individual under the age of 65, if the trust is established for the individual's benefit by a parent, grandparent, legal guardian, or the court. Upon the beneficiary's death, the remaining assets must be used to reimburse the state for Medicaid outlays. Any remaining assets would then pass to recipients designated by the trust.

Distinguish between support and discretionary trusts. The former may be available to the trust beneficiary and thus available to Medicaid or creditors. Assets placed in supplemental needs trusts, on the other hand, may be used to pay for "supplemental" needs of the disabled individual, such as non-medical living expenses (if living in the community) or extra care (if institutionalized). (See Chapter 8.)

Under recent Medicaid law, assets can also be placed in a *master trust* established by a not-for-profit corporation, which could then pay for a disabled person's supplemental needs such as a companion or other non-Medicaid-covered expense out of a separate trust account set up for that individual. Funds not expended during the beneficiary's lifetime could be left in the trust for the benefit of others after the individual's death.

In any event, living trusts are subject to scrutiny when the grantor applies for Medicaid. Remember that a testamentary trust is not a Medicaid disqualifying trust.

There are many categories of trusts, and hybrids within each category. Trust law is a field strewn with landmines for the innocent; only an experienced practitioner can determine which kind of trust is best for you. We don't recommend setting up a trust without a lawyer. This is a complex and rapidly changing area, requiring close attention to federal and state laws. You should consult an attorney who specializes in trusts and estates and elder law, preferably one with experience in government entitlements for the disabled.

What if my child's disability passes?

If recovery is possible, you should include it in your plans. A trust may include a termination clause, based on a functional assessment of the child's capabilities. It could be structured on a time-release basis, distributing the principal in yearly or other periodic increments to ensure that the disability is ended before the trust terminates.

▌ EDUCATION AND HOUSING

Other major rights of children with disabilities include the right to education, established by the Education for All Handicapped Children Act and its successor, the Individuals with Disabilities Education ACT (IDEA), which mandate free appropriate education for children with disabilities.

Under IDEA, your local school district must provide a free appropriate education for your disabled child, in accordance with an evaluation of your child's needs and an individualized education program (IEP) devised for expressly for him or her. Related services such as speech and language therapy, counseling, physical therapy, and various other supports may also be required. The law provides that each child be educated in the *least restrictive environment*, although many school districts oppose "inclusion" of children with disabilities as detrimental to children in both "general" and "special" educational programs.

If no appropriate public school setting is available, the school district must educate your child in a private school *at no cost to you*. If this includes residential placement (usually for only the most severely handicapped), the school district will pick up the cost. (The school district is not responsible for all private school costs for the child—only those in cases where it can't locate an appropriate public placement.)

Under federal regulations, you have the right to have an impartial hearing if you contest the evaluation, placement or services provided for your child. An impartial hearing officer can order modifications in the IEP or make other changes in services and placement. You also have the right to pursue further action in state or federal court. If you are having difficulty with the school district, we suggest contacting an advocacy group or private lawyer familiar with this field.

Although the protections of these laws have traditionally extended to compulsory school age children (generally 5 to 21 years of age), more recent laws have increased options for children in the 3-to-4-year-old age group who are assessed as needing help. Preschool children with disabilities may be entitled to related services and programs.

At the other end of the spectrum, older students must be provided with transition services to ease their transition from school to post-school activities, which may include post-secondary education, vocational training, adult services, or independent living.

As children with disabilities become adults with disabilities, appropriate living arrangements become an important issue. Under a federally financed program, states provide comprehensive living services, including support to help people with disabilities live independently in the community. (For more information, contact the local parent support or advocacy group concerned with your child's particular disability; see also Chapter 20 on assisted living programs.)

The ADA also offers a range of legal protections for persons with disabilities seeking jobs as well as transportation services in the community with which you should be familiar. There are discussed in Chapters 16 and 20. Chapter 20 also describes Fair Housing Act safeguards against discrimination in housing.

Discrimination in receiving services is also forbidden under Section 504 of the Rehabilitation Act and the Americans with Disabilities Act. (For more information on these laws, you may also contact agencies listed in the Resources section at the end of this book.)

FINDING HELP

As a general rule, local parent support or advocacy groups concerned with particular disabilities are excellent sources of referrals for parents. There are also state protection and advocacy agencies for the disabled in each state, established under federal mandate, which may assist you. (See Resources section.)

Some private organizations have begun to help in planning for disabled children. These offer future-care plans on a contract basis, structured to conform with family wishes. Services may include advocacy before public agencies, arranging health care and social service delivery, monitoring living arrangements, and coordinating supplemental services that may be provided through trusts. Lifetime assistance programs are operating in several states.

Private programs designed to function as surrogate families may be of particular help in the future, when children may need an extra voice advocating on their behalf, for instance arguing for housing services or making a legal claim under the Americans with Disabilities Act. These programs may provide an extra measure of security in your planning. Contact support or advocacy groups or protection agencies for referrals in your area. The National Planned Lifetime Assistance Network and the National Alliance for the Mentally Ill are also sources for information and referrals. (See Resources section.)

13

■■

GUARDIANS AND
PROTECTIVE SERVICES

W e've seen that various legal strategies such as powers of attorney and trusts can help manage the affairs of an incapacitated person and maintain him or her in the community when appropriate. When these devices are not in place or not working effectively, the appointment of a guardian or conservator to manage an individual's personal and financial affairs may be necessary.

Guardianship is the judicial appointment of a person with the power and duty to make decisions concerning personal or financial affairs on behalf of another who is considered incapable of doing so for herself or himself. In this it is similar to a power of attorney, except that it is a judge—not you—who decides who is going to serve.

Guardianship was once an all-or-nothing affair in which the incapacitated person relinquished all status and basic rights such as the right to vote, to marry, and to enter into contracts. But an aging society means an increase in the number of functionally disabled older people, a category that includes those with chronic physical disorders as well as the cognitively impaired. An estimated 23 percent of those aged 65 to 74 experience difficulties with specific activities of daily living (ADLs), making it harder for them to remain in the community without help. By age 85, the percentage of those experiencing such difficulties rises to 45 percent. According to a recent survey, nearly 70 percent of older people seek or receive help with day-to-day tasks such as preparing meals or managing money.

The ability to exercise decisional autonomy can be affected by functional abilities. But decreased abilities as often as not lead to partial or incremental impairment in decision-making ability, necessitating new forms of intervention. For those in need of such limited help, guardianship laws may offer some additional options, such as conservatorships and limited guardianships. At the same time, guardianship does entail

161

a loss of control, and the all-or-nothing concept persists in a number of states and in some of the practices of all states.

Protective services agencies also provide an array of services, from social support to legal intervention to help maintain the elderly in the community. A variety of demographic and other factors has given rise to a sharp increase in the incidence of personal and financial elder abuse. Interventions by protective services agencies have taken on new significance as the problem of elder abuse has become more prevalent in our society.

 ## THE LAW OF GUARDIANSHIP

Guardianship dates back to ancient Rome and medieval England. Under the doctrine of *parens patriae*, the king as sovereign had an obligation to take care of those under disability. In contemporary times, these royal duties have devolved onto the government. In Europe, guardianships are generally administered by public agencies. In the United States, guardianship proceedings are brought in the state courts—usually a probate court or surrogate's court—seeking the appointment of an individual to act as a guardian.

There are two ways of looking at guardianship:

- It is a well-intended and benign process designed to afford protections to people in need of them by assigning the power to exercise the rights of an incapacitated person, who is not in a position to do so in his or her own best interests, to someone who can do so on his or her behalf. According to this view, the guardianship process should be flexible and easy to use so that it is readily available to people in need of its help.
- It is, in effect, the taking away of an individual's rights and freedoms, a deprivation of constitutional magnitude under any circumstances and not necessarily in the best interests of an incapacitated person, who is not always able to protest. In this view, only the strictest application of due process standards will safeguard against potential abuse and conflicts of interest.

Which view is right? Both are. Guardianship is an important tool to help manage the affairs of people incapable of doing so themselves. At the same time, transferring control of people's property creates an enormous potential for abuse. And even the most well-intentioned may harbor ageist stereotypes which keep them from recognizing the need for continued autonomy among older people or seeking less drastic alternatives to help them.

Autonomy versus paternalism. Expect to see this dichotomy reflected in your own state guardianship laws—powers and flexibility granted with one hand and restrictions and safeguards imposed with the other in order to achieve a "balanced" approach. Guardianship questions focus on these major stages:

- *Defining the nature of incapacity What* does incapacity mean?
- *Determining incapacity When* and under what conditions does a guardianship become effective?
- *The role of the guardian What is* covered by a guardianship order?
- *Choosing the guardian Who* is eligible for selection?
- *The hearing process How* are the issues resolved?
- *Enforcement and monitoring How* will a guardianship be supervised?

The law of guardianship has its own vocabulary. A person for whom a guardianship is established is called a *ward*, or a *legally incapacitated person*. In some jurisdictions, a guardian is appointed over personal affairs, while a *conservator* or *committee* is used to manage financial affairs. Don't be confused by terminology, which differs from state to state. What's important is not the jargon, but whether an appointment is validly made and what powers are conferred upon the guardian.

THE NATURE OF INCAPACITY

Who needs a guardian or conservator? Once upon a time, the answer would have been a person who was an "idiot," "insane," or later, "incompetent." Such labels assigned people to vague and generally unhelpful categories.

Today the generally accepted response would be someone who, due to physical or mental incapacity or illness, is incapable of taking care of himself or herself, or someone who is incapable of making or communicating informed or responsible decisions.

The definition of incapacity is an evolving area of law. Recent reform efforts across the country calling for guardianships tailored to the least restrictive alternative have focused on decision-making and communicating capacity and functional assessment criteria in areas such as personal care, hygiene, nutrition, health care, residence, safety, and daily money management. Depending on the nature of the tasks involved, each area has its own standards of capacity. A person may be incapable of the tasks associated with money management, for example, while continuing to be capable in all others. New Hampshire and the District of Columbia, among others, now require information about a potential ward's functional capacity.

DETERMINING INCAPACITY

The most critical legal issue in guardianship is the assessment of an older person's decision-making capacity, which precedes a determination of the necessity for appointment of a guardian.

Older state statutes still require proof of a particular physical or mental condition as well as a resultant inability to manage one's personal or financial affairs. By contrast, newer laws establish a different measure, requiring an inability to perform and a lack of understanding of the consequences.

This kind of assessment is about specific behavior and limitations. These components should be addressed in any incapacity hearing. With the least restrictive form of guardianship, the ward's decision-making capacity and rights are respected. Nationwide the trend has been to tailor the guardians's powers to the functional limitations of the person. Among the states with comprehensive reform measures are Florida, New York, Michigan, New Mexico, and Washington. For example, New York's new guardianship law focuses on functional level and decision-making incapacity.

Is age a "condition" for guardianship purposes?

A number of states still list "advanced age" as a condition upon which a finding of sufficient impairment may be based. Mississippi and Nebraska are two states that have eliminated advanced age as a statutory condition.

THE ROLE OF THE GUARDIAN

The role of the guardian over a ward's personal affairs is usually spelled out in the court order appointing him or her, in a general statement giving the guardian broad powers over care, custody, and control of the ward.

The power and the responsibility of a guardian vary from state to state. Despite advocates' calls for limited grants of power, guardians continue to be granted broad powers to manage their wards' financial affairs or personal affairs, or both. These powers may include the rights to

- Consent to medical treatment
- Decide where to live
- Make a nursing home placement
- Ensure clothing, food, housing, medical care, and personal needs are met
- Initiate divorce or separation proceedings when it is in the ward's best interests
- Make contracts
- Bring and defend lawsuits
- Apply for government benefits

In the past, guardianship proceedings have commonly resulted in the automatic loss by wards of basic rights such as marrying, voting, working, traveling, and seeking employment and government benefits. In some states, such restrictions are still common. In others, such wholesale forfeiture of rights are no longer the rule. In Massachusetts, for example, express court authority may be needed for placing a ward in a nursing home;

similar court sanction is required in New Jersey before consenting to or refusing medical treatment on behalf of a ward. (As a general rule, you cannot deprive a ward of the right to have counsel or access to the courts.)

The role of the guardian over financial matters is expressed as the power to manage property, finance, and business affairs. In some state laws, it includes a duty to preserve the estate from loss or damage. Powers granted over financial affairs may include the right to

- Enter agreements
- Bring lawsuits
- Manage property
- Invest assets
- Rent or sell apartment or home
- Control money, and determine distribution for food, shelter, and living expenses
- Receive income
- Make gifts or disposition of property

These lists are by no means exhaustive, nor are all guardians granted all these powers in all jurisdictions. The specific powers of a guardian depends on state law and the court's order.

Under what circumstances may a guardian make gifts or dispose of property?

This is an important power. A guardian can make gifts to fulfill support obligations of a ward, for tax planning and Medicaid planning purposes, and to carry out a plan of charitable giving.

What is a limited guardianship?

A limited guardianship is a grant of powers of a lesser magnitude than the common broad authority over a ward's person or property. It may even limit powers otherwise authorized by statute. Such an order is allowed in most states. Courts have the inherent power to fashion orders without specific statutory authority, although some states have so provided.

New Mexico's laws allow guardianship only to the extent required by the limitation of the ward, who retains all other rights. Florida and New York are among those states which have redrafted their laws authorizing limited guardianship.

While limited guardianships may be appropriate only for some wards, for those it is very important. Wherever possible, ask for a limited guardianship to help preserve the ward's autonomy. The los of autonomy is keenly felt by all people—no less so by those who've already conceded some.

CHOOSING THE GUARDIAN

A number of state statutes provide an order of priority of persons from whom to choose a guardian. As a general rule, the order is spouse, children, grandchildren, or other next-of-kin.

Often, there is neither friend nor relative available to serve as a guardian. In such cases, courts may appoint lawyers or community agencies (in community and public guardian programs). Banks may also be appointed where substantial assets are involved.

States impose a patchwork quilt of rules and restrictions on the choice of guardian, trying to serve competing interests and policy considerations. Often these rules are an attempt to minimize the potential for abuse, by ensuring that persons are not appointed as guardians who have interests (financial or personal) that conflict with those of the ward. In Florida, for example, a health care provider cannot serve as a guardian except with a specific court finding that there is no such conflict and that the agent is acting in the best interests of the ward. California courts require a statement of whether a petitioner is a creditor of the person over whom conservatorship is sought. In New York, relatives of judges are ineligible.

These rules vary from state to state. A more progressive approach to many of the difficulties encountered in guardianship may be found in Florida's new guardianship law, which imposes comprehensive training requirements on guardians.

Can someone other than a relative be chosen?

All jurisdictions allow judges to refuse an appointment not in the best interests of the proposed ward. In states without priority statutes, preference may be given to a friend.

Can I choose my own guardian?

A number of states allow a person to name his or her own future guardian, in anticipation of such an appointment becoming necessary. This can be done by making the nomination in a power of attorney or a separate document. Designation works something like a power of attorney. In Florida, a competent person can name his or her future guardian. At the very least, the person designated in advance will be given priority status in consideration by the court.

The person who acts as your guardian should have your best interests at heart; ideally, it would be you who chooses the guardian. Remember, if you have a durable power of attorney, living will, and health care proxy, you will already have made your appointments to manage your future personal and financial affairs—and avoided the need for a guardian.

THE HEARING PROCESS

The process by which a guardianship is imposed on a ward takes place in court. The subject of the hearing is whether the proposed ward has any incapacity, the extent of incapacity, powers needed to manage his or her affairs, and the choice of the guardian. This is usually heard in probate court or surrogate's court, but it may also be before a county court, circuit court, or any other tribunal designated by the state.

A guardianship involves taking away some of a ward's very basic constitutionally protected rights of liberty and property which are protected under the 14th Amendment of the Constitution. A hearing may be formal or informal, but, at a minimum, the proposed ward is entitled to due process of law, including notice and an opportunity to be heard.

Notice and petition. The court is asked to appoint a guardian in a document that is filed with it called the *petition.* The petition must state the grounds upon which the request for guardianship is based and the statutory basis for that request. There are different requirements in different states. Some require a guardian plan or one for rehabilitation in the petition.

The right to be present. Under most circumstances, an opportunity to be heard means the right of the person to be heard *in person.* Guardianship proceedings often ignore this requirement. Some argue that it is not necessarily in the best interests of the proposed ward, who may be confused and unable to make a good presentation before the court. Sometimes the proposed ward is truly unavailable, in a coma or otherwise incapacitated, incapable of understanding or contributing to the proceeding.

If necessary, arrangements can and should be made to facilitate the proposed ward's appearance at the hearing. Scheduling and transportation may need special accommodation. Under appropriate circumstances, a hearing may be held at a hospital or nursing home.

Representation by counsel and appointment of a guardian ad litem. Depending on state law, the guardianship process may require an attorney, a guardian *ad litem,* both, or neither. In many jurisdictions across the country, a guardian *ad litem* (literally, "for the suit") is appointed by the court to protect the interests of the ward. A guardian *ad litem* is a person appointed for the hearing only, usually a lawyer, who functions *both* as an advisor to the court and a representative of the ward. Sometimes a *court evaluator* is appointed as well.

Difficulties arise in the dual role of the guardian *ad litem.* The guardian *ad litem*'s opinion of the proposed ward's best interests may be in direct conflict with the proposed ward's own expressed views, but it is the guardian *ad litem*'s responsibility to tell the court his or her own view, rather than advocating the ward's.

This inherent conflict has led to calls for reform and institution of mandatory counsel to represent the ward throughout the guardianship process. Although implemented in a few jurisdictions like Minnesota, this kind of reform has been successfully resisted in most states by opponents who question the need for an adversarial approach to the most common, noncontested situations. These are called "plain vanilla" cases, because no one is questioning the need for the loss of rights by people who have lost some or all of their capacities. In our view, it is this acquiescence that speaks loudest for reform. Who needs legal representation more than people who are unable to speak up for themselves?

What is the difference between a guardian ad litem and a guardian appointed to manage a ward's personal or financial affairs?

A guardian *ad litem* is *not* a guardian other than for the narrowly-defined purpose of representing the ward's interests before the court and advising the court. Unlike the guardian, the guardian *ad litem* has no powers or responsibilities over a ward's personal affairs or property. If you're dealing with a guardian *ad litem*, or someone functioning in a similar capacity, remember that his or her first loyalty is not to any "client" but to the court.

Can a person file his or her own petition?

Yes. Several states provide for the alleged incompetent or incapacitated person to file.

Can a guardianship be revoked or terminated?

Yes. A guardianship may be ended through a process called a *restoration hearing*, authorized in all states. The ward would have to show that the condition upon which the guardianship was based no longer exists. If the grounds for which the petition was granted in the first place are gone, then the court may restore the ward's rights. The guardian would be asked to show cause why the services of a guardian are still needed.

Can a guardian be removed?

A guardian may always be removed for cause, such as abuse of powers. Most states allow any interested third party to bring an action for removal. Upon the guardian's removal, a substitute guardian will be appointed.

Can a guardian withdraw as guardian and relinquish powers to the ward?

No. A guardian cannot withdraw on his or her own initiative. The guardian has fiduciary responsibility for the ward and is accountable to the court. Even if the ward regains full capacity to manage both personal and financial affairs, application must be made to the court.

MONITORING GUARDIANSHIP

A guardianship usually lasts the rest of a ward's life. Yet with the exception of a few states, guardianship has been subject only to limited review or oversight. Guardianships over personal affairs have been subject to even less supervision than those over financial affairs.

In recent years, guardianship accountability has been the goal of substantial reform efforts. Three-quarters of the states require annual or periodic financial accounting. A number of new guardianship statutes impose on a guardian the requirement to report annually on the ward's personal status, including physical and mental health, social condition, services and treatment, and names of treating physicians, and setting forth the basis for continuing guardianship. Requirements of this nature are in force in Florida, Oklahoma, Michigan, and New Mexico. Most states limit their reviews to investigations of complaints, although some, such as California and Maryland, have attempted to impose more regular review requirements.

A number of programs offer training for guardians and at least one state, Florida, has instituted a mandatory course in guardianship, which must be completed within one year of appointment. The eight-hour training program, approved by the court system, includes training on guardian duties, rights of wards, local resources, and preparation of annual reports, financial accounts, and guardianship plans. There is also a national professional association for guardians, which has drafted standards.

Who pays for guardianship?

The ward pays the guardian. Usually the fee is either a percentage of the estate or reasonable compensation approved by the court, subject to statutory fee schedules.

What provision is made for those with small estates?

Public guardianship may be available for the incapacitated without funds. These kinds of programs are often operated by a court or not-for-profit organization. Public guardianships are now authorized in 34 states.

 ## ALTERNATIVES TO GUARDIANSHIP

A number of programs available through local resources may be used as a viable alternative to guardianship. Although unregulated, they may provide help in daily money management and other services with which older people may be having difficulty. Programs of this sort may be found through senior centers, hospitals and social services agencies.

Remember, the best alternative to guardianship is advance planning, making use of power of attorney, living will, and health care proxy.

ELDER ABUSE AND THE LAW

According to national surveys, incidents of abuse, neglect and exploitation of the elderly rose at a dramatic pace in the 1980s, reaching 1.5 million a year by the end of the decade. Across the nation, elder abuse has now been estimated to affect upwards of 2 million older people annually. Only one out of 14 cases is ever reported to a public agency.

Revelations of abuse and neglect in nursing homes in the 1970s gave way to discovery of the larger, *sub rosa* problem of abuse outside the institutional setting. In fact, elder abuse is more often a family problem. With the rapidly aging population, increasing rates of abuse can be expected.

Elder abuse in the home setting is addressed at the state level. All 50 states have enacted some type of statute addressing the problem of elder abuse and neglect, most within their already existing adult protective services legislation. Adult protective services commonly provide preventive, supportive, and surrogate services to enable the elderly to maintain independent living in the community and avoid abuse and exploitation.

The contents of state statutes vary, but all include two main components: services for adults at risk, including prevention, support, and treatment services, and the power of the state or local jurisdiction to intervene as needed.

IDENTIFYING ELDER ABUSE

Elder abuse is not easily identified, in part because of misconceptions about just what constitutes mistreatment. Barriers to identifying abuse arise from societal attitudes about aging which ascribe otherwise treatable conditions of frailty and functional decline to the aging process. There is also a notable reluctance among physicians as well as the general public to address family violence. Older adults in institutions are also at risk, vulnerable to mistreatment by facility staff with inadequate training and experience, and without recourse or redress.

Legal definitions of abuse and neglect vary from state to state (including variations in the age for defining the "elderly" population). However, the basic principles may be described by reference to guidelines, issued not by legislators but by the American Medical Association, which define elder mistreatment to include:

- *Physical abuse.* This includes acts of violence that may result in pain, injury, impairment or disease.
- *Physical neglect.* This is characterized by a caretaker's failure to provide goods or services necessary for optimal functioning or to avoid harm. This may include not providing eyeglasses or hearing aids.
- *Psychological abuse.* Psychological abuse involves conduct that causes mental anguish. This includes verbal berating, harassment, or intimidation, threats of punishment or deprivation, treating the older person like an infant, or isolating the older person from family, friends, or activities.
- *Psychological neglect.* Psychological neglect is the failure to provide a dependent elderly person with social stimulation.
- *Financial or material abuse.* This is the misuse of a person's assets or income for the personal gain of another, i.e. the caretaker. This includes stealing money or possessions, either directly or by forcing the older person to sign contracts or assign power of attorney or change a will.
- *Financial or material neglect.* This is failure to use available resources needed to sustain or restore the health and well-being of the older person.

- *Violation of personal rights.* This occurs when caretakers and providers ignore the older person's capacity and desire to make decisions about his or her life, and to otherwise assert autonomy as a human being. This includes denying privacy, denying participation in health care and other personal decisions, and forcible eviction and/or placement in a nursing home.

(Source: Diagnostic and Treatment Guidelines on Elder Abuse and Neglect, American Medical Association, 1992.)

Is there a profile of a typical abused person?

An estimated two-thirds of elder abuse victims in home settings are females. While this statistic may not seem surprising, consider its corollary: one-third of victims of elder abuse are male.

Mistreatment of the elderly occurs throughout all racial, ethnic, and socioeconomic groups. The median age of victims is 78.8. One study reported that those 80 years or older made up more than 40 percent of reported cases.

Who abuses?

The highest incidence of abuse of neglect is by an adult child or a spouse. However, caregivers, paid and otherwise, may also be involved. (Self-neglect among the elderly is also a major concern for health and legal professionals.)

 REPORTING ELDER ABUSE

All states require reporting of elder abuse, although there is variation among states in requirements for identifying and reporting.

Forty-two states have passed mandatory reporting laws in recent years, but state officials are skeptical about their effectiveness in combating elder abuse. Illinois and Pennsylvania, for example, chose not to pass mandatory reporting laws after pilot studies. In a 1991 survey by the federal government, a majority of officials rated awareness among professionals and the public as the best way to discover abuse. (Prevention of abuse was linked to the provision of home care.)

Categories of people required to report vary from state to state, making comparisons for purposes of assessing reporting laws difficult if not impossible. Mandatory reporting rules in many states cover doctors and other health care providers, professionals and paraprofessionals. Members of a total of fifty professional groups are required to report. All states grant some legal immunity for making a complaint or report. (See Resources section for a list of State Adult Protective Service Agencies.

Elder abuse is underreported for a number of reasons. An abused person is often ashamed to admit victimization by family members, a feeling which is further complicated by guilt as a parent. Add to that dependence on the abuser and apprehension about unknown alternatives, such as removal to a nursing home. To the victimized elderly person, the devil you know is often preferable to the devil you don't know.

INVESTIGATION AND SERVICES

Investigation processes also differ among states. Generally, upon a report, a visit is made and interviews conducted with people having knowledge of the matter under investigation. Some states require on-site investigation; others don't. If a situation merits action under statutory criteria, a range of social services may be offered, from standard casework (including food delivery and preparation, personal care, housecleaning, and visiting nurse services) to special fiscal and legal services.

If the victim does not agree to accept help or lacks the capacity to consent, legal options may include

- Guardianship
- Conservatorship or committee
- Financial management assistance
- Orders of protection

As a general rule, however, state agencies have insufficient staff with limited experience and training, limited funding, and limited powers.

Local police, sheriff's offices, and district attorneys may investigate and prosecute elder abuse, particularly cases involving sexual abuse, assault, theft, or fraud. In states with statutes making elder abuse a crime, laws generally require suspected abuse to be reported to a law enforcement agency.

ABUSE IN NURSING HOMES

In institutional settings, federal law applies. Under the Nursing Home Reform Act, which provides national standards for care in nursing homes, residents have certain rights, among them the right to be free from verbal, sexual, physical, or mental abuse, corporal punishment, and involuntary seclusion.

Federal guidelines under this Act define abuse as "the willful infliction of injury, unreasonable confinement, intimidation, or punishment with resulting physical harm or pain or mental anguish, or deprivation by an individual, including a caretaker, of goods or services that are necessary to attain or maintain physical, mental, and psychological well-being."

Use of physical and chemical restraints is also regulated. Residents have the right to be free from physical restraints or psychoactive drugs administered for purposes of discipline or the convenience of staff. (See Chapter 4 for a discussion on restraints.)

In addition, several states, among them California, Delaware, Florida, Georgia, Maryland, Massachusetts, Missouri, New Mexico, and Oregon, have laws that address abuse in institutional settings. Federal law mandates that the states have long-term care ombudsmen to investigate the quality of care in and complaints about nursing homes, although these positions are often filled on a volunteer basis. However, just the existence of a system for reporting and investigating deters some abuse.

The courts may also provide remedies for institutional abuse for those who file complaints or lawsuits. See Chapter 4 for a discussion of your rights against nursing homes.

14

■ ■

WILLS AND ESTATE
PLANNING

When a person dies without a will, his or her property passes to the closest relatives, as set forth in the laws of the state of residence. If there are no next-of-kin, the property of the deceased will go to the state.

A will allows you to direct how your property will be disposed of after you die. It allows you to divide it the way you choose, to give property to friends and charities as well as relatives, and to set up legal structures to protect your beneficiaries. It also allows you to name the person or persons who will be responsible for carrying out your instructions.

An extra benefit of the will-making process is that it offers you the opportunity to review your financial situation and to plan. This is of considerable importance for another reason—planning for the financing of unanticipated medical expenses or long-term care. In deciding how your estate will be distributed, you will need to consider the possibility that you will need such care, and the best ways to pay for it without dissipating your estate.

UNDERSTANDING THE BASICS

Wills and estate planning involve a number of terms and concepts that require explanation.

Testator. The person making a will is called the *testator* (a woman is sometimes called the *testatrix*). The testator must be an adult and have the mental capacity to make the will in order for it to be a valid instrument. This is called *testamentary capacity.* Physical disability is irrelevant. At the time of the signing, the testator must understand what he or she is doing. That's why wills often contain the phrase "being of sound mind."

Legatees and heirs. The people named to receive bequests in a will are called *legatees.* They are also called *beneficiaries.* An individual's *heirs* are family members who would inherit the estate if there were no will. In some states, these heirs are called *distributees.*

You can divide your money among as many persons as you wish or leave it all to one. It's your call. (Spouses have special rights, which we'll discuss later.)

You can and should state whether the bequest will go to your legatee's heirs or estate if the legatee does not survive you or if the bequest will "lapse." In some states, "anti-lapse" laws provide that bequests to certain heirs automatically go to *their* heirs if they die before the testator, unless the will provides otherwise. If you want to make an alternative disposition, you need to say so. Making this clear will avoid the need to make a new will every time a legatee dies.

Consider a bequest in your will that provides, "I give $5,000 to my brother Bob Smith." What happens if Bob dies before you? Do you want the bequest to lapse? Go to Bob's wife? His children? In a state that has an anti-lapse law, it would probably go to Bob's children. You need to spell out your wishes, by stating, for example, "I give $5,000 to my brother Bob Smith if he survives me, but if not, to his wife Sally Smith, if she survives me."

Estate. The estate is the total assets owned at the time of death which will pass to the descendant's survivors either under a will or through intestacy. This is often referred to as the *probate estate.*

Assets in your probate estate include real estate, bank accounts, investment accounts, stocks, bonds, mutual funds, and money owed to you by others. It also includes personal possessions such as jewelry, works of art, furniture, and cars.

Your probate estate does not include property which you own in joint ownership with someone else, bank accounts or United States "E", "EE," or "H" bonds payable on death (POD) to another person, life insurance benefits for which you have designated a policy beneficiary, or pension plan or retirement benefits for which you have designated a beneficiary. These assets will pass "outside" of your estate. They are referred to as *non-probate assets* and are not affected by the provisions of your will. (They are, however, subject to taxation as part of your *taxable estate.* This is discussed in Chapter 15.)

Bequests can be of specific items of property such as "my antique gold watch" (called *specific bequests*), set amounts or percentages of your estate (called *general bequests*), or the balance of your estate after the specific and general bequests are paid (called *residuary bequests*).

Executor, administrator. The executor (in some states, the *personal representative*) is the person named in the will to dispose of the estate according to your instructions. If there is no will, in most states the person who performs these duties is called the *administrator* (or *administratrix*), although some use the term personal representative. This person's responsibilities include arranging for probate if there is a will, gathering the assets, paying debts and expenses, filing the necessary income and estate tax returns and paying any taxes due, investing the estate's assets prudently, and, finally, distributing the assets as instructed in the will or in accordance with state intestacy laws. (We discuss probate below.)

Being an executor is not an easy job. The selection depends on a number of factors. An executor should be trustworthy and capable of assuming the responsibilities. It may be that the people you are leaving your money to do not have both these characteristics. Other possibilities include your attorney, accountant, a bank, or a trusted friend. Some jurisdictions impose additional requirements for being an executor, such as state residency or being a relative.

Executors receive payment for their work, from your estate. The fee is set by statute, commonly fixed at a percentage of the total estate. You can appoint a person to serve as executor without fee, but no one is obligated to accept appointment. Usually close family members, especially those who are the beneficiaries, will forego fees, but there may be some cases where taking fees has some tax advantages.

You should always appoint a successor executor in case your first choice is unavailable or declines, is disabled and cannot serve, or dies before you.

Probate.   Your executor is charged with the responsibility of gathering and distributing your assets. The first step is probate of your will, to determine whether it is a legal and valid document. Probate means, literally, *proving the will.* This is a court proceeding, done in a probate or surrogate's court. After probate, the executor is authorized to proceed. The court then issues *letters testamentary.*

Domicile.   Where you are domiciled affects your will in a number of respects. The states have different will execution requirements and rules governing the rights of family members. Since a few states have inheritance taxes, your place of domicile can affect the taxation of your estate. You may have several residences but only one domicile—the place where your actions and intent demonstrate that you choose to make your primary residence.

If I name my life insurance beneficiary in my will, will it be counted as part of my probate estate?

You cannot change the beneficiary of a life insurance policy by saying in your will who is to get the proceeds of that insurance policy. Nor can you change the designation of who is to get your IRA account. Making changes in beneficiary designation for non-probate assets must be done in accordance with the insurance policy contract or the rules governing the IRA.

I want to be sure to leave specified property to my nieces and nephews. How can I be sure they will get what I've left them?

Sometimes it's not a good idea to be too specific. Leaving "my 100 shares of Widget, Inc. to my nephew Billy" is not a good idea. If you sell that stock before you die, Billy won't get anything. You'd be better off giving Billy a dollar amount equal to the value of the stock.

I'm concerned that no single member of my family will be in a position to act as executor of my estate. Would it be a good idea to name two or more of them to act as co-executors?

Naming more than one executor is not always a good idea. Since executors are entitled to payment for their services, having two or more co-executors can become expensive. And there is always the possibility that the co-executors may not work well together, leading to disputes that will hinder the smooth administration of an estate.

YOUR WILL AND ESTATE TAXES

The federal government imposes a tax on the transfer of wealth from one generation to another, an estate tax when transfer takes place at death and a gift tax when given during one's lifetime. The gift and estate tax is a unified system which allows individuals tax-free transfers of $600,000, reflecting a tax credit of $192,800. Estates above that amount are taxed at a rate starting at 37 percent, subject to certain exceptions. There is no gift or estate tax imposed on gifts or bequests to charities or to spouses who are U.S. citizens. (Non-citizen spouses are not eligible for this *unlimited marital deduction.*)

In drafting your will, there are a number of important estate tax planning tools that you need to consider. The way your will is worded can have a significant effect on the estate tax imposed on your estate. (We discuss estate taxes in more detail in Chapter 15.)

Can I use a do-it-yourself will kit?

We don't advise it. No matter how small or simple your financial affairs or how basic your wishes, this area of law is extremely technical and highly specialized. Moreover, the consequences of making an error—both financial or otherwise—may be great. A kit will not point out all the legal considerations or give you answers to any special problems. The cost of a will prepared by a lawyer is generally a good investment. (Don't forget to ask about fees before you engage a lawyer.)

BEQUESTS TO SPOUSES, CHILDREN, AND OTHER FAMILY MEMBERS

Leaving money outright to the people you love is a nice gesture, but it may cost them money. The rules on inheritance are very tight when it comes to family bequests and the tax consequences of uninformed largesse can be appalling.

Bequests to Spouses

As we described above, property left to your spouse will not be taxed in your estate. It will be taxed in your spouse's estate later at his or her death, when the unlimited marital deduction will likely no longer apply. For that reason, a simple will leaving everything to your spouse may not be the best approach. It is probably better to set up a trust for your spouse of the first $600,000 of your estate. The funds in this trust will be available to him or her, but will not be taxed either in your estate or your spouse's, and will eventually pass estate-tax-free to your other heirs. (See Chapter 15.)

A trust is also a valuable device for providing for a spouse who is ill or incapacitated. Another benefit of a trust is that you can provide for a beneficiary during the beneficiary's lifetime but retain the right to control the ultimate disposition of the trust fund when the beneficiary dies. The trust is particularly useful in second, later-life marriages, allowing you to leave your estate in trust for your spouse but ensuring that your estate will be left to your children by your first marriage if that is your wish.

I have been married three times, a fact my spouse doesn't know. My ex-wives have no legal interest in my estate, so do I have to tell my lawyer or mention them in the will?

By all means, tell your lawyer. Previous marriages may affect both planning and how your will is drafted. For example, your will should always name people, in addition to describing them by relationship, e.g. leaving money "to my wife Alice Adams" as opposed to just "my wife."

Bequests to Children and Grandchildren

In the language of wills, children and grandchildren descended from you are referred to as your *issue*. Wills commonly leave bequests to unnamed descendants by referring to them as issue, for example, "I leave everything to Jane Doe, and if she does not survive me, to her issue, *per stirpes*."

"*Per stirpes*" indicates that if Jane Doe's issue receive an inheritance, it will be divided among them as if all her children were living, and if any are not, the shares of any predeceased children will be passed on to their issue (who, literally, "step into the parent's shoes"). The alternative bequest, leaving it to her issue *per capita*, would leave the bequest divided equally among those still living. (The chart on p. 179 describes the different results from *per stirpes* and *per capita* bequests.)

Remember that family bequests to "issue" may not necessarily include family members such as adopted children, stepchildren, half-siblings, and non-traditional relations. This is vitally important in today's family, when people are living longer and in more complicated family situations than in prior years. You have the right to leave your money to anyone you want, but you may have to make special reference to an adopted child or grandchild or a half-sibling who may otherwise be excluded. The same applies if you want to exclude someone who would otherwise be included. A lawyer will help sort out who's who, and who's legally entitled to a portion of your estate.

BEQUESTS TO CHILDREN AND GRANDCHILDREN
PER STIRPES AND *PER CAPITA*

Bequests *per stirpes*	Bequests *per capita*
Bequest: I leave everything to Jane Doe and if she does not survive me, to her issue *per stirpes*.	Bequest: I leave everything to Jane Doe and if she does not survive me, to her issue *per capita*.

Jane Doe	Jane Doe
Jane Doe's Children	Jane Doe's Children
Amy Bob Carl	Amy Bob Carl

Jane Doe's Grandchildren	Jane Doe' Grandchildren
Ann-Bill Cal-Dan Ed	Ann-Bill Cal-Dan Ed

• If Jane Doe has died and all her children are alive, her children Amy, Bob, and Carl will share equally in the bequest.	• If Jane Doe has died and all her children are alive, her children Amy, Bob, and Carl will share equally in the bequest.
• If Jane Doe has died and Bob is also not alive, Amy and Carl will get their 1/3 shares, and Bob's two children Cal and Dan will share Bob's 1/3 share, getting 1/6 each.	• If Jane Doe has died and Bob is also not alive, Amy and Carl will get 1/2 shares, and Bob's two children Cal and Dan will take nothing. (No grandchildren will inherit.)
• If Jane Doe has died and all three of her children have also died, her grandchildren Ann and Bill will share the 1/3 share that would have been Amy's, Cal and Dan will share the 1/3 share of Bob, and Ed will take the 1/3 share of Carl.	• If Jane Doe has died and all her children have also died, all her grandchildren Ann, Bill, Cal, Dan, and Ed will share equally, each taking a 1/5 share.

Be careful not to leave money outright to minors. Those bequests to grandchildren may seem like a good idea but in fact be nothing but trouble. Minors can't own assets, so funds you leave to them can be collected only by a court-appointed guardian who will be severely restricted in using the funds, even for things like college tuition. These guardians, even if they are the parents of the grandchild, will have to go to court to get permission to spend the funds and the court may decline, stating that the funds are to be preserved because the parents have the obligation to pay for college out of their own funds. Bequests to minors should be left in a trust for them or the will should allow the executor to retain the funds until the minor comes of age, using it for their care in the meantime. The same problem applies to funds your grandchildren may receive from you from in ITF ("in trust for") accounts, POD ("paid on death") government bonds, or life insurance.

DISPOSING OF YOUR PERSONAL EFFECTS

In legal terminology, your furniture, art, silverware, china and glassware, jewelry and automobiles, to list just a few things you may own, are called *tangible personal property.* You can specify bequests of these items in your will, but usually this is not necessary. You can give all such property to your spouse or another heir, for example, by simply stating that "I give all of my tangible personal property to my wife, Sally."

If your effects are to be divided among several people, another option is to leave them to one person and "request" that person "distribute the property in accordance with the instructions I will set forth in a letter" to be given to that person. This approach allows you to change your mind without having to redo your will every time. While in most jurisdictions the person you designate is not legally obligated to honor your instructions, you will presumably choose a trustworthy person who will respect your wishes. Some states such as Florida have adopted this kind of procedure in their will laws, making a statement or letter of this nature legally binding.

BURIAL INSTRUCTIONS

Many people choose to include funeral service and burial instructions in their wills. Although there is no reason not to do so, keep in mind that a will may not always be available to the family at the time of death. Technically, your will has no legal effect until it is admitted to probate. So it is important to tell your family or friends of your funeral and burial wishes and set them out in a separate letter of instructions.

I want to donate my organs for use after my death. Can this be included in my will?

Under the Uniform Anatomical Gifts Act, a version of which has been adopted by every state, you can make a "gift" or some or all of your organs upon your death through your will. You can indicate the conditions under which you will donate and further include any burial instructions following donation of organs.

An alternative is to also carry a *uniform donor card,* signed and witnessed, which may be more likely to be found in time to be useful. (Organ and tissue donation is discussed in Chapter 10.)

DISINHERITING YOUR HEIRS

Most states have provisions preventing you from disinheriting your spouse. These laws give surviving spouses a *right of election* to take a share of the deceased spouse's estate, often one-half or one-third. But these laws are often easily avoided in some states because the "estate" of the deceased spouse for the purpose of making a spousal right of election does not always include "non-probate" property such as assets owned jointly with persons other than the spouse or assets in trust for the benefit of persons other than the spouse. While some states such as New York are tightening their laws protecting spouses, many states have a long way to go. (Under federal law, spouses have special rights to pensions, discussed in Chapter 17.)

Spouses can "waive" this right, a common practice in prenuptial agreements signed by couples entering into later-life marriages. Keep in mind that even though you have signed a prenuptial agreement, you can always provide your spouse with more than the agreement calls for.

Disinheriting a child is another matter. Other than a spouse in a state with a "right of election" law, you have no obligation to provide for anyone. In most states, it is not necessary to mention a disinherited child or to leave him or her a nominal sum, although it is required in a few jurisdictions to ensure that a child is not unintentionally omitted. There is no requirement to give a reason, although you can if you like.

An exception to this rule applies when a child is born to you after the date you make your will and not mentioned in it (either by name or as part of an inclusive reference to "children" or "issue"). The new child will be given the equivalent of an intestate share on the premise that you forgot to change your will and provide for him or her. If you wish to disinherit a child in this situation, you need to "republish" your will by making a new one or signing a codicil stating that you do not want to make a provision for that child.

BEQUESTS TO CHARITIES

The common law as adopted in many states had limitations on the percentage of one's estate that could be left to charity when the testator was survived by a spouse or children. The purpose of the limitations was to prevent undue influence from religious bodies. These laws—known as *mortmain statutes*—have been largely superseded by the spousal right of election laws, which have been deemed to protect spouses adequately. But it is a good idea to check your state's law in this regard if you plan to leave substantial amounts to charity.

JOINTLY OWNED PROPERTY

Upon the death of one of the joint owners of property, it becomes the sole property of the surviving *joint tenant*. It does not pass under the deceased person's will or form part of his or her probate estate.

Joint ownership has some advantages. In small estates, property passes to the spouse quickly without the need for the probate of a will or other administration.

There are disadvantages as well. There may be unexpected gift tax implications when property is placed in joint ownership. For example, parents often set up joint accounts with children. When a parent places stocks in joint ownership with a child, the act may result in a gift of one-half the value of the property. This gift, although probably unintended, may nevertheless result in the imposition of a substantial gift tax. (Other non-estate problems are discussed in Chapter 11.)

Moreover, with joint ownership, you lose control. Except for joint bank accounts, you do not retain the power to sell or dispose of 100 percent of the assets at any time (nor does your co-owner). Nor can your will undo joint ownership. If you made your daughter co-owner of a bank account or stock certificate, you can't leave that account or stock to another child.

 ## COMMUNITY PROPERTY STATES

Eight western and southwestern states have community property laws that treat assets acquired during marriage as owned equally by the spouses. These are Arizona, California, Idaho, Louisiana, Nevada, New Mexico, Texas, and Washington. In these states property is deemed either *community property* or *separate property*. While the rules outlined in this chapter generally apply in community property states, there are some differences which may affect you. Make sure to consult your local counsel.

WITNESSES AND OTHER FORMALITIES

The first step in probate of a will is determining whether it a legal and valid document. A valid will requires compliance with a number of formalities. These execution requirements vary according to the state in which you reside, but there are some general rules.

- *Age.* A will must be completed by an adult. A will executed by a minor is not a valid document and won't be recognized by law. In most states, the *age of majority,* at which time a person ceases to be a minor, is 18.
- *Testamentary capacity.* The testator must be legally capable of making a will. This is called testamentary capacity. Most states define this as knowing and understanding who your natural heirs are and the nature and extent of your property.
- *Form.* Most states require wills to be written. Oral wills are recognized in very limited circumstances such as that of a soldier in combat.
- *Signature and date.* Wills must be signed by the testator at the end and dated.

- *Witnesses.* Witnesses are required in all but the most limited circumstances. Witnesses confirm your signature on the will, the voluntariness of your signing your will, your competence to do so, your declaration that it is your will, and each other's signatures as well. States usually require two witnesses, although some require three. Witnesses must generally be adults and competent. Some states have additional requirements concerning who they may be, and, more importantly, who they may not be. A beneficiary under a will may not be a witness. In some states the signature of a witness who is also a beneficiary may be recognized as valid if the amount received through the will is less than the share he or she would receive if there were no will or if he or she gives up the right to inherit. This penalty may be avoided by not using a beneficiary as a witness.
- *Notarization.* Wills are not notarized. However, many states have adopted a system known as a "self-proving" will which allows the probate of a will without having to locate witnesses and bring them to court to "prove" the will. In a self-proving will, the witnesses confirm by separate affidavit that the formalities of will execution were followed; the *affidavit* is signed, notarized, and attached to the will.

How many copies do I sign?

Only one! If you execute more than one original and any of the signed copies cannot be found when the time comes to probate the will, the missing copy may be presumed to have been destroyed by you with the intent to revoke it. Never sign more than one copy of a will.

Can my executor be witness to my will?

Yes, unless he or she is also a beneficiary named in your will. Technically, there's no prohibition if the share designated under your will is less than his or her share would be if you had no will. But this is not always possible to determine. The best way to proceed is to select witnesses who are not beneficiaries.

Where can I get witnesses? I don't want people knowing my business.

Your witnesses do not have to be told the contents of your will. All you need to do is declare to them that the document you are asking them to witness is your will (this is called *publication* of your will), that it expresses your wishes, and that you are requesting them to be your witnesses. Anything more is nobody's business but yours. Your attorney will usually provide witnesses, so your family, friends, and neighbors don't even have to know that you're preparing a will.

I want to change a part my will. Can I do that with a codicil?

A codicil, the technical name for an amendment to a will, is valid if executed with the same formalities required for your will. While a codicil may be simpler than redoing your entire will, it's not always the wisest way to proceed. In most states, if you change your will by a codicil, anyone whose interests are adversely affected will learn of the change and could challenge the codicil. If you incorporate the change in a new will, the earlier provisions are no longer part of the document and it becomes much more difficult to challenge it.

I have a handwritten will stating my intentions. That should be good enough. Why should I give good money to lawyers?

Sorry. Handwritten wills are not valid. Nor are wills that you type yourself, unless they are witnessed and the other execution formalities described above are followed. In a few states, a handwritten will (called a *holographic* will) is valid under limited circumstances without requiring the usual formalities.

When should I update my will?

When your family or financial circumstances change considerably or you change your wishes. Or when tax or other laws affecting your financial plans change, as happens frequently.

Events such as marriage, the marriage of a child, the birth of another child or grandchild, or a significant improvement in your financial situation are the most frequent causes of reviewing wills and estate plans. Or there might be a divorce or other family rift causing you to want to take someone out of your will, or a family member may die or become seriously ill or incapacitated. (We discuss planning for a disabled child in Chapter 12.) You may also want to change the executor (or trustee) if the circumstances of the person or persons you have nominated have changed or if you have lost confidence in them.

Must I change my will when I move to another state?

It's not usually necessary but may be a good idea. All the states will recognize a will drawn in another state if it was properly executed under the laws of that state. But a move to another state is one of the life events that should prompt you to review and update your will.

How do I make the necessary changes? Can I mark up the old one?

No! This could invalidate your will. Your existing will had to be properly witnessed; so must your changes. Either redo the whole will or execute a *codicil* (amendment) with the same formalities with which you signed the will itself. It is generally preferable to redo the entire will, one reason being that any persons you may be eliminating from your will do not get to see the earlier provisions.

How do I revoke my will?

You revoke your will by making a new one and stating in the new one that the old will is revoked, or by physically destroying the old will. Be careful if you want to revoke it by tearing it up or burning it. Someone could later allege that it was destroyed accidentally. To revoke a will by destroying it you must destroy it with the *intent* to revoke it, so it is probably a good idea to do this before witnesses and tell them that you mean to revoke it.

Where do I keep it?

The best place is to leave the original will with your lawyer, provided he or she will keep it in a bank vault or a fireproof safe in his or her office. You will get *conformed copies* which you can keep at home and give to your heirs and executor. Other possibilities include keeping the original at home or in your bank safe deposit box.

Keeping it at home has risks—someone could find and destroy it, it could easily be misplaced, or it could be destroyed in a fire. A bank safe deposit box is not a bad choice, but keep in mind that in many states safe deposit boxes are sealed upon the death of the owner (or joint owner) and it takes a court order to get into the box even to remove a will.

 ## DYING WITHOUT A WILL

If you die without a will, your property is distributed under your state's laws of intestacy, which prescribe strict orders of distribution. An individual who dies without a will has died *intestate*; the persons who will receive the estate under the intestacy laws are usually called *intestate distributees*. In effect, the state is writing a will for you, and it may not be the will you would have wanted.

Generally, state laws will distribute your property in the following way, although the states do differ.

- If you are survived by your spouse and one or more children, your estate will be divided among them. Usually your spouse will get one third and your children will share the balance. The children of a child who dies before you (a *predeceased child*) will usually take that child's share.
- If you are survived by your spouse but have no children, your spouse will receive your entire estate, although in some states your parents may get a share.
- If you are survived by children but not your spouse, your children will share the entire estate. The children of predeceased children will inherit their parent's share. If all your children have predeceased you, your grandchildren will take the whole estate (in some states, *per stirpes*, in others *per capita*).
- If you have neither spouse nor children, your parents will receive your estate. In some states it will be shared with your siblings.
- If you are survived by neither your spouse, descendants, nor parents, your estate will be paid to your siblings and the children of predeceased siblings. If all of your siblings have also died, your nieces and nephews will inherit the estate.

State laws also specify who will be appointed as *administrator* of the estate.

The "will" the state makes for you is probably not going to be the will you would have written for yourself. You might want your entire estate given to or held in trust for your spouse during his or her lifetime and not want to give anything to your children at the time of your death. Or, if you do wish to leave property to your children outright, you may want to make unequal bequests or leave a child's share in trust. Perhaps you want to provide for a parent. Your wishes and the statutory scheme of intestacy may be very different in many ways. But the statutory format will take precedence unless you act.

If the state's intestacy laws make the same provision as I would in a will, why do I need a will?

It's never exactly the same. Without a will, your court-appointed administrator may have to post a bond. A will may also ensure that taxes are paid out of your estate and the liability not distributed among your heirs.

RENOUNCING AN INHERITANCE

While it may be hard to imagine, an inheritance is not always what you want. You can't be forced to accept a gift or an inheritance and you have the right to refuse it. This is call a *disclaimer* or a *renunciation*. Under the tax laws, property you disclaim is treated as never having belonged to you, so that you are not liable for gift taxes on the transfer to the person who will get the disclaimed property.

Disclaimers are tricky. The rule is that if a person disclaims, it is treated as if he or she had died immediately before the death of the person whose estate is to be distributed. Under this construct, whether the will makes an alternative disposition takes on critical importance. You don't want to make a disclaimer if the bequest will go to a stranger. Make sure you know who will take the disclaimed property.

There are a number of situations in which, for reasons of family relations or tax planning a disclaimer may make sense or be appropriate. For example, a man may die intestate, with only one-third of his estate going to his widow and the children to inherit the remaining two-thirds. That may not have been what he wanted. The surviving spouse may have limited assets. The children could disclaim their interests and the property would pass to the spouse, *if there are no grandchildren*. But if the children have children, it is those grandchildren of the decedent who would receive the disclaimed property. (If they are minors, the disclaimer won't be valid. In that case, the children would have to gift their share to their mother, with possible gift tax consequences.)

A disclaimer might also be a good idea for tax reasons. Remember that assets passing to the spouse are not subject to estate tax, but that property going to children is taxable. It might be better to have the estate unreduced by estate taxes as long as the spouse survives.

A disclaimer is often used by a child with substantial means to have a bequest pass directly to his or her children, thus avoiding having the assets taxed again as part of his or her estate later on. Disclaimers are also quite common in situations where a person leaves the entire estate to the surviving spouse and the estate is greater than $600,000. In this case, it might be wise for the surviving spouse to disclaim assets up to $600,000, having them pass immediately to their children, for tax planning reasons. Of course, this should only be done where the surviving spouse has adequate resources and income to justify giving up the disclaimed assets.

Disclaimers cannot be used to qualify for Medicaid. While disclaimers work fine for tax purposes, keep in mind that for Medicaid planning purposes property disclaimed is considered to be an asset and a disclaimer will be considered as a disqualifying transfer.

Specific rules for disclaiming property are contained in the Internal Revenue Code and state laws. Disclaimers must be made within nine months of the creation of the property interest being disclaimed. In the case of a bequest made under a will, the nine-month period begins with the date of the testator's death. If you are disclaiming an asset from a trust, the time period begins at the time of death of the person whose trust interest comes before you.

Disclaimers need to be valid under state law as well. Most jurisdictions require a written document acknowledged by a notary public. Some jurisdictions prescribe a time period during which a disclaimer must be made and filed in court to be effective.

 ## THE USE OF TRUSTS

A trust is simply a legal agreement by which a person gives property to a "trust," which is administered by a trustee or trustees. Assets must actually be deposited into the trust, which becomes the nominal owner by re-registering the assets. The principal and the income are administered and applied for the benefit of the trust beneficiaries in accordance with the instructions in the trust agreement. (Trusts are a common and useful device for the concerns of older people. Other models are discussed in Chapters 8, 11, and 12.)

A *testamentary trust* is created by a person's will, and takes effect upon his or her death. A testamentary trust may be advisable when

- You think your spouse or child will be unable to manage a large sum of money
- The beneficiary may be ill or incapacitated
- The beneficiary may need Medicaid and you want your bequest to supplement the care provided by Medicaid
- You want to control where your property will go after your the initial beneficiary dies

Another popular form of trust is the *living trust* (in Latin, an *inter vivos* trust), created by you to take effect during your lifetime. A living trust can accomplish many of the goals of a testamentary trust.

A common method of "avoiding probate" is to create a revocable living trust, name yourself as both trustee and beneficiary, and transfer all your assets into it. Upon death, your assets can then be transferred without the formalities and expense of probate. In a few states, you cannot be the sole trustee of such a trust but must name a co-trustee. The revocable living trust has no tax consequences whatsoever during your lifetime.

Unfortunately, while revocable living trusts have useful purposes and can reduce estate administration expenses to a limited extent, the advantages are greatly overestimated in many situations. Other methods exist for estate tax savings which may be preferable to a revocable living trust. You should obtain legal counsel and explore the advantages and disadvantages of revocable trusts fully before you transfer your assets into one.

I have a living trust. My lawyer says I still need a will. Why?

A *pourover will* is a necessary accompaniment to a living trust. Although distribution of your assets is controlled by the your living trust, with a pourover will you can have the terms of your trust govern the distribution of any other assets you may own or later receive that weren't put into your living trust during your lifetime.

Part 4

■ ■ ■ ■ ■ ■ ■ ■ ■ ■ ■ ■ ■ ■ ■ ■ ■ ■ ■ ■

You and Your Taxes

Every decision you make in the context of planning for the future has tax consequences. That makes it critical for your financial planning that you have a basic understanding of how gift, estate, and income taxes may affect you. So important is this point that we've set apart our discussion of taxes for the older citizen for emphasis.

Shifting funds for Medicaid planning, creating trusts to manage your assets or provide for a family member's care, using financial strategies such as reverse mortgages to reap current income or accelerated life insurance benefits to help pay for health care—all of these may have significant tax implications for you.

One word of caution. This chapter provides general guidelines to help you understand the potential impact tax issues may have on your planning; it is *not* intended as advice on your specific financial or tax situation. Before you take any action altering the ownership or distribution of your assets or income, you should seek professional tax counsel.

15

PLANNING AND TAX
IMPLICATIONS

Life planning does not take place in the abstract. In all your planning decisions and actions, you must take into account the effect on your taxes. Tax considerations apply to almost all the planning choices available: creating a trust, purchasing or collecting on insurance, planning your estate, purchasing an annuity, purchasing a lifecare contract, moving to another state. Although we cannot offer legal advice on any particular tax situation, here are some general guidelines for understanding the gift, estate, and income tax implications of decisions you may face.

Giving assets away. If you are considering gifts to support or aid family members or make yourself Medicaid-eligible, you must consider these questions:

- Will this transfer cause gift tax or future estate tax liability?
- Are the funds free from eventual estate tax?
- Am I liable for taxes on the income on gifted money?
- Are transfers or payments tax-deductible?

Arranging to receive money or assets. If you are using a device that will result in your receiving additional cash payments, such as accelerated life insurance benefits or reverse mortgage, you must consider:

- Will payments I receive count as income for income tax purposes?
- Will payments count as income for determining tax liability on my Social Security income?

Medicaid and taxes. Tax considerations are made even more difficult by the question of safeguarding your potential Medicaid eligibility. Whether you are transferring assets or arranging to receive them, you must also ask:

- Will giving money away or arranging to receive payments affect Medicaid eligibility?

Often these two considerations can conflict, a fact not readily apparent to people making life decisions under stressful conditions. For example, if you give your home to your children so that it is not available to Medicaid, the tax bill resulting from the gift may be substantially greater than any Medicaid benefits you obtain. In order to avoid this kind of Catch-22, you need expert guidance. Remember, both tax rules and benefit eligibility rules are subject to swift change. (We discuss Medicaid eligibility rules in Chapter 8.)

 GIFT AND ESTATE TAXES

Death and taxes are inevitable, and inevitably they go together. Whether or not you have a will, upon your death your estate may be subject to taxes.

As a general rule, only estates with assets over $600,000 are subject to federal estate tax liability. Under the federal system, individuals are allowed a *lifetime exclusion* of $600,000, reflecting a tax credit of $192,800 (roughly equivalent to the tax on $600,000). The tax rate for estates over $600,000 starts at 37 percent, and goes up to over 55 percent for larger estates.

The estate tax is part of a "unified" tax system for gift and estate taxes. Gifts were made part of the system to ensure that people wouldn't escape estate taxes by giving away their money. At the time of death, the computation of the gross estate against which tax will be assessed includes any gifts made over the years (above the annual exclusion, discussed below).

Several states also have an estate tax. Some of these states impose an *inheritance tax*, which taxes those receiving an inheritance for their share, rather than a tax on the entire estate.

Federal Estate Taxes

Everything you own is taxable as part of your estate when you die. All the property which you own or control or in which you have an interest at the time of death, whether or not it passes through your will, is part of your *taxable estate*. This includes assets in your name or assets owned jointly with another, *POD* (payable on death), or *ITF* (in trust for). Your gross estate will include real estate, stocks, bonds, life insurance, retirement plan funds, IRAs, jointly owned property, and certain transfers made during your lifetime. (This is not the same as your *probate estate*, which is limited to assets passing through your will.)

For example, property you have placed in a trust, whether revocable or non-revocable, will be taxed in your estate if you receive the income from the trust during your lifetime. The basic rule is that if you keep an economic interest or retain control of the use of assets you've placed in a trust, your estate will be taxed on it.

Federal estate tax is due nine months after the decedent's death. Under certain limited circumstances where assets are not liquid, such as a farm or a business, estates may be allowed to pay their taxes in installments (with interest).

Exceptions. The basis for successful estate planning is found in the exceptions. The most common and useful of these techniques to reduce the amount of taxable estate are the annual exclusion and the marital deduction, although there are a number of other techniques you can use. Remember, you don't want to give away more than you can afford (or give up too much control).

Annual exclusion. We explained before that the gift and estate taxes operate as a unified tax system. This means that the *lifetime exclusion of $600,000* applies to gifts made over the course of your lifetime as well as bequests made upon your death.

The annual exclusion is the amount you may give to a donee or donees each year without incurring any tax liability. Over the course of your lifetime, you can make gifts of up to $10,000 per donee ($20,000 per couple), using the annual exclusion. You can make unlimited gifts up to this amount to any number of people without paying tax.

Annual exclusion gifts do not reduce the $600,000 lifetime transfer privilege. Gifts of $10,000 or less are not taxed by virtue of the tax exclusion. Gifts over the annual exclusion amount are subject to a gift tax, unless a portion of the lifetime $600,000 exclusion is used. The tax advantage of making annual exclusion gifts is that those gifts will not be included in figuring your gross estate, thus reducing your estate and its tax liability.

Education and medical expenses. There is no upper limit on the amount you can pay for education or medical expenses for another person, without tax liability, so long as the amount is paid directly to the provider, i.e. the educational or health care institution. For example, if you want to pay for your grandchild's college tuition, you can arrange to make direct payments to the university. And you can still make your grandchild an annual exclusion gift of up to $10,000 (or $20,000 if you're making the gift as a married couple).

Marital deduction. The marital deduction allows gifts and bequests to be made to a spouse without any federal tax liability. All property given or bequeathed to a spouse is free of federal taxes, provided that the spouse receiving the property is a citizen of the United States. Some states do tax at least a portion of such gifts or bequests.

Taking advantage of the marital deduction is a two-edged sword. It softens the blow on a surviving spouse when the first spouse dies, but leaves that spouse at a disadvantage in planning his or her own estate, now larger and more vulnerable. Under the marital deduction, tax is *deferred*, not eliminated. Planning is needed for the eventual death of the surviving spouse, because that's when the big tax bite will hit.

USING THE LIFETIME EXCLUSION AND MARITAL DEDUCTION

If you and your spouse have, or expect to have, assets worth more than $600,000, you want to make sure your heirs get the maximum benefit of $600,000 and don't lose it. If all your assets (including joint assets) are worth over $600,000 and you leave everything outright to your husband or wife, it will be lost. Joint property owned by husband and wife may pass to the survivor at the death of the first spouse and will qualify for the estate tax marital deduction, but the benefit of the $600,000 estate tax exemption equivalent will be lost. The survivor will wind up with more than $600,000, and subsequent heirs will be taxed for everything above that amount at estate tax rates of 50 percent or higher.

The lifetime exclusion can be used to your advantage. Couples should *split their estates* and not have wills leaving everything outright to each other. Each spouse should create a "credit shelter trust" or "bypass trust" of the first $600,000 of assets (the exempt amount) of which the surviving spouse can have use but which will pass tax-free to heirs when the surviving spouse dies. By this means, as much as $1,200,000 can be sheltered from estate tax.

For example, if you and your spouse have $1.2 million in assets, you can divide the total between you, each then leaving up to $600,000 in a trust for the benefit of the other. Upon the first spouse's death, the surviving spouse will have $600,000 in assets and the use of $600,000 in trust. At the latter's death, the $600,000 assets plus the remaining trust principal (including any growth) will pass tax-free to heirs.

SELECTED TRUST STRATEGIES

A variety of strategies exist for minimizing the tax bite on your federal estate, such as the *qualified personal residence trust* (QPRT) or the *family partnership*, in which assets (your home or your business) transferred on a discounted basis during your lifetime can be used to leverage your annual exclusion gift rights and your $600,000 lifetime exclusion. Strategies of this level of sophistication require consultation with a lawyer. Other strategies include:

Charitable deduction and the charitable remainder trust. There is no gift or estate tax imposed on gifts or bequests to charities. The *charitable remainder trust* is a device which allows you to put your property in trust for a charity while allowing you the income from the trust during your lifetime or that of your spouse or your child. Its chief advantage is that it minimizes estate tax and avoids capital gains tax. One disadvantage is that the principal is not available and cannot be invaded for possible emergency medical needs of the surviving spouse. Another is that your heirs won't receive the property.

The ideal way to use this device is to transfer your appreciated property to the charitable remainder trust now, which allows you to get the benefit of the charitable deduction immediately, have the trust sell the appreciated property and reinvest the proceeds of the sale—unreduced by capital gains tax—in higher yielding investments, so that the trust will pay you a higher return. For example, if you own a property worth $1 million, presently earning 2 percent or $20,000 yearly and subject to eventual estate taxation at a 50 percent rate, you can transfer the property, getting an annuity from the trust of between $60,000 and $90,000 depending on your age and life expectancy, and use the extra money to purchase a $500,000 life insurance policy. That way, you have the benefit of extra income, a charitable deduction, and when you die, your heirs will receive the same $500,000 inheritance.

Life insurance trust. Although it passes outside of your will and is not part of your probate assets, life insurance is part of your taxable estate. A useful device for removing life insurance from taxation is to assign it to an irrevocable life insurance trust. That way money available to the surviving spouse will not be taxed in his or her estate.

If you already own life insurance and assign it to a trust, you will be subject to a three-year rule during which period it may still be taxable. In that case, it may be possible for the trustee to buy a new policy, which will never have been in your estate. Whether this is desirable depends on the relative costs of your original policy and a new, more expensive one measured against the potential tax savings. You can make gifts to the trust to pay insurance.

QTIP trust. QTIP is an acronym for *Qualified Terminable Interest Property Trust.* This kind of trust allows the testator, who sets it up, to provide for his or her surviving spouse *and* name the beneficiary upon the surviving spouse's death.

The QTIP trust qualifies for the marital deduction if a number of conditions are met. Among them:

- The trust must distribute all income to the surviving spouse for life on at least an annual basis.

- The executor must make an irrevocable election to treat it as a QTIP trust.

Use of the QTIP trust is governed by a number of technical rules set forth in the law and IRS regulations. Like any other estate or trust instrument, this requires consultation with a lawyer expert this area. (The QTIP is discussed in Chapter 14.)

I'm happily married and plan on leaving my spouse a marital deduction share outright. Is there any reason I shouldn't?

It depends. A QTIP trust allows you greater control over the disposition of your assets. If you have children from a previous marriage, a QTIP trust is especially desirable for ensuring the eventual receipt of assets by children who might otherwise get nothing in the later disposition of your spouse's estate. It also can be used to protect the interests of children in the event of subsequent marriage by the surviving spouse.

INCOME TAXES

In the context of elder law, there are a number of income tax issues which may have an effect on your planning. These include:

- Income tax on Social Security and Medicare benefits
- Income tax on reverse mortgages
- Income tax on long term care insurance benefits, and deduction for premiums
- Income tax on accelerated benefits
- Income tax on viatical life insurance policy
- Income tax on estates
- Additional standard deduction for individuals over 65 or blind
- Tax credit for the elderly and disabled

Remember, this discussion is not intended as legal advice on your taxes. Only a competent professional familiar with your particular financial situation can counsel you.

Income tax on social security benefits. Social Security benefits are not subject to income tax liability except when your income exceeds a certain limit. As a general rule, you are liable for income taxes on a portion of your Social Security benefits if your other income is more than $25,000 (or $32,000 for a married couple).

The determination of whether you are liable, and if so, for how much, is a two-part calculation:

(1) *Am I liable?*

The formula for determining whether your income meets the $25,000/$32,000 threshold amount adds:

- Your regular earned income, tax-exempt income, and one-half of your Social Security benefits. For this computation, include in your total Social Security benefits any Medicare premiums withheld from your check and workers compensation pay.

  If the total exceeds $25,000 for an individual or $32,000 for a married couple, then a portion of your Social Security benefits will be taxable.

(2) *How much am I liable for?*

- You will be taxed on one-half the amount exceeding $25,000 (or $32,000 for a married couple) or one-half your Social Security benefits, whichever is less.

  If you make more than $34,000 (or $44,000 if you are a married couple), than you will be taxed on 85 percent of the amount exceeding that amount or 85 percent of your benefits, whichever is less.

For example, if a married couple filing jointly receives $17,000 in income, $12,000 in tax exempt interest income, and $10,000 in Social Security benefits, their gross for determining tax liability for their Social Security benefits is $34,000 ($17,000 plus $12,000 plus 1/2 of $10,000), making some portion of their Social Security liable for taxation. That portion is the lesser of the amount exceeding $32,000 ($2,000) or half their benefits ($5,000). Therefore, $2,000 is added to their $17,000 income, for a total of $19,000 which will be subject to federal tax.

Taxes on your Social Security benefits are subject to change, always hard to predict. A few states with income taxes also tax Social Security, usually linked to your federal return, although a smaller number of states treat benefits separately as taxable income. (See Chapter 18 for more on Social Security.)

I purchased annuities precisely because the interest was tax-exempt. Now you're saying they can be included in my taxes? Is this legal?

Yes, this indirect taxation of your tax-exempt interest has been upheld by the courts. Technically, it's your Social Security benefits which are being taxed, but you're right that the tax-exempt interest boosts the base upon which your tax liability is calculated. If you have investment shelters, you should discuss with your accountant whether they are subject to this calculation.

Income tax on reverse mortgages. With reverse mortgages, older home owners can use the equity built up in their homes as collateral and receive lump-sum or periodic payments from a bank. As a general rule, these reverse mortgage payments are not taxable. (Nor will they affect your Social Security or your Medicaid benefits.) Make sure you consult a lawyer familiar with your state's regulations before getting a reverse mortgage.

(See Chapter 19 for a discussion of reverse mortgages, as well as rollover and exclusion benefits available to older Americans upon sale of their homes.)

Income tax on long-term care insurance benefits and deduction for premiums. Under present law, the benefits you receive from a long-term care insurance policy will be treated as income for tax purposes. Your premiums for long-term care insurance are not deductible as a medical expense, unlike the premiums you pay on your other health insurance.

Legislative note. At this writing, there is legislation pending in Congress to change the Internal Revenue Code to exclude the receipt of benefits from income and to allow the deductibility of long-term care insurance premiums as a medical expense if you itemize deductions.

Income tax on accelerated benefits. Accelerated benefits payments and viatical settlement payments are treated as income to your under present law. Some states, such as New York, do not tax accelerated benefits.

Legislative note. There are proposals for changes in the Internal Revenue Code which would exempt accelerated benefits payments from income taxation. At this writing, however, accelerated benefits are still taxable and reported as such to the IRS.

Income tax on viatical life insurance policy. Viatical settlement payments are treated as income. Unfortunately, the proposed change to exempt accelerated benefits payments does not include viatical settlements. In our view, this is manifestly unfair, penalizing people in dire need for ready cash to meet medical bills and related expenses.

Income tax on estates. This is a tax on income of the estate, during that window of time when the estate is being administered and the assets have not yet been distributed to beneficiaries. Trust income is taxed as well.

Additional standard deductions for individuals over 65 or blind. Taxable income is calculated by taking a taxpayer's gross income, making certain deductions to reach an adjusted gross income (AGI), then deducting personal exemptions and standard or itemized deductions.

The standard deduction, available to taxpayers who do not itemize their deductions, may be increased for individuals who are 65 or older and for individuals who are blind. For 1995 returns, the standard deduction allowed a married couple was $6,550 ($3,275 if filing separately). An additional deduction of $750 was allowed each spouse who is 65 or older, and an additional $750 to each spouse who is blind. Both partners are entitled to the extra deductions, if they meet the qualifications. A single taxpayer, granted a $3,900 standard deduction in 1995, would be entitled to an additional deduction of $950 for age and $950 if blind. (These amounts are indexed annually for inflation.)

To qualify for the additional deduction, you cannot itemize your deductions. If you are a married taxpayer filing separately and your spouse itemizes deductions, this will also disqualify you. Estates and trusts are not eligible for the standard deduction. (There is also no extra "exemption" for the elderly or the blind.)

Can I deduct payments I make on behalf of my aging parent or disabled child?

Yes, under certain circumstances. If you furnish over 50 percent of the support of your parent or adult or infant child, you can deduct *all* the unreimbursed medical expenses incurred by that parent or child (to the extent that such expenses exceed 7.5 percent of your AGI). This applies whether or not the person's income exceeds the specified limit to allow you an extra exemption on your return. Remember, you cannot deduct itemized medical expenses and claim the standard deduction or the additional deductions available for individuals over 65 or blind.

Under this rule, you can deduct medical, dental, and prescription drugs expenses for any of the following relatives who qualify as your dependents by virtue of your providing over one-half of their support:

- Your child, stepchild, adopted child, grandchild, or great-grandchild
- Your son-in-law or daughter-in-law
- Your parent, stepparent, parent-in-law
- Your grandparent or great-grandparent
- Your brother, sister, half-sibling, step-sibling, brother-in-law, or sister-in-law
- Your aunt, uncle, nephew, or niece (if related by blood)

Your dependent must be a citizen of the United States or a resident of Canada or Mexico. A married person filing a joint return is generally not eligible to be your dependent.

Tax credit for the elderly and disabled. A tax credit is available to a taxpayer who is:

- Sixty-five or older
- Retired on disability and permanently and totally disabled at the time of retirement

The credit is 15 percent of a base which may be as high as $5,000 for a single taxpayer or married taxpayer filing jointly (where only one spouse qualifies), $7,500 for married taxpayers filing jointly (where both spouses qualify), and $3,750 for a married taxpayer filing an individual return. For people qualifying as disabled, this base amount is limited to disability income. The base is also subject to further reduction for single taxpayers with income over $7,500 and married taxpayers filing a joint return with income over $10,000. In any event, the credit cannot exceed the individual's tax.

 STATE TAXES

States often give tax breaks to their older taxpayers, in the form of credits or deductions. These breaks may include a flat rate income tax credit, a tax credit based on the size of your federal tax bite, a tax credits to older taxpayers, and an exemption for those 65 and older.

Some states also provide tax relief for those who support elderly relatives in their home. A few count only a portion of the income of people in continuing-care or nursing home facilities. Connecticut exempts owners over 65 from state tax on the sale of their homes. Often, too, states have specific tax relief programs for property taxes which allows reduced or deferred payments. (See Chapter 19 for a description of these plans).

Taxes and tax programs change each year. With a new Congress, federal tax changes portend state changes with promises of greater relief from current tax burdens. It remains to be seen whether these promises will be kept and just who will reap the benefits of such changes.

Part 5

■■■■■■■■■■■■■■■■■■■■■■■■

Working and Retirement

Recent years have seen a small revolution in work in the United States. In no small part due to the demographics of our aging population, the linear path from trainee to retiree has been replaced with a new and often bewildering maze of options. With the disappearance of mandatory retirement, many people want to work past traditional retirement age and many more—in need of income or health benefits—have to work past retirement age. More than 13.5 million people over 55 are currently in the work force. It's estimated that 6 million unemployed Americans over the age of 55 are ready and able to work.

These trends have had direct impact on older workers in a variety of ways, from changes in Social Security eligibility and benefits to cutbacks in, and increased cost-sharing for, benefits to employees and retirees to bankrupt companies and lost pensions. At the same time, there are more protections afforded workers than ever before, more options for retirees and more safeguards for their families.

This section offers a short course on work and retirement issues that you may face. Chapter 16 explains laws designed to protect you on the job, offering advice on how to identify discrimination and what to do about it. Chapter 17 discusses some of the factors that go into your decision to retire, as well as your legal rights to benefits and pensions, and the protections you have against changes to them. In Chapter 18, we give you the grand tour of Social Security retirement and disability benefits, making sure you understand how to assert your rights in the complicated world of government benefits.

16

■■

PROTECTIONS IN THE
WORKPLACE

The older worker has long presented a contradictory image to American business. The "early retirement decade" of the 1980s reinforced a view of the older worker as unproductive members of the work force to be "riffed" (from "reduction in force") as soon as possible. At the same time, with 13.5 million people over 55 in the work force and another 6 million unemployed and ready to work, public policy and legislation were based on a portrait of the older worker as offering significant benefits to his or her employer and to the nation's economy.

As this stronger, more positive portrait of older worker emerged, there was a noticeable shift in public opinion, in large part brought about by changes in employment practices and employment laws. Some labor-strapped companies showed renewed interest in older workers, offering part-time work, flex-time schedules, and retiree job banks. Laws at the federal, state, and local level recognized the disadvantages faced by older workers in their efforts to obtain and retain employment and sought to promote treatment of older persons based on their abilities rather than age, while prohibiting arbitrary discrimination.

The centerpiece of federal legislation affording older workers protection from age discrimination is the Age Discrimination in Employment Act, passed in 1967. More than a quarter century later, it has been joined by the Americans with Disabilities Act, offering new protections to older workers, and the Family and Medical Leave Act, entitling workers to needed leave for medical or family caretaking purposes. Numerous state and local laws, many patterned on these federal laws, provide different or stronger protections.

AGE DISCRIMINATION IN EMPLOYMENT ACT (ADEA)

Age discrimination? It's as old as Lear, forced out of the family business and into early retirement without a pension. Then as now older workers were more vulnerable to loss of employment based on age stereotypes and arbitrary age limits unrelated to ability.

The nation's work force has aged, becoming an older (and more experienced) cadre of workers since 1967, when Congress passed the Age Discrimination in Employment Act extending anti-discrimination protections to people from 40 to 65. Current projections forecast that the median age of the country's workers will reach 38.9 years by the year 2000.

What was once revolutionary now passes unremarked. Virtually all states have laws on age discrimination of some sort or another, as do a number of local governments.

New laws on the books, however, do not translate immediately into changes in practice. In the 1980s, more than a quarter-million complaints of age bias were brought before the Equal Employment Opportunity Commission (EEOC) and local and state agencies. Seventy percent of them charged wrongful dismissal or involuntary retirement.

As a matter of fact, federal age anti-discrimination efforts get mixed reviews at best, largely due to enforcement problems. To its credit, the law has proven an effective curb on bias in corporate downsizing, but it has been largely ineffective at dealing with discriminatory hiring.

State and local laws often have different rules concerning what constitutes discrimination, to whom they apply, and where to complain and when. Ironically, some states offer greater protection than does the federal government, something which may be important for you.

 ## YOUR RIGHTS UNDER THE ADEA

The Age Discrimination in Employment Act of 1967 (ADEA), as amended, prohibits employment discrimination based on age against persons 40 years of age or older.

The Age Discrimination in Employment Act forbids employers to do any of the following to employees or potential employees over 40:

- Fire or refuse to hire, or otherwise discriminate with respect to compensation, terms, conditions, and privileges of employment, on the basis of age
- Limit, segregate, or classify employees in any way that would tend to deprive any individual of employment opportunities or adversely affect his or her status, on the basis of age
- Retaliate for opposing an illegal practice or otherwise exercising rights established by the law

Basic cases under ADEA allege unfair treatment based upon age. Such treatment includes not only dismissals based on age but other adverse job decisions, such as demotion, withholding promotions, or not hiring based on age alone. Within that basic prohibition, a number of exceptions have been carefully drawn. Examples of employer actions permitted under the ADEA include:

- Firing an individual for good cause; for example, incompetence or insubordination. It is legal to discharge or otherwise discipline employees for good cause, regardless of their age. The ADEA offers no extra protections to employees who otherwise deserve to be fired.
- Laying off older workers as part of a wholesale reduction in force (RIF). Reasonable factors other than age may justify a decision which impacts older workers.
- Not hiring or promoting an individual because of failure to meet *bona fide* occupation qualifications. These are qualifications an employer has established as reasonably necessary to the normal operation of the particular business.

It is up to the employer to justify an occupational qualification based on age. An employer must show both that the age qualification is reasonably necessary in that those over the given age are unable to perform the job competently or that individual assessments would be impossible or highly impractical. For example, an upper age limit might be justified for hiring or retiring airline pilots or traffic controllers.

I work for a small employer. Does my employer have to comply with the law?

The Age Discrimination in Employment Act applies only to employers with 20 or more employees, working at least 20 or more calendar weeks.

Federal and state government are subject to the law, regardless of the number of employees. Local government is also covered, although only if employing 20 or more, under the 20-employee rule. Labor unions and employment agencies are also regulated under the law.

Who qualifies as an employee or prospective employee?

Under the law, employees and potential employees are protected. You are not protected if you are an independent contractor or partner (although what qualifies as a partnership may be subject to interpretation).

Is all age discrimination banned or only discrimination against older people? What age group is protected under the law?

The good news in that there's no longer an upper limit on those covered by the Age Discrimination in Employment Act. The original upper age limit of 65 was first extended (to 70), then removed. Exceptions exist for those not covered by the act. For example, judges and elected state and local officials can be terminated at age 70.

However, there's still a lower limit, and if you're younger than 40, you are *not* protected by the ADEA. Discrimination against people who are 39 or 17 may be wrong, but it is not protected by the federal age discrimination laws. Some states and municipalities have age discrimination laws that cover a greater age range.

Can companies advertise for employees by age?

Employment notices or advertisements indicating any preference, limitations, or specification based upon age are prohibited under the law. Help Wanted ads with terms like "girl," "boy," or "recent college grad" discriminate against older workers (and demean younger ones). The prohibitions on help wanted ads apply to employers, employment agencies, and labor organizations.

If a company against which you have a grievance publishes an illegal help wanted ad, hold onto it! In addition to forming the basis for a complaint, it may be of use as evidence should you file a complaint about improper firing or failure to hire.

Can companies ask how old I am?

Not before they hire you. The only preemployment question concerning age which is appropriate and legal is whether you are between 18 and 65. Once you're employed, age becomes an appropriate part of your employment record. (Note that questions asked prospective employees are even more circumscribed by the Americans with Disability Act, discussed later in this chapter).

Does the law apply to employee benefits?

Yes. A 1989 Supreme Court ruling in *Public Employees' Retirement System of Ohio v. Betts* interpreted the Age Discrimination in Employment Act as applying only to nonfringe benefit aspects of employment, such as compensation, terms, and conditions of employment. The *Betts* decision held that the law's discrimination prohibition did *not* apply to retirement plans, unless they were a subterfuge for discrimination in nonfringe benefits. This ruling was overturned by Congress in 1991. The Older Workers benefits Protection Act provides that an employer who has a benefit plan must provide equal benefits to older workers, or incur the same cost as providing them to younger workers.

Can a company demand that I sign an agreement when I'm hired or when I'm retiring promising not to sue?

Prior to 1991, the answer was, unbelievably, Yes. Although the average employee has a bargaining position about as strong as that of a homeless person challenging the clauses of a standard lease, until 1991 the courts found these waivers and releases to be legal. In one restrictive ruling, the United States Supreme Court upheld a similar clause in an employment contract which mandated compulsory arbitration in lieu of an age discrimination lawsuit.

What's the point of a waiver? Theoretically, your employer confers valuable benefits on you in exchange for your "voluntary" departure. Even if you have a good age discrimination complaint, you've bargained it away.

In 1990, Congress passed the Older Workers Benefit Protection Act. Under the new law, the answer is still Yes, but only if certain conditions are met. Title II of the law sets out minimum criteria which must be satisfied before any waiver of a claim or right under the Age Discrimination and Employment Act will be considered a "knowing and voluntary" waiver:

- The waiver must be part of an agreement that is written in a manner understandable by you (or by the average individual eligible to participate).
- The waiver must specifically refer to rights and claims under the Age Discrimination in Employment Act.
- The waiver does *not* apply to any claims arising after the date you sign.
- The waiver must be in return for "consideration"—you must be getting something in addition to what you would be getting without any waiver
- You must be advised in writing to consult a lawyer before signing.
- You must be given at least 21 days to consider signing—45 days if it's part of an exit incentive or other employment termination program being offered to a group of employees.
- You must be given a period of at least seven days to revoke your waiver—even after you've signed it.
- If it's an exit incentive or other employment termination program, you must be informed in writing of the class of individuals being covered, eligibility factors, applicable time limits, job titles and ages of everyone in the group, and ages of everyone in the same job classification or organizational unit *not* eligible or selected for the program.

The Older Workers Benefit Protection Act, applicable to all new plans, became effective September 15, 1991.

AMERICANS WITH DISABILITIES ACT (ADA)

An even more revolutionary event occurred in 1990, when the Americans, with Disabilities Act (ADA) was signed into law. The ADA was designed to protect the rights of an estimated 43 million people with disabilities in the United States. This landmark civil rights law contains a sweeping design that mandates a range of protections in public accommodations, commercial facilities, transportation and communication services, and employment. Title I of the ADA sets forth employment protections which may cover older as well as younger persons with disabilities.

The protections of the ADA are not limited to older people. However, as disabilities increase with age in both number and severity, its impact is greater among older workers. According to the Health and Retirement Study conducted by the Institute for Social Research at the University of Michigan and the National Institute for Aging, the four most common reasons for leaving jobs were given as back problems, heart condition, diabetes, and chronic lung disease—all more prevalent among older workers.

One of the trickiest things about the new disability law is that many older people with a disability may not recognize it—or they may not consider themselves to have a disability. As a result, they also may not recognize discrimination when they encounter it.

Don't equate the term *disability* with major impairment. In fact, the law is written to reflect functional abilities—so that you may have a limitation which qualifies you for ADA protection without realizing it.

Identifying discrimination. Remember that if you have a disability, you may face discrimination based on disability alone, not age. Or you may encounter discrimination for your disability coupled with age discrimination.

 ## YOUR ADA RIGHTS

Title I of the Americans with Disabilities Act prohibits discrimination against any qualified individual with a disability, because of the disability, in regard to job application procedures, hiring, advancement, discharge, compensation, job training, and other terms, conditions, or privileges of employment. Employers may not discriminate against an individual with a disability in hiring or promotion if the person is otherwise qualified for the job.

The law applies to employers with 15 or more employees. It prohibits discrimination in hiring, promotion, assignments, evaluations, termination, layoff and recall, discipline, training, leave and benefits. It also prohibits employers from limiting, segregating, or classifying an individual in a way that limits or otherwise denies job opportunities because of disability.

Who is a person with disabilities covered by the law?

In order to be covered by the ADA, you must meet the statutory definition of disability. You are considered an individual with a disability if you:

- have a physical or mental impairment that substantially limits one or more major life activities or
- have a record of such an impairment or
- are regarded as having such an impairment

This impairment must cause a *substantial limitation* in one or more major life activities:

- Caring for oneself
- Performing manual tasks
- Walking
- Seeing
- Hearing
- Speaking

- Breathing
- Learning
- Working

This list is not exhaustive. Other examples of major life activities would include sitting, standing, lifting, and reaching.

By substantial, the law factors in the nature and severity of the impairment, its duration or expected duration, and its long-term impact or expected impact.

Test: Are you qualified to perform the essential functions of the job?

Under the ADA, an individual claiming disability discrimination must be qualified for the job. This means that you must

- Satisfy the requisite skill, experience, education, and other job-related requirements of the employment position and
- Be able to perform the essential functions of the job, *with or without reasonable accommodation*

This is the crux of the employment provisions of the ADA. The test is whether you can do the job. Once that test is met, if you need "reasonable accommodations" to accomplish that, they must be provided.

What are essential job functions?

These are the basic job duties you as an employee must be able to perform. In analyzing the basic functions and tasks required for your job, factors to consider include

- Whether the reason the position exists is to perform that function
- The number of other employees available to perform the same function or among whom the function is distributed
- The degree of expertise or skill required

What are reasonable accommodations and when are they required?

If you have a disability under the law, you are entitled to reasonable accommodations to enable you to enjoy equal employment opportunity:

- In the application process
- In performing the essential functions of the job
- In the benefits and privileges of employment

Reasonable accommodations may include modifications or adjustments such as job restructuring, part-time or modified work schedules, reassignment to a vacant position, buying or modifying equipment or devices, appropriate adjustment or modification of examinations, training materials or policies, providing qualified readers or interpreters, as well as making facilities accessible to and usable by individuals with disabilities. It is your responsibility to inform your employer of your need for accommodation.

Exception for Employer Hardship

Reasonable accommodations are not required if they will cause an employer undue hardship to business operations in the form of significant difficulty or expense. In determining whether there is undue hardship on an employer, the following factors are considered:

- The nature and cost of the needed accommodation
- The overall financial resources of the employer, the number of persons employed, and the effect on expenses and resources

Expense alone does not constitute undue hardship.

What questions are permissible during a job interview? Can an employer question me about my need for reasonable accommodations?

No. Asking a prospective employee about disability is forbidden. Employers are restricted to asking whether the applicant can do the job—with or without a reasonable accommodation. They can ask about your ability to perform the job, but not whether you have a disability. Nor may they use tests that tend to screen out those with disabilities.

An employer's initial offer to you may not be conditioned on whether or not you need accommodation. After an offer is made, the question of whether an accommodation is reasonable may be discussed.

Can I be denied employment because of my spouse's disability?

No. The ADA also prohibits discrimination due to your relationship with a person with a disability. However, your employer is *not* required to provide accommodation for you to care for a disabled relative; it is the *employee* with a disability who is entitled to accommodation under the law. (You may be entitled to leave, however, under the Family and Medical Leave Act, discussed later in this chapter.)

Can I be refused work because of concern about the effect on a company's health care costs?

According to the Equal Employment Opportunity Commission (EEOC), which administers the employment portion of the ADA, the answer is No. In a policy statement, the EEOC has stated that insurance cannot be used as a subterfuge to evade the purposes of the law.

Disabled employees must be given equal access to any health insurance provided to other employees. Distinctions may be made in broad categories, but there may not be a lower level of benefits for a specific illness such as diabetes, deafness, AIDS, kidney disease, or cancer. Exclusions based on experimental drugs and treatments are allowed.

If I have a covered disability, does that mean I have to be hired?
No.

What is an acceptable disability? Does mental illness count? Overweight?

There is no list of "acceptable" disabilities. Federal regulations define physical impairment as any "physiological disorder, or condition, cosmetic disfigurement, or anatomical loss affecting one or more of the following body systems: neurological, musculoskeletal, special sense organs, respiratory (including speech organs), cardiovascular, reproductive, digestive, genito-urinary, hemic and lymphatic, skin, and endocrine."

A mental impairment may be any "mental or psychological disorder, such as mental retardation, organic brain syndrome, emotional or mental illness, and specific learning disabilities."

The law includes persons with visual, speech, and hearing impairments, cerebral palsy, epilepsy, muscular dystrophy, multiple sclerosis, diabetes, heart disease, cancer, HIV or AIDS, as well as individuals with mental retardation, emotional illness, and some learning disabilities. The EEOC has said that under certain conditions, obesity may be a disability as defined by the law; however, it must be an impairment, as defined, and limiting to at least one major life activity.

Physical or emotional characteristics are not disabilities, nor is advanced age by itself, although conditions associated with age such as Alzheimer's, arthritis, cancer, diabetes, osteoporosis, and vision and hearing impairments may be. Alcoholism may also qualify as a disability. However, the ADA does not cover compulsive gamblers, kleptomaniacs, pyromaniacs, or people with sexual disorders.

Is age an impairment?

No. Advanced age, in and of itself, does not constitute an impairment under the Americans with Disabilities Act. However, various medical conditions commonly associated with age, such as hearing loss, osteoporosis, or arthritis would constitute impairments within the meaning of the law.

Does the fact that I receive disability benefits qualify me as disabled?

The fact that you may receive disability benefits under any other program, such as Social Security or Supplemental Security Income (SSI), does not mean you are qualified under this law. All laws have their own definitions and eligibility requirements.

ENFORCING YOUR RIGHTS

The Age Discrimination in Employment Act is administered by the Equal Employment Opportunity Commission (EEOC), which also enforces the Americans with Disabilities Act's Title I provisions against employment discrimination on account of disability.

The Equal Employment Opportunity Commission is a federal agency, responsible for enforcing a number of equal employment opportunity laws and regulations. EEOC will investigate your charge of employment discrimination (under both the ADEA and ADA) and may litigate those charges, on its own or your behalf. This process also applies to complaints against labor unions and employment agencies, which are regulated under the ADEA.

A number of state laws also proscribe age discrimination. Whether to proceed through the state or federal system with a given complaint should be discussed with a lawyer. (See discussion of state discrimination laws, later in this chapter.)

Bringing a Complaint Before the EEOC

In order to bring a complaint of discrimination, either on the job or in applying for a job, you must file a charge with the EEOC. To do so, you need only allege that some act of discrimination has taken place, and you must specify the act, the date it occurred, and the law that was violated.

Notice and filing. You must file a charge of discrimination with the EEOC within certain time frames. There are strict deadlines which must be observed if you are going to preserve your claim.

Charges may be filed in person, by mail or by telephone by contacting the nearest EEOC office. The EEOC has 50 district and field offices that investigate and resolve charges of employment discrimination filed with it. For a listing, consult the Resources section at the end of this book.

Filing deadline. For both ADA and ADEA claims, you have the option of filing within the following time periods:

- 180 days after the alleged discriminatory act
- in states or localities with antidiscrimination laws, 300 days after the act, or 30 days after receiving notice that the state or locality has terminated its proceeding, *whichever is earlier*

In order to determine your filing deadline, you must first determine when your case arises (*accrues*). Figuring out when the discriminatory act occurred is not as clear as you may think. As a general rule, the clock starts running when you know (or should know) that you've been discriminated against.

This leaves some room for interpretation. Sometimes the clock doesn't start running until you actually discover you've been discriminated against (which may happen some time after your company acts).

Contents of complaint. The complaint must contain

- Your name and address
- Names of all persons who committed the act
- A record of specific events

The complaint must be signed and sworn to. It is not necessary to overstate your case. Resist the temptation to be dramatic; be brief and specific.

EEOC Investigation

Upon receipt of your complaint, the EEOC opens a case file and conducts an investigation. (As of 1995, private sector employment discrimination charges are categorized according to priority, and some cases are immediately dismissed without investigation.)

As part of its investigation, EEOC staff will

- Interview you
- Notify your employer (or would-be employer) of your charge, and request relevant information
- Interview any other witnesses with direct knowledge of the alleged discrimination

When its investigation is completed, EEOC makes a determination that there either is or is not reasonable cause to believe discrimination occurred.

- If EEOC determines that the evidence shows reasonable cause to believe discrimination occurred, it will attempt to conciliate. Conciliation is a legal process that involves voluntary negotiation with the employer to persuade him or her to remedy the violation. If conciliation fails, EEOC may initiate a court action.
- If EEOC determines that there is no reasonable cause to believe discrimination occurred, it will notify both you and the employer—and issue you a *right-to-sue letter*. This means you may take the employer to court yourself (not possible without the right-to-sue letter).

When does the EEOC attempt to conciliate?

Under the ADEA, generally, conciliation must be attempted before EEOC seeks to determine the validity of the charge. Conciliation may also be tried after the determination is made.

If conciliation fails, must EEOC initiate a court action?

No. EEOC initiates very few court actions. Most charges are conciliated or settled, making further action unnecessary. If your case is not, and the EEOC, as is likely, does not not initiate court action, you will usually be able to bring court action on your own behalf.

How long does it take for EEOC to process a complaint?

You may have to wait several months, perhaps more than a year. That's a long time at any age. Ironically, age discrimination complaints used to have priority because charging parties had only two years from the time of the alleged discrimination to take offending parties to court. However, the Civil Rights Act of 1991 removed this time limit, and age discrimination cases—up to 24,000 claims annually—are no longer given priority.

The EEOC is also subject to strict budgetary constraints, which limits its effectiveness. With ADA cases added to its workload, the agency's caseload increased more than 50 percent, yet its funding increased only slightly to its current $233 million. At the end of 1994, the EEOC had a backlog of 100,000 unresolved cases of all types.

In general, the EEOC's rate of "no cause" determinations has been high for years. In 1992, of 68,000 discrimination charges processed on all accounts, fewer than one out of 40 resulted in "reasonable cause" findings:

2.4 percent "reasonable cause" findings

6.4 percent settled through conciliation

6.8 percent settled through withdrawal and payment of monetary benefits

23.4 percent closed for administrative reasons

61.0 percent "no cause" findings

Because of increased workloads, decreased resources, and new civil rights laws, the EEOC brings only a limited number of cases to court itself. In 1992, it litigated only 447 cases. In response, many employers have established alternative policies for resolving discrimination and other employment complaints. Mediating employment disputes through other processes are discussed later in this chapter.

How long do I have to wait for the EEOC in order to sue?

You are required to go through the process before you can proceed to court on your own. You may, after 180 days have passed since you filed your claim, request that the EEOC issue you a "right-to-sue" letter. Once you receive a right-to-sue letter, you have 90 days in which to file suit.

 BACK PAY AND OTHER RELIEF

The available universe of relief that may be sought in an action includes:

- Back pay
- Hiring, promotion, reinstatement, benefit restoration, front pay, and other affirmative relief
- Damages for actual pecuniary loss other than back pay (ADA only)
- Liquidated damages (ADEA only)
- Compensatory damages for future monetary losses and mental anguish (ADA)
- Punitive damages (ADA)
- Posting of a notice advising employees of rights under laws and the right to be free from retaliation
- Corrective or preventive actions to cure the source of the identified discrimination and minimize the chance of its recurrence
- Stopping of the specific discriminatory practice

In the 1980s, the EEOC collected more than $400 million on behalf of those claiming age discrimination.

Under the Civil Rights Act of 1991, employment discrimination on account of disability under the ADA may entitle you to compensatory damages, *if* it is shown that you were the victim of intentional discrimination. The total amount is limited by the statute and dependent upon the number of employees the company has:

15–100 employees	$ 50,000
101–200 employees	100,000
201–500 employees	200,000
more than 500 employees	300,000

Can I get punitive damages for my ADA claim?

Punitive damages are designed not to compensate you for your injury, but to punish the offending employer. An award of punitive damages is made only in cases of intentional discrimination *and* where the employer's conduct was wanton, willful or reckless.

The monetary limits of the Civil Rights Act, however, apply to monetary awards, whether they are for compensatory damages alone or for compensatory and punitive damages.

 MEDIATING EMPLOYMENT DISPUTES

Many employers have adopted alternative methods for mediating complaints of discrimination and other employment disputes. For reasons including time, cost, and employee relations, both small and large employers use one or more alternative approaches for resolving disputes in order to achieve conciliation between the parties outside the EEOC and court process:

- *Mediation.* A process for resolving disputes in which a neutral trained person (from inside or outside the company) helps negotiate a mutually agreeable solution.
- *Arbitration.* A process similar to a legal challenge, in which the dispute is submitted to a neutral third party for decision, which is usually binding on the parties.
- *Fact finding.* A process in which a neutral person (from inside or outside the company) investigates and develops findings for use in resolving the dispute.
- *Negotiation.* A process in which employee and employer, each with the aid of counsel, discuss the dispute with the goal of coming to settlement.
- *Peer review.* A process in which employees (sometimes including managers) sitting as a panel hear and try to resolve employment complaints.

From an employee point of view, these methods have advantages and drawbacks. Time is the greatest advantage, in that most alternative dispute resolution methods will prove faster than going through the EEOC. Very often, employees will have no choice in the matter, being bound to arbitration or another method by a collective bargaining agreement or by waiver signed as a condition of employment.

Employer policies vary considerably in matters which have great importance, such as selection of the arbitrator or other neutral decision-maker. Some call for employee participation in selection, while others provide for unilateral selection by the employer. Although many company policies are silent on the subject, you generally have a right to be represented by counsel or other representative of your choosing.

The ADA encourages the use of alternative means of dispute resolution. In 1995, EEOC established a voluntary program using mediation to handle some workplace discrimination charges. Under the program plan, complaining employees and their employers work with a neutral mediator. If settlement cannot be reached through this process, the claim will be returned to the regular EEOC process.

If I agree to mediation, do I waive my right to seek enforcement under the law?

You may. Many companies use arbitration, peer review courts, and other forms of alternative dispute resolution as "private courts" to allow rapid resolution of employment disputes. These forums do not necessarily apply the same laws or standards as the courts. Your agreement to submit your claim to mediation or arbitration may preclude you from seeking relief in the courts. Provisions for alternative dispute resolution are becoming more common in collective bargaining agreements and employment contracts. Note that under the voluntary process set up by the EEOC, an unresolved claim would not preclude your right to pursue regular EEOC enforcement.

STATE DISCRIMINATION LAWS

All states have some sort of law banning discrimination on account of age. The specific prohibitions, enforcement mechanisms, and remedies available to the successful complainant vary from state to state.

Forty-six states, forty localities, and the District of Columbia have established fair employment practices agencies to investigate employment discrimination. Most states have a system that parallels the federal structure. The state agency investigates complaints filed with it, and in appropriate cases will attempt conciliation or bring a court action against the employers. Some states have a dual system, with available forums in both an administrative agency and the state courts. New York has a dual system, as do New Jersey, Pennsylvania, Maine, Minnesota, Oregon, Idaho, West Virginia, and the District of Columbia. A few states allow only for private action.

Some jurisdictions have a work-sharing arrangement, in which case the charge may be processed initially by either EEOC or the state or local agency. The ADA requires that the EEOC defer charges of discrimination to state or local Fair Employment Practice Agencies (FEPAs). State agencies conduct roughly half of current investigations.

Different strategies bring different results. If you choose to go the administrative route before an agency, you may waive your right to pursue the matter in court. You'll want to consult with a lawyer before making any determination about how to proceed.

What do I do if I suspect that I'm the victim of discrimination?

- *Identify.* First of all, recognize it. The first step in combating age discrimination is being able to identify it.
- *Investigate.* You are your own best detective. Who knows better the whys and wherefores of your case? See what you can find out about your company's actions which may have bearing on your claim, particularly any disparate treatment among you and your colleagues.
- *Document.* Make a paper trail. If at all possible, document your claim with written memoranda sent to you or by you. Keep a log of things said to you. Don't depend on your memory, and don't depend on the memories of witnesses. Although many cases rely on indirect or circumstantial evidence, often on statistics culled concerning the treatment of other older workers similarly treated, direct evidence is always the best.
- *Get outside help.* Age discrimination is hard to identify, still harder to prove. Your best bet is to contact your local EEOC office or state agency. You may want to file a charge with EEOC or your state's human relations agency.
- *Get a lawyer.* Lawyers who specialize in this field are called employment lawyers. Call your local bar and ask for a referral. If you have a case, your lawyer will tell you. If not, he or she will tell you that, too. These are hard cases to win. Your lawyer will be able to help you determine whether to sue in state court or go to the EEOC, or whether you have a claim at all.

I believe that I've been discriminated against in my job because of my age, which is 30. Do I have any recourse?

Some states and municipalities have laws affording greater protections to a larger age range than the federal laws. For example, people 18 and over are afforded discrimination protection in Iowa, Kansas, Minnesota, New York, Oregon, Vermont, and the District of Columbia. Others, including Alaska, Connecticut, Florida, Maryland, Michigan, New Jersey, and New Mexico, have no statutory age range. Check with your state human rights agency to see what protections your state offers.

 ## FAMILY AND MEDICAL LEAVE ACT

On a brighter note, the Family and Medical Leave Act was passed by Congress in 1993 in recognition of the need for greater balance between work and family life. The demands on American workers have increased steadily in recent years. The growing numbers of elderly dependent on working family members only added to that burden. In many cases older workers, particularly women, have been forced to leave the workforce in order to care for an older relative.

The law gives workers some assurance that they will not have to choose between meeting their obligations at home or on the job. If you qualify under its provisions, you must be granted up to 12 work weeks of unpaid leave during any 12-month period for one or more of these reasons:

- Birth or placement of a child for adoption or foster care
- To care for an immediate family member (spouse, child, or parent) with a serious health condition
- Medical leave when unable to work because of a serious health condition

In order to qualify, you must work for:

- Any public employer
- A private employer, engaged in commerce, with 50 or more employees working at least 20 work weeks in the current or preceding calendar year

And you must meet the following conditions:

- Have worked for a covered employer for a total of at least 12 months
- Have worked at least 1,250 hours over the prior 12 months
- Work at a location where at least 50 employees are employed by the employer within 75 miles.

Under the Family and Medical Leave Act, the employee is entitled to this leave, with no loss of health or other benefits, and with job restoration when the leave is concluded. If you take a leave under the Family and Medical Leave Act, you must be restored to your original job, or to an equivalent job with equivalent pay, benefits, and other terms and conditions.

The employer's obligation under this law terminates if informed by you that you will not return (although you may still be eligible for continuation coverage, as described in Chapter 6.)

What happens to my health care coverage when I go on a leave?

If you take a leave under the Family and Medical Leave Act, you must continue to get coverage under the same group plan that would have been provided if you remained at work. If you generally make a contribution to the costs, you would still be required to do so. You can decline coverage during your leave period without jeopardizing your right to be restored to full coverage on your return, but don't give up your health care coverage unless you will be receiving comparable coverage from another source. If you do not return to work at the end of your leave, your right to continuation coverage under federal law would be measured from that date. (See Chapter 6.)

My aunt is sick and needs care. Must I be granted leave to tend to her?

No. The biggest weakness of the act is that it mandates leave only for "an immediate family member." This is defined to mean an employee's spouse, son or daughter, or parents. You are not guaranteed leave to care for your aunt or uncle, or your in-laws, or your grandparents.

The narrow definition of parent and family member ignores the half of the entire problem for which the law was introduced, the working woman upon whom most of these duties invariably fall. If you are a member of the so-called "sandwich generation," simultaneously taking care of children and parents, you are guaranteed leave from your job only if you are caring for your own mother and father, not your mother-in-law or father-in-law.

It remains to be seen whether having drafted the law this way will encourage more adult sons to take care of their own parents, with leave available to them. The law provides no relief for those thousands of women—dutiful daughters-in-law—for whom that will not be the case.

Can my employer count my paid vacation and leave time against the unpaid leave time due me under this law?

It's up to your employer and company policy. Remember, the law allows you a full 12 weeks of leave time.

My employer approved my leave for care of my elderly mother, but now keeps pestering me about her recovery. How do I deal with this?

You may be required to submit medical verification of your mother's health condition. However, your employer is not permitted to question you about the details of your family situation.

My mother has a chronic condition that doesn't require medical care. Can my employer deny me leave to care for her?

No. Chronic illness qualifies as a serious health condition under the law. Note also that you can space out your leave up to the 12-week limit; you need not take it as consecutive days.

I am a public school teacher. Can I get leave during the school term?

As a general rule, your leave must be taken in blocks of time when the leave is needed intermittently or is required near the end of the school term or semester. These rules apply for teachers and employees of local education agencies.

Enforcing Your Rights

It is unlawful for any employer to interfere with or deny you your rights under the Family and Medical Leave Act. It is also unlawful to discriminate or discharge you for attempting to enforce your rights under this law.

The Family and Medical Leave Act is administered by the Department of Labor, Employment Standards Administration, Wage and Hours

Division, which has issued regulations to help companies develop leave policies conforming with the law's requirements.

The Department of Labor is charged with investigating complaints of violations. If your complaint is not resolved, the Department may bring an action for compliance. Complaints may be made to the Department of Labor, Employment Standards Administration, Wage and Hours Division, at your regional office. (The address and telephone number are in your local directory.)

The law is relatively new, and thus far compliance has been spotty. Employers' implementation has been characterized by misinformation and disinformation about its requirements. Companies have failed to develop policies and procedures regarding leaves, and training has been non-existent. In the first year of the law, the Department of Labor investigated 965 complaints, of which 60 percent were deemed violations. Nine out of 10 were settled in the employees' favor.

 ## STATE FAMILY LEAVE LAWS

Two-thirds of the states and the District of Columbia have enacted family leave laws for their residents. The federal Family and Medical Leave Act does not restrict or preempt these laws in any way. If your state's law is more generous than the federal one, then by all means make sure you assert your state rights in this regard. For example, your state's law may provide a greater leave period than the federal law or apply its law to employers with fewer employees. Depending on where you live, you may be able to coordinate your leave under both laws.

In addition, many corporations also have leave policies that are more generous than the federal law. And a number of government agencies allow reduced work schedules for employees under a *leave bank* or *leave pool* program. Check with your employer's human resources division.

17

PENSIONS AND BENEFITS

Financial planners talk about the "three-legged stool" upon which your retirement income is based: savings and investments, Social Security, and pension.

Your pension is critical to how you will live after you retire. Your right to a pension, how your pension works, what changes may be made by your employer, its very security—all these are governed by laws with acronyms instead of names, such as ERISA, REA, and COBRA. These laws are your protection for your pension and benefits.

Recent proposals offer a potpourri of reforms, including a Pension Bill of Rights, guaranteed inclusion and fair treatment, increased funding requirements, portability, and protections against fraud and abuse.

A word about pension law. Your pension plan is a contract. Federal laws provide minimum requirements for pension plans in order to afford you basic protections. You and your employer are also governed by the terms and conditions of the contract, that is, your company's pension plan. This is an important point for you to understand. Your company's plan cannot restrict rights granted you under federal law, but it can be more liberal than the federal law and afford you additional rights which you can enforce.

As a corollary, the application of general rules governing pension plans to individual employees under their company plans depends on a number of factors, such as the type of plan, the time and length of service, employee earnings, and the terms and conditions of the plan. For specific advice on your pension, you must contact your plan administrator or seek advice from the Department of Labor or a lawyer with expertise in pensions and benefits.

THE LAW OF PENSION PLANS

A pension plan is basically a structure for investing money. Funds are paid by a company into a pension fund, which then invests it. Eventually, the invested funds will be used to pay monthly benefits to retirees, under specified conditions.

There are two kinds of pension plans:

- A *defined benefit plan* tells you what benefits the plan will pay out. The final amount may be based upon a percentage of your final year's salary or a flat rate which increases based on the number of years of service. Under this kind of plan, the company is wholly responsible for structuring the plan and funding it; the actual amount of money put into the plan each year can change.
- A *defined contribution plan* sets out how much money your employer will pay into the plan. The company puts a fixed dollar amount, often into a separate account on your behalf. Some plans allow employees to direct investment of their accounts. Defined contribution plans include stock option, profit-sharing, and 401(k) plans. In the typical 401(k) plan, an employer will make matching contributions to an employee's, and the employee decides on investment.

Defined benefit plans, common among the larger, older corporations in the United States, were once the accepted standard for pensions. They also proved to be the most vulnerable to mismanagement, underfunding, bankruptcies, and all the calamities that can affect companies.

Remember the Studebaker? Calls for government backing of pension benefits date back to the car manufacturer's collapse in the early 1960s. Thousands of workers lost their benefits when the Indiana factory closed its doors a few days before Christmas in 1963.

Ten years later, the result was the *Employment Retirement Income Security Act of 1974* (ERISA). ERISA was passed by Congress to reform employee pension and welfare benefits programs by providing fiduciary standards for pension funds and some guarantee of benefits. The law requires that minimum standards be met in eligibility, participation, earning benefits, vesting, making claims, and disclosure of information. The Retirement Equity Act (REA) passed in 1984 and the Tax Reform Act (TRA) passed in 1986 amended ERISA rules on participation and vesting and added additional protections for spouses.

My company is setting up a defined contribution plan. How does this affect me?

With a defined contribution plan, you have no idea of what your benefit will be until you actually retire. And that benefit will be a function of the risk you took, not the company. Defined contribution plans are *not* insured by the Pension Benefit Guaranty Corporation.

From a practical point of view, investments in defined contribution plans tend to be conservative, and ultimately less profitable for workers. Since ERISA, companies have tried to reduce their risk by moving from defined benefit plans to defined contribution plans. When ERISA was passed, contributions to defined benefit plans were nearly twice those to defined contribution plans; since then, the balance has shifted in the other direction—payments to defined contribution plans now lead three to one.

YOUR RIGHT TO PARTICIPATE

The first step in establishing your right to a pension is to establish your eligibility and qualify for participation in your company's pension plan. You are a participant when you become a member of the plan. This is an absolute prerequisite for any legal claim to a pension.

A few general comments on your rights to participate in a pension plan:

- There's no legal requirement that your company have a pension plan.
- Even if your company has a pension plan, the law doesn't say that you must be covered. Pension plans usually cover categories of employees, and may exclude certain positions. As many as 30 percent of lower-income workers can lawfully be excluded from a plan.
- Your company may have different plans for different employees. Make sure you know under which plan you're covered.
- If you are covered, you may be required to work for your employer for a period of one year before becoming eligible. The one-year service requirement is usually measured as 1,000 hours during a 12-month period, although you may actually qualify with fewer than 1,000 hours, depending on the terms of your plan. (A two-year requirement may be imposed for plans with full and immediate vesting.)
- Once you are eligible, you must be allowed to become a member of the plan within six months or at the start of the next plan period, whichever is earlier.

The bottom line is, never assume you have pension coverage. Make sure of it. Make sure you know if your company's plan covers you. Make sure you know *which plan* covers you. Remember, there's no law that says you must be covered. And you must put in the time to qualify for participation.

Can my employer impose age requirements on participation in the company's pension plan?

If you're under 21, you may have to wait until six months after your 21st birthday (assuming you've worked for one year prior to that date). If you work for a tax-exempt educational institution that provides a plan with immediate 100 percent vesting, you may be subject to an age requirement of 26 years.

You cannot be denied membership because you're too close to retirement age. That's against the law.

Can I be excluded from coverage under my company's pension plan if other employees in the same job classification are eligible for the plan?

No. Although coverage may lawfully exclude categories of employees, no one person within a single category can be excluded from eligibility. You still have to put in the time to qualify for membership.

Can I waive participation in my company's plan?

Under the law, the company must allow you to participate in its pension plan if you are eligible. But that doesn't prevent a company from asking older workers to waive participation in the company's pension plan before they are hired. You may be caught between a rock and a hard place on this one. If you refuse, you may not get the job—and it would be a difficult age discrimination claim to prove. If you agree to a so-called "voluntary" waiver that meets the requirements of the Older Workers Benefits Protection Act (discussed in the last chapter), it will keep you from collecting benefits later.

Watch out for these one-sided negotiations. Remember, federal law provides that these waivers are revocable for seven days after you sign. (For more on the Older Workers Benefits Protection Act, see age discrimination in Chapter 16.)

 VESTING RULES

Participation in a pension plan does not by itself establish your right to a pension. Your legal right to receive a pension at retirement age becomes effective when the pension vests. Your pension vests after you have met a minimum threshold in length of employment as set forth in your employer's pension plan.

Before ERISA, vesting rules often provided for strict, sometimes onerous requirements before an employee could be eligible for pension. A requirement such as 15 or 20 years of full-time service without a break was not uncommon.

ERISA was passed in part to remedy just such injustices and to promote fairness. Vesting rules now provide for a maximum vesting period of either

- *Five years:* 100 percent vested pension to an employee with five years of service
- *Seven years:* graded vesting at a specified percentage after three years, and the remaining percentage proportionately for each subsequent year, or
- *Ten years:* 100 percent vested pension after ten years (for union-negotiated multi-employer pension plans only)

These rules became effective in 1989; workers who retired prior to that date are subject to prior vesting requirements.

These are minimum requirements; plans can be more generous to employees. If the plan is "top-heavy," meaning that managers and owners receive more than 60 percent of benefits, the scheduling of vesting must be even quicker.

All plans must provide for vesting prior to retirement. Once your benefits have vested, they are yours. They cannot be taken away from you. The same is true for benefits due you as a surviving spouse. Once they are vested, they cannot be taken away from you. (We discuss survivor's benefits below.)

My employer says my "break-in-service" (a two-year absence after four years of work) counts against me and I have lost all credit toward my pension. Have I forfeited my rights?

Probably not. Breaks-in-service are subject to special rules under ERISA. These govern when your pension credits may be reduced (for vesting and benefit accrual) and when your service prior to the break must be recognized by your employer when you return to work.

As a general rule, you can't forfeit vesting or benefit credit unless you've had five consecutive one-year breaks-in-service. Service prior to your break must be recognized unless you've had five consecutive one-year breaks, or consecutive one-year breaks equaling or exceeding the years of service earned before your break, whichever is greater. (If you are talking about a past break-in-service, be aware that some of these laws may have taken effect since the time of your break.)

A break-in-service shorter than one year cannot be counted against you. For most plans, this means the equivalent of 500 hours; if you work less than this amount, you may lose credits towards vesting as well as reducing your benefits later on. (Exceptions may apply for birth, adoption, and caring for a child.)

Protections may vary, depending on the terms of your plan. If you want to protect your pension benefits, make sure you examine your plan's break-in-service provisions, preferably *before* you take a break or reduce your hours. ERISA rules are minimum requirements designed to minimize the likelihood of your exclusion from your pension. Your company's plan may be more liberal.

What happens to my pension when I change jobs?

If you change employers before your pension has vested, you will probably lose all your pension credit, other than your own contributions. Most likely, you will not be entitled to a pension from this job when you retire. However, if you work in an industry that has negotiated an industry-wide pension plan, such as construction or trucking, your participation may continue as you change employers within the same industry.

RECEIVING PENSION BENEFITS

Pension plans generally provide for benefits paid out monthly over the lifetimes of participants and their surviving spouses. In this regard, ERISA requires that two options be offered you:

- **Maximum pension** gives you a life-only payout; the pension ends with your death.
- **Joint-and-survivor** gives you a pension at a fixed percentage (usually 80 percent) of a lifetime pension, but pays your spouse from 50 to 75 percent of your pension if you die first.

Some pension plans offer other options. Your plan may give you to option of having it paid out over a fixed number of years or allow you to collect your money in a single lump-sum payment. A lump-sum benefit theoretically lets you invest the principal or shop for annuities to provide you a larger monthly income.

Lump-sum payments are based on actuarial tables that estimate how long you'll live and the anticipated investment earnings of the plan. *One recent change in law to note*: new pension calculations mandated by GATT (General Agreement on Tariffs and Trade) may alter, and in some cases significantly reduce, the amount you'll receive in a lump-sum payment under a defined benefit plan.

A few observations about lump-sum payments:

- If your plan doesn't provide for lump sum payment, your company can't be forced to provide it.
- Under the Retirement Equity Act, your spouse's agreement is necessary to authorize lump-sum withdrawal.
- If your total pension is $3,500 or less, your plan can require that you take in the form of a lump-sum payment.
- You will have to pay taxes on a lump-sum payment unless you roll it over into an IRA (as well as a special penalty tax if you're under 59 and a half). It must be a direct rollover; partial rollovers are also authorized under the law. You may also be able to roll it over to a new employer's pension plan. These should be discussed with your accountant, to avoid incurring unnecessary taxes or penalty.

My company's pension plan provides for "integration" of benefits. How does this affect me?

This is a raw deal. Despite your pension rights, an integrated plan may allow your employer to deduct a substantial portion from its expected payments, based on your anticipated Social Security benefits. By "integrating" with the federal system, many plans deduct as much as half the amount of the Social Security payment from employees' checks!

SURVIVOR PENSIONS

If your spouse has vested rights to a pension, then your rights to a survivor's pension in the event of his or her death are also vested. Under the Retirement Equity Act of 1984, you will collect a survivor's pension unless you have given a written waiver.

The amount of your survivor's pension must be 50 percent of the amount your spouse receives or would have received had he or she lived to retirement age.

I am separated and in the process of getting a divorce from my spouse. Will I have any entitlements to my ex-spouse's pension?

Under federal law, none. But your divorce is governed by state law, your spouse's pension is property, and the terms of your separation and divorce are subject to negotiated agreement and judicial decree. A court order can direct your spouse's pension plan to pay a share of your spouse's pension benefits directly to you. It may also provide for survivor benefits in the event of your spouse's death.

MAKING A CLAIM

You pension plan has a claims procedure for filing a claim for benefits. It is your responsibility to file a claim in accordance with your plan requirements. According to ERISA, the claims procedure must be included in the plan summary you are given.

ERISA requires that your plan must respond to your written benefits claims. Within 90 days, you must be provided with either notice of a decision or notice of a 90-day extension.

If the decision on your claim is yes, you will receive the benefits you claim. If the decision is a denial, it must state the reasons, and reference to the provision in the plan upon which the denial is based. If you don't get an answer within the 90-day statutory time frame, you can treat that as a denial also.

If the decision is not in your favor, you will have to take action to enforce your rights by appealing the decision. A process for appeals will also be included in the plan summary you are given. (Plan summaries and appeals are discussed in the next section.)

GETTING INFORMATION ON YOUR PENSION

The first step in enforcing your rights is knowing what they are. ERISA sets forth detailed requirements concerning information and disclosure about pension plans.

A summary plan description must be given to participants. The summary outlines requirements for participation, accrual of benefits, vesting, conditions of forfeiture, and procedures for claims and remedies. The law requires that the summary plan description be given to you within 90 days after your coverage begins. You'll also get a summary of any material amendments in the year following the year the plan was changed. If there are changes, you'll get an updated summary plan description, supplied every five years; if there are no changes in the plan, the plan description is due every ten years. You must also be given a summary annual report.

The plan administrator must also furnish to each plan participant a statement of the nature, form, and amount of deferred vested benefits after your employment has ended, and information on pension plan survivor coverage.

On your written request, your plan administrator must furnish you a statement of benefits accrued and benefits vested, if any, or the earliest date on which accrued benefits will become vested. This statement need only be provided once in a 12-month period. (This requirement doesn't necessarily apply to multi-employer plans.)

In addition, within 30 days of your written request, your plan administrator must supply you with additional copies of the latest updated summary plan report, the latest annual report, and documents under which the plan was established or operated such as plan rules or trust agreement. Be prepared to pay reasonable costs, which the law allows. (The latest annual report and plan documents must also be made available to any participant at the principal office of the plan administrator.)

Summary plan descriptions, financial reports, and other documents must also be filed with the Department of Labor in Washington, D.C., where they are available for inspection. Copies may be purchased at a charge of ten cents per page. Write the Department of Labor, Public Disclosure Room, 200 Constitution Avenue N.W., Washington DC 20210, or call 202/523-8771 or a regional office.

Be informed! Read your plan! The summary description will tell you your plan requirements, eligibility rules, and other information that will allow you to be an informed participant and enable you to ensure that you receive the benefits due you.

Although the plan itself is the controlling document, the summary plan may be Exhibit A in any appeal or action you take to claim your benefits. It may not be dispositive, but it's evidence of the plan's representations to you.

 APPEALING A CLAIM DECISION

If your benefits claim is denied, the denial must state the reasons, and make reference to the provision in the plan upon which the denial is based. You can appeal that decision according to the procedures set forth in your plan.

You have 60 days from receiving your notice of denial to appeal the decision. You must appeal in writing, and your appeal should contain your reasons for believing the denial is wrong, along with copies of supporting documents. Pay attention to the reason given for the denial and the provision quoted in the claim decision, and respond to them. Keep copies of anything you send.

This process is called a *fair review*. There is no requirement under ERISA that you be allowed to appear in person, although your plan can grant you that right. Some plans authorize the use of alternative grievance or arbitration procedures for the claims process. If yours is one of them, you may invoke that process, but make sure you don't waive any rights you have to review by the courts.

You are entitled to a decision within 120 days from the plan's receipt of your appeal. (The 120-day time is applicable to most plans). If the appeal decision upholds the denial of your benefits, it must state the reason and make reference to the provision of the plan upon which it is based. This will be important for subsequent legal action.

You may appeal a claim denial in court, if you have first exhausted your remedies through the administrative process. Whether this should be state or federal court likely depends upon the basis for your claim, which may be noncompliance with ERISA provisions or violation of contract provisions in your pension plan.

You will want to consult a lawyer experienced in pensions and benefits. Issues concerning interpretation of ERISA will go to federal court; if you're claiming that legal obligations of the contract are not being met, you will probably sue for compliance in state court. As a federal law, ERISA preempts all state rules, and its rules will be applied in either court.

 PENSION PLAN TERMINATIONS

Under ERISA, defined-benefit pension plans are required to pay insurance premiums to the federal Pension Benefit Guaranty Corporation. This means that if your employer goes out of business or terminates your pension plan, you may have some benefit protection.

The Pension Benefit Guaranty Corporation insures more than 100,000 pension plans with assets totalling almost $1 trillion. Whether there will be remedies available for you depends on what kind of pension plan you have and whether your pension has vested.

- Participants in defined-benefit pension plans whose pensions have vested will receive all or some of their pension benefits.
- The protection of the Pension Benefit Guaranty Corporation does not extend to benefits which have not vested.
- Defined-contribution plans are not insured or protected; the account is already in your name and the investment risk is yours.

For pension plans terminating in 1996, the maximum guaranteed amount will cover you up to $2642.05 a month ($31,704.60 yearly, adjusted for inflation). However, a number of limitations make this less generous than it first appears:

- Benefits are insured for the full amount only if they have been in existence and unchanged for more than five years.
- The maximum monthly payment must be reduced if your benefit is paid or payable to you before age 62, or is paid in a form other than an annuity for your life alone (such as the traditional joint-and-survivor payout).

- Insurance protections are for "basic benefits" only. They do not cover anything else: medical, disability, death, and other benefits are not protected.

ERISA requires that the Pension Benefit Guaranty Corporation be self-financing. However, the Corporation, which finances its operations from terminated plans, employer premium payments, and investment, is criticized as being underfunded itself. Despite the Pension Protection Act of 1987, which required sponsors of underfunded defined-benefit plans to make additional contributions to their funds, underfunding in single-employer plans rose to an unprecedented $50 billion in 1992. Under federal law, the United States government is *not* responsible for any obligation or liability incurred by the Corporation.

Can I demand a pension guarantee from my employer?

Some executives do demand and receive pension guarantees to protect themselves against the threat of takeovers or bankruptcies. ERISA prohibits corporations from granting pension guarantees above the maximum defined benefit allowed by the tax code, $100,000.

I work as a school teacher. How secure is my public sector pension?

An estimated $1 trillion is in public sector pensions ranging from the grossly underfunded to those with large surpluses. These funds are not eligible for insurance by the Pension Benefit Guaranty Corporation. The pensions of public employees must rely on the soundness of their government, whether state, municipal, or other locality.

State governments can't go bankrupt, but cities can. So can school districts. Public pension funds are also vulnerable to invasions for balancing state budgets, as well as questionable investments for public works.

How safe is an underfunded plan?

A pension fund does not actually have to be 100 percent funded to be self-sustaining. After all, not all beneficiaries will draw benefits simultaneously (except in the case of a bankruptcy). At the same time, the average retirement age has dropped to 62 while the average length of retirement—the time retirees will be drawing benefits—has lengthened to 20 years. It's been estimated that fully one-third of companies declared underfinanced are in trouble. The Pension Benefit Guaranty Corporation has assailed underfunding in pension funds by four big industries—auto, steel, tire, and airlines.

What does the future hold for pension guarantees?

The Pension Benefit Guaranty Corporation has an estimated $6 billion in assets, some $2.5 billion less than liabilities. And despite modifications, there is an underlying problem with its funding scheme based on the number of companies leaving the insurance fold, through terminations. Annuities bought by new owners to finance pension obligations are not insured by the Pension Benefit Guaranty Corporation. From a funding point of view that means no insurance premiums are being paid in.

From a plan participant's point of view, of course, it may spell disaster. Almost 400,000 Americans were directly dependent on the Pension Benefit Guaranty Corporation for pensions their employers or former employers had not funded sufficiently.

My company switched from its pension plan and bought annuities. Is my pension safe?

Many annuities are bought by pension plans for plan participants; terminating pension plans are *required* to buy annuities for all participants. The U.S. General Accounting Office estimates that 3 to 4 million of 10 million retired U.S. workers don't get their pension checks directly from their employers, relying instead on income from annuity contracts. As a general rule, individuals in pension plans have no say in which insurance company gets the annuity contract. Often, they don't even realize where their checks are coming from. If you're receiving or counting on insurance-backed annuities for retirement, remember that the switch to annuities will cut you off from Pension Benefit Guaranty Corporation protection. Some coverage may still be available under state insurance guaranty funds.

BENEFITS AND WELFARE PLANS

Health benefits, offered after World War II as a way of giving extra benefits to employees restricted by wage freezes, became a common part of employment packages in the 1950s and 1960s as a result of collective bargaining gains. Since that time, benefits have been extended to retirees as well as active employees, in packages as varied as the capitalistic landscape. Benefits offered by employers have included hospitalization and surgery, sickness, accident, death, disability, unemployment, day care, scholarship, legal services, holiday, severance, and training.

At the time ERISA was passed, concern was focused on pensions. Yet ERISA also applied to welfare plans, defined as

> . . . any plan, fund, or program established or maintained by an employer or an employee organization for the purpose of providing medical, surgical, or hospital benefits, or other "fringe benefits" through insurance or otherwise.

Under ERISA, employers who provide welfare benefits are held to these requirements:

- Reporting and disclosure standards, including a mandate that employees be given a summary plan setting forth their rights
- Claims procedures (see description in the preceding section)

However, the protections afforded by ERISA for pension plans were not duplicated for health benefits. Health nd welfare benefit packages do not have any legal requirements ensuring minimum capitalization, vesting rules, or guarantees.

CHANGING EMPLOYEE BENEFITS

Employers can change their health benefit plans, so long as they reserve the right to do so in either the benefit plan documents or collective bargaining agreements. Court opinions have upheld the right of companies to alter or amend health care benefits under ERISA. Almost all employers have done so.

What is the net effect for you? Read your plan. The courts have said that the right to change depends on the plain language in the plan. Many plans contain express reservations by the company of its right to change or terminate the plan. Courts have been reluctant to look at other evidence. But if the language in the plan is ambiguous, other evidence may be referred to, such as oral statements and brochures. Under limited circumstances, benefits may "vest" when you retire.

Can my employer cancel health care benefits?

Unless you have a contract or collective bargaining agreement that provides to the contrary, the answer is yes. With rising health care costs, health and welfare plan modifications are subject to change and more change. Change one year may beget change the next year. Your employer may shift costs by various strategies, such an increasing your contributions toward insurance premiums, eliminating specific benefits such as prescription drugs, or terminating your health benefits entirely (a far less likely possibility).

Am I protected under a self-insuring health benefit plan?

An increasing number of companies are "self-insuring" their health plans, primarily to avoid taxes on premiums as well as state-mandated coverage. This is within the law. Large firms have generally always been self-insured. Among small to medium-sized firms, two-thirds had self-insured plans by 1992. State health care reforms in this area have been largely unsuccessful, ironically because ERISA's authority over employee benefit plans has preempted state regulation.

Can my former employer cancel my health care continuation coverage?

Your continuation coverage can be terminated only if your former employer stops coverage for all active employees. Group health plans are required to provide former employees increased opportunity to have their health care coverage continued, under ERISA amendments contained in the Consolidated Omnibus Budget Reconciliation Act (COBRA).

COBRA applies to medical benefits provided by insurance or any other mechanisms including trusts, self-insured plans, reimbursement, and health maintenance organizations. Medical benefits may include inpatient and outpatient hospital care, physician care, surgery and other major medical, prescription drugs, and other medical benefit such as dental and vision care. COBRA does not apply to life insurance. (For an explanation of continuation coverage, see Chapter 6.)

Can my employer cancel my health care benefits or switch me to continuation coverage when I am on leave under the Family and Medical Leave Act?

No. Under this law, the employer must continue your coverage under the same group plan, as if you were still working. If you notify your employer of your intention not to return to work, then your right to continuation coverage would kick in.

RETIREE BENEFITS

Retiree benefits took a hit with the imposition of a change in accounting standards by the Financial Accounting Standards Board in 1990. Under the new standards, employers were required to accrue and disclose retiree health benefit liabilities in their financial statements. This spurred employers to reduce liabilities and control growth by cutting their retiree health benefit costs.

The standards didn't affect how much employers paid for health care benefits nor did it require them to set aside any given amount or percentage. But health care costs were reflected as a bottom-line liability. And health care costs for early retirees cost as much as four times as much as the same health care provided through Medicare.

Are your benefits secure? Can they be cut back? Under the right circumstances, and within the law, they can be modified or totally eliminated. In a recent survey by the Commonwealth Fund, more than half the employers reported expecting to reduce benefits for future retirees.

I'm a retiree. What happens to my health care coverage if my former employer goes out of business?

As your employer goes, so goes your health benefits. If the company goes out of business or ends coverage for its current employees, you are not protected.

What happens if my former employer goes bankrupt?

Under the Retiree Benefits Protection Act of 1988, retirees' health benefits are given priority status in bankruptcy cases. Moreover, a company in bankruptcy cannot change a plan without consent of the retirees' representatives or unless ordered by the court. (This is not as good as it sounds, however. Judges have been more willing to approve change than retirees would like. And this protection does not apply to banks and insurance companies, which are subject to separate state regulation.)

You may still be eligible for COBRA continuation coverage if your former employer is a subsidiary of another company which still provides group health benefits for its employees.

18

■■

SOCIAL SECURITY AND
DISABILITY

The odds are that you're either paying Social Security or getting Social Security. If you're not, someone in your household is. Social Security affects nearly everyone in the United States. In 1993, 37 million people collected Social Security benefits totalling $302 billion.

Is it welfare? Is it insurance? A pension fund? The history of social security dates back to Otto von Bismarck, who as Chancellor of Imperial Germany in the latter part of the 19th century instituted a state system of "social security" for Germans over 70 years old. Bismarck's adoption of the biblically-sanctioned threescore and ten as the benchmark for when retirement benefits would begin was later changed by officials to age 65. Social Security was the law in most European nations long before the New Deal made it a reality in the United States in the 1930s.

In 1995, according to Labor Department reports, 56 percent of the 13.2 million current retirees 65 and older depend entirely on Social Security for their income. And almost three and a half million of those receiving Social Security and private pensions get less than $10,000 yearly.

With corporate cutbacks in staff and only half of today's workforce employed by companies with pension plans, and only a quarter of those entitled to future benefits, that three-legged stool of retirement planning is looking a little wobbly. For many lower-income workers, it's already collapsed; an estimated 42 million workers don't have pensions. Social Security represents 100 percent of their retirement plan.

Today's Social Security system is not only a provider of retirement income for the worker. Social security also provides

- Retirement benefits for spouses of workers
- Disability benefits to disabled workers and their dependents
- Survivor benefits to spouses and children of deceased workers

- Supplemental Security Income (SSI) for low-income people 65 and over, or blind and disabled of any age

Social Security is financed by taxes on employers and employees. (The SSI portion is funded from general revenues.) Problems raised by an aging workforce and a reduced labor pool make the financial structure uncertain. When Social Security was enacted in the 1930s, there were 40 workers for each retiree. By 1950, that figure had dropped to 15 workers. In 1985, there were 3.4 workers for each retiree; by the year 2030, there will be only 2 workers for each retiree.

Critics predict that the Social Security disability fund will be in deficit in 2034 and that the pension fund will go broke in 2050. More optimistic estimates forecast that Social Security will continue, relying less on trust fund surpluses and more on pay-as-you-go financing.

Calls for restrictive changes in Social Security are invariably met by resistance on behalf of those across the economic spectrum who feel their financial future threatened. Current proposals before Congress to limit benefits call for increasing the retirement age to 70 and impose some form of means testing in order to receive benefits. Other proposals would increase benefits to working retirees age 65 to 69 by raising the limit on their earnings and rolling back income taxes on the benefits of higher-income retirees.

SOCIAL SECURITY ELIGIBILITY AND BENEFITS

Eligibility for Social Security is determined by *credits*. As a worker, you earn Social Security credits up to a maximum of four per year. The general rule is that you need 40 credits, representing 10 years of work, to qualify for benefits.

The amount of money you have to earn to qualify for credits goes up each year. For example, in 1996, one credit is earned for each $640 in earnings. Credits used to be called "quarters," referring to the quarter-year theoretically represented by each. The four credits need not be spread out over four quarters, however, but can be earned any time over the calendar year.

Your benefit is figured to give you an average of 42 percent of your lifetime working income. (This figure is applicable to a worker with average earnings. The earnings-replacement rate is different for low, average, and maximum earners. Because the benefit formula is weighted to favor lower-income workers, with theoretically less opportunity to save and invest, the percentage is higher for them and lower for people in higher income brackets.)

The formula is very complicated; here is a brief summary. Benefits depend on your average monthly earnings, figured over a number of years.

The number of years of earnings is used as a base. That number is figured at 35 for retirement benefits. (For disability and survivor benefits, your actual record is used.) Earnings are adjusted for inflation, and then your average adjusted monthly earnings are determined, according to the base number of years. This is then multiplied by a fixed number set forth in the law.

It's difficult to predict exactly what you'll get because of any number of factors, including future benefits adjustments, related Congressional action, and your own uncertain future earnings. Social Security will provide you with an estimate of your future benefits, but it will be a rough one at best. As you approach retirement age, the estimate will better approximate the benefits you will actually receive.

Your personalized estimate will include an accounting of

- Earnings history and amount paid in to Social Security
- Estimates of retirement benefits at ages 62, 65, and 70
- Estimates of survivor and disability benefits

In order to get an estimate, you can get Form SSA-7004, Request for Earnings and Benefits Estimate Statement, from your local Social Security office or by calling toll free to 800/973-2000.

Starting in 1995, Social Security began sending statements to people over 60 who are not yet collecting benefits. By the year 2000, annual reports should be going out to people 25 and older.

Make sure you check your records! If there's an error and you're not receiving credit for time you've worked, you want to correct it in time. We recommend checking the record at least once every three years.

How exactly is my benefit calculated?

By a complicated formula. Your earnings since 1951 are adjusted for changes in average wages over the years to make them comparable with current earnings. Earnings are adjusted for each year up to the year you reach age 60. From this list, the 35 highest years of earnings are selected to figure your benefit. The earnings for these years are totaled and divided by 420 (the number of months in 35 years) to get your average monthly earnings.

This is the number used to figure your benefit rate. A three-level formula, readjusted each year for people reaching 62, is applied to your average monthly earnings to arrive at an actual benefit rate. A fixed dollar amount of your monthly earnings (the amount itself changes each year) is multiplied by 90 percent, a larger amount by 32 percent, and any remaining amount by 15 percent. The total is your basic full retirement-age benefit rate. Whether you retire at 62 or later, the formula used is based on the year you turn 62.

RETIREMENT AND EARLY RETIREMENT

The retirement age for Social Security purposes is an artificial construct, chosen by legislators with their eye on the bottom line. When Bismarck picked 70, the average life expectancy in Germany was 45 years. When the Social Security Act was signed into law by President Franklin D. Roosevelt, the average life expectancy in the United States was 61.7. Today's life expectancy exceeds the statutory retirement age by more than a decade.

When are you eligible? It depends:

- **Age 65:** You are eligible for your full retirement benefit at age 65, *if* you were born before 1938.
- **Age 65 to 67:** For those born after 1938, the full benefit age is being increased starting in the year 2000. If you were born in 1940, your retirement age will be 65 years and six months. If you were born in 1950, it will be 66. Those born in 1960 will reach their retirement age in 2027, at the age of 67.
- **Age 62:** You are eligible for reduced benefits at age 62, no matter what year you were born in.

If I begin collecting my Social Security benefits when I'm 62, how much less will I receive? Is this a good deal or not?

If you choose the early retirement benefit, your benefits are reduced by a certain percentage for each month prior to your full benefit age. A reduction of 20 percent applies at age 62, prorated for those who retire between 62 and 65. The monthly percentage is five ninths of one percent, or .0055 repeating. For example, if you retire 20 months before your full retirement age, your benefit will be decreased by 20 x .0055, or 11.1 percent, making it 88.9 percent of what it would be at age 65.

On the average, you would probably need to collect benefits for 12 years at the full rate to catch up to the amount you're getting starting at 62. Remember, as the full benefit age increases in the coming years, the total amount of the reduction in your benefit amount will reflect the increased number of months between your early retirement and the full retirement age.

In making a decision to retire early, there are a number of factors to take into account, including both your benefits and spousal benefits due your mate. Don't forget to consider pension benefits from your job. These also may be reduced if you leave work before a certain age, especially if they are tied to your Social Security benefits.

 APPLYING FOR SOCIAL SECURITY BENEFITS

You can apply for Social Security benefits by telephone or at any Social Security office. The information and documentation needed by Social Security will include

- Your Social Security number and the worker's
- Your birth certificate
- Your marriage certificate if widowed (for survivor's benefits)
- Your divorce papers (if applying as divorced spouse)
- Children's birth certificates and Social Security numbers (if applying for survivor benefits)
- Deceased worker's W-2 forms or self-employment tax return for recent year
- Checkbook or savings passbook for direct deposit

You should file your application a few months before you plan to retire, if possible. Retroactive benefits can be paid for up to six months prior to the date of filing. The timing is more critical if you're retiring before age 65, in which case you can only be paid as of the month you file. Benefits are not retroactive for early retirees.

WORKING PAST RETIREMENT AGE

For many people, the question of early retirement is of purely academic interest. For better or worse, you may be among those thousands of people who continue to work past the "traditional" age—whether out of desire or financial need—at their old jobs, or, often at new careers.

The good news is, you still have a job.

The bad news is, Social Security imposes restrictions on the amount you can earn:

- *Age 62 through 65*: In 1996, for example, if you're receiving benefits, you can earn up to $8,280 without affecting your benefits. Beyond this maximum amount, the *2-for-1 rule* applies: you'll lose $1 in benefits for every $2 you earn.
- *Age 65 through 69*: In 1996 you can earn up to $12,500 without affecting your benefits. Beyond this amount, it's *3-for-1*: you lose $1 in benefits for every $3 you earn.
- *Age 70*: You may earn whatever you can with no effect on your Social Security benefits.

For those between 65 and 69, new legislation increases the ceiling on what you can earn without adverse effect on your benefits, with the "earnings limit" reaching $30,000 by the year 2002.

The decision to continue to work may mean having to defer benefits. If you defer collecting till past your retirement age, there are two consequences:

- *Increased average earnings.* Your continued income will probably increase your average earnings and your future benefit, although by a very small amount.
- *Benefit credit.* You will actually be given a credit for the time you continue to work. Your annual benefit will be increased by a certain percentage for each month you work past the full retirement age. For those who turned 65 in 1994, this amounts to 4.5 percent per year. This rate will be increasing in future years, to 6 percent in the year 2000 and 8 percent in 2008 and after. Critics say this will not be actuarially fair until 2008 (and wholly ineffective for widows).

If you will be working and receiving benefits at the same time, you are required to advise Social Security of your anticipated earnings and verify the year's earnings by April 15th on the following year.

My retirement income comes mainly from my pension and investments. Does this income limit my Social Security benefits?

No. The limitation on earnings applies only to money you earn at work and after you begin receiving benefits. Investments, pensions, annuities, even Social Security benefits, are not counted in determining the amount of your earnings applied to this maximum allowable figure.

Do these earnings limitations apply to my disability or SSI benefits?

No. These limitations apply only to people under 70 collecting Social Security retirement, survivor, or dependent benefits. People who work and collect disability or SSI benefits are subject to different earnings requirements. Keep in mind that if you're working you may not meet the requirements for disability or SSI benefits.

TAXING SOCIAL SECURITY

For decades, Social Security was considered sacrosanct. But with 650,000 millionaires collecting benefits, it was inevitable that the tax collector would come calling. At the present time, people whose incomes exceed a certain specified limit are subject to federal taxation on half or more of their benefits. (Not surprisingly, proposals to roll back these taxes are currently before Congress.)

Unfortunately, for purposes of determining whether your benefits will be taxed, your "combined income" includes income not otherwise taxed—counting not only your adjusted gross income (AGI) of wages, interest, and dividends but also any tax-exempt interest and half your Social Security benefits.

If you file an individual income tax return reflecting between $25,000 and $34,000 combined income, you will have to pay taxes on 50 percent of your Social Security benefits or half the income amount above the $25,000 threshold, whichever is less. If you make above $34,000, 85 percent of your Social Security benefits or 85 percent of your income above $34,000 will be subject to taxation. Couples filing jointly will have to pay taxes on the lesser of 50 percent of their Social Security benefits or income over $32,000, and the lesser of 85 percent of their benefits or income over $44,000. (See Chapter 15 for a description of how tax liability for Social Security is calculated.)

What if I win the lottery? How will that affect my Social Security?

Your check will keep coming—restrictions on your earnings under age 70 apply only to earned income. Depending on the amount of the award, however, it might affect your tax liability, boosting you into another tax bracket *and* subjecting a portion of your Social Security benefits to taxation.

 ## SPOUSAL BENEFITS

If you are 62 or older, you can get Social Security benefits on your own record or on the record of your retired spouse. Generally you will be allowed to take the higher benefit rate.

Your benefits as a spouse may be as much as half of your retired spouse's benefits. There is a limit on the total amount that can be paid to your entire family in so-called "derivative benefits." The limit is generally no more than 150 to 180 percent of the benefits of the worker upon whose record these payments are based. In such a case, family members' benefits will be reduced proportionately; the worker's benefits will not be reduced.

When am I eligible for spousal benefits?

When your spouse retires. If you are a married woman, you may get more money through your husband's benefits than through your own. As a married man, you have the same right to derivative benefits from your wife's earnings. If your spouse doesn't want to retire, you can still take retirement based on your own earnings, and early retirement at age 62.

What if my spouse retires early?

If you retire along with your spouse (upon whose earnings your benefits will be based), your benefits will also be reduced, up to 25 percent at age 62. If you don't retire but continue to work, and you qualify for spousal benefits (which you may elect as greater than your own benefit), you will receive 50 percent of what your spouse's full benefit would have been had he or she not retired until age 65.

My ex and I have been divorced two years. Am I eligible for spousal benefits?

If you are divorced from a person who is at least 62, whether collecting benefits or not, you are eligible for spousal benefits *provided* that the marriage lasted at least 10 years and the divorce was over two years prior to the application. There is no two-year waiting period for divorced spouses whose mates are already collecting benefits. (You're also eligible for survivor benefits. See the next section.)

SURVIVOR BENEFITS

Social Security is not just a retirement system. A significant part of the Social Security system is survivors insurance, which provides benefits to family members of covered workers. Family members may include widows and widowers, former spouses of deceased workers, children, and dependent parents:

- A widow or widower can get full benefits at age 65 or reduced benefits as early as 60. A disabled widow or widower can get benefits at 50.

  A widow or widower is eligible at any age if he or she is taking care of a child under 16 or a child who is disabled and entitled to or receiving benefits.
- Unmarried children under 18, under 19 if attending elementary or secondary school full-time, are entitled to benefits. Children with disabilities incurred before age 22 may get benefits with no age limit on receipt.
- Dependent parents age 62 or older may be eligible for survivor benefits, if they were dependent on the deceased for at least half of their support.

Survivor benefits are payable, depending on the deceased's benefit, at the following rates:

- 100 percent for a widow or widower age 65 or older
- between 71 percent and 94 percent for a widow or widower age 60 to 64
- 75 percent for a widow or widower under 60 with a child under 16
- 75 percent for children

There is an additional one-time death benefit of $255 generally available to a surviving spouse or minor children.

As a divorced spouse, am I entitled to survivor benefits?

Yes, if your marriage lasted at least 10 years. (No time limits apply if you are a divorced spouse taking care of a disabled child.) Benefits paid to a divorced spouse will not affect the benefit rates for others eligible for survivor benefits.

Can I get survivor benefits if I remarry?

Yes, under certain circumstances. If you remarry after age 60, you can still get benefits based on your former spouse's record—or you can choose to receive benefits based on your new spouse's record, whichever affords you higher benefits. If you're disabled and remarried, you can qualify for survivor benefits at age 50.

Which are better, retirement benefits or survivor benefits?

There's no easy answer to that question. You can switch from one form of benefit to another, depending on your individual situation.

If you're already getting benefits on your own record and your spouse dies, you can change to survivor benefits, which may give you more. Or, if you're receiving survivor benefits, you can switch over to your own retirement benefits at a reduced rate as early as 62. It's also possible to begin one benefit at a reduced rate and switch to the other at an unreduced rate at age 65.

These are complicated calculations, and you have to sit down with someone who is familiar with Social Security to figure them out. A Social Security representative will also discuss options with you.

 SOCIAL SECURITY OVERPAYMENTS

By law, Social Security must seek repayment of any overpayments it has given. If this occurs in your case, you will receive a notice informing you of the amount overpaid and your right to appeal or request a waiver. Repayment is usually made by direct refund within 30 days or withholding from future benefits checks.

One possibility is a waiver of repayment. *If* the overpayment wasn't your fault in any way, and *if* you couldn't meet necessary living expenses if you had to pay it back or repayment would cause severe financial hardship, you may not have to pay it back. But you must bear no scintilla of responsibility for the overpayment and could not have known that the amount was not correct. If you didn't report excess earnings, for example, you wouldn't qualify for a waiver. (There is also provision for waiver, rarely invoked, when repayment would be "against equity and good conscience.")

If you disagree with a determination of overpayment, you may challenge it through the appeal process. Unfortunately, notices of overpayment are often inadequate in this respect, not detailing amounts paid or due, or the reasons. An appeal will stay the collection of the overpayment. (Appeals are discussed later in this chapter.)

 SOCIAL SECURITY DISABILITY INSURANCE

Disability benefits are available under two programs: the Social Security disability insurance program and the Supplemental Security Income (SSI) program (discussed later in this chapter). The disability insurance program is authorized under Title II of the Social Security Act. Under its provisions, disability benefits are available for people who've worked and qualified.

In 1993, disability insurance provided nearly $35 billion to 5.3 million disabled workers and their dependents. The disability program, however, is characterized by backlogs and delay. There is an average wait of 75 days for a determination of eligibility—as long as four months in some states! Appeal of an unfavorable decision may drag on for a year.

Unprecedented increases in claims have further exacerbated problems with both disability and SSI. A million more claims were filed in 1993 than the 1.6 million filed in 1989. Recent government forecasts have estimated that the disability rolls will nearly double to more than 6 million workers over the next 10 years.

DISABILITY ELIGIBILITY AND BENEFITS

In order to qualify for Social Security disability insurance, you must have a recent work record of sufficient length. Your work history is determined by your number of credits, earned at the same Social Security rate of four per year, with the minimum requirement dependent on age:

- *Under 24*: You need six credits in the three-year period prior to your disability.
- *24 to 31*: You need credit for working half the time between 21 and the time of your disability (for example, 12 credits—half of six years—if you're disabled at age 27).
- *Over 31*: You need 20 credits from the ten years immediately preceding your disability, and an additional two credits for each two years of age over 42 up to 62 (for example, 26 credits at age 48, 40 credits at age 62).

In addition to benefits for yourself, disability benefits for your family may also be available based on your work record, much in the same way as retirement benefits are available for your family. Members of your family who may be eligible include:

- Your husband or wife, if 62 or older (and not collecting a higher Social Security benefit in his or her own name);
- Your husband or wife, if caring for a child under 16 or a child who is disabled and entitled to or receiving benefits; and
- Your children, if unmarried and under 18 (or under 19 but still in public school, or disabled since before age 22.)

A disabled widow, widower, or divorced spouse (if the marriage lasted ten years) may also qualify for benefits, if he or she is over the age of 50.

Benefits start on the sixth full calendar month of your disability. For example, if you become disabled by a stroke on February 15, your benefits will begin as of August, which is the sixth full calendar month you are disabled.

Disability benefits continue until your condition improves or you return to substantial work. You can receive disability benefits at any time. At 65, they become retirement benefits, although the amount remains the same.

Social Security provides a number of work incentives for people receiving disability benefits, including a trial work period of nine months (not necessarily consecutive), in which you can work as much as you can without affecting your benefits.

 ## DETERMINING DISABILITY

Social Security has a very strict definition of disability. It is based entirely on your ability to work, and does not cover partial disability. Nor does it cover any short-term disability.

For Social Security purposes, a disability is a physical or mental impairment which is expected to keep you from doing any "substantial" work for at least one year.

These rules apply to the disability insurance program run by Social Security. The rules for qualifying under any other plan, for example your employer's plan or another government agency's, do not necessarily apply.

Applying for Benefits and Determining Disability

There is a five-step evaluation process to determine disability under Social Security law. It requires that you as the applicant give the right answer to each of the following questions *in sequence*.

1. Are you working?
2. Is your condition severe?
3. Is your condition found in the list of disabling impairments?
4. Can you do the work you did previously?
5. Can you do any other type of work?

The Social Security office determines your non-medical eligibility under Step 1, including whether you are insured or have recently worked. Then your application is forwarded to your state's Disability Determination Services office for an evaluation of whether you are sufficiently disabled to qualify for benefits (Steps 2 through 5). The determination is done by a state Disability Determination Services team, consisting of a physician (or psychologist) and a disability evaluation specialist. Your application will proceed through these last four steps until a determination is made of "disability" or "no disability."

The disability services team is responsible for evaluating your medical records, looking at your condition and treatment, and requesting information about your ability to do work-related activities. You may be asked for an examination, performed by your own or another doctor. Most disability claims focus on this determination. If your claim is denied, you can appeal it.

Step 1. Are you working?   More to the point, are you currently working at substantial gainful activity? Disability benefits can be paid only if you are unable to do any substantial work.

What constitutes "substantial" work? The amount of your earnings is the key.

- In general, if your wages average more than $500 a month (after allowable deductions), you are performing substantial work.
- If your average monthly earnings are between $300 and $500 a month, your work could be considered substantial if the amount and quality of your work are about the same as that done by workers in your area who are not disabled. Factors considered include the time, energy, skill, and responsibility involved in your work.
- Earnings of less than $300 a month are not considered substantial.

If you are self-employed, more consideration will be given to the amount of time you spend in your business than the amount of your income.

Steps 2 and 3. What constitutes sufficient impairment?   In Step 2, you are examined to see if you have an impairment that is severe and that will last 12 months (or result in death). A short-term disability, however severe, will not qualify.

Assuming you pass Step 2, Step 3 is a reference to the *Listing of Impairments.* If your condition is on the list, or is similar enough to be medically equivalent to one on the list, you will be allowed disability benefits.

There are 125 impairments defined in the adult listings, descriptive of mental and physical illness and characterized generally by body system, neurological impairment, or mental disorder. Each impairment is defined in terms of specific medical signs, symptoms, or laboratory test results. To match a listing, you must feel *all* the specified criteria. If you display only some, no matter how severe, you will not qualify.

The list is designed to define impairments that would preclude an applicant from any gainful activity. It functions as a presumption of disability, streamlining the process. Under the law, however, the list cannot be the final test.

The law allows disability to someone who is prevented from performing "substantial gainful activity." If your condition is not on the list, the evaluation will proceed to Step 4.

Steps 4 and 5. What constitutes sufficient functional impairment? These steps evaluate your ability to perform work, either work of the kind you have done in the past or generally available work. They measure "residual functional capacity" of what you can still do despite your limitations.

For mental impairments, residual capacity is generally expressed in psychological terms. For physical impairments, it relates to your abilities to perform physical activities, such as walking, lifting, standing, and sitting.

An estimated 25 percent of adult claimants qualify for benefits under Steps 4 and 5.

Step 4 questions whether you can still perform work you have done in the past. According to the Social Security Administration, Step 4 is strictly a denial step. Either you are denied because you have the capacity to perform past work, or the evaluation proceeds to step 5.

Step 5 evaluates your ability to perform generally available work, subject to some modification. Under the law, your age, work experience, and education must be factored into a determination as to whether you are able to perform any other kind of work. Moreover, the work must "exist" in the national economy.

Step 5 rules for those who cannot do their past work are more lenient for older workers. The rules reflect the belief that age affects significantly a person's ability to adapt to new types of work, assuming the ability to adjust to a significant number of jobs at age 50 and less ability to adjust to any new work at age 55. At age 60, the factor of "skill marketability" is added.

Those aged 55 and over are required to adjust to other work if (1) past work required moderate to heavy levels of physical exertion and (2) the applicant has no skills readily transferrable to lighter work. Moreover, people aged 60 to 64 do not have to adjust to other work if their skills are not highly marketable. Nor do applicants with at least 35 years of arduous, unskilled physical labor and marginal education.

CONTINUING DISABILITY REVIEW

Under the law, Social Security must conduct a review every three years to determine your continuing eligibility for disability benefits. This is required for all but the permanently disabled. Since 1987, however, fewer than half the required reviews have been performed. An estimated 30,000 ineligible people remain on the rolls.

The review is performed by the same state disability determination services office that conducts initial application reviews. A full review, much like the application review, includes a face-to-face meeting with a Social Security representative, evaluation by a disability examiner, and frequently a doctor's examination. About 90 percent of such reviews result in a finding of continued eligibility.

If you are denied continued benefits, you may challenge the decision through the appeals process. Forty percent of those denied benefits are successful at the appeals stage, winning back their benefits. (See the discussion of appeals later in this chapter.)

SUPPLEMENTAL SECURITY INCOME (SSI)

The Supplemental Security Income (SSI) program was enacted by Congress in 1972 to assist individuals over 65, blind, or disabled by setting a guaranteed minimum income level for them. SSI is not funded by the Social Security trust fund or Social Security taxes. Its financing comes from general federal revenues. In effect, the federal government took over public assistance benefits for these categories of people.

The maximum federal SSI payment in 1996 is $470 a month for an individual and $705 a month for a couple. More than half the states provide an additional state supplement bringing the SSI benefit level up, although it still falls below the poverty level in almost all the states.

In 1993, SSI provided about $24 billion to 6 million recipients. SSI is one of those government programs under attack for eligibility rules that allow benefits to many elderly immigrants as well as the native-born poor. In fact, many elderly people have never heard of SSI or imagined that there is any program other than Social Security to provide them with income. In any year an estimated 1.5 million elderly people potentially eligible for SSI never even apply for it.

Many people who are not eligible for Social Security may be eligible for Supplemental Security Income. In addition, people who receive Social Security retirement or disability benefits which are below SSI allowances may qualify concurrently for benefits under both the Social Security retirement or disability insurance program and SSI.

SSI ELIGIBILITY

To be eligible for SSI, you must

- Be age 65 or older, blind, or disabled (children can also get SSI in some circumstances)
- Have assets and income less than certain amounts

If you are single, you can have no more than $2,000 in assets and be eligible for SSI. The limit for a couple is $3,000. In measuring your assets to determine eligibility for SSI, the following resources will not be included:

- Your home and the land it's on
- Your personal and household goods
- Your car (up to $4,500; there is no limit when needed for medical or employment reasons)
- Burial plots for you and members of your immediate family
- Life insurance and burial funds up to $1,500 for you and up to $1,500 for your spouse

The amount of income you can have each month and still get SSI depends partly on where you live. (You can call 800/772-1213 to find out the income limits in your state.)

Social Security does not count the following when deciding SSI eligibility:

- The first $20 of most income received in a month
- The first $65 a month you earn from working and half the amount over $65
- Food stamps
- Most food, clothing, or shelter you get from private nonprofit organizations
- Most home energy assistance

An applicant with resources above the specified limits may be able to "spend down" resources to qualify for SSI. For example, a widow over 65 years old having a savings account of $2,500 would be ineligible for SSI because her assets were above the limit. However, if she took $750 from her savings and opened a separate burial fund, then her non-exempt assets would be $1,750, under the $2,000 amount.

This is the same technique we described in Chapter 8 to qualify for Medicaid. Don't forget that a transfer of assets may affect your eligibility for Medicaid. (As a general rule, your SSI eligibility does not affect Medicaid eligibility.)

You must also be a United States citizen, lawfully admitted for permanent residence, or permanently residing in the United States under "color of law." In addition, you must be residing both in the United States *and* in the state where you apply. An individual who leaves the United States for 30 days becomes ineligible for benefits.

 APPLYING FOR SSI

SSI must be applied for at the Social Security office. If you live in a state that provides a state supplement, you may also have to apply at a state agency.

The law gives states the option of having the federal government administer the state supplement, with the state picking up the administrative costs. In states that choose this option, a single application covers both the federal and state payments.

Some states choose to administer their own supplement. In those states, application for the supplement must be made with the state agency. States that administer their own supplement are Alabama, Alaska, Arizona, Colorado, Connecticut, Florida, Idaho, Illinois, Indiana, Kentucky, Louisiana, Maryland, Minnesota, Missouri, Nebraska, New Hampshire, New Mexico,

North Carolina, North Dakota, Ohio, Oklahoma, Oregon, South Carolina, South Dakota, Virginia, and Wyoming.

When filing an SSI application with either Social Security or the state agency, you should bring:

- Your Social Security card or number
- Your birth certificate or proof of age
- Information about the home where you live, such as your mortgage or your lease
- Payroll slips, bank books, insurance policies, car registration, burial fund records, and other information about your income and the things you own
- If you're applying for disability, the names, addresses, and telephone numbers of doctors, hospitals, and clinics that have seen you

You can call the Social Security hotline (800/772-1213) to make an appointment at your local Social Security office or to apply over the phone. If you apply over the phone, you will be mailed an application for signature and a notice of what documents you must submit.

SSI BENEFITS

In 1996, the maximum federal SSI payment is $470 a month for an eligible individual living alone and $705 a month for an eligible couple. Benefits are lower for individuals or couples living with others or in another's household. An individual living with others or a disabled person living with parents would be eligible for a maximum of $313.34 monthly (one-third off the maximum benefit rate). Those with other income will also receive less.

For example, a widow over 65 years old receiving $235 a month in Social Security retirement benefits and living alone would have her SSI benefits calculated in the following way. Her $235 income would be reduced by a fixed "non-countable" $20, leaving an income of $215. The $215 income would be deducted from the maximum benefit of $470, giving her an SSI benefit of $255 monthly. (This example does not include any state supplement she might receive.)

Note that the federal benefit will be reduced to $30 if the recipient is institutionalized (unless a doctor certifies that the stay will be for less than 3 months and the recipient demonstrates a need for the money to maintain the non-institutional living arrangement.

More is available in most states through the state supplement. You can call Social Security at 800/772-1213 to find out the amounts for your state. Although the federal amount is increased yearly, the supplement amount may not change, depending on the state.

SSI DISABILITY RULES

The medical requirements for disability payments and the process for determining disability are the same as under the Social Security disability insurance program described in the previous section. The disability determination services teams are the same, and subject to the same standards as those concerning medical review for eligibility and continued eligibility determinations.

Other Social Security and SSI rules are different. For example, a disabled person under Social Security's disability insurance program is not paid benefits for five months *from* the date the disability began. But SSI disability benefits can be paid *retroactively* to the date the person filed his or her claim. SSI also applies different rules from Social Security's for people with disabilities who want to go back to work.

 APPEALING A SOCIAL SECURITY DECISION

If you don't agree with a decision about Social Security or SSI regarding your eligibility for benefits, or the amount of benefits awarded you, you can appeal the decision. About two million SSI claims are adjudicated each year.

Social Security has a three-part appeal process, after which you may sue in federal court. However, you must proceed in order. The steps in the process are called: reconsideration, hearing, and review. Don't be intimidated by the names of these processes, which have no legal significance other than the convenience of telling them apart.

Step 1: Reconsideration

A reconsideration involves review by a Social Security representative, who will look at all the evidence submitted when the original decision was made. He or she will also look at any new evidence you may wish to submit.

You must request a reconsideration within 60 days of the original decision. The law requires that reconsideration be handled by someone who didn't take part in the initial decision you're challenging. If you're not satisfied with the decision after the reconsideration, you have a right to a hearing.

Step 2: Hearing

A hearing is conducted by an administrative law judge (also called an ALJ) who had nothing to do with any prior decisions made regarding your case. You must request a hearing within 60 days of the reconsideration decision. The hearing will usually be held within 75 miles of your home. If after the hearing you still disagree with the decision, you can ask for a review by the Appeals Council.

Step 3: Review

The Social Security Appeals Council conducts reviews of hearing decisions. You must request a review within 60 days of the hearing decision. The Appeals Council does not review all cases that are appealed. If it does decide to review your case, it will either render a decision or return it to an ALJ for further review. The Appeals Council is located in Falls Church, Virginia.

After Steps 1 through 3, your appeal to Social Security is over. If you're dissatisfied with the result, you have 60 days to file a suit in a federal district court.

Must I be present for Social Security appeals?

It depends. Whether or not you are present for the reconsideration depends upon the kind of decision being considered. Many reconsiderations are strictly "file review," conducted solely by reference to the written documents and without the opportunity for you to meet with a representative. In other circumstances, you will be given the choice. For example, if you've been receiving disability benefits and are going to be cut off, you will be given the opportunity to meet with a disability hearing officer.

For disability claimants, the reconsideration process allows you the option to meet face-to-face with the person who is reconsidering your case to explain why you feel you are still disabled. You can submit new evidence or information and can bring someone who knows about your disability. This special hearing does not replace your right to also have a formal hearing before an ALJ (the second appeal step) if your reconsideration is denied.

At the hearing level, you always have the opportunity to appear in person—and you always should. It is much harder for an ALJ to make a decision against a sympathetic person who has been present than it is when all the judge has seen is the dry-as-dust files. If you don't choose to appear, the ALJ may decide your presence is required. Otherwise, and far more likely, he or she will make a decision based on all the information in your case, including any new information given. You must inform Social Security in writing that you don't wish to attend.

Will I continue to receive payment during the time of my appeal?

Yes, if you want to. You can continue to receive payments if you are appealing a decision that you are no longer eligible for Social Security disability benefits because your condition has improved, that you are no longer eligible for SSI, or that your SSI payment should be reduced. You must inform Social Security of your desire to have payments continue during your appeal within 10 days of the date you receive the notice of the decision about your benefits from Social Security. If you ultimately fail in your appeal, you may have to pay back the money if you were not eligible to receive it.

How does the hearing work?

You will be notified by the ALJ of the time and place of the hearing. You may bring witnesses and a representative to the hearing. The ALJ will question you and any witnesses you choose to bring. You may look at the information in your file and give new information.

The ALJ's decision will be made after the hearing. You will be sent a copy, along with a notice.

Do I need a lawyer? What if I can't afford one?

You are entitled to a lawyer or a non-lawyer "representative" to help you or to appear on your behalf. He or she can act for you in most matters and will receive a copy of any decisions made about your claim. (Your representative must get permission from Social Security to charge you or collect a fee.)

There are groups that can help you find a lawyer or that provide free legal services if you meet certain qualifications. Your local Social Security office should have a list of such groups.

The Social Security Administration determines fees for lawyers, based on regulations setting forth the services performed by the lawyer and the complexity of your case. Your attorney's fee must be approved before he or she may bill you. And you have the right to appeal a determination about the amount of the fee. (So does your lawyer.) At the federal court level, the court has the power to set the fees.

 CREDITOR PROTECTION FOR YOUR BENEFITS

Under the law, your Social Security and SSI benefits cannot be attached by a creditor. Even the IRS cannot get them if you owe back taxes. They are "judgment-proof."

 YOUR SOCIAL SECURITY NUMBER

About 10 million new numbers are assigned each year. The Social Security Administration has issued an estimated total of 365 million Social Security numbers.

There's actually a law, a little-known section of the Privacy Act of 1974, which governs use of the Social Security number for anything other than the reasons for which it was created. Under the law, you cannot be denied a government benefit for refusing to divulge your Social Security number (unless there is a statute authorizing its use).

Are my Social Security records confidential?

Generally, yes. However, several other government agencies are permitted by law to use Social Security numbers. For example, some state death records are matched to Medicare records using Social Security numbers to uncover Medicare and Social Security fraud.

When do I have to give my Social Security number out?

First, for anything that reflects your income. Or to account for retirement and survivor benefits. For example, banks and other financial institutions use the numbers to report interest earned on accounts to the IRS for income tax purposes.

The law does not prohibit the use of Social Security numbers by the private sector. If a business or other enterprise asks you for your Social Security number, you may refuse to give it to them. That may mean doing without the purchase or service for which your number was requested. But remember, your Social Security number is a "universal identifier," of particular appeal to criminals and con artists as well as advertisers, employers, and bureaucrats. Armed with your number, people can get all sorts of information about you and your credit rating, bank accounts, and finances, without your knowing about it until it's too late.

Part 6

■ ■

Meeting Your Housing Needs

For older people, living arrangements take on great importance. Most people seek to remain in their own homes, and housing expenses represent a major budget item. On fixed retirement incomes and budgets, they feel the financial pinch. Some may experience difficulties in managing a household or performing chores, but for many, staying in their own homes is worth the extra effort. Witness the vast numbers of those in the over-85 age group who still live in their own homes, often getting care to cope with frailty and ill health.

This section takes a look at legal and financial issues of housing you should consider and discusses the options and opportunities available to you. In Chapter 19, we discuss your status and rights as tenants and homeowners. We give you the tools to help you keep autonomy over your living arrangements, much as you are trying to retain control of your finances, and show you how to deal with discrimination in housing.

For some, circumstance or necessity may compel other choices. In Chapter 20, we turn to the latest trend in retirement living, the adult-living communities, which have become a $7 billion industry in this country. We tell you what you can expect, what to watch out for, and what your legal rights are in alternative housing arrangements ranging from continuing care facilities to assisted-living communities.

1 9

■■

TENANTS AND
HOMEOWNERS

Surveys indicate that more than 86 percent of older Americans want to stay in their homes. And in fact, according to census data, 75 percent do remain in their homes after retirement. A full 96 percent stay in the same state. For these citizens, housing expenses represent a major budget item. This is true for both renters and homeowners.

 ## TENANTS' RIGHTS

If you are a renter, your landlord-tenant relationship is spelled out in your lease and, to some extent, in state laws and judicial decisions. Tenants have rights in these important areas:

Condition of the premises. Tenants have the right to adequate heat, hot water, and a "habitable" home. Under general principles of law, landlords also have the duty to make repairs and ensure safety.

Occupancy. State and local occupancy laws deal with your right to remain in your home. These laws, generally applicable to public housing and to some private housing, frequently provide that the landlord cannot refuse to renew your lease, so long as you continue to pay the rent. They generally do not apply to housing with fewer than a given number of units. If you live in housing with fewer than the number of units specified in your state's laws, the laws may afford you limited or no protection and allow termination of your lease.

Other rights include the right to form tenant groups, to distribute literature, and to be free from retaliation from your landlord for making complaints.

Your landlord also has rights, including the right to timely payment of rent and the right of access to your apartment in emergencies.

My elderly mother is in the hospital and may be transferred to a nursing home. Is she obligated to continue to pay rent on her apartment?

254

It depends on the law where you live. Many jurisdictions provide for termination of the lease in specific cases. For example, in New York, your mother would have the right to terminate her lease upon entering a skilled nursing facility.

HOUSING REGULATION

State laws on the rights of tenants vary from state to state. However, all states have legal rules governing "habitability," contained in building codes and warranty-of-habitability laws. These laws and regulations apply to privately owned buildings.

States, counties, and most municipalities have administrative agencies charged with handling complaints governing housing matters such as landlord-tenant disputes, including complaints about heating, services and conditions, and rent overcharge.

In addition some states provide affordable-housing programs, ensuring lower-cost housing by subsidizing renters with modest incomes. There are similar federal programs, as well. Many elderly qualify for these programs, but are unaware of their existence.

Some states and municipalities limit rent increases as well, and have special programs regulating increases for qualified older tenants. Applying to these programs can lead to substantial rent reductions or smaller rent increases. For example, the Senior Citizens Rent Increase Exemption (SCRIE) program in New York limits rent increases for people over 62 with incomes below $20,000 yearly who spend at least a third of their incomes on rent.

Renters also get some tax relief in the form of rebates, credits, or refunds in a number of states, including California, Michigan, Missouri, Nevada, North Dakota, Oregon, New Mexico, and Pennsylvania. Some states such as Illinois and Connecticut provide direct grants or help with rent. Eligibility for and amount of relief from these programs often depend on income.

RENTAL ASSISTANCE

Elderly renters are particularly affected by high housing costs, the impact of which are made greater by their fixed incomes. As many as half of poor elderly renters spend more than 45 percent of their incomes on housing.

For poorer renters among the elderly, low-cost public housing or federal subsidies are made available under programs dating back to the 1930s and passage of the United States Housing Act in 1937. As a general rule, income must be very low to qualify for these programs. Eligibility criteria vary considerably.

Public housing. Elderly people occupy nearly 45 percent of the country's 1.3 million public housing units. These are federal Housing and Urban

Development (HUD) projects, administered by more than 3,000 public housing authorities across the country. Public authorities may be city agencies or independent authorities. (The former provide more safeguards, along with the inevitable red tape.)

Some of these projects are fairly old, with inadequate insulation, roofing, electric and plumbing systems. Despite nationwide reports of deteriorating facilities, delays by HUD and local authorities have caused backlogs for modernization projects in the $9 billion range. Long-term solutions to sustaining these projects have become mired in partisan politics.

Under Section 504 of the Rehabilitative Act of 1973, five percent of a public housing authority's units must be made accessible to the disabled. This means accommodations of benefit to the elderly, including exit and entrance ramps and doors equipped for wheelchairs. (Related protections in the Fair Housing Act and the Americans with Disabilities Act are discussed later in this chapter.)

According to government reports, most new public housing projects have been designed exclusively for the elderly. However, the percentage of elderly actually benefiting from public housing is declining as a result of increases in the population of eligible nonelderly people with mental or physical disabilities. And funding for these projects has declined markedly over the past decade.

Section 202 housing. Section 202 housing is designed to give the elderly and handicapped an independent living environment with necessary support services. Residents pay 30 percent of income, and the difference is paid by HUD. Although certain services are required by HUD regulations, they need not be provided on-site. There are waiting lists of one year and longer for this type of housing. Of 138,000 units in 1988, 94 percent were occupied by elderly.

Section 8 subsidies. The federal Section 8 program provides rental assistance to low-income people. "Section 8" refers to Section 8 of the United States Housing Act, enacted in 1937 and amended several times since. The elderly amount to about 44 percent of the 2.5 million participants receiving Section 8 benefits.

- *Certificates and vouchers* provide subsidies for the difference between 30 percent of the renter's income and the "fair market" rent. The difference between a certificate program and a voucher program is that rentals in the certificate program have a fair market rent ceiling established by federal regulations. In the voucher program, participants can live in apartments with higher rents and pay the difference out of pocket. In a tight housing market, vouchers give you more control over where you live. At this writing, unfortunately, cutbacks in federal funding have frozen commitments for new tenant-based subsidies for the past two years. Current tenants may find themselves vulnerable to rent increases under proposed eligibility restrictions.

- Section 8 also runs *project-based programs*, which provide assistance for low-income people living in privately owned rental housing. In a project-based program, you and your family must live in designated properties. Again, you are required to pay 30 percent of your income for rent. Your rights are governed by the contract and the regulatory agreement. Unlike the certificate and voucher programs, tenants who move from these Section 8 facilities lose their rental assistance (unless they move to another subsidized property).

HUD has quality standards for safe, decent, and sanitary housing. For HUD-assisted properties, the contract provides for yearly inspection by HUD. Standards require that assisted properties be maintained by owners in good condition. Tenants in Section 8 housing must be provided with

- Properly operating sanitary facilities
- Adequate security
- Properly operating heating and air conditioning
- Ceilings and walls without serious defects

Owners who fail to comply with these standards can be barred or suspended from further participation in Section 8 contracts. In cases of serious physical neglect, payments for individual units can be suspended and the current contract can be ended.

However, this provision is of little help—and may perhaps do harm—to tenants living in subsidized substandard apartments who could be displaced if no other funding and no long-term alternative housing assistance were available. The threat of a future funding cutoff is effective only against owners who wish to keep participating in HUD programs. Moreover, enforcement by HUD is spotty. Recent reform laws allow owners to be assessed up to $25,000 per violation. These penalties apply only to certain properties, however, and so far have had limited effect on owners with protected assets.

 SHARED HOUSING

Homesharing has become increasingly popular over the past two decades for reasons that include added income, companionship, and a measure of extra security provided by housemates. The number of people sharing homes has increased to well over a million.

No matter how amicable the arrangement, the homesharing relationship is nevertheless a legal one, with concomitant rights and responsibilities which should be codified in a written contract. While the form of the contract can be as simple as a letter or as formal as a lease, the wording should contain basic lease clauses regarding term, notice of termination, and rent amount. The arrangement between the homeowner and the homesharer should be drafted with care. It is more intimate than a regular landlord-tenant relationship, and rights and responsibilities should be spelled out, especially in an arrangement in which an older person is sharing his or her home with a younger one. Expectations concerning the use of the telephone, shared expenses, guests, and other such details should also be made explicit. Remember, too, in figuring the amount, rental income is taxable.

One possible legal obstacle: local housing ordinances may not allow unrelated parties in a single home. You should check with your local housing authority.

Local agencies may be a source for homesharing candidates, matching compatible older people. One source for information, including a sample lease agreement, is the Shared Housing Resource Center (telephone: 802/223-2627).

I am receiving home care services from Medicaid. I have thought about renting out a room in my home in exchange for personal care.

The income might put your Medicaid eligibility in jeopardy, or you could forfeit your extra income. Make sure you consult a lawyer first (See Part 7, Getting Help, and Resources section for a list of organizations that provide lawyer referrals.)

HELP FOR HOMEOWNERS

Housing costs can be a real drain on the limited resources of older homeowners as well as tenants. These problems are compounded by the difficulties owners face as they age. Often homes need to be adapted to changing conditions, to ensure safety as well as comfort, particularly in bathrooms and kitchens. A few federal programs exist to help low-income homeowners repair their homes or make alterations to accommodate their changing needs.

The poorer you are, the worse your problems may be. Although the vast majority of older homeowners own their own houses mortgage-free, as many as half of poor homeowners over 65 report spending more than 45 percent of their income on housing expenses such as real estate taxes, insurance, and utilities.

Assistance for homeowners comes in a number of forms. Among the possibilities of aid for repairs and maintenance are public subsidies and deferral loans as well as tax relief. (Contact your local housing department or Area Agency on Aging.)

Taxes. Tax exemptions, tax abatements, tax credits, and other forms of tax relief based on the value of your home are available in a number of states. Eligibility requirements usually include a minimum age of 65, although some are as low as 55, and specify the value of your home, your income, and the length of your residency. Some states (New Jersey is one) include provision for residents in adult communities under certain conditions.

Home repair loans and loans for paying property taxes. There are publicly financed loan programs for low- or moderate-income people, including property tax deferral programs and deferred-payment loans. In these kinds of programs, the costs are lower than for private sector loans. Typically the money can be used only for certain purposes, that is, for paying property taxes or for making repairs or improving your home. Acceptable improvements include roof, stair, and floor repairs, plumbing, heating, wiring, and accessibility features such as ramps and rails.

Property taxes deferred under such programs do not have to be paid until you leave your home. You can get a one-time deferral or a new deferral every year. Deferred taxes under these programs are loans. The taxes are not forgiven. Upon your death, payment will be due against the home. (The payment will not come due if a surviving spouse inherits, but the lien continues.)

Programs to lend money are available in many states, including California, Colorado, Georgia, Illinois, Maine, Oregon, Tennessee, Texas, Utah, Virginia, Washington, and Wisconsin. Connecticut, Florida, Iowa, Massachusetts, and New Hampshire also support local programs. Check with your local property tax collector or contact your Area Agency on Aging.

Utility assistance. Some gas and electric companies offer loan programs and deferral loans for insulation and weatherizing. Relief and some help is offered for utility bills in some states, including Connecticut and Wisconsin. All such programs are at the mercy of legislatures and may fall to the ax in budget-cutting times.

 ## REVERSE MORTGAGES

Many older homeowners find themselves in the dubious position of being house-rich and cash-poor. With their houses paid off and no money owed the bank, they are suddenly faced with unanticipated housing costs ranging from increased tax payments to roof repairs for which they simply don't have the money. At the same time, they may incur significant expenses for other unexpected needs, such as home care.

One solution designed to supplement other income is the *reverse mortgage*. Reverse mortgage programs permit elderly homeowners to convert the equity in their homes into cash, without having to sell their homes. A reverse mortgage is a type of home equity loan designed expressly for older homeowners. Using their homes as collateral, homeowners can borrow money and postpone repayment until a future time.

Technically, this is a *home equity conversion mortgage*. The reason it's called a *reverse mortgage* is that it reverses the way a regular mortgage works.

Instead of your making a payment to your lender each month, the lender pays you.

The benefit is that, unlike other home equity loans, you're not required to pay back the loan for as long as you live in the house. And reverse mortgages can be used for any purpose. If you qualify, you can continue to own and live in your home while receiving either a lump sum or periodic payments. Under most plans, repayment is not due until the home is sold or the owner dies.

Reverse mortgages have been on the market for more than a quarter of a century. There are three basic types of reverse mortgages offered by banks and savings and loan associations. These are:

FHA-insured reverse mortgages. The FHA-insured reverse mortgages provide funds in a lump sum payment, monthly, or whenever you choose. The Federal Housing Administration puts limits on the amount of cash you may get, as a condition of its insuring such loans. This insurance is an important guarantee: if the lender defaults, you will continue to be paid. "Home Equity Conversion Mortgages" sponsored through the Department of Housing and Urban Development (HUD), of which the FHA is a part, are available through FHA-approved lenders nationwide. Under FHA rules, independent counseling is also provided.

Private insurance. Reverse mortgages backed by private insurance may offer greater cash advances than FHA-insured reverse mortgages. The biggest disadvantage of such insurance is the risk connected to the financial stability of the lender. As with any insurance, you should check the financial soundness of the company.

Uninsured. Uninsured reverse mortgages are for fixed terms. Monthly payments are available for terms varying from 3 to 10 years. The loans must be repaid in full when the term ends.

QUALIFYING FOR A REVERSE MORTGAGE

Different programs apply different qualifying restrictions. Basic eligibility requirements are:

- Borrowers must be at least 62 years old.
- Borrowers should owe little or no money on their homes. (As you're not expected to make regular payments, income is not a factor in your eligibility for a reverse mortgage.)
- Homes must be single-family, one-unit owner occupied dwellings.
- Condominiums must be FHA-approved to be eligible.

I live in a cooperative apartment. Am I eligible for a reverse mortgage?
No. Mobile homes, cooperatives, and multiple unit dwellings are not eligible for reverse mortgages. Legislation is pending in some states to allow loans on cooperatives.

LOAN AMOUNT AND PAYMENT OPTIONS

Total loan amount. Loans made as reverse mortgages are calculated on an amount fixed at the maximum the FHA will insure. The total amount you may receive depends on

- The value of your home
- Your age
- The area in which you reside

The maximum amount varies per locality, from $67,500 in low-cost rural areas to $151,725 in costlier housing markets. This cap determines the total amount from which your cash payments will be made. If your home value is less, the cap will be less.

The amount will also vary depending on your age. Payments are based on actuarial tables. The percentage you receive will vary from 37 percent of the limit for a 62-year-old to 83 percent for a 95-year-old.

Payment options (what you get). Once approved, the homeowner has various options for receiving payment. The type of payment chosen also alters the amount.

- Lifetime monthly payments. Also called *tenure plans.* These will vary depending on your age. The older you are, the higher the monthly amount will be. (For couples, the younger person's age will determine the payout, as his or her life expectancy is how long the house is likely to be kept.) In some plans, monthly payments may be increased in later years
- Monthly payments for a fixed term
- A one-time lump-sum payment
- A line of credit, from which withdrawals may be made

These same options are available through FHA-backed and private lender reverse mortgages. A combination is also possible, such as monthly payments and a line of credit. Under FHA rules, options can be changed, at an administrative fee of no more than $20.

Amount due (what you owe). In addition to the full loan amount, you are liable for fees, as with any mortgage, including application fees, points, closing costs, insurance premiums, plus all interest. Interest and closing rates are generally higher than those in conventional mortgages.

Your potential liability is limited to the value of your home. You can't be made to pay from other assets as you may have. No costs, including insurance premiums, are collected until the loan is due.

Counseling. You must get counseling from a mortgage counselor from an HUD-approved agency. This protects both you and the bank.

Warning. A reverse mortgage is a loan. It becomes due when you move, sell your home, or die, or in some cases, at the end of a determinate loan period. You could lose your home if the reverse mortgage is not repaid, or use up your equity and have to move. Remember, that once your home equity is spent, it is no longer available to you or your heirs. Make sure you consult with your lawyer or accountant before agreeing to a reverse mortgage.

What happens when my spouse dies?

No repayment is due until the last surviving borrower dies or sells or moves from the home.

Is my home safe? What if I have to go to a nursing home or a facility? Should I sell my home?

Most reverse mortgage plans address the issue of what will happen when your home is unoccupied for a long period of time. Depending on the provisions in your plan, you might be required to repay the loan amount. A forced sale under equity conversion may force spend-down of proceeds. And any equity you use up will not be available to your spouse or heirs.

TRUTH IN LENDING REQUIREMENTS

The federal Truth in Lending Act requires lenders to inform you about the terms, conditions, and costs of your reverse mortgage plan. This includes an explanation of payment terms, annual percentage and variable rates, credit charges and other fees. There is a Truth in Lending form that tells you what the loan actually costs.

The law also requires mortgage counseling from a third party who is not the lender. The information you are given must include

- Other options available to you, including home equity conversion
- Financial implications of the plan
- Tax and estate consequences of the plan
- The consequences of the plan for your eligibility for government benefits

Your right to *rescission* is also spelled out in notice from your lender. You have three business days after signing and receiving your Truth in Lending disclosures to reconsider your decision to take out the loan.

Reverse mortgages are complicated legal transactions, combining elements of home equity loans, life insurance, and annuities. You should not be proceeding without a professional adviser to counsel you concerning the terms and their implications for you.

REVERSE MORTGAGES AND GOVERNMENT BENEFITS

Reverse mortgage payments are not taxable. Nor are they counted as income for purposes of determining eligibility for Social Security, SSI,

Medicare, or Medicaid benefits. However, reverse mortgage payments may nevertheless effect your eligibility in the following way. Although the monthly payments you receive from a reverse mortgage are not "income" for Medicaid or SSI purposes, if the funds are not spent, you may accumulate assets in excess of the allowable amounts (see Chapter 8). By the same principle, annuity payments or a lump-sum payment to you may jeopardize your eligibility. This is an important issue, so make sure you consult a lawyer familiar with federal SSI requirements and your state's Medicaid regulations before getting a reverse mortgage.

FINDING A REVERSE MORTGAGE

At the present time, FHA-insured reverse mortgages are offered through lenders in 47 states and the District of Columbia. Privately insured and uninsured reverse mortgages are also available in several states.

A list of programs offering reverse mortgages is available from the National Center for Home Equity Conversion (telephone 612/953-4474). The names of FHA-insured lenders are available from the Federal National Mortgage Association (Fannie Mae), (telephone 800/7-FANNIE). The American Association of Retired Persons (AARP) also supplies information on private and public reverse mortgage lenders (telephone 202/434-6030). See the Resources section of this book for complete listings.

A listing of reverse mortgage counseling agencies, approved by HUD, can be obtained from lenders in your area. Nonprofit agencies which provide information and initial contacts for reverse mortgages are also available in your area. Complaints or questions should be directed to the Federal Trade Commission.

SALE LEASEBACK

Another way of tapping the equity in your home is the sale leaseback. In a sale leaseback transaction, you sell your home and lease it back from the person who bought it. The buyer of your home is in effect an investor, who grants you a life tenancy (or specified term of years) allowing you to remain in your home.

Like a reverse mortgage, the sale leaseback gives you access to the equity tied up in your home without forcing you to move. In the sale leaseback, the homeowner assumes the roles of seller, buyer and lender:

- *Seller.* As a seller, you receive a lump sum or monthly mortgage payments from the buyer.
- *Buyer (or tenant).* As a buyer, you are purchasing a life tenancy or lease term, for which rental payments are due (and theoretically will be deducted from the amounts you receive).

- *Lender.* As a lender, you're financing the purchase. Payments represent the mortgage due you.

In a sale leaseback, your income is protected by your mortgage and/or annuity purchase. Unlike reverse mortgages, the installment payments in a sale leaseback deal are taxable income, and may be subject to both capital gains and income taxes. Tax considerations should dictate the specific arrangement which is best for you. Your lawyer should be familiar with lease, sale and financing.

 SELLING YOUR HOME

Your home is a *capital asset*. If you sell it for more than your purchase cost, including both the original price plus certain improvements, you must pay an income tax on your gains. This is the *capital gains tax.*

The Internal Revenue Code provides some tax breaks in these specific instances:

Rollover. The Internal Revenue Code provides that the proceeds from the sale of your home can be "rolled over" into the purchase of another home without current income tax liability, provided that

- You purchase the new home within two years before or after the sale of the former residence and
- The cost of the new home exceeds the sale price of the old one (If the new home costs less than the sale price for the former home, you may be liable for taxes on the unspent portion of your proceeds.)

The rollover of sales proceeds is available to sellers of any age. Note that the income tax is not avoided but only deferred until the new home is sold.

One-time $125,000 exclusion. A seller 55 or older, who has owned and resided in his or her home for three out of the five years preceding a sale, is eligible for a one-time exclusion of up to $125,000 from capital gains tax on the proceeds. Only one to a customer (or a couple).

Some states with income tax also give you a tax break.

My future husband and I both own homes from our first marriages. Can we each use the exclusion?

Not after you marry. If two seniors are planning to marry, they should sell their homes first.

Can I use my rollover when I move from my present home into an adult community?

Yes, if you're buying an apartment or other housing unit. If you're merely entering into a lease or contract for services including housing, it may not constitute an ownership interest sufficient to qualify for this tax break, in which case you'll be taxed on any gains from the sale of your home.

Can I use both the rollover and exclusion in selling my home?

Yes, if you meet the requirements for each benefit. Remember, you can only use the $125,000 exclusion one time. Keep in mind that you would only need to use the one-time exclusion if the cost of your new home was less than your previous home.

My house is on the market now. My husband used an exclusion when he sold the residence he and his former wife lived in. Will I still be able to get my one-time exclusion?

No. As long as you're married to your husband, his use of the exclusion precludes you from using it.

MOVING TO ANOTHER STATE

If you are among the 4 percent of retirees who opt to move to another state after retirement, your plans require consideration of additional factors.

In addition to your basic housing costs, you must consider the implications for your tax liability. Investigate the differences in taxes under your new state's laws, including:

- Income taxes
- Sales taxes
- Real property taxes
- Tangible or intangible personal property taxes
- Gift and estate taxes

Taken individually or together, these may add considerably to the expenses of your planned move.

The other major area to check is public benefits, particularly if paying for long-term health care costs may present a problem for you. As we discussed in Chapter 8, your potential eligibility for public benefits may change, especially if you are moving to an "income cap" state or one with other restrictive rules. *This is especially important now, with states taking an increasing role in determining how their Medicaid moneys will be spent—and cutting back on expenditures for the elderly in areas like home care.* If you are unsure, speak to a lawyer or other professional familiar with the Medicaid rules in your new state.

Reminder. If you do move to another state, instruments such as your will, power of attorney, living will, and health care proxy may need to be reviewed and revised to comply with the requirements of your new home state.

ZONING AND AGE DISCRIMINATION

When it comes to housing, older people are doubly disadvantaged. Many are unaware of their housing rights. Many more are unable to represent their own interests because of the very conditions associated with their age—disabilities and frailty.

In addition, older persons are frequently subject to discrimination, which isolates them. Fear of reprisal also keeps some from seeking to enforce their rights.

Federal law provides some legislative tools for addressing these issues. The Fair Housing Act provides for reasonable accommodations which may allow older tenants to retain their housing, and their independence, as they age.

 ## FAIR HOUSING LAWS

The Fair Housing Act is a federal law that prohibits discrimination in housing on account of race, national origin, religion, sex, familial status, or handicap. It does not have a separate category for age but it does prohibit discrimination on account of handicap—and requires reasonable accommodation be made for them.

As we discussed in Chapter 16, the definition of "handicap" may apply to many people who do not think of themselves as handicapped. You may be protected from housing discrimination if you

- Have a physical or mental disability that substantially limits one or more major life activities, *including* hearing, mobility, and visual impairments, chronic alcoholism, and chronic mental illness or
- Have a record of such disability or
- Are regarded as having such a disability

What that means is that if a potential landlord discriminates against you thinking you are impaired in regard to your mobility, you are in the protected class.

The Fair Housing Act covers most housing, both private and public, in this country. The only exemptions are for owner-occupied buildings with no more than four units, single-family housing sold or rented without a broker, and housing operated by organizations and private clubs that limit occupancy to members.

The law's prohibitions relating to the sale and rental of housing are extensive. Under its provisions, no one can take any of the following actions based on race, national origin, religion, sex, familial status, or handicap:

- Refuse to rent or sell you housing
- Refuse to negotiate for housing
- Make housing unavailable
- Set different terms, conditions or privileges for sale or rental of a dwelling
- Provide different housing services or facilities
- Falsely deny that housing is available for inspection, sale or rental

- Deny access or membership related to sale or rental of housing

Specific prohibitions related to handicap give you the following additional protections:

- Your landlord must allow you to make *reasonable modifications* necessary for you to use your dwelling (or common use area), *at your expense.*
- Your landlord must make reasonable accommodations in any rules, policies or services if necessary for you to use the housing.

Elder Community Exemption

Buildings and communities may not discriminate against people based on familial status. That means they can't discriminate against families with one or more children under 18 living with:

- A parent
- A person who has legal custody of the child or children
- The designee of a parent or legal custodian, with written permission

Housing for older persons is exempt from this prohibition if

- The HUD Secretary determines that it is specifically designed for and occupied by elderly persons under a federal, state, or local government program or
- It is occupied solely by persons who are 62 or older or
- It houses at least one person who is 55 or older in at least 80 percent of the occupied units; it has significant services and facilities for older persons; it adheres to a published policy statement that demonstrates an intent to house persons 55 or older

Making a Discrimination Complaint

If you have a complaint of discrimination, you should write HUD or call the Hotline at 800/669-9777. (800/927-9275 TDD; in Washington, D.C., 202/708-0836. See Resources for full HUD contact information.)

Conciliation. HUD will try to reach an agreement with the person against whom you've made your complaint. If a conciliation agreement is breached, HUD will recommend the Attorney General file suit.

Complaint referrals. HUD may refer your complaint to a state or local agency with jurisdiction. That agency must begin work on your complaint within 30 days.

Immediate help. HUD may go to court immediately to seek an injunction if necessary.

Administrative hearing. If after its investigation HUD finds reasonable cause to believe discrimination has occurred, your case will be sent for an administrative hearing within 120 days. (Or, alternatively, it may be taken to a Federal district court.)

HUD attorneys will represent you before the Administrative Law Judge, unless you wish to be represented by your own attorney.

The ALJ has the power to order a number of penalties:

- Money damages to compensate for your actual damages, as well as for any pain and suffering
- Injunctive relief, if needed
- Civil penalty, between $10,000 and $50,000, payable to the Federal government
- Attorneys' fees

SOME HELP FROM THE ADA

The Americans with Disabilities Act (ADA) does not apply to housing, and prohibitions on discrimination in housing are located in the Fair Housing Act and Amendments, described before. However, the ADA does provide protections in other areas which may directly benefit older citizens (as well as younger people with disabilities) to allow them to remain in their homes and their communities.

In this regard, the ADA governs various aspects of

- Public services (including transportation)
- Public accommodations (including hotels, retail stores, restaurants and other private businesses)
- Telecommunications (including emergency telephone services)

The ADA's protections apply to anyone who has or is regarded as having a physical or mental impairment substantially limiting a major life activity. This broad definition covers many people who do not think of themselves as disabled. (For more on who qualifies, see Chapter 16.)

Public services. Individuals with disabilities cannot be excluded from the benefits of public transportation services. Title II of the ADA prohibits discrimination in public transportation and requires that new public transportation equipment be accessible to the disabled. Transportation facilities must also be accessible; those that are not must be made so. This applies to private contractors as well as direct government providers.

The requirements of Title II are designed to increase the mobility of people with disabilities by ensuring access to, around, and in a particular mode of transportation:

- Paratransit and specialized transportation services comparable to those provided the general public
- Lifts and ramps

- Equipment maintenance
- Personnel training
- Information for people with visual, hearing, and cognitive impairments

Eligibility for special transit services may be limited to individuals with temporary or permanent disability who can't access the fixed route services.

Alternative transit services must meet standards relating to hours and days of service, service area, response time, fares, and reservation capability.

My community has a special van service for people using wheelchairs. Can they restrict the number of trips I make?

No. That's not permitted under the law. And no waiting lists limiting service are allowed.

If I use a hotel shuttle, do they have to make any accommodation for me?

Yes. These provisions of the ADA apply to businesses whose primary business is transporting people, whether they are public or private.

Public accommodations. Title III of the ADA prohibits discrimination in any place of public accommodation and requires that such places be made accessible.

ADA regulations focus on eliminating physical, architectural, and communication barriers that may limit access to goods and services offered by these types of facilities. Detailed requirements govern items as diverse as:

- Pathways to and from facilities
- Entrances, doors, and gates
- Elevators, stairs and alternative pathways
- Toilets and rest room stalls
- Drinking fountains
- Parking spaces
- Telephones
- Hotel rooms
- Restaurants and cafeterias
- Location of signs

Private businesses subject to ADA accessibility requirements include hotels, motels, restaurants, bars, theaters, concert halls, museums, libraries, office buildings, banks, doctors' and medical offices, recreation facilities, service establishments such as dry cleaners and beauty shops, and sales establishments such as clothing stores, grocery stores, and shopping centers.

Telecommunications and emergency telephone services. This part of the law requires relay services for non-voice terminal users, and full 24-hour seven-day-a-week service. Telephone emergency services are operated by many public entities to allow individuals to seek help from police, fire, ambulance, and other emergency services. Direct access to these services is required under the law.

Compliance efforts with ADA requirements have been hampered for a number of reasons, including a statutory exception for financial burdens. The regulatory scheme for the statute is a complicated one, dividing enforcement authority among various agencies. State and local public housing complaints may be made to the Department of Housing and Urban Development (telephone 800/669-9777). Inquiry and complaints concerning transportation services can be made to the Department of Transportation's Federal Transit Administration (telephone 202/366-4011). Questions about architectural barriers may be directed to the Architectural and Transportation Barriers Compliance Board (telephone 800/USA-ABLE; 202/272-5449 TDD) or to the Department of Justice (telephone 202/514-0301, 202/514-0381 TDD). (See Resources for full listings.)

20

■■■

ADULT LIVING
COMMUNITIES

For many older people, staying in their own homes is not an option. Health problems, even relatively minor physical impairment, may make living alone too difficult to manage. A spouse with a similar medical condition may make the situation even more difficult. Unfortunately, home care, community assistance, and financial assistance provided through programs such as Medicare and Medicaid do not offer a solution to everyone's needs. Short of moving into a nursing home, what options are there?

If you are among the growing number of those seeking security or assistance that cannot be provided in your home, the answer may be an *adult living community*. Adult living communities come in different varieties designed to meet a range of needs.

- *Retirement communities* as they are commonly called, are designed for healthy and frequently younger retirees who seek independent living but with some conveniences and services.
- *Continuing care facilities* provide a place to live, three meals a day, and the availability of a nurse to deal with medical emergencies as needed.
- *Assisted living facilities* provide a broader menu of services for those who need greater non-medical help and some medical supervision.

In general, an adult living community provides the shelter of a home along with extra services and care, from housekeeping help to a range of personal services and heath care comparable to what is provided by a nursing home. Monthly costs range from $1,000 to $4,000—steep but nowhere near comparable costs for a nursing home.

By any name, these communities have become a billion-dollar industry. The most well-known companies include Marriott, Classic Residences by Hyatt, and Sunrise Retirement Homes. A 1992 report by *Consumer Reports*

271

estimated 230,000 people were living in 800 continuing care retirement communities nationwide. For retiring people, one quarter of those moving out of state move to planned adult communities in other states. About 600,000 people currently reside in over 10,000 developments built to provide some form of assisted living.

If you're thinking about an adult community, there are a number of factors for you to consider. After all, you are seeking both a residence *and* medical services in one form or another.

- For the housing part of the equation, the first question is whether you should buy or rent. While the adult living community industry has offered mostly owner-occupied housing, this trend is changing. More and more rental housing, with the same facilities and services, is appearing on the market. Whether you rent or buy, you need to find out just what rights in your apartment you will have—and under what circumstances you could lose the apartment.
- You have to examine the provisions of the "insurance" part of the package you are buying. Consider your future long-term care needs—whether there are limits in the package you are buying, what those limits are, and what the implications are for your ability to finance nursing home care down the road. Depending on your needs, your money might be better spent investing in long-term care insurance.

This chapter explains what to look for in an adult living community. And if you are contemplating a move to an adult community, remember to consult with a knowledgeable professional. Although these facilities are marketed like vacation condos, what you are seeking is both your home and your future medical care. You wouldn't do either of these things without long, hard consideration and professional advice, would you? There is no substitute for such advice when you are considering an adult community.

TYPES OF COMMUNITIES

Although adult living communities are undergoing a radical transformation, coming in almost as many varieties as there are customers, they all derive or borrow features from the traditional *continuing care* retirement communities. These include structures that provide every level of service:

- *All-inclusive or life-care facilities.* These facilities provide traditional long-term care as part of their package.
- *Modified or continuing care facilities.* These provide similar care, but with some limitations as to duration and service.

- **Fee-for-service facilities.** In fee-for-service housing, you pay for additional services provided on an *a la carte* menu. These are increasingly popular.

(Source: American Association of Homes for the Aging)

As the industry and its market grow, different offerings and service packages have appeared, under a variety of guises. These may be called *adult living communities, assisted living,* or just plain *retirement housing.*

What these facilities provide is housing *plus* a menu of services, whether included in a package fee or on a fee-for-service basis:

- **Medical services,** including dental, ophthalmological, and podiatric services, checkups and assisted living services such as personal care and help with activities of daily living (ADLs)
- **Hospitality services,** including housecleaning, meals and meal service, laundry, utilities, telephone, and TV
- **Support and social services,** including health club, exercise classes, lectures, library, sports activities, and transportation

Not all of these services are available in all types of facilities, and not all of these services will be available to you. *The services you are eligible to receive—and the services you do receive—depend on the kind of facility you choose and the contract you sign.* State regulations offer limited protections in some areas, but not all facilities are subject to their rules.

For many facilities, you may have to meet extra qualifications to obtain services, particularly medical ones, and you may have to pay additional costs for them as well. This puts the burden on you to examine closely what you are being offered before you sign on the dotted line. Remember, although you may not need those services now, your needs progress as you age.

CONTRACTUAL AGREEMENTS

Buying an interest in an adult community is like buying a combination home and insurance policy. Only you usually don't have an insurance adviser or a lawyer protecting your interests (a mistake, in our opinion). What are the risks? After all, you have a threefold investment at stake: your money, your health, and your home. Each one deserves protection. Any transaction that involves all three deserves your full attention and the advice of any experts you can muster.

The first thing to do is to get a copy of the offering brochure and the contract from the facility. *Then read them.* Reading a contract is always an intimidating experience. Take your time. If you have questions, ask. If you find a clause objectionable and someone tells you "they don't really mean that part," then have it crossed out!

Initially there are two major considerations—the financial soundness of the facility and quality of services. These are discussed in the next section.

I am considering an adult living facility that doesn't offer a contract, just a lease. The facility provides two meals a day. Is this desirable or not?

If you're moving into a rental community, without buying, you will usually be given only a lease. A lease is a contract that specifies your rights and your landlord's rights to your apartment. In some cases, the lease will also spell out the other services you will receive. Sometimes, these benefits and services will be set forth in a separate contract, called a *service agreement*. Both lease and service agreement are enforceable in the courts.

Whether you buy or rent, stay away from any community that offers you neither a contract nor a lease and service agreement. If the deal is that you get two meals a day, this must be specified in writing. Don't take an oral promise that "all residents get breakfast and dinner." If breakfast is eliminated the next year, you may have no recourse. If they won't put it in writing, you have no way to enforce your claims.

 FINANCIAL SOUNDNESS

If you are shopping for an adult living community, you must investigate the fiscal soundness of any facility you are considering. *This may be the most important part of your search.* Too many community residents have been left high and dry by bankrupt facilities or those with finances so shaky that services are unavailable. Low occupancy and inadequate reserves spell trouble for a number of communities, and state regulation on reserves is often inadequate. While sponsorship by a parent organization may sound nice in a brochure, it may afford you little legal guarantee in the way of protecting your investment. You need to know:

Corporation information
- Who the owners are, i.e., the principals and any others with an interest in the facility
- Whether there are any outstanding lawsuits or administrative proceedings against the owners or the parent organization, if there are any liens or other financial obligations which could affect the financial viability of the development
- Whether there are any license restrictions
- What are the corporate assets, current funds, reserve funds, projected income and liabilities of the facility
-

Actuarial and utilization data
- Market studies, population projections, occupancy rates, and service costs
- Projected and actual data on use of health care services

You're entitled to receive audited financial statements and other certified documentation providing this information. You should have the information reviewed the way you would information about a house before closing, by either an attorney or an accountant. You should also check with local service organizations, consumer groups, and government agencies for information about the project and the owner.

Many states require that you be given this information, although that in itself is no guarantee that it will be given to you. It doesn't matter whether your state requires it or not—don't even bother with a facility that won't give you financial information.

A special note. Make sure the name of the facility on the information you receive matches the name of the facility that appears on the contract. Be wary of facilities that advertise they're sponsored by nonprofit groups such as churches. In some cases where ownership is nonprofit, the management company calling the shots is for-profit. In others, there may be no legal relationship at all.

What else should I find out?

You should inquire about fees. Current rates are only half the story. You want to know whether they've increased in recent years and by how much, as a gauge of your potential future obligations.

 ## ENTRANCE FEES AND PAYMENTS

The cost of adult living varies by the type of facility and by the level of service you're buying. Other variables to be considered include the size of your residence, and the number and age of the people who will be living in it. Cost also varies by geographic area.

Entrance fees. Entrance fees should be detailed in the contract, including whether they are refundable, to what extent, and under what conditions. Often there are limitations on the amount you will be refunded, depending on the payment structure:

- Cash up front. Total fee paid in advance, particularly in lifecare communities
- Entrance fees, with additional monthly fees. By far the most common form of contract
- Rental agreements, with fee-for-service available
- Ownership arrangements, such as cooperative or condominium arrangements, with care services. These are growing in popularity

Other fees. The contract should also specify

- Monthly payments and increases
- Extra costs, if any, upon your transfer to a nursing facility
- Fee increases
- Spousal fees

The contract should also spell out any other entrance requirements, such as a physical examination of the kind you would have to qualify for insurance, in order to establish your ability to live independently. Your finances may be checked to confirm your ability to meet monthly payments. The contract should also spell out your rights and the facility's rights in regard to termination.

Can I cancel the contract and have my entrance fee refunded?

There should always be some sort of probationary period provided, in which you can cancel the contract and get your money back.

Many states provide a "free look" period of a week or 30 days, in which the law provides that you can cancel the contract.

Can I cancel after the probationary period and get my entrance fee back?

It depends on the contract. It's not required by law, although a number of facilities are beginning to offer "fully refundable" entrance fees. Some contracts provide for a portion of the entrance fee to be reclaimed, in part, at the end of the residency term. This protects people who don't want to pay a hefty fee which will be forfeited no matter how long they remain in the facility. Non-refundable fees will probably be lower.

What protections do I have against fee increases?

Very few. Contracts may provide for notice, but rarely do they have limits on the number or rate of fee increases.

See if there is any provision to keep on residents who run out of money. Some nonprofit facilities' contracts provide this.

What if my spouse has to be transferred? What happens to my fees?

It depends on the contract. But couples, who usually pay more in the first place, need to understand the fee implications should either of them require a change in the level of care provided or where that care will be given.

Under what circumstances can my contract be ended?

The contract should include a *termination clause*, which spells out both your rights and the facility's rights in regard to termination. Usually you are entitled to a probationary period, during which you may cancel the contract. Facilities protect themselves with clauses allowing them to cancel the contract if you are disruptive or a risk to health or safety of yourself or others. Cancellation is also a possibility if there is fraud on either party's part.

If a facility is threatening to invoke the termination clause in a contract against you, you should consult a lawyer. Some state laws impose limitations on when your contract and residency may be terminated against your will, e.g., only for good cause, upon adequate notice to you, and after you have been afforded the opportunity to "cure" the defect.

HOUSING AND RELATED SERVICES

Continuing care facilities have traditionally been akin to rental arrangements, with ownership of the residence remaining in the hands of the facility. More recently, co-ops and condominiums have entered the market.

If you are "renting," your accommodations should be clearly defined in the contract. For one thing, make sure the unit which is to be yours is specified, as well as what is provided with it.

You should also know what your rights are in making changes or alterations. Are moves allowed, and under what circumstances? More importantly, under what circumstances can you be forced to give up your unit or transfer to another? (These determinations are often tied to changes in your or your spouse's need for nursing or medical services. See Assisted Living and Nursing Services, below.)

Other services included in housing and hospitality service packages include food, housekeeping, and laundry. Make sure you know whether your accommodations include kitchen facilities, and if there are any restrictions on their use. Are meals provided, and if so, are these in a communal dining room? Fees, schedules, and facilities for housekeeping and laundry services should be clearly indicated.

 ## SOCIAL AND SUPPORT SERVICES

A number of people join retirement communities because their friends are there, or because they want the companionship of people in a certain kind of community. They may also want specific activities to keep them engaged in their lives. To many older people, social and support services are critical to maintain their quality of life as they age, including:

- Sports
- Recreation facilities
- Spa and gym facilities
- Entertainment
- Movies
- Transportation
- Beauty salons

A picture in a brochure does not mean a service is available. Social and support services must be spelled out in the contract. Again, fees, schedules, and facilities for services should be clearly indicated. The availability of services and their continuation should *not* be left to the discretion of the facility.

 ## ASSISTED LIVING AND NURSING SERVICES

One of the reasons you enter an adult living community or continuing care facility is the availability of assistance in daily living and nursing care if you need it. This is a very important part of the package you are buying. You don't want any surprises when you need medical attention.

You need to know when you're entitled to care, under what circumstances, and what level of care:

- When you can get assisted living services
- What your rights are to services, including what services will be provided under what conditions
- When you can get nursing care
- Your rights for entry to assisted living or nursing care when you need it
- Where care will be provided (on-site or off-site)
- Whether you will have private accommodations
- What your rights are to a bed, and what provisions are made if one is not available
- What the terms of care are
- What quality guarantees you have concerning care

You need to know when others may make determinations about the care to which you're entitled, under what circumstances, and what your rights are then.

- When you can be moved to assisted living or nursing care
- Your rights to challenge that move
- Your rights to retain your assigned apartment upon your entry to assisted living or nursing care
- Your rights to remain in your assigned apartment upon your spouse's entry to assisted living or nursing care

Read the contract closely. This is very important. Not all facilities and not all levels of care offered may be licensed or regulated by the state. If it is not in the contract, you may have no protection at all.

What protections do I have against being moved against my will?

This is a key question, as important to you as why you chose this community in the first place. The trigger for a move from an independent unit to an assisted one or a nursing unit should be clearly spelled out in the contract. These provisions are often left vague and undefined.

This is not to your advantage. If you are going to be transferred to assisted living or nursing care, you need to have some say in the matter. At a minimum, a transfer determination should be subject to

- Written criteria for transfer
- Designation of decision-maker
- Your right to involvement in the decision
- An appeal process for challenging the decision

GOVERNMENT BENEFITS

Often people buy into lifecare and continuing care arrangements to avoid Medicare and Medicaid issues. By this method, they intend to purchase care for the rest of their lives.

Depending on the type of contract you have and your facility's participation in Medicare and Medicaid, you may still need or want to apply for Medicaid to meet additional long-term care needs. If your assets are high, you may have to spend down to qualify. Your contract may also be counted as an asset.

Many communities also require residents to maintain certain insurance, either Medicare Part B coverage or supplemental Medigap coverage as well.

The facility we looked at said we would have to purchase long-term care insurance to enter. Is this a legitimate entrance requirement?

This is a double whammy. If you are already paying them to provide nursing care, why do you need the insurance? If you're getting long-term care coverage, what do you need them for?

RESIDENTS' RIGHTS

Residents' rights should be spelled out in the contract. These may include the rights to:

- Appeal transfer decisions
- Participate in residents' councils
- Register grievances through a complaint mechanism
- Participation in or representation before management

In addition, representation of tenants' grievances can be had through residents' councils or mandated participation on boards of directors.

Can my rights be changed?

All rules should be incorporated into the contract. However, policies not included in the contract may be part of a supplemental handbook of rules. Generally, the handbook cannot change rights established by the contract, unless the contract allows it.

My contract says I waive all claims against the retirement facility when I enter it. Can I sue if I fall?

Such "waiver of liability" clauses are common in contracts. They are generally not enforced by the courts.

CHANGES IN YOUR FAMILY

Usually, you purchase an apartment or unit in an adult community as a basic family unit. But what happens if you divorce or your spouse dies? You may want a new roommate or spouse who falls below the facility's age limit.

The eligibility requirements for a new resident, spouse, or roommate should be included in the contract. Additional fees, if any, should be spelled out, as should your options if a new spouse fails to meet eligibility requirements. The contract should also include any restrictions as to number or duration of visits by family and friends.

REGULATING ADULT LIVING COMMUNITIES

Continuing care facilities are regulated in more than 30 states. Of these, fewer than half require anything more than disclosure of financial information. State regulation of mandated reserve funding is generally considered inadequate.

Oregon has been a pioneer in assisted living programs, supported by state policy favoring choice for people outside of nursing homes.

Several states have statutes providing specific resident rights for continuing care residents, similar to their statutory protections of nursing home residents.

One problem of regulation is definition. Although your state may have regulations, the adult living facility you are looking at may not be subject to them, for any number of reasons. The overlapping jurisdictions of insurance, housing, and health authorities leave many gaps. (State authorities are listed in the Resources section.)

Accreditation may be available through the Continuing Care Accreditation Commission for continuing care residential communities. The commission has established standards in finance, health care, and residence, and will send you a list of accredited communities. (See Resources section for the Commission's address.) The Assisted Living Facilities Association (also listed in Resources) is also seeking to establish industry standards of care. Neither are regulators, however. Although their imprimatur may be a good sign, it does not substitute for your own investigation.

Part 7

■ ■ ■ ■ ■ ■ ■ ■ ■ ■ ■ ■
Getting Help

This book describes numerous laws and regulations written for your protection and strategies for making sure you can avail yourself of that protection. Federal, state, and local governments have passed countless laws designed to help you make decisions about your health, where you'll live, and how you'll protect your assets and plan for your and your children's future.

But these legal provisions aren't worth the paper they're printed on, unless you take action to enforce them. This last, all-important chapter tells you how to go about protecting your rights—what actions you can take on your own, when and how to find and hire a lawyer, and what agencies and organizations to contact for assistance.

21

PROTECTING YOUR RIGHTS

Protecting your rights is first and foremost a matter of identifying what those rights are. This book provides the blueprint to do just that. In the preceding chapters, we've laid out the basic areas of elder law and several strategies to deal with problems that you may face in health care, money management, caretaking of others, work and retirement, pensions and housing. This information will help clarify your position and understand your legal rights and the issues you may be facing.

Once you've identified your rights, the question is what are you going to do about them? We've discussed strategies for action under many different circumstances, but these are not tailored to your individual problem and may not answer your specific questions. Here are some guidelines for where you can turn for help.

ASSERTING YOUR POSITION

Your first line of help is *you*. You are your strongest and best advocate. You know what the problem is, you may have a solution in mind, and you probably know where to complain.

Do it! No matter what your complaint is, it will not be resolved unless you make it known. You must communicate your grievance as effectively as possible to those who can do something about it. Most people are reluctant to pursue their complaints, either because they are too busy or intimidated—and government agencies and private companies rely on that in turning you down.

Don't be intimidated, and don't let bureaucrats give you the runaround. If they tell you it's policy, ask to see the policy. If you're still not satisfied, demand to speak to a supervisor or the manager. Remember, the squeaky wheel gets the grease. Ask for the decision and an explanation in writing.

Put your complaint in writing. You would be surprised how many companies will back down if they get reasonable, written objections. If at all possible, type letters. This has two benefits—it gives a businesslike appearance and it makes it easier for people responding to you. Make sure you date and sign all communications, and include your address and daytime phone number. Keep copies of everything you send.

Put *everything* in writing. If you make a telephone call, keep a record of it. Note the date of your call and the name of the person who spoke to you. A log of your communications with an agency or company is essential to keeping track of your actions.

If you can't get any action from a government agency or insurance company or feel you're not being treated fairly, try contacting the director of the agency or the president of the company, by phone or in writing. We guarantee you'll get a response then.

"IN-HOUSE" ASSISTANCE

Often large organizations have individuals designated to assist aggrieved or dissatisfied consumers or clients. There are people in agencies whose job is to help you. For example, the patient advocate in a hospital can help with various problems you may encounter, from informal complaints to formal appeals.

Ask them to tell you whether there is anyone to assist you or with whom you can talk. Remember that persistence pays off.

APPEALING DECISIONS

As a general rule, you have the right to appeal decisions made by government agencies (federal, state, and local) as well as industries regulated by government, such as insurance and nursing homes.

An appeal is simply a challenge to a decision. If you are unhappy with a decision, you can appeal it to a designated forum, usually *not* the original decision-maker. Appealing a decision is the same as making an informal complaint, except that the process generally has rules spelling out time and place for filing, time and place of the hearing, whether a complainant has the right to appear in person, whether there is a right to further appeal, and other provisions.

Your rights in these matters will be set forth in policy, regulation, or contract. You may also have additional rights in the law. The process you will have to follow will also be spelled out—and it may be explained as well in written information you are sent about your claim or complaint. If not, ask for a copy of appeal procedures. Remember, there may be specified time frames for appeal which must be observed. You must always file by the prescribed deadline dates.

Although people are intimidated, it never hurts to appeal an adverse decision. What have you got to lose? Nearly two thirds of Medicare Part B appeals result in reversed decisions. An estimated 30 percent of insurance company rejections are the result of error.

FEDERAL AND STATE HELP

A government regulatory agency can be of particular help to you in pursuing a complaint within its jurisdiction. At the state level, there are agencies responsible for housing, health, and insurance, among others. The long-term care ombudsman in each state investigates nursing home complaints. Others may provide useful information or referrals.

Additionally, a number of federal agencies have responsibility for matters with direct bearing on your life. A federal agency may be able to direct you for help or listen to your complaint. For example, the Medicare hotline will take complaints of fraud and abuse. Many offer valuable information as well. Those agencies charged with specific duties are noted in the text. A full listing of government agency help is available in the Resource section of this book.

THE OLDER AMERICANS ACT

The Older Americans Act (OAA), a federal law passed in 1965, authorizes grants to the states to provide specific benefits to the elderly. The law was designed to promote the development of programs to help the nation's over-65 population. To its initial mission of community planning, subsequent amendments have added legal assistance and advocacy.

Under the law, states are required to establish a program for ensuring legal and advocacy assistance for elder rights. State and Area Agencies on Aging and other local agencies provide legal assistance along with other programs. Unfortunately, funding has been cut back at all levels of government, affecting many OAA programs. (See Resources for a listing of State Agencies on Aging.)

LEGAL PROBLEMS OF THE ELDERLY

Several national organizations specialize in the *legal problems* of the elderly. These include organizations such as the National Senior Citizens Law Center and the American Bar Association's Commission on Legal Problems of the Elderly. These programs generally provide assistance to lawyers, but can also provide helpful information to you or refer you to someone who can.

Other national associations which may be of help include the National Academy of Elder Law Attorneys, which can refer you to a lawyer specializing in elder law. The National Association of Professional Geriatric Care Managers may also be of help.

Depending on your need, there are support and advocacy groups and agencies with specific missions which can help you. For example, Choice in Dying provides information and assistance in dealing with enforcing treatment decisions, "right-to-die" issues and advance health care directives. The Medicare Beneficiaries Defense Fund provides advice about Medicare and how to appeal Medicare decisions. It can also refer you to a lawyer in your area for more help.

 ## HIRING A LAWYER

Lawyers make great punchlines for comics, but the bottom line is, when you need a lawyer, get one! The government has lawyers, insurance companies have lawyers, landlords have lawyers. Why shouldn't you? Don't hesitate to get a lawyer when you need one.

When do you need a lawyer?

- *When planning.* This is when you need a lawyer before you need one—to avert a crisis, to make sure documents are in place and assets structured so that you won't be scrambling for help when it may be too late.
- *When reviewing contracts and documents.* If you're entering a facility, buying an insurance policy, or negotiating retirement with your employer—these all require professional help.
- *When appealing decisions.* Get a lawyer for appeals above a certain level, where expertise in complicated government regulations is needed. And get a lawyer for anything that has big consequences, such as a denial of a Medicaid eligibility claim. (Better yet, get one before—so you can plan when to apply.)
- *When there's a crisis.* Even with planning, you may need a lawyer to help enforce your rights in a crisis.

Having a lawyer on your side expands your team. A letter from your lawyer to an agency or company is often worth the fee by itself—because it may avert lengthy future action. Don't try to save money by not hiring a lawyer; it may wind up costing you more. Most problems can be handled for relatively modest costs.

Finding a lawyer. The best lawyer is one who specializes in your problem, whether it is an issue of trusts and estates, Medicaid planning, real estate, or health care. You can get a lawyer through personal recommendations, through the organizations described in this chapter (and others listed in the Resources section of this book), through referrals by other lawyers, or from local bar associations which may have legal referral services or elder law sections or committees. The National Academy of Elder Law Attorneys will provide names of members in your area.

Depending on your problem, you can also get referrals from organizations dedicated to the subject area in which you need assistance, such as the Alzheimer's Association, the Social Security Office, or the National Citizens Coalition for Nursing Home Reform.

On a local level, your Area Agency on Aging may be able to refer you to a lawyer. Good local attorneys may be found through your local city or county bar association, or through people you know.

Interviewing a lawyer. Schedule a consultation—ask in advance what the charge for that will be—and make sure you bring any documents you have pertaining to your problem. The way to avert possible problems is to have an understanding up front of what the cost will be, what work the lawyer will do, and what results may occur.

Make a list of questions and bring the list with you. Your questions should relate to the substance of your problem, the lawyer's background, and costs.

- *The substance of your problem.* Ask what steps he or she proposes to resolve your problem, how long it will take, what may happen, and if there are any other alternatives.
- *Lawyer's background.* Ask about the lawyer's general background, years of practice, education, area of expertise, time devoted to elder law, and particular expertise in the area. Will he or she handle all parts of your problem, including appeals or trials if needed? Who will you be talking to?
- *Cost.* This is the most important consideration. You must ask this question. More and more attorneys are willing to go over your costs with you, explaining their charges and what will be. Ask if the lawyer can take your case on a *contingent fee* basis, taking as his or her fee a percentage of the money you may eventually be awarded. This arrangement is common in personal injury suits. If an attorney will not discuss costs with you, find another one who will.

Do not hire anyone who doesn't answer your questions satisfactorily or completely.

AGING ORGANIZATIONS AND AGENCIES

There are numerous agencies in your community which can assist you in legal and non-legal matters, in finding programs and in enforcing your rights. There are a number of national, state, and local agencies whose missions are just that.

On the national level, there are two kinds of agencies which may be of help to you. The first is national organizations set up to assist the elderly, such as the Gray Panthers, the Older Women's League (OWL), and the

American Association of Retired Persons (AARP). They have strong information and assistance programs to aid you in almost any conceivable problem you may have.

A number of organizations exist for help with specific diseases. They may also provide referrals for the services you need. These include organizations such as the Alzheimer's Association and the American Cancer Society. (See Resources.)

Don't forget your own backyard. Many communities have programs which provide assistance for local residents. There may be a local chapter of one of the national organizations. You can consult your local Area Agency on Aging for information on these.

The last word. Elder law is a system of tools, built upon strategies to help you with problems you may face. You must pick up the tools to make them work.

Don't be afraid to take action when it is needed. Ask questions. Ask more. When you need help, get it. Remember, you are not alone. You have the information in this book to help you to plan and to deal with problems that you have not anticipated in your planning. Remember, you are your own best planner, your own best advocate, and your own best resource for shaping your future.

Resources

APPENDIX I:
WHERE TO GET
INFORMATION OR HELP

PART 1: PLANNING FOR YOUR HEALTH CARE NEEDS

Doctors and Hospitals

American Board of Medical Specialties
hotline certification: 800/776-2378

American Board of Internal Medicine
202/289-1700

American Academy of Family Practice
800/274-2237

American Hospital Association
1 North Franklin Street
Chicago IL 60606
312/422-3000

American Medical Association
312/464-5000

Association of State and Territorial
Health Officials
415 2d Street NE
Washington DC 20002
202/546-5400

Joint Commission on the Accreditation
of Healthcare Organizations
1 Renaissance Boulevard
Oak Brook Terrace IL 60181
312/642-6061

Community Health Assessment Program
800/847-8480

National Practitioner's Data Bank
301/443-2300

Public Citizen Health Research Group
1600 20th Street NW
Washington, DC 20009
202/588-1000

Medical Information

Alzheimer's Association
800/272-3900

American Cancer Society
800/ACS-2345

Cancer Information Center
800/4-CANCER

Nutrition Hotline
American Institute for Cancer Research
800/843-8114

Medical Information, for a fee

Health Access
914/232-6628

Michigan Information Transfer Source
313/763-3620

Medical Information Services
Palo Alto Medical Foundation
3000 Sand Hill Road
Building 2, Suite 260
Menlo Park CA 94025
800/999-1999

Local Referrals, Second Opinions, QMB Program, Medigap Information

Medicare hotline
800/638-6833

Information on Life-sustaining Technology, State Laws, and Sample State Forms

Choice in Dying
200 Varick Street
New York NY 10014
212/366-5540
800/989-WILL

Home Care

National Association for Home Care
519 C Street NE
Washington DC 20002
202/547-7424

National HomeCaring Council
Foundation for Hospice and Homecare

513 C Street NE
Washington DC 20002
202/547-6586

Community Health Accreditation
Program
National League for Nursing
350 Hudson Street
New York NY 10014
212/989-9393
800/669-1656

Home Care Accreditation Services

Joint Commission on the Accreditation
of Healthcare Organizations
1 Renaissance Boulevard
Oak Brook Terrace IL 60181
312/642-6061

National Council on the Aging
409 Third Avenue SW
Washington DC 20024
202/479-1200

Adult Day Care Referrals

National Eldercare Locator
(sponsored by the Administration on
Aging)
800/677-1116

National Association of Professional
Geriatric Care Managers
1604 North Country Club Road
Tucson AZ 85716
602/881-8008
(NY chapter 212/222-9163)

Children of Aging Parents
1609 Woodburne Road
Suite 302A
Levittown PA 19057
215/945-6900

Aging Network Services
4400 East-West Highway, Suite 907
Bethesda MD 20814
301/951-8589

National Citizens' Coalition for
Nursing Home Reform
1424 16th M Street NW
Suite 202
Washington DC 20036
202/332-2275

For-profit Nursing Homes

American Health Care Association
1201 L Street NW
Washington DC 20005
202/842-4444

Not-for-profit Nursing Homes

American Association of Homes for
the Aging
1129 20th Street NW
Washington DC 20036
202/296-5960

Friends and Relatives of the
Institutionalized Aged (FRIA)
11 John Street, Suite 601
New York NY 10038
212/732-4455

National Association of Area Agencies
on Aging
1112 16th Street
Washington DC 20036
202/296-8130

National Association of State Units on
Aging (NASUA)
1225 I Street NW
Suite 725
Washington DC 20005
202/898-2578

Restraint Minimization

Jewish Home & Hospital for the Aged
120 West 106th Street
New York NY 10025
212/870-5000

Medigap Counseling

National Association of Area Agencies
on Aging
800/677-1116

PART 2: MANAGING AND PAYING FOR A HEALTH CRISIS

Medicare/Medicaid

Health Care Finance Administration
(HCFA)
200 Independence Avenue SW
Washington DC 20201
202/690-6726

Medicare fraud hotline
800/368-5779
800/638-3986 (Maryland)

Center for Medicare Advocacy
203/456-7790
800/262-4414

Medicare Beneficiaries Defense Fund
1460 Broadway, 8th floor
New York NY 10036
212/869-3850

Medicare-Medicaid Assistance Program
AARP
1909 K Street
Washington DC 20049
202/728-4843

Rating Services

A.M. Best
212/439-2200 or 908/439-2200
(for ID code)
then 900/420-0400

Standard & Poor's
25 Broadway
New York NY 10004
212/208-1527

Moody's Investors Service
99 Church Street
New York NY 10007
212/553-0377

Duff & Phelps
55 East Monroe Street
Chicago IL 60603
312/368-3157

Weiss Research
P.O. Box 109665
Palm Beach Gardens FL 33410
800/289-9222

Accreditation Information

Blue Cross and Blue Shield Association
676 No. St. Clair Street
Chicago IL 60611
312/440-6000

National Commission of Quality
Assurance
2000 L Street NW, Suite 500
Washington DC 20036
202/955-3500

Insurance Claims, Information, and Referrals

National Insurance Consumers
Organization (NICO)
121 North Payne Street
Alexandria VA 22314
703/549-8050

Medicare Supplemental (Medigap) Insurance

National Insurance Consumer Helpline
(sponsored by the American Council of
Life Insurance, Health Insurance
Association of America and Insurance
Information Institute)
800/942-4242

National Association of Insurance
Commissioners
120 West 12th Street
Kansas City MO 64105
816/842-3600

Health Insurance Association of
America
1025 Connecticut Avenue NW
Washington DC 20036
202/223-7780

Long-term Care Insurance Partnerships

New York State Partnership for
Long-term Care
800/633-3088

Connecticut Partnership
203/424-4943

PART 3: LIFE PLANNING FOR YOU AND YOUR FAMILY

Living Wills, Health Care Proxies, and Powers of Attorney for Health Care

Choice in Dying
200 Varick Street
New York NY 10014
212/366-5540
800/989-WILL

Disabled Children

Clearinghouse on Disability
Information
Office of Special Education and
Rehabilitative Services
Department of Education

330 C Street SW, Room 3132
Washington DC 20202
202/205-5465

Community Trust Federation of
Employment Guidance Services
9745 Queens Boulevard
Rego Park NY 11374
718/896-9090

Disabled and Alone/Life Services for
the Handicapped
352 Park Avenue South, Suite 703
New York NY 10010
212/532-6740
800/995-0066

Health Resource Center for People
with Disabilities
800/544-3284

National Information Center for
Children and Youth with Disabilities
800/628-1696

National Association of Protection and
Advocacy Agencies
900 Second Street NE, Suite 211
Washington DC 20002
202/408-9514
202/408-9521 (TDD)

National PLAN Alliance
(Planned Lifetime Assistance Network)
195 Woodlawn Avenue
Saratoga Springs NY 12866
518/587-3372

Planned Lifetime Assistance Network
(PLAN of New York)
432 Park Avenue South, Suite 1201
New York NY 10016
212/545-7063

Proxy Parent Services Foundation
1336 Wilshire Boulevard, 2nd Floor
Los Angeles CA 90017
213/413-1130

National Alliance for the Mentally Ill
200 North Glebe Road, Suite 1015
Arlington VA 22203
703/524-7600

Guardianship

American Bar Association
Commission on Legal Problems for
the Elderly

1800 M Street NW
Washington DC 20036
202/331-2297

Elder Abuse

National Aging Resource Center on
Elder Abuse (NARCEA)
810 First Street NE, Suite 500
Washington DC 20002
202/682-2470
202/682-0100

Organ Donation

The Living Bank
P.O. Box 6725
Houston TX 77265
800/528-2971
800/GIFT-4-NY (NY office)

Organ Donor Hotline
North American Transplant
Coordinator Organization
800/24-DONOR

United Network for Organ Sharing
800/243-6667

PART 5: WORKING AND
RETIREMENT

Discrimination Complaints

Equal Employment Opportunity
Commission
1801 L Street NW
Washington DC 20507
800/669-EEOC
800/800-3302 (TDD) (and regional
offices)
202/663-4264

Americans with Disabilities Act

US Department of Justice
Civil Rights Division
Coordination & Review Section
P.O. Box 66118
Washington DC 20035-6118
202/514-0301
202/514-0381, 0383 (TDD)

Persons with Disabilities

Disability Rights Education and
Defense Fund Inc.
1633 Q Street NW, Suite 220
Washington DC 20009

202/986-0375 (Voice and TDD)
800/466-4232

Jobs Accommodation Network
800/526-7234

National Association of Protection and
Advocacy Agencies
900 2nd Street NE, Suite 211
Washington DC 20002
202/408-9514
202/408-9521 (TDD)

Family and Medical Leave Act

Department of Labor
Employment Standards
Administration, Wage and Hours
Division
200 Constitution Avenue
Washington DC 20210
202/219-4907

9 to 5 National Association of Working
Women
hotline 800/522-0825

Pensions and Benefits

Department of Labor
Pension & Welfare Benefits
Administration
200 Constitution Avenue NW
Washington DC 20210
202/523-8771 (or a regional office)

Employment Standards Administration
Pension Benefit Guaranty Corporation
Technical Assistance
1200 K Street, Suite 930
Washington DC 20005
202/326-4000
202/326-4179 (TDD)

Pension Rights Center
202/296-3776

Social Security and Disability

Social Security Administration
hotline 800/772-1213
earnings estimate 800/973-2000

PART 6: MEETING YOUR HOUSING NEEDS

Shared Housing

Shared Housing Resource Center
136 ½ Main Street

Montpelier VT 08602
802/223-2627

Reverse Mortgages

National Center for Home Equity
Conversion
7373 147th Street West, Suite 115
Apple Valley MN 55124
612/953-4474

FHA-insured Lenders

Federal National Mortgage Association
(Fannie Mae)
800/7-FANNIE

AARP Home Equity Conversion
Service
1909 K Street NW
Washington DC 20049
202/434-6030

Federal Trade Commission
6th Street and Pennsylvania Avenue
NW
Washington DC 20580
202/326-2180

Fair Housing and Discrimination Complaints

US Department of Housing and
Urban Development
Office of Fair Housing and Equal
Opportunity
Room 5204
Washington DC 20410
202/708-0836
800/669-9777
800/927-9275 (TDD phone for the
hearing impaired)

HUD User
US Department of Housing & Urban
Development
P.O. Box 6091
Rockville MD 20850
301/251-5154
800/245-2691

Department of Transportation
Federal Transit Administration
Office of Chief Counsel
400 7th Street SW
Washington DC 20590
202/366-4011

US Department of Justice
Civil Rights Division
Coordination and Review Section
P.O. Box 66118
Washington DC 20035
202/514-0301
202/514-0381, 0383 (TDD)

US Architectural and Transportation
Barriers Compliance Board
1331 F Street NW, Suite 1000
Washington DC 20004
800/USA-ABLE
202/272-5449 (TDD)

Regional Disability and Business
Technical Assistance Centers
800/949-4232 (Voice/TDD)

Adult-living Communities

American Health Care Association
1201 L Street NW
Washington DC 20005
202/842-4444

Continuing Care Accreditation
Commission
1129 20th Street NW, Suite 400
Washington DC 20036
202/828-9439

Assisted Living Facilities Association
9411 Lee Highway
Fairfax VA 22031
703/691-8100

PART 7: GETTING HELP

Aging Organizations

Older Women's League
666 11th Street, Suite 700

Washington DC 20001
202/783-6686

American Society on Aging
833 Market Street, Suite 512
San Francisco CA 94103
415/882-2910

Legal Assistance or Lawyer Referrals

Legal Counsel for the Elderly/AARP
1909 K Street NW
Washington DC 20049
202/833-6720

Center for Social Gerontology
2307 Shelby Avenue
Ann Arbor MI 48103
313/665-1126

National Senior Citizens Law Center
1815 H Street NW
Washington DC 20006
202/887-5280

National Academy of Elder Law
Attorneys
1604 North Country Club Road
Tucson AZ 85716
602/881-4005

Institute of Law and Rights of
Older Adults
Brookdale Center on Aging
425 East 25th Street
New York NY 10010
212/765-5710

American Bar Association
Commission on Legal Problems for
the Elderly
1800 M Street NW
Washington DC 20036
202/331-2297

■■■■■■■■■■■■■■■

APPENDIX II:
STATE AGENCIES AND
REGIONAL FEDERAL
OFFICES

1. State Units on Aging and Adult Protective Services Agencies
2. State Long-term Care Ombudsmen
3. State Protection and Advocacy Agencies
4. State Insurance Departments
5. State Health Departments
6. EEOC District and Regional Offices

1. STATE UNITS ON AGING AND ADULT PROTECTIVE SERVICE AGENCIES

(Source: National Association of State Units on Aging)

ALABAMA

Elder Abuse Hotline
In-State: 800/458-7214

Martha Murph Beck
Executive Director
COMMISSION ON
AGING
Suite 470
770 Washington Avenue
Montgomery AL 36130
205/242-5743

Chris Kendall, Director
ADULT SERVICES DIVISION
Dept. of Human Resources
50 Ripley Street
Montgomery AL 36130
205/242-1350

ALASKA

Connie Sipe, Director
DIVISION OF SENIOR SERVICES
Department of Administration
3601 C. Street., Suite 380
Anchorage AK 99503
907/563-5654

ARIZONA

Richard Littler, Director
AGING AND ADULT
ADMINISTRATION
Dept. of Economic Security
1789 W Jeffferson 950A
Phoenix AZ 85007
602/542-4446

Faustina Encinjas
Operations Manager
Adult Protective Service
AGING AND ADULT
ADMINISTRATION
Dept. of Economic Security
1789 W Jefferson #950A
Phoenix AZ 85007
602/542-4446

ARKANSAS

Elder Abuse Hotline
In-State: 800/482-8049
or 800/922-5330

Herb Sanderson, Director
DIVISION OF AGING AND
ADULT SERVICES
Dept. of Human Services

P.O. Box 1437, SLOT 1412
7th and Main Streets
Little Rock, AR 72201
501/682-2441

CALIFORNIA

Robert Martinez, Director
DEPT. OF AGING
1600 K Street
Sacramento CA 95814
916/822-5290

Robert Barton, Chief
ADULT SERVICES BRANCH
Dept. of Social Services
744 P Street
Sacramento CA 95814
916/387-4582

COLORADO

Rita Barreras, Manager
AGING AND ADULT SERVICES
Dept. of Social Services
110 16th Street, 2nd Floor
Denver CO 80202-1714
303/620-4127

Joanne Marlatt, Program
Administrator for Adult
Protection/Assisted Living
AGING AND ADULT SERVICES
Dept. of Social Services
110 16th Street, 2nd Floor
Denver CO 80202-1714
303/620-4137

CONNECTICUT

Thomas Corrigan, Director
DEPARTMENT OF SOCIAL SVS
25 Sigourney Street
Hartford CT 06106
203/424-5281

Pamela Giannii
Manager Adult Protective Services
DEPARTMENT OF SOCIAL SVS
25 Sigourney Street
Hartford CT 06106
203/424-5281

DELAWARE

Eleanor Cain, Director
DIVISION OF SERVICES FOR
AGING & ADULTS WITH
DISABILITIES
1901 North DuPont Highway

New Castle DE 19720
302/577-4791

Cindy Solge, Administrator
DIVISION OF SERVICES FOR
AGING & ADULTS
W/DISABILITIES
Adult Protective Services
C.T. Building
1901 North DuPont Highway
New Castle DE 19720
302/577-4660

DISTRICT OF COLUMBIA

Jearline Williams, Director
OFFICE ON AGING
One Judiciary Square
441 4th Street NW, 9th Floor
Washington DC 20001
202/724-5622

Karel Cornwell
Chief of Social Service
FAMILY SERVICES
ADMINISTRATION
Dept. of Human Services
Randall Building
First and I Streets SW
Washington DC 20024
202/727-0113

FLORIDA

Elder Abuse Hotline
In-State: 800/96-ABUSE

Bentley Lipacomb, Secretary
DEPARTMENT OF ELDER
AFFAIRS
Building E - Room 317
1317 Winewood Boulevard
Tallahassee FL 32301
904/922-5297

Christopher C. Shoemaker
Program Administrator
AGING AND ADULT SERVICES
Dept. of Health & Rehabilitative
Services
Building 2, Room 823 H
1317 Winewood Boulevard
Tallahassee FL 32399-0700
904/488-2881

GEORGIA

Judy Hagenbak, Director
OFFICE OF AGING
878 Peachtree Street #632, NE

Atlanta GA 30309
404/894-5333

Sara Brownlee, Unit Chief
for Adult Services
DIVISION OF FAMILY &
CHILDREN SERVICES
Social Services Section
Dept. of Human Resources
Suite 503
878 Peachtree Street, NE
Atlanta GA 30309-9844
404/657-8409

HAWAII

Marilyn Seely, Director
EXECUTIVE OFFICE ON
AGING
Office of the Governor
835 Merchant Street #241
Honolulu HI 96813
808/586-0100

Patricia Snyder
Program Administrator
ADULT SERVICES
Dept. of Human Services
P.O. Box 339
Honolulu HI 96809
808/586-5701

IDAHO

Ken Wilkes, Director
OFFICE ON AGING
Room 108 - Statehouse
Boise ID 83720
208/334-3833

David DeAngelis, Chief
BUREAU OF ADULT SERVICES
Department of Health and Welfare
450 W State Street
10th Floor
Boise ID 83720
208/334-5531

ILLINOIS

Elder Abuse Hotline
In State: 800/252-8966

Maralse Lindley, Director
DEPT. ON AGING
421 East Capitol Avenue
Springfield IL 62701
217/785-2870

INDIANA

Adult Abuse Hotline
In-State: 800/992-6978

Geneva Shedd, Director
BUREAU OF AGING/
IN-HOME SERVICES
Room E-431
402 W Washington Street
Indianapolis IN 46207-7083
317/232-7020

Arlene Franklin
Director of Advocacy Services
DEPARTMENT OF HUMAN
SERVICES
P.O. Box 7083
Indianapolis IN 46207-7083
317/232-1750

IOWA

Elder Abuse Hotline
In-State: 800/362-2178

Betty Grandquist, Director
DEPT. OF ELDER AFFAIRS
Suite 236, Jewett Building
914 Grand Avenue
Des Moines IA 50309
515/281-5187

Sandy Koll, Program
Manager for Adult Services
BUREAU OF ADULT, CHILDREN,
& FAMILY SERVICES
Dept. of Human Services
Hoover Building, 5th Floor
Des Moines IA 50319
515/281-6219

KANSAS

Elder Abuse Hotline
In-State: 800/432-3535

Thelma Hunter Gordon, Director
DEPT. ON AGING
Docking State Office
Building, 122-S
915 SW Harrison
Topeka KS 66612-1500
913/296-4986

Rosilyn James-Martin
Adult Abuse Program
COMMISSION ON ADULT
SERVICES
Dept. of Social & Rehabilitative
Services

Smith-Wilson Building
300 S.W. Oakley
Topeka KS 66606
913/296-2575

KENTUCKY
Adult Abuse Hotline
In State: 800/752-6200

S. Jack Williams, Director
DIVISION OF AGING
SERVICES
Cabinet for Human Resources
CHR Building - 6th West
275 East Main Street
Frankfort KY 40621
502/564-6930

Richard Newman Branch Manager
ADULT SERVICES
Division of Family Services
Dept. of Social Services
Cabinet for Human Resources
275 East Main Street
Frankfort KY 40621
502/564-7043

LOUISIANA
Robert Fontenot, Director
OFFICE OF ELDERLY AFFAIRS
4550 North Boulevard, 2nd Floor
Baton Rouge LA 70898
504/925-1700

MAINE
Elder Abuse Hotline

In-State: 800/452-1999

Christine Gianopoulos, Director
BUREAU OF ELDER & ADULT
SERVICES
Dept. of Human Services
State House - Station #11
Augusta ME 04333
207/624-5335

MARYLAND
Sue Ward, Director
OFFICE ON AGING
State Office Building
801 West Preston Street
Room #1004
Baltimore, MD 21201
410/225-1100

Handy Brandenburg
Program Manager

ADULT PROTECTIVE
SERVICES
Dept. of Human Resources
811 W Saratoga Street, 5th Floor
Baltimore MD 21201
410/767-7043

MASSACHUSETTS
Elder Abuse Hotline
In-State: 800/922-2275

Franklin Ollivierre, Secretary
EXECUTIVE OFFICE OF ELDER
AFFAIRS
1 Ashburton Place, 5th Floor
Boston MA 02108
617/727-7750

Donna Reulbach, Director
Protective Services
EXECUTIVE OFFICE OF ELDER
AFFAIRS
1 Ashburton Place, 5th Floor
Boston MA 02108
617/727-7750 ext. 302

MICHIGAN
Diane Braunstein, Director
OFFICE OF SERVICES TO THE
AGING
P.O. Box 30026
Lansing MI 48909
517/373-8230

Ralph Young, Director
OFFICE OF ADULT AND
EMPLOYMENT SERVICES
Dept. of Social Services
236 S. Grand Avenue #504
P.O. Box 80037
Lansing MI 48909
517/873-2869

MINNESOTA
Elder Abuse Hotline
In-State: 800/652-9747

Jim Varpness, Executive Director
BOARD ON AGING
444 Lafayette Road
St. Paul MN 55155-3843
612/296-2770

Elmer Pierre, Supervisor
AGING AND ADULT
SERVICES
Board on Aging
444 Lafayette Road

St. Paul MN 55155-3843
612/296-4019

MISSISSIPPI

Elder Abuse Hotline
In-State: 800/354-6347

Eddie Anderson, Director
COUNCIL ON AGING
Division of Aging and
Adult Services
750 North State Street
Jackson MS 39202
601/359-4929

Marva Hayes, Manager
ADULT PROTECTION SERVICES
Dept. of Human Services
P.O. Box 352
Jackson MS 39205
601/359-4484

MISSOURI

Elder Abuse/Neglect
Hotline In-State: 800/392-0210

Gregg Vadner, Director
DIVISION ON AGING
Dept. of Social Services
615 Howerton Court
P.O. Box 1337
Jefferson City MO 65102-1837
314/751-3082

MONTANA

Charles Rehbein, Acting Aging
Coordinator
THE GOVERNORS' OFFICE
ON AGING
State Capitol Building
Capitol Station, Room 219
Helena MT 59620
406/444-3111

Donald Sekora, Program Officer
ADULT PROTECTIVE SERVICES
Program Bureau
Program and Planning
Division - Dept. of Family Services
P.O. Box 8005
Helena MT 59604
406/444-5900

NEBRASKA

Elder Abuse Hotline
In-State: 800/652-1999

Dennis Loose, Director
DEPARTMENT ON AGING
P.O. Box 95044
301 Centennial Mall-So.
Lincoln NE 68509
402/471-2306

Mary J. Iwan, Administrator
SPECIAL SERVICES FOR
CHILDREN AND ADULTS
Medical Services Division
Dept. of Social Services
P.O. Box 95026
301 Centennial
Mall-South, 5th Floor
Lincoln NE 68509-5026
402/471-9345

NEVADA

Suzanne Ernst, Administrator
DIVISION FOR AGING SERVICES
Dept. of Human Resources
State Mail Room Complex
Las Vegas NV 89158
702/486-8545

Dale Capurro, Director
ADULT PROTECTIVE SERVICES
Dept. of Human Resources
Welfare Div. Medicaid
Capitol Complex
2527 North Carson Street
Carson City NV 89710
702/687-4588

NEW HAMPSHIRE

Elder Abuse Hotline
In-State: 800/852-3345

Ronald Adcock, Director
DIVISION OF ELDERLY &
ADULT SERVICES
115 Pleasant Street
Annex Building #1
Concord NH 03301-6501
603/271-4680

NEW JERSEY

Elder Abuse Hotline
In-State: 800/792-8820

Ruth Reader, Director
DIVISION ON AGING
Dept. of Community Affairs
101 South Broad & Front Streets
Trenton NJ 08625-0807
609/292-4833

Elga Mercer
State Coordinator APS
Office of Adult Services
Division of Community Affairs
101 South Broad & Front Streets
Trenton NJ 08625-0807
609/292-0920

NEW MEXICO
Elder Abuse Hotline
In-State: 800/432-6217

Michelle Lujan-Grisham, Director
STATE AGENCY ON AGING
4th Floor
La Villa Rivera Building
224 East Palace Avenue
Santa Fe NM 87501
505/827-7640

Dr. Jesus Brada, Bureau Chief
ADULT SERVICES
Social Services Division
Human Services Dept.
P.O. Box 5160
Santa Fe NM 87502-5160
505/827-8438

NEW YORK
Maribeth Bersani, Acting Director
OFFICE FOR THE AGING
Agency Building #2
New York State Plaza
Albany NY 12223
518/474-4425

Greg Guiliano, Director
BUREAU OF COMMUNITY
SERVICES
State Dept. of Social Services
40 North Pearl Street
Albany NY 12243
518/432-2980

NORTH CAROLINA
Elder Abuse Hotline
In-State: 800/662-7030

Bonnie Cramer, Director
DIVISION OF AGING
CB 29531
693 Palmer Drive
Raleigh NC 27626-0531
919/733-3983

Vicki Kryk, Program Consultant
for APS
ADULT AND FAMILY SERVICES

Division of Social Services
Dept. of Human Resources
325 North Salisbury Street
Raleigh NC 27611
919/733-3818

NORTH DAKOTA
Linda Wright, Director
AGING SERVICES DIVISION
Dept. of Human Services
P.O. Box 7070
Northbrook Shopping Center
North Washington Street
Bismarck ND 58507-7070
701/328-2577

OHIO
Elder Abuse Hotline
In-State: 800/686-1581

Judith Brachman, Director
DEPT. OF AGING
50 West Broad Street
9th Floor
Columbus OH 43266-0501
614/466-5500

Erika Taylor, Chief
BUREAU OF ADULT SERVICES
Division of Adult & Child
Care Services - Family,
Children, & Adult Services
Dept. of Human Services
65 E. State Street, 5th Floor
Columbus OH 43266-0423
614/644-6140

OKLAHOMA
Elder Abuse Hotline
In-State: 800/522-3511

Roy Keen, Division Administrator
AGING SERVICES DIVISION
Dept. of Human Services
P.O. Box 25352
Oklahoma City OK 73126
405/521-2327

Barbara Kidder
Program Supervisor
ADULT PROTECTIVE SERVICES
Aging Services Division
Dept. of Human Services
312 N.E. 28th Street
Oklahoma City OK 73105
405/521-3660

OREGON

Elder Abuse Hotline
In-State: 800/232-3020

Jim Wilson, Administrator
SENIOR AND DISABLED
SERVICES DIVISION
500 Summer Street NE
2nd Floor
Salem OR 97310
503/945-5811

Aileen Kaye, Program Manager
ABUSE AND PROTECTIVE
SERVICES
Senior Services Division
2nd Floor, NE
500 Summer Street
Salem OR 97310
503/945-6399

PENNSYLVANIA

Fraud and Abuse Hotline
In-State: 800/992-2433

Richard Browdie, Secretary
DEPARTMENT OF AGING
400 Market Street, 6th Floor
Harrisburg PA 17101-2301
717/783-1550

James L. Bubb, Jr., Aging Services
Specialist
DEPARTMENT OF AGING
400 Market Street, 6th Floor
Harrisburg PA 17101-2301
717/783-6007

PUERTO RICO

Ruby Rodriguez, Executive Director
GOVERNORS OFFICE
FOR ELDERLY AFFAIRS
Corbian Plaza Stop 23
Ponce De Leon Avenue
#1063, U.M. Office C
San Turec PR 00908
809/721-5710

Maria I. Soldevila-Walsh, Program
Director
SERVICES TO ADULTS
Dept. of Social Services
P.O. Box 11398
Fernandez Juncos Station
Santurce PR 00910
809/723-2127

RHODE ISLAND

Elder Abuse Hotline
In-State: 800/322-2880

Barbara Ruffino, Director
DEPARTMENT OF
ELDERLY AFFAIRS
160 Pine Street
Providence RI 02903-3708
401/277-2858

Robert F. McCaffrey, Administrator
ADULT SERVICES
Dept. of Human Services
600 New London Avenue
Cranston RI 02920
401/464-2651

SOUTH CAROLINA

Constance Rinehart
Director
DIVISION ON AGING
Office of the Governor
Building, Suite 301
202 Arbor Lake Drive
Columbia SC 29223
803/737-7500

Tim Cash, Director
DIVISION OF ADULT SERVICES
Office of Children, Family, and Adult
Services
Dept. of Social Services
P.O. Box 1520
Columbia SC 29202-1520
803/734-5670

SOUTH DAKOTA

Gail Ferris, Director
OFFICE OF ADULT SERVICES
AND AGING
700 Governors Drive
Pierre SD 57501-2291
605/773-3656

TENNESSEE

Emily Wiseman, Director
COMMISSION ON AGING
Andrew Jackson Building
500 Deaderick Street, 9th Floor
Nashville TN 37243-0860
615/741-2056

Marilyn Whalen
Program Manager
ADULT PROTECTIVE
SERVICES

Social Services Programs
Dept. of Human Services
Citizens Plaza
400 Deaderick Street
Nashville TN 37248-9700
615/741-5926

TEXAS
Elder Abuse Hotline
In-State: 800/252-5400

Mary Sapp, Executive Director
DEPARTMENT ON AGING
P.O. Box 12786 Capitol Station
1949 III 35, South
Austin TX 78741-3702
512/444-2727

Judith Rouse, Director
ADULT PROTECTIVE SERVICES
Dept. of Protective & Regulatory
Services
P.O. Box 149030
Austin TX 78714-9030
512/450-3211

UTAH
Jim Quast, Director
DIVISION OF AGING AND
ADULT SERVICES
Dept. of Social Services
120 North - 200 West
Box 45500
Salt Lake City UT 84145-0500
801/533-3910

VERMONT
Elder Abuse Hotline
In-State: 800/564-1612

Lawrence Crist, Commissioner
AGING AND DISABILITIES
103 South Main Street
Waterbury VT 05676
802/241-2400

Mark Schroeter, Chief
ADULT PROTECTIVE SERVICES
Aging and Disabilities
Ladd Hall
103 South Main Street
Waterbury VT 05671-2306
802/241-2345

VIRGINIA
Thelma Bland, Commissioner
DEPARTMENT FOR THE AGING

700 Centre, 10th Floor
700 East Franklin Street
Richmond VA 23219-2327
804/225-2271

Joy Duke, Program Supervisor
ADULT PROTECTIVE SERVICES
Bureau of Adult and Family Services
Division of Service Programs
Dept. of Social Services
730 East Broad Street 2nd Floor
Richmond VA 23219-1849
804/692-1299

WASHINGTON
Charles Reed, Assistant Secretary
AGING AND ADULT SERVICES
ADMINISTRATION
Dept. of Social and Health Services
P.O. Box 45050
Olympia WA 98501-5050
206/586-3768

Vicki Gawlik, APS Program Manager
ADULT PROTECTIVE SERVICES
PROGRAM
Dept. of Social and Health Services
P.O. Box 45600
Mail Stop 5600
Olympia WA 98504-5600
206/493-2537

WEST VIRGINIA
Elder Abuse Hotline
In-State: 800/352-6513

David K. Brown, Executive Director
COMMISSION ON
AGING
Holly Grove-State Capitol
Charleston WV 25305
304/558-3317

Ronald Nestor, Director
SERVICES TO THE
AGED, BLIND AND DISABLED
Social Services Bureau
Dept. of Human Services
State Capitol Complex
Building 6, Room 13850
Charleston WV 25305
304/558-7980

WISCONSIN
Donna McDowell, Director
BUREAU OF AGING
Division of Community Services

Suite 300
217 South Hamilton Street
Madison WI 53707
608/266-2536

WYOMING
Elder Abuse Hotline
In-State: 800/528-3396

Morris Gardner, Administrator
COMMISSION ON AGING
Hathaway Building #139

Cheyenne WY 82002-0710
307/777-7986

Joe Nies, Program Manager
FAMILY SERVICES
Division of Public Assistance and Social
Services
Dept. of Health & Social Services
Hathaway Building #349
Cheyenne WY 82002-0049
307/777-6082

2. STATE LONG-TERM CARE OMBUDSMEN

Key contacts for information and assistance regarding residents' rights or to resolve complaints in long-term care facilities. Some states have toll-free 800 numbers; these can only be used for in-state calls.

Source: (National Long Term Care Resource Center, National Association of State Units on Aging)

ALABAMA
Marie Tomlin
Commission on Aging
RSA Plaza, Suite 470
770 Washington Avenue
Montgomery AL 36130
205/242-5743

ALASKA
William O'Connor
Office of the LTC Ombudsman
Division of Senior Services
3601 C Street, Suite 260
Anchorage AK 99503-5209
907/279-2232
(accepts collect calls from older
persons)

ARIZONA
Rosalind Webster
Aging and Adult Administration
P.O. Box 6123-950A
1789 West Jefferson 950A
Phoenix AZ 85007
602/542-4446

ARKANSAS
Raymon Harvey
Division of Aging and Adult
Services
1417 Donaghey Plaza South
POB 1437 - Slot 1417

Little Rock AR 72203-1437
501/682-2441

CALIFORNIA
Vacant
Department on Aging
1600 K Street
Sacramento CA 95814
916/323-6681
800/231-4024

COLORADO
Virginia Fraser
The Legal Center
455 Sherman Street
Suite 130
Denver CO 80203
303/722-0300
800/332-6356

CONNECTICUT
Barbara Frank
Department of Social Services
25 Sigourney Street
Hartford CT 06106
203/424-5242

DELAWARE
Maxine Nichols
Division of Services for Aging &
Adults w/Physical Disabilities
1113 North Church Avenue
Milford DE 19963

302/422-1386
800/223-9074

DISTRICT OF COLUMBIA
Anne Hart, Ombudsman
Legal Counsel for the Elderly
4th Floor, Building A
601 E Street NW
Washington DC 20049
202/662-4933

FLORIDA
Vacant
State LTC Ombudsman
Council
Office of the Governor
Carlton Building
501 S. Calhoun Street
Tallahassee FL 32399-0001
904/488-6190

GEORGIA
Becky Kurtz
Division of Aging Services
Department of Human
Resources
#2 Peachtree Street, NW
18th Floor
Atlanta GA 30303
404/657-5319

HAWAII
Marilyn Seely
Office on Aging
335 Merchant Street
Room 241
Honolulu HI 96813
808/586-0100

IDAHO
Arlene Davidson
Office on Aging
State House Room 108
Boise ID 83720
208/334-3833
208/334-2220

ILLINOIS
Neyna Johnson
Department on Aging
421 East Capitol Avenue
Springfield IL 62701
217/785-3140

IOWA
Carl McPherson
Department of Elder Affairs

Jewett Building
Suite 236
914 Grand Avenue
Des Moines IA 50309
515/281-5187

INDIANA
Robyn Grant
FSSA/DDARS
Bureau of Aging/In Home Services
Room W-454
P.O. Box 7083
Indianapolis IN 46207-7083
317/232-7134
800/622-4484

KANSAS
Myron Dunavan
Department on Aging
Docking State Office Building
122-South
915 S.W. Harrison
Topeka KS 66612-1500
913/296-4986
800/432-3535

KENTUCKY
Gary Hammonds
Division for Aging Services
Cabinet for Human Resources
CHR Building, 5th Floor West
275 East Main Street
Frankfort KY 40621
502/564-6930
800/372-2291

LOUISIANA
Linda Sadden
Governor's Office of Elderly Affairs
4550 North Building, 2nd Floor
PO Box 80374
Baton Rouge LA 70898-0374
504/925-1700

MAINE
Brenda Gallant
Legal Service for the Elderly
P.O. Box 2723
Augusta ME 04338-2723
207/287-4056

MARYLAND
Elizabeth Kirk
Office on Aging
301 West Preston Street, Room 1004

Baltimore MD 21201
410/225-1098

MASSACHUSETTS
Mary McKenna
Executive Office of Elder Affairs
1 Ashburton Place, 5th Floor
Boston MA 02108-1518
617/727-7750

MICHIGAN
Hollis Turnham
Citizens for Better Care
416 North Homer Street
Suite 101, Alpha Building
Lansing MI 48912
517/336-6753
800/292-7852

MINNESOTA
Sharon Zoesh
Board on Aging
Office of Ombudsman for
Older Minnesotans
444 Lafayette Road, 4th Floor
St. Paul MN 55155-3843
612/296-0382
800/652-9747

MISSISSIPPI
Anniece McLemore
Council on Aging
750 North State Street
Jackson MS 39202
601/359-4929

MISSOURI
Carol Scott
Division of Aging
Department of Social Services
P.O. Box 1337
615 Howerton Court
Jefferson City MO 65102
314/751-3082

MONTANA
Doug Blakley
The Governor's Office on Aging
P.O. Box 8005
Room 219
Helena MT 59604
406/444-4676
800/332-2272

NEBRASKA
Geri Tucker
Department on Aging

301 Centennial Mall S
Lincoln NB 68509-5044
402/471-2306
402/471-2307

NEVADA
Candice Rutledge
Ombudsman Program
Compliance Investigator
Department of Human Resources
340 North 11th Street, Suite 203
Las Vegas NV 89101
702/486-3545

Gilda Johnstone
Division for Aging Services
445 Apple Street, Suite. 104
Reno NV 89502
702/688-2964

NEW HAMPSHIRE
Doris Beck
Division of Elderly and Adult Services
State Office Park South
115 Pleasant Street, Annex Building #1
Concord NH 03301
603/271-4375
800/442-5640

NEW JERSEY
Bonnie Kelly
Office of the Ombudsman for the
Institutionalized Elderly
101 South Broad Street
CN808
Trenton NJ 08625
609/292-8016
800/624-4262

NEW MEXICO
Tim Covell
State Agency on Aging
LaVilla Rivera Building, Suite A
228 East Palace Avenue
Santa Fe NM 87501
505/827-7640

NEW YORK
Faith Fish
Office for the Aging
Agency Building, #2
Empire State Plaza
Albany NY 12223
518/474-7329

NORTH CAROLINA
Michael McCann
Department of Human Resources
Division of Aging
CB-29531\693 Palmer Drive
Raleigh NC 27603
919/733-3983

NORTH DAKOTA
Jo Hildebrant
Aging Services Division
Department of Human Services
1929 North Washington Street
PO Box 7070
Bismarck ND 58507-7070
701/328-2577
800/472-2622

OHIO
Beverley Laubert
Department of Aging
50 West Broad Street, 9th Floor
Columbus OH 43266-0501
614/466-1221
800/282-1206

OKLAHOMA
Esther Allgood
Division of Aging Services
Department of Human Services
312 N.E. 28th Street
Oklahoma City OK 73105
405/521-6734

OREGON
Meredith Cote
Office of LTC Ombudsman
2475 Lancaster Drive NE
Building B, #9
Salem OR 97310
503/378-6533
800/522-2602

PENNSYLVANIA
Linda Jackman
Department of Aging
400 Market Street, 6th Floor
Harrisburg PA 17101-2301
717/783-7247

PUERTO RICO
Norma Venegas
Governor's Office for Elderly Affairs
Call Box 50063
Old San Juan Station
San Juan PR 00902
809/724-1515

RHODE ISLAND
Denise Medeiros
Department of Elderly Affairs
160 Pine Street
Providence RI 02903-3708
401/277-2858

SOUTH CAROLINA
Mary B. Fagan
State LTC Ombudsman
Division on Aging
Office of the Governor
202 Arbor Lake Drive, Suite. 301
Columbia SC 29233
803/737-7500

SOUTH DAKOTA
Jeff Askew
Office of Adult Services & Aging
Department of Social Services
Richard F. Kneip Building
700 North Governors Drive
Pierre SD 57501-2291
605/773-3656

TENNESSEE
Vacant
Commission on Aging
Andrew Jackson Building
500 Deaderick Street, 9th Floor
Nashville TN 27243-0860
615/741-2056

TEXAS
John Willis
Department on Aging
P.O. Box 12786
1949 IH 35, South
Austin TX 78711
512/444-2727
800/252-9240

UTAH
Carol Bloswick
Division of Aging & Adult Services
Department of Human Services
120 North-200 West, Room 401
Box 45500
Salt Lake City UT 84145-0500
801/538-3924

VERMONT
Deb Hamel
Dept. of Aging & Disabilities

103 South Main Street
Waterbury VT 05676
802/241-2400
800/642-5119

John Michael Hall, Director
Vermont Legal Aid
18 Main Street
St. Johnsbury VT 05818
802/748-8721

VIRGINIA

Mark Miller
Department for the Aging
700 E. Franklin Street, 10th Floor
Richmond VA 23219-2327
804/225-2271
800/552-3402

WASHINGTON

Kary Hyre
WA State LTCO Program
South King County
Multi-Service Center
1200 South 336th Street
Federal Way WA 98003

206/838-6810
800/562-6028

WEST VIRGINIA

Carolyn Riffle
Commission on Aging
State Capitol Complex
1900 Kanawha Boulevard East
Charleston WV 25305-0160
304/558-3317

WISCONSIN

George Potaracke
Board on Aging and LTC
214 North Hamilton Street
Madison WI 53703
608/266-8944

WYOMING

Debra Alden
State Ombudsman Program
P.O. Box 94
953 Water Street
Wheatland WY 82201
307/322-5553

3. STATE PROTECTION AND ADVOCACY AGENCIES

(Source: New York State Commission on Quality of Care for the Mentally Disabled)

ALABAMA

Reuben W. Cook, Executive Director
Alabama Disabilities Advocacy Program
The University of Alabama
P.O. Box 870395
Tuscaloosa AL 35487-0395
205/348-4928
205/348-9484 TDD
800/826-1675

ALASKA

Rick Tessandore, Executive Director
Advocacy Services of Alaska
615 E. 82nd Avenue, Suite 101
Anchorage AK 99518
907/344-1002
800/478-1234

ARIZONA

Timothy M. Hogan, Executive Director
Arizona Center for Law in the Public

Interest
3724 North Third Street, Suite 300
Phoenix AZ 85012
602/274-6287

ARKANSAS

Nan Ellen East, Executive Director
Advocacy Services, Inc.
Evergreen Place, Suite 201
1100 North University
Little Rock AR 72207
501/324-9215
800/482-1174

CALIFORNIA

Catherine Blakemore, Executive
Director
California Protection & Advocacy, Inc.
100 Howe Avenue, Suite 185N
Sacramento CA 95835
916/488-9950

800/766-5746
818/546-1631 LA
510/839-0811 OK

COLORADO
Mary Anne Harvey, Executive Director
The Legal Center
455 Sherman Street, Suite 130
Denver CO 80203
303/722-0300

CONNECTICUT
Eliot J. Dober, Executive Director
Office of P&A for Handicapped &
DD Persons
60 Weston Street
Hartford CT 06120-1551
203/297-4300
203/566-2102 MI
800/842-7303
(statewide)

DELAWARE
Christine Long, Administrator
Disabilities Law Program
144 E. Market Street
Georgetown DE 19947
302/856-0038

DISTRICT OF COLUMBIA
Vivianne Hardy-Townes, Executive
Director
Information Protection and Advocacy
Center for Handicapped Individuals, Inc.
4455 Connecticut Avenue NW, Suite
B100
Washington DC 20008
202/966-8081
202/966-2500 TTY

FLORIDA
Marcia Beach, Executive Director
Advocacy Center for Persons with
Disabilities
2671 Executive Center, Circle West
Webster Building, Suite 100
Tallahassee FL 32301-5024
904/488-9071
800/342-0832
800/346-4127TDD

GEORGIA
Patricia Powell, Executive Director
Georgia Advocacy Office, Inc.
1708 Peachtree Street NW, Suite 505
Atlanta GA 30309

404/885-1234
800/282-4538

HAWAII
Gary L. Smith, Executive Director
Protection and Advocacy Agency
1580 Makaloa Street, Suite 1060
Honolulu HI 96814
808/949-2922

IDAHO
Shawn deLoyola, Executive Director
Co-Ad, Inc.
4477 Emerald, Suite B-100
Boise IA 83706
208/336-5353

ILLINOIS
Zena Naiditch, Director
Equip for Equality, Inc.
11 East Adams, Suite 1200
Chicago IL 60603-6303
312/341-0022

INDIANA
Mary Lou Haines, Executive Director
Indiana Advocacy Services
850 North Meridian Street, Suite 2-C
Indianapolis IN 46204
317/232-1150
800/622-4845

IOWA
Mervin L. Roth, Director
Iowa Protection & Advocacy Service,
Inc.
3015 Merle Hay Road, Suite 6
Des Moines IA 50310
515/278-2502

KANSAS
Joan Strickler, Executive Director
Kansas Advocacy & Protection Services
2601 Anderson Avenue
Manhattan KS 66502
913/776-1541
800/432-8276

KENTUCKY
Gayla O. Peach, Director
Office for Public Advocacy, Division
for Protection & Advocacy
100 Fair Oaks Lane, 3rd Floor
Frankfort KY 40601
502/564-2967
800/372-2988

LOUISIANA

Lois V. Simpson, Executive Director
Advocacy Center for the Elderly &
Disabled
210 O'Keefe, Suite 700
New Orleans LA 70112
504/522-2337
800/662-7705

MAINE

Paul Vestal, Executive Director
Maine Advocacy Services
32 Winthrop
P.O. Box 2007
Augusta ME 04338-2007
207/626-2774
800/452-1948

MARYLAND

Elizabeth Jones, Executive Director
Maryland Disability Law Center
1800 North Charles Street
Baltimore MD 21201
410/234-2791
410/234-2792-93

Maryland Disability Law Center
2510 Street Paul Street
Baltimore MD 21218
800/233-7201
410/235-4227

MASSACHUSETTS

Susan Herz, Executive Director
Disability Law Center, Inc.
11 Beacon Street, Suite 925
Boston MA 02108
617/723-8455

MICHIGAN

Elizabeth W. Bauer, Executive Director
Michigan Protection & Advocacy
Service
106 West Allegan, Suite 210
Lansing MI 48933-1706
517/487-1755

MINNESOTA

Luther A. Granquist, Deputy Director
Minnesota Disability Law Center
430 First Avenue North, Suite 300
Minneapolis MN 55401-1780
612/332-1441

MISSISSIPPI

Rebecca Floyd, Executive Director
Mississippi Protection & Advocacy

System for DD, Inc.
5330 Executive Place, Suite A
Jackson MS 39206
601/981-8207

MISSOURI

Cynthia North Schloss, Director
Missouri Protection & Advocacy
Service
925 Country Club Drive, Unit B-1
Jefferson City MO 65109
314/893-3333
800/392-8667

MONTANA

Kris Bakula, Executive Director
Montana Advocacy Program
316 North Park, Room 211
P.O. Box 1680
Helena MT 59624
406/444-3889
800/245-4743

NEBRASKA

Timothy Shaw, Executive Director
Nebraska Advocacy Services, Inc.
522 Lincoln Center Building
215 Centennial Mall South
Lincoln NE 68508
402/474-3183

NEVADA

Travis Wall, Director
Office of Protection & Advocacy, Inc.
Financial Plaza
1135 Terminal Way, Suite 105
Reno NV 89502
702/688-1233
800/922-5715

NEW HAMPSHIRE

Donna Woodfin, Director
Disabilities Rights Center
P.O. Box 19
18 Low Avenue
Concord NH 03302-0019
603/228-0432

NEW JERSEY

Sarah Wiggins Mitchell
Executive Director
New Jersey Protection and
Advocacy, Inc.
210 South Broad Street, 3d Floor
Trenton NJ 08608
609/292-9742

NEW MEXICO
James Jackson, Executive Director
Protection & Advocacy System, Inc.
1720 Louisiana Boulevard NE,
Suite 204
Albuquerque NM 87110
505/256-3100
800/432-4682

NEW YORK
Clarence J. Sundram, Chairman
N.Y. Commission on Quality of Care
for the Mentally Disabled
99 Washington Avenue
Albany NY 12210
518/473-4057

NORTH CAROLINA
Cindy Crouse-Martin, Executive
Director
Governor's Advocacy Council for
Persons w/Disabilities
1318 Dale Street, Suite 100
Raleigh NC 27605
919/733-9250
800/821-6922

NORTH DAKOTA
Barbara Braun, Executive Director
North Dakota Protection &
Advocacy Project
400 E. Broadway, Suite 515
Bismarck ND 58501
701/224-2972
800/472-2670
800/642-6694 (24 Hour)

OHIO
Carolyn Knight, Executive Director
Ohio Legal Rights Service
8 East Long Street, 6th Floor
Columbus OH 43215
614/466-7264
800-282-9181

OKLAHOMA
Steve Novick, Executive Director
Oklahoma Disability Law Center, Inc.
4150 South 100th East Avenue, 210
Cherokee Bldg
Tulsa OK 74146-3661
918/664-5883

OREGON
Robert Joondeph, Executive Director
Oregon Advocacy Center

Board of Trade Building
310 Southwest 4th Avenue, Suite 625
Portland OR 97204-2309
503/243-2081

PENNSYLVANIA
Kevin Casey, Executive Director
Pennsylvania Protection and
Advocacy Inc.
116 Pine Street
Harrisburg PA 17101
717/236-8110
800/692-7443
800/238-6222

PUERTO RICO
Juan Rivera
Ombudsman for the Disabled
P.O. Box 4234
San Juan PR 00902-4234
809/721-4299
800/981-4125
809/725-3606

RHODE ISLAND
Ray Bandusky, Executive Director
Rhode Island Protection & Advocacy
System (RIPAS), Inc.
151 Broadway, 3rd Floor
Providence RI 02903
401/831-3150

SOUTH CAROLINA
Betty Easler, Executive Director
S.C. Protection & Advocacy System
for the Handicapped, Inc.
3710 Landmark Drive, Suite 208
Columbia SC 29204
803/782-0639
800/922-5225

SOUTH DAKOTA
Robert J. Kean, Executive Director
South Dakota Advocacy Services
221 South Central Avenue
Pierre SD 57501
605/224-8294
800/658-4782

TENNESSEE
Dick Tanner, Executive Director
Tennessee Protection & Advocacy, Inc.
P.O. Box 121257
Nashville TN 37212
615/298-1080
800/342-1660

TEXAS

James Comstock-Galagan
Executive Director
Advocacy, Inc.
7800 Shoal Creek Blvd., Suite 171-E
Austin TX 78757
512/454-4816
800/252-9108

UTAH

Phyllis Geldzahler, Executive Director
Legal Center for People with
Disabilities
455 East 400 South, Suite 201
Salt Lake City UT 84111
801/363-1347
800/662-9080

VERMONT

Bill Sullivan, Executive Director
Vermont Protection and Advocacy
21 E. State Street, Suite 101
Montpelier VT 05602
800/229-1355

Judy Dickson, Director
Vermont DD Law Project
12 North Street
Burlington VT 05401
802/863-2881

VIRGINIA

James Rothrock, Director
Department for Rights of Virginians
w/Disabilities
James Monroe Building
101 North 14th Street, 17th Floor
Richmond VA 23219

804/225-2042
800/552-3962
(TDD & Voice)

WASHINGTON

Mark Stroh, Executive Director
Washington Protection & Advocacy
System
1401 E. Jefferson, Suite 506
Seattle WA 98122
206/324-1521

WEST VIRGINIA

Linda Leasure, Executive Director
West Virginia Advocates, Inc.
Litton Building, 4th Floor
1207 Quarrier Street
Charleston WV 25301
304/346-0847
800/950-5250

WISCONSIN

Lynn Breedlove, Executive Director
Wisconsin Coalition for Advocacy, Inc.
16 North Carroll Street, Suite 400
Madison WI 53703
608/267-0214

WYOMING

Jeanne A. Thobro, Executive Director
Wyoming Protection and Advocacy
System, Inc.
2424 Pioneer Avenue, #101
Cheyenne WY 82001
307/638-7668
307/632-3496
800/624-7648

4. STATE INSURANCE DEPARTMENTS

ALABAMA

Commissioner of Insurance
135 South Union Street
Post Office Box 303351
Montgomery AL 36130
334/241-4101

ALASKA

Director of Insurance
P.O. Box 110805
Juneau AK 99811
907/465-2515

ARIZONA

Director of Insurance
2910 North 44th Street,
Suite 210
Phoenix AZ 85018
602/912-8456

ARKANSAS

Insurance Commissioner
University Tower Building
1123 South University
Avenue, Suite 400

Little Rock AR 72204
501/686-2909

CALIFORNIA
Insurance Commissioner
45 Fremont Street, 23rd Floor
San Francisco CA 94105
415/904-5410

COLORADO
Commissioner of Insurance
1560 Broadway, Suite 850
Denver CO 80202
303/894-7499

CONNECTICUT
Insurance Commissioner
Insurance Department
P.O. Box 816
Hartford CT 06142
203/297-3802

DELAWARE
Insurance Commission
Rodney Building
841 Silver Lake Boulevard
Dover DE 19904
302/739-4251

DISTRICT OF COLUMBIA
Commissioner of Insurance
Department of Consumer and
Regulatory Affairs
One Judiciary Square
441 4th Street NW
8th Floor North
Washington DC 20001
202/727-8000

FLORIDA
Insurance Commission
State Treasurer's Office
State Capitol
Tallahassee FL 32399
904/922-3100

GEORGIA
Commissioner of Insurance
7th Floor West Tower, Floyd Building
2 Martin Luther King Jr. Drive
Atlanta GA 30334
404/656-2056

HAWAII
Insurance Commissioner
Department of Commerce and
Consumer Affairs

P.O. Box 3614
Honolulu HI 96811
808/586-2790

IDAHO
Director of Insurance
P.O. Box 83720
Boise ID 83720
208/334-4250

ILLINOIS
Director of Insurance
State of Illinois
320 West Washington Street
Fourth Floor
Springfield IL 62767
217/782-4515

INDIANA
Commissioner of Insurance
311 West Washington
Street, Suite 300
Indianapolis IN 46204
317/232-3520

IOWA
Commissioner of Insurance
Lucas State Office
Building
Des Moines IA 50319
515/281-5523

KANSAS
Commissioner of Insurance
420 S.W. 9th Street
Topeka KS 66612
913/296-3071

KENTUCKY
Insurance Commissioner
215 West Main Street
P.O. Box 517
Frankfort KY 40602
502/564-6027

LOUISIANA
Commissioner of Insurance
P.O. Box 94214
Baton Rouge LA 70804
504/342-5423

MAINE
Superintendent of Insurance
State House, Station 34
Augusta ME 04333
207/582-8707

314 THE ELDER LAW HANDBOOK

MARYLAND
Insurance Commissioner
501 Street Paul Place, 7th Floor
Baltimore MD 21202
410/333-2521

MASSACHUSETTS
Commissioner of Insurance
470 Atlantic Avenue
Boston MA 02210
617/521-7794

MICHIGAN
Insurance Commissioner
P.O. Box 30220
Lansing MI 48909
517/373-9273

MINNESOTA
Commissioner of
Commerce
133 East 7th Street
St. Paul MN 55101
612/296-6694

MISSISSIPPI
Commissioner of Insurance
1804 Walter Sillers Building
P.O. Box 79
Jackson MS 39205
601/359-3569

MISSOURI
Director, Department of Insurance
301 West High Street,
6 North P.O. Box 690
Jefferson City MO 65102
314/751-4126

MONTANA
Commissioner of Insurance
Mitchell Building
P.O. Box 4009
Helena MT 59604
406/444-2040

NEBRASKA
Director of Insurance
Terminal Building
941 O Street, Suite 400
Lincoln NE 68508
402/471-2201

NEVADA
Commissioner of Insurance
Capitol Complex
1685 Hot Springs Road
Suite 152
Carson City NV 89710
702/687-4270

NEW HAMPSHIRE
Insurance Commissioner
169 Manchester Street
Concord NH 03301
603/271-2261

NEW JERSEY
Commissioner of Insurance
20 West State Street
CN 325
Trenton NJ 08625
609/292-5350

NEW MEXICO
Superintendent of
Insurance
P.O. Drawer 1269
Santa Fe NM 85704
505/827-4500

NEW YORK
Superintendent of Insurance
160 West Broadway
New York NY 10013
212/602-0429

NORTH CAROLINA
Commissioner of Insurance
430 North Salisbury Street
Dobbs Building
P.O. Box 26387
Raleigh NC 27611
919/733-7349

NORTH DAKOTA
Commissioner of Insurance
600 East Boulevard, 5th Floor
Bismarck ND 58505
701/328-2440

OHIO
Director of Insurance
2100 Stella Court
Columbus OH 43215
614/644-2651

OKLAHOMA
Insurance Commissioner
1901 North Walnut
P.O. Box 53408
Oklahoma City OK 73152
405/521-2828

OREGON
Insurance Commissioner
440 Labor and
Industries Building
Salem OR 97310
503/378-4100

PENNSYLVANIA
Insurance Commissioner
Strawberry Square, 13th Floor
Harrisburg PA 17120
717/783-0442

RHODE ISLAND
Director of Business
Regulation and Insurance
Commissioner
State of Rhode Island
233 Richmond Street, Suite 233
Providence RI 02903
401/277-2223

SOUTH CAROLINA
Chief Insurance Commissioner
1612 Marion Street
P.O. Box 100105
Columbia SC 29202
803/737-6160

SOUTH DAKOTA
Director of Insurance
910 East Sioux
Pierre SD 57501
605/773-3563

TENNESSEE
Commissioner of Commerce and
Insurance
500 James Robertson Parkway
Nashville TN 37243
615/741-2241

TEXAS
Commissioner of Insurance
333 Guadalupe Street
Austin TX 78701
512/463-6464

UTAH
Commissioner of Insurance
3110 State Office Building
Salt Lake City UT 84114
801/538-3804

VERMONT
Commissioner of Banking, Insurance,
and Securities
89 Main Street, Drawer 20
Montpeller VT 05620
802/828-3301

VIRGINIA
Commissioner of Insurance
Tyler Building
P.O. Box 1157
Richmond VA 23209
804/371-9694

WASHINGTON
Insurance Commissioner
Insurance Building
P.O. Box 40255
Olympia WA 98504
360/753-7301

WEST VIRGINIA
Insurance Commissioner
2019 Washington Street, East
P.O. Box 50540
Charleston WV 25305
304/558-3354

WISCONSIN
Commissioner of Insurance
121 East Wilson Street
P.O. Box 7873
Madison WI 53707
608/266-0102

WYOMING
Insurance Commissioner
Herschler Building
122 West 25th Street - 3 East
Cheyenne WY 82002
307/777-7401

5. STATE HEALTH DEPARTMENTS

ALABAMA
Department of Public Health
434 Monroe Street
Montgomery AL
36130
205/242-5095

ALASKA
Division of Public Health
P.O. Box H
Juneau AK 99811
907/465-3030

ARIZONA
Department of Health Services
1740 W. Adams Street
Phoenix AZ 85007
602/542-1000

ARKANSAS
Department of Health
4815 W. Markham Street
Little Rock AR 72205
501/661-2111

CALIFORNIA
Department of Health Services
714 P Street
Sacramento CA 94234
916/445-4171

COLORADO
Department of Health
4210 E. 11th Street
Denver CO 80220
303/320-8333

CONNECTICUT
Department of Health Services
150 Washington Street
Hartford CT 06106
203/566-4800

DELAWARE
Division of Public Health
P.O. Box 637
Federal Street
Dover DE 19901
302/739-4726

DISTRICT OF COLUMBIA
Department of Public Health
1660 L Street NW
Washington DC 20036
202/673-7700

FLORIDA
Department of Health and
Rehabilitative Services
1317 Winewood Boulevard
Tallahassee FL 32399-0700
904/488-0294

GEORGIA
Division of Public Service
Department of Human Resources
878 Peachtree Street, NE
Atlanta GA 30309
404/894-7505

HAWAII
Department of Health
P.O. Box 3378
Honolulu HI 96813
808/586-4400

IDAHO
Department of Health and Welfare
450 W. State Street
Boise ID 83720
208/334-5500

ILLINOIS
Department of Public Health
535 W. Jefferson Street
Springfield IL 62761
217/782-4977

INDIANA
State Board of Health
1330 W. Michigan Street
P.O. Box 1964
Indianapolis IN 46206
317/633-0100

IOWA
Department of Public Health
Lucas State Office Building
East 12th and Walnut Streets
Des Moines IA 50319
515/281-5787

KANSAS
Department of Health and
Environment
Landon State Office Building
Topeka KS 66612
913/296-1500

KENTUCKY
Department of Health Services
275 East Main Street
Frankfort KY 40621
502/564-7736

LOUISIANA
Office of Public Health
P.O. Box 60630
New Orleans, Louisiana 70160
504/568-5050

MAINE
Bureau of Health
State House, Station 11
Augusta ME 04333
207/289-3201

MARYLAND
Department of Health and Mental
Hygiene
201 W. Preston Street
Baltimore MD 21201
301/225-6860

MASSACHUSETTS
Department of Public Health
150 Tremont Street
Boston MA 02111
617/727-0201

MICHIGAN
Department of Public Health
P.O. Box 30195
Lansing MI 48909
517/335-8000

MINNESOTA
Department of Health
717 Delaware Street SE
Minneapolis MN 55440
612/623-5000

MISSISSIPPI
State Health Department
2423 North State Street
P.O. Box 1700
Jackson MS39215
601/960-7400

MISSOURI
Department of Health
P.O. Box 570
Jefferson City MO 65102
314/751-6400

MONTANA
Department of Health and
Environmental Services
Cogswell Building
Helena MT 59620
406/444-25444

NEBRASKA
Department of Health
301 Centennial Mall, South
P.O. Box 95007
Lincoln NE 68509
402/471-2133

NEVADA
Department of Health
505 E. King Street
Carson City NV 89710
702/687-4740

NEW HAMPSHIRE
Department of Health and Human
Services
6 Hazen Drive
Concord NH 03301
603/271-4685

NEW JERSEY
Department of Health
CN 360
Trenton NJ 08625
609/292-7837

NEW MEXICO
Department of Health
1190 Street Francis Drive
P.O. Box 26110
Santa Fe NM 87502
505/827-0020

NEW YORK
New York State Health Department
Corning Tower
Empire State Plaza
Albany NY 12237
518/474-2121

NORTH CAROLINA
Division of Health Services
Department of Environmental
Health and Natural Resources
1330 Street Mary Street
Raleigh NC 27605
919/733-7081

NORTH DAKOTA
Department of Health
State Capitol
600 E. Boulevard Avenue
Bismarck ND 58505
701/224-2370

OHIO
Department of Health
246 North High Street
P.O. Box 118
Columbus OH 43266
614/466-3543

OKLAHOMA
Department of Health
1000 NE 10th Street
P.O. Box 23551
Oklahoma City OK 73152
405/271-4200

OREGON
Health Division
Department of Human Resources
1400 Southwest Fifth Avenue
P.O. Box 231
Portland OR 97201
503/378-3033

PENNSYLVANIA
Department of Health
Health and Welfare Building
P.O. Box 90
Harrisburg PA 17108
717/787-5901

RHODE ISLAND
Department of Health
3 Capitol Hill
Providence RI 02908
401/277-2231

SOUTH CAROLINA
Department of Health and
Environment Control
2600 Bull Street
Columbia SC 29201
803/734-4880

SOUTH DAKOTA
Department of Health
445 East Capitol Avenue
Pierre SD 57501
605/773-3361

TENNESSEE
Department of Public Health
344 Cordell Hull Building
Nashville TN 37247
615/741-3111

TEXAS
Texas Department of Health
1100 W. 49th Street
Austin TX 78756
512/458-7111

UTAH
Department of Health
288 North 1460 West
Salt Lake City UT 84116
801/538-6101

VERMONT
State Health Department
60 Main Street
Burlington VT 05401
802/863-7200

VIRGINIA
State Health Department
Main Street Station
1500 East Main Street
Richmond VA 23219
804/786-3561

WASHINGTON
Department of Health
MS ET-21
Olympia WA 98504
206/586-5846

WEST VIRGINIA
Department of Health
1800 Washington Street
Charleston WV
25305
305/348-0045

WISCONSIN
Division of Health Services
P.O. Box 7850
Madison WI 53707
608/266-3681

WYOMING
Department of Health and Human
Services
117 Hathaway Building
Cheyenne WY 82002
307/777-7656

6. EEOC DISTRICT AND REGIONAL OFFICES

ALABAMA
1900 3rd Avenue North
Birmingham AL 35203
205/254-1166
205/731-0083

ARIZONA
4520 North Central Avenue, Suite 300
Phoenix AZ 85012
602/261-3882
602/640-5000

ARKANSAS
320 West Capitol, Suite 621
Little Rock AR 72201
501/324-5060

CALIFORNIA
1313 P Street, Room 103
Fresno CA 93721
209/487-5793

3660 Wilshire Building, 6th Floor
Los Angeles CA 90010
213/251-7278

1333 Broadway, Suite 430
Oakland CA 94612
415/273-7588

880 Front Street, Room. 4521
San Diego CA 92188
619/293-6288
619/557-6288

901 Market Street, Suite 500
San Francisco CA 94103
415/744-6500

84 West Santa Clara Avenue
Room 300
San Jose CA 95113
not listed

COLORADO
1845 Sherman Street
Denver CO 80203
303/866-1300

DELAWARE
No office.

DISTRICT OF COLUMBIA
1801 L Street NW
Washington DC 20507
202/663-4264

FLORIDA
Metro Mall
1 N.E. 1st Street, 6th Floor
Miami FL 33132
305/350-4491
305/536-4491

501 E. Polk Street
Timberlake Annex
Building, Suite 1020
Tampa FL 33602
813/228-2310

GEORGIA
75 Piedmont Avenue NE
Atlanta GA 30335
404/331-6093

ILLINOIS
536 South Clark Street
Room 910A
Chicago IL 60605
312/353-2713

INDIANA
46 East Ohio Street, Room 456
Indianapolis IN 46204
317/226-7212

KENTUCKY
600 Dr. Martin Luther King Jr. Place
Room 268
Louisville KY 40202
502/582-6082

LOUISIANA
701 Layola Avenue, Suite 600
New Orleans LA 70113
504/589-3842

MAINE
No office.

MARYLAND
711 West 40th Street, Suite 210
Baltimore MD 21211
301/962-3932

MASSACHUSETTS
150 Causeway Street, Suite 1000
Boston MA 02114
617/223-4535

MICHIGAN
477 Michigan Avenue
Detroit MI 48226
313/226-7636

MINNESOTA
220 2nd Street S, Room 108
Minneapolis MN 55401-
2141
612/370-3330

MISSOURI
207 W. Amite Street
Crossroads Fielding
Jackson MO 39201
601/965-4537

911 Walnut, 10th Floor
Kansas City MO 64106

816/374-5773
816/426-5773

625 North Euclid Street, 5th Floor
St. Louis MO 63108
314/425-6585

NEW JERSEY
60 Park Place, Room 301
Newark NJ 07102
201/645-6383

NEW MEXICO
505 Marquette NW, Suite 1105
Albuquerque NM 87102
505/766-2061

NEW YORK
28 Church Street, Room 301
Buffalo NY 14202
716/846-4441

90 Church Street, 15th Floor,
Room 501
New York NY 10007
212/264-7161

NORTH CAROLINA
5500 Central Avenue
Charlotte NC 28212
704/563-2501

324 West Market Street
Room B-27
Greensboro NC 27402
919/333-5174

1309 Annapolis Drive
Raleigh NC 27608-2129
919/856-4064

OHIO
550 Main Street, Room 7015
Cincinnati OH 45202
513/684-2379

1375 Euclid Avenue, Suite 600
Cleveland OH 44115
216/522-7425

PENNSYLVANIA
1421 Cherry Street, 10th Floor
Philadelphia PA 19102
215/597-7784

1000 Liberty Avenue, Room 2038
Pittsburgh PA 15222
412/644-3444

SOUTH CAROLINA
300 E. Washington Street, Suite B41
Greenville SC 29601
803/233-1791

TENNESSEE
1407 Union Avenue, Suite 621
Memphis TN 38104
901/722-2617

50 Vantage Way, Suite 202
Nashville TN 37228
615/736-5820

TEXAS
1900 Pacific, 13th Floor
Dallas TX 75201
214/767-7015

Common 4171
North Missa Building, C100
El Paso TX 79902
915/543-7596
915/534-6440

1919 Smith Street
7th Floor
Houston TX 77002
713/653-3320

5410 Fredericksburg
Suite 200
San Antonio TX 78229
512/229-4810

VIRGINIA
252 Monticello Avenue
Norfolk VA 23510
804/441-3470

3600 W. Broad Street, Suite 229
Richmond VA 23230
804/771-2692

WASHINGTON
2815 Second Avenue
Suite 500
Seattle WA 98121
206/553-0968

WISCONSIN
310 W. Wisconsin
Avenue, Suite 800
Milwaukee WI
53203-2292
414/297-1111

Index